Cultivating Cannabis

in the 21st Century

C.K. Watson

Cultivating Cannabis

in the 21st Century

C.K. Watson

Green Candy Press

Published by Green Candy Press

San Francisco, CA

www.greencandypress.com

Photography: Cover photo: Royal Haze by Dinafem Seeds is courtesy and copyright of Dinafem Seeds, http://dinafem-seeds.com. Interior and back cover photographs are copyright © by 420Clones.com, 420Magazine, Alpine Seeds, Andre Grossman, BadBoy Lighting Systems, BreedBay.co.uk, Bubble Man, Cannaseur.co.uk, Ch9 Female Seeds, C.K. Watson, Delta 9 Labs, Dr. Greenthumb Seeds, D. Strange, Dutch Passion Seeds, Ed Borg, Gardenscure.com, Green Born Identity, Green Devil Genetics Seed Company, Green House Seed Co., Jong-Young Han, HydroHuts, Hydroplex, Hy Pro, Ian Phillips, KC Brains Seeds, LF Images, marijuana.com, MG Imaging, MoD, No Mercy Supply Paradise Seeds, Pepper Design, Sagarmatha Seeds, Sativa Steph, Sensi Seeds, Short Stuff Seeds, Spliff Seed Company, Subcool, Sweet Seeds, TGA, TH Seeds, Weado, and weedfarmer.com.

Printed in Canada by Transcontinental Printing Inc.

Massively distributed by P.G.W.

ISBN 978-1-931160-75-9

Contents

Acknowledgments

I would like to thank my God, Jesus Christ, for the opportunity to write this book and of course for creating this amazing plant; my mom and dad for inspiring me to pursue gardening and my ambitions; my wife for the love and support she has shown me; my brother / best friend for helping me with this enormous task and for always being there when I needed him; my auntie for helping me with editing; and my Tia for helping out with legal matters.

I would also like to thank all the people, growers, and breeders that contributed to this book: Bubble Man, The_Seed, Monkey, Roberto from FutureGarden.com, Motaco, Professor from Simply Hydro.com, TheNewGuy, ChiefSmokingBud, HydroRascal, Rob Christopher of the UKCIA, George Kuepper of the NSAIS, ToB, JoeShmoe, Elevator Man, Mrs. Fly, Don de Marco, Beancounter, Grasshopper, Black Bart, Rainha Ginga, GrowGreen, Oldjoints, Pig&PotFarmer, Cofi, Jubei, OBSoul33T, Closet Funk, Suby, Fredster420, Dr. Jay R. Cavanaugh, Henk from Dutch Passion, TGA_BadBoy, The Mole, Max Yields, CBF, Texas Kid, FarmerMike1187, Grow Green, Crazy Composer, Rellikbuzz, Nuclear Nuggets, Shipperke, Krusty, 3LittleBirds aka TheFlintstoners, Brothers Grimm Soul and Sly, MarijuanaMat, LC, Vic High of the BCGA, Kumquat, Closet Funk, Nomad, Tie Down, subcool, Contagis, and all those Overgrow members whose names were lost but whose information lives on. This book would be nowhere near as good without the information y'all have contributed. Thank you.

Finally, thanks to Robert Connell Clarke and Mel Frank for making great works that have educated and inspired many.

Dedication

I dedicate this book to anyone that is in search of true knowledge of cannabis and to all the victims and families who have been affected by this senseless war on freedom.

This bud is nearing maturity as indicated by the swelling calyxes, withering pistils and copious trichomes.

Introduction

And God said, let the earth bring forth grass, the herb yielding seed, and the fruit tree yielding fruit after his kind, whose seed is in itself, upon the earth: and it was so. And the earth brought forth grass, and herb yielding seed after his kind, and the tree yielding fruit, whose seed was in itself, after his kind: and God saw that it was good.
—Genesis 1:11-13
Make the most you can of the Indian hemp seed and sow it everywhere.
—President George Washington, 1794

The purpose of this book is to educate those who aspire to know more about this miraculous plant. All facets of cannabis will be covered: its history, breeding, and cultivation; how to grow it securely; how to cook it; and much more. We will cover it in ways that have never been done before. Instead of duping the customer into buying several different books—one for cooking, one for growing, one for history, one for breeding, one for hash, one for security—I have written this book so it's all in one place, at one low price. I promise you that no matter how long you have been growing or breeding, you will not read this book and walk away empty-handed.

Since cannabis is illegal, there is no mandate for the information published concerning it. This means that anyone who can get their book into print can have whatever so-called information they want made available to the public. This is why some "grow guides" totally contradict others. My advice to you is to use your best judgment; if it sounds too good to be true, it usually is.

I didn't write this book to become rich or famous—I don't even make a dollar a book—and of course it's not my real name. I have read so many books about growing cannabis and have seen so much misinformation and disinformation that it made me question if many published authors had even grown cannabis. There are many aspects of cannabis—both in terms of cultivation and general information—that

A Canadian Cannabis activist exercising his rights.

have been left out of these other books; some of this information is scattered in hard to find places on the Internet; some of it has heretofore not been documented (at least to my knowledge); and all of it is recorded here. (This includes work drawn from the famous Overgrow texts, on which more later.) Misinformation pertaining to the growth of cannabis has been a principal motivating factor in my writing, and I guarantee that all the information contained in this book has been tried and verified by experienced cannabis growers and breeders.

Whether you are a novice or an expert, there is a wealth of information here that a grower of any level can appreciate and learn from. For the novice grower: I have a chapter just for you. It will tell you of common mistakes that inexperienced growers make, and also show you the ropes with several step-by-step, how-to sections. For the experienced grower: I have an advanced techniques chapter unlike any before, and a breeding chapter that eliminates those (in my opinion) confusing punnett squares, ratios, and so on, and provides you with real methods and results. The breeding chapter also features an extensive account of characteristic traits, with pho-

This photo of Canadian Cannabis activist Will Hung-Bong was taken at the Marijuana March in Toronto, Canada.

tographs, so you know exactly what to look for. And for growers of any experience level: I have devised whole new investigations of security, outdoor growing, and building your own grow room and greenhouse.

I am proud to say that this book is the first to feature a truly extensive online cannabis section. In it, I discuss which seed banks, seed breeders, and forums are the best, and I have given each a grade on various aspects of business. Also, this book deals solely with organic gardening; but don't worry: you will learn how to grow a killer crop without the need for environmentally harmful chemical fertilizers.

Several guest authors have helped out in order to make each subject as thoroughly comprehensive as possible. An extensive portion of the hash and extraction chapter was written by the king of full melt himself, Bubble Man. He provides a step-by-step tutorial, documented with photographs, on all his hash-making methods: the Bubble Box, Bubble Bags, as well as the new Bubble Now; he also provides a section on resin quality. While this book mainly deals with soil-grown cannabis, we have an extensive hydroponic / aeroponic chapter, written by an expert who has been building his own systems for more than 18 years. He has used his knowledge to aid several large companies and organizations that are using his systems to feed starving people in various countries. I am also pleased to feature an extensive, up-to-date history of cannabis, compiled by Rob Christopher of the UKCIA.

No other plant has the economic and environmental capabilities of cannabis. It has been documented throughout history, by many different cultures and countries, as one of the most useful on plants on earth. Yet the U.S. government and many others continue to outlaw this wonderful plant. I urge the readers of this book to march in your city's Global Marijuana March, or to donate time and / or money to organizations such as MPP (Marijuana Policy Project), CAMP (Coalition Against Marijuana Prohibition), SAFER (Safer Alternative For Enjoyable Recreation), LEAP (Law Enforcement Against Prohibition), and NORML (National Organization for the Reform of Marijuana Laws). Most of these organizations have been fighting to change these unjust laws for decades. I strongly encourage you to support them.

Visit norml.com or hightimes.com for a list of cannabis-friendly politicians in every election year.

Don't hate the government, *change* the government!

Note: I am not currently, nor have I ever grown, smoked, or even seen, real marijuana. All of the photographs shown here are not my own. Any and all information contained in this book is strictly for educational / entertainment purposes only. Neither the author nor publisher condones the violating of any laws.

Now that we got that out of the way, let's get on with the show.

The Basics

This is a purple kush cola. A cola is comprised of numerous calyxes which make up bracets and bracets grow together to form a nice long cola, if you're growing right!

Chapter 1

History

CHINA

Cannabis is believed to have originated in Asia, in the Himalayas, or the Altai Mountain ranges. However, there is some evidence that it originated near present day Iran and Iraq, near the Tigris and Euphrates rivers. Cannabis's first documented use, however, was in 8,000 B.C., in what would today be known as China. (It was also recorded for medical use in China around 2,700 B.C., ritual use in India around 2,000 B.C., and as hashish in the Middle East around 1,000 A.D.) The most detailed of these ancient descriptions comes from China.

The earliest indirect evidence of hemp's use is found in decorated Chinese Neolithic pottery, pieces of which were found to have hemp cord impressions on them. Painted pottery from Honan province belonging to the Neolithic Yang-shao culture also indicates the probable presence of cultivated hemp. Pieces of what are thought to be hemp cloth have been found on the inside of a jar belonging to a Neolithic culture at a site in the western province of Gansu. The hemp fiber was primarily used for clothing and nets. Only the emperor wore hemp clothes, until it became available to the masses; silk was then used to clothe the emperor.

The world's oldest pharmacopoeia, the Chinese *Shen-nung Pen Ts'ao Ching*, written 2,000 years ago, refers to cannabis as "Ma." The book lists more than 100 ailments that may be treated with various parts of the cannabis plant. It was used for reducing the pain of rheumatism and treating digestive disorders, constipation, and diarrhea. It was also prescribed as an anesthetic prior to surgical operations, as well, so as to lessen the symptoms of patients with malaria and beriberi. Another Chinese text, written by Li Shih Chen in 1578, speaks of cannabis as an anti-nausea agent, an antibiotic, and as a means of stopping hemorrhaging.

There is also evidence of cannabis being used recreationally in ancient China. The Taoists used cannabis as a hallucinogen by adding it to other ingredients in incense

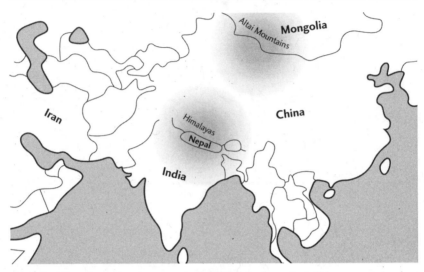

Cannabis' first documented use was in 8,000 B.C., in ancient China.

burners. In the sixth-century A.D., the *Wu Tsang Ching*, or "Manual of the Five Viscera," contained the following instructions for aspiring magicians: "If you wish to command demonic apparitions to present themselves you should constantly eat the inflorescences of the hemp plant." It was also believed that using cannabis and ginseng together gave one the ability to see into the future. Smoking it was uncommon in ancient China; instead, patients would use it in liquid and food preparations, extracts, and topical preparations. Despite the numerous Chinese references to cannabis, it has never played a comparable role in Chinese social life such as achieved in India.

SOUTH ASIA

The Aryans introduced cannabis to India 4,000 years ago. Literature from that time period describes cannabis as a treatment for similar medical conditions to those of China. The earliest Indian account of it was in the four Vedas (circa 1,400–1,000 B.C.). The *Atharva Veda*, one of the four Vedas, calls cannabis a "reliever of stress and anxiety."

Sushruta, an ancient Indian healer, recommends cannabis for relieving congestion and as part of a cure for fevers. Ayurveda, a traditional Hindu medicinal system practiced in India since 1,000 A.D., cites cannabis as a appetite stimulate, digestive aid, pain reliever, and sleeping potion. Cannabis has been grown for fiber and as a source of medicine for several thousand years, but until 500 A.D. the use of its psychoactive properties was almost exclusively confined to India. Various psychoactive preparations containing cannabis were considered sacred in Hinduism, and were associated with the gods Shiva and Indra.

In Cambodia the plant is sometimes boiled and a small amount of the liquid is then sprinkled on tobacco and smoked. The smoking of cannabis resin in this region seems to be due to recent foreign influence. Until the current "drug problem" introduced by Western foreigners, it was commonplace in Thailand to employ cannabis for its analgesic and other medical uses. An infusion of the flowers was given in small quantities at meal times to women who had just given birth. Similar practices are reported from Cambodia.

THE WORLD

Other literature about the ancient use of cannabis comes from Africa, ancient Greece, and the Roman Empire. They variously cite cannabis as being able to quicken the mind, enhance concentration, eliminate stress, create joyful feelings, and enhance sexual pleasure. Muslims popularized hashish, pressing trichomes into bricks and balls. Islam strongly influenced African cannabis use. However, some ancient African rituals clearly predate Islam's influence. To this day, some African tribes seal treaties and special ceremonies with the passing of the Dagga pipe and by blowing a puff of smoke. The Dogon tribe of Africa has been using cannabis recreationally for centuries; in fact, they have a ritual in which they are high for almost every waking moment of an entire year!

Potted histories of cannabis often imply that hemp's intoxicating properties were virtually unknown in Europe until the eighteenth and nineteenth centuries, when travelers to Egypt and other parts of the East "discovered" the drug. These tales are built on the false premise that alcohol is and always has been the standard of European culture and that other substances, like cannabis and opium, are recent arrivals. In fact, palaeobotanical studies have shown that hemp was cultivated, presumably as a fiber, in eastern England by the Anglo-Saxons from 400 A.D. onwards. Cannabis was known by numerous names—neck weed, gallows grass, and Welsh parsley among them. In certain parts of Britain the seeds of the hemp plant were used in a very specific form of folk divination. In order to see a vision of her future husband, a girl would have to retire alone at the witching hour to a churchyard, and whilst throwing the seeds over her left shoulder, chant the following short rhyme:

Hempseed I sow, hempseed, grow
He that is to marry me,
Come after me and mow

During the 19th century, European interest in the drug was aided by two scientific reports, the first by W. B. O'Shaughnessy in 1839, and the second by Queen Victoria's physician, Russell Reynolds; the latter report prescribed hashish cubes for Queen Victoria's menstrual cramps. Both men recommended its medical use for a variety of ailments and to provide mild euphoria. Napoleon's army was interested in the drug's pain relieving and sedative effects. It was used during, and to a greater extent, following his rule in France. Cannabis received highly laudatory testimonials from the medical profession of the day and was readily available without prescription. Interest in cannabis was furthered by popular writers who used and spoke of hashish enthusiastically, including Charles Baudelaire, Arthur Rimbaud, and Pierre Gautier. Baudelaire and Gautier were in fact members of the Club des Hachischins, in which a number of writers and intellectuals gathered and experimented with the recreational use of hashish. Although the public delighted to read of the French writers' drug experiences, the majority of the public did not care to engage in the same kind of activity; most found that their experiences were frightening and repugnant.

THE AMERICAS

Cannabis's first introduction to North America is shrouded in a veil of controversy. Some say that the Columbians brought it over, others that it began during the slave trade, and still others that it began during the Mexican immigration. The first cultivation of hemp in the Americas seems to have been in Nova Scotia in 1606, and it subsequently became widely grown across North America for its use as a fiber. It seems, however, that there was no awareness of its psychoactive properties until the middle of the nineteenth century. The earliest flags were made from hemp and the Declaration of Independence is written on Dutch hemp paper. Most early American clothes were made from hemp fiber; even the first Levi's jeans were made from it. American production of hemp was encouraged by the government in the 17th century for the production of rope, sails, and clothing. In 1619, the Virginia Assembly passed legislation requiring every farmer to grow hemp. Hemp was allowed to be exchanged as legal tender in Pennsylvania, Virginia, and Maryland. In 1775, Kentucky started the American hemp industry. By 1860 Kentucky produced 40,000 tons a year, second only to cotton. Domestic production flourished until the Civil War, when imports and other domestic materials replaced hemp for many purposes. In the late nineteenth century, cannabis became a popular ingredient in many medicinal products and was sold openly in public pharmacies.

The first outlawing of an intoxicating substance occurred in 1875, by the Californian government, who forbade Chinese immigrants from smoking opium in "opium dens." This law applied only to Chinese immigrants; Caucasians could freely enjoy opium on the streets if they so chose. The next outlawing was against African-Americans in 1914, around Louisiana, and this time the substance was cocaine. After the Mexican Revolution of 1910, Mexican immigrants flooded into the U.S., introducing American culture to the recreational uses of cannabis. Cannabis became associated with the Mexican immigrants, and the fear and prejudice about the Spanish-speaking newcomers became associated with it. Anti-drug campaigners warned against the encroaching "Marijuana Menace," and many terrible crimes were attributed to cannabis and the Mexicans who used it.

During the Great Depression, massive unemployment increased public resentment and fear of Mexican immigrants, escalating public and governmental concern about the "problem" of cannabis. This instigated a flurry of "research" which linked the use of cannabis with violence, crime, and other socially deviant behaviors. Propaganda films such as *Reefer Madness* portray the supposed effects of cannabis. California was the first state to label cannabis as "poison" and classified it as a hard narcotic. By 1929, 16 western states had passed cannabis restrictions, and by 1935 almost all states had passed cannabis restrictions in some form. The final act against cannabis came in 1937 with the passing of the Marijuana Tax Act. The only opponent of the Marijuana Tax Act (cannabis prohibition) was the American Medical Association, which argued:

There is positively no evidence to indicate the abuse of cannabis as a medicinal agent or to show that its medicinal use is leading to the development of cannabis addiction. Cannabis at the present time is slightly used for medicinal purposes, but it would seem worthwhile to maintain its status as a medicinal agent. . . There is a possibility that there are studies of the drug by modern means that show other advantages to be derived from its medicinal use.

Of course, they failed to persuade Congress and the Marijuana Tax Act passed. Cannabis was removed from the American pharmacopoeia in 1941.

The Marijuana Tax Act was then imposed, which made growing and selling cannabis legal if you had a $1.00 Stamp; the only problem was that the stamps were never made available. The first victim of marijuana prohibition was Samuel R. Caldwell in 1937. On the very day that the new law passed, police raided the Lexington Hotel and arrested Caldwell for selling two ounces of dried cannabis flowers. The judge sentenced Caldwell to four years of hard labor in Leavenworth penitentiary, plus a $1,000 fine! Caldwell served everyday of his sentence and died one year after his sentenced ended.

The passing of this act, in addition to being racially motivated, was also fueled by greed and political ambition. William Randolph Hearst printed false statements in his newspapers; this was due to the vast fortune he would lose if hemp were allowed to

Cannabis growers are forced to be more innovative than the typical gardener. This is a sea of green on a balcony with a sheet of opaque plastic to hide everything while still allowing sunlight to reach the plants.

be used over his wood pulp in printing processes. DuPont Industries also faced destruction from hemp, which was a direct competitor for its new fiber products rayon and nylon. Most of Harry Anslinger's readings to Congress came directly from Hearst's slanderous lies about the menace marijuana. Anslinger argued that the "Marijuana Menace" would cause death, insanity, and addiction. However, he changed his tune when the La Guardia Marijuana Report was released; now Anslinger said that cannabis use would make the youth too complacent to fight in any wars that America participated in. The "facts" about cannabis would continue to be changed over the years. It was said to lead to heroin use and abuse, thus starting the "gateway theory" about cannabis. All of these lies came on the heels of an article in Popular Mechanics that called hemp the new Billion Dollar Crop. How convenient for Hearst and DuPont.

For a plant to be such a menace to our society, it might be surprising to learn just how much we relied on cannabis during the Second World War. American cotton production wasn't enough to cover the amount needed and the government promoted a program called Hemp for Victory. The reinvigorated hemp industry produced 63,000 tons in 1943. After the war was won, though, the hemp was ordered to be destroyed and this wondrous plant was once again placed under a black cloud. Some stands of hemp still survive in states like Kentucky and Missouri.

The prejudice placed against cannabis has intensified in recent years. In 1973, Richard Nixon combined the Bureau of Narcotics and Dangerous Drugs and the Office of Drug Abuse Law Enforcement to create the Drug Enforcement Administration (DEA). This new super-acronym administration was commissioned with the task of enforcing the laws against the illegal drug trade. The DEA has a particularly nasty stance towards cannabis. Believing it to have no medical value, they zealously hunt down any users of cannabis, medicinal or not, despite all of the studies done to show its obvious application to the medical sciences. As such, many believe the DEA demonizes cannabis in order to keep the large budget that it receives for the hunting down of cannabis users. During the Reagan Administration, the DEA further sharpened its claws with the beginning of the War on Drugs. This so-called war bolstered the DEA's budget and boldness. In a recent review by the Justice Department, close to $616 million dollars of money seized by the DEA is either unaccounted for or is missing. This leads to obvious thoughts of theft by the agents and their superiors in the DEA. Regan's bold stance against cannabis was continued by his successor George H. W. Bush. From 1977–79, Bush served as director for Eli Lilly, which stood to lose a fortune on its monopoly of the synthetic THC molecule found in cannabis should cannabis become legal. This could shed light on why the Bush family are such starch anti-cannabis activists. (However, hemp helped save George's life when he bailed from a plane over the Pacific—his parachute was made entirely of hemp.)

Six states sponsored state research for Medical Marijuana: New Mexico, California, New York, Tennessee, Michigan, and Georgia. They concluded that cannabis could help lessen cancer patients' nausea and increase the appetites of AIDS and cancer patients suffering from chemotherapy.

Cultivating Cannabis in The 21st Century

In November 1996, an enlightened stride was taken towards the decriminalization of cannabis. California, ironically the first state to prohibit cannabis, became the first state to promote and sponsor medical marijuana; Arizona quickly followed. Over the next few years, state after state approved medical marijuana. California saw an amendment to Proposition 215 with Senate Bill 420. This Bill set guidelines stating that no more than 8 dried ounces may be possessed by any one patient and caregiver at anytime. Alaska, Oregon, Washington, Maine, Hawaii, and Colorado followed suit, and over the next few years Montana, Nevada, Maryland, New Mexico, Rhode Island, and Vermont passed similar measures. In total, there are 13 states that have approved of the use of cannabis as a medicine.

Proof that the "war on drugs" isn't working is the fact that there have been over 381 million arrests of non-violent cannabis users since the Marijuana Tax Act in 1937. Some of these non-violent arrests have included more prison time than rapists and murderers. The U.S. has the highest prison population rate in the world; over 55% of the people in prison are non-violent drug offenders. On average, it takes $32,000 dollars in tax payer money to convict a drug dealer, and the drug dealer will get, on average, ten years in prison, which will cost tax payers $24,000 for each year the individual is incarcerated, and a total of $243,000 for the entire period of incarceration.

Cannabis' use as a drug aside, hemp has more potential than any other plant to serve as an economic aid. On an annual basis, one acre of hemp will produce as much fiber as 2–3 acres of cotton. This hemp fiber will be stronger and softer than cotton, will last twice as long, and will not mildew. Unlike cotton, hemp is frost tolerant, requires moderate amounts of water, and can be cultivated in all 50 states. Over half of the world's pesticides and herbicides are used on cotton, while hemp requires no pesticides or herbicides and only moderate amounts of fertilizer. In the next 20 years, global demand for paper will increase drastically; if a tree-free source of paper is not found, massive deforestation and environmental damage will occur. Hemp is the most promising source for tree-free paper. Hemp paper is superior to tree-based paper; for one thing, it can be recycled many more times than tree-based paper and can last hundreds of years without degrading. Hemp can also make stronger and lighter plastics than other plants—as Mercedes Benz knows; the car company is currently using hemp to manufacture automobile bodies and dashboards. The oil from hemp can be used to produce non-toxic diesel fuel, paint, varnish, detergent, ink, and lubricating oil. Hemp possesses more biomass than any other plant, including corn, which makes it ideal for making ethanol. As well as providing a strong economic staple, Hemp seeds contain a higher protein than that of soybeans, and anything that is made from soybeans can be made from hemp, including tofu, veggie burgers, cheese, salad oils, ice cream, milk, and so on.

A CANNABIS CHRONOLOGY

The following is a timeline taken from www.UKCIA.org, and was compiled by Rob Christopher.

Cannabis sativa appears to have originated in Central Asia and was probably first cultivated for its fiber. It has been grown in China for at least 4500 years. It is thought to have reached Europe by 1500 B.C.

2700 B.C.	First written record of cannabis use, in the pharmacopoeia of Shen Nung, one of the fathers of Chinese medicine.
550 B.C.	The Persian prophet Zoroaster gives hemp first place in the sacred text, the Zend-Avesta, which lists over 10,000 medicinal plants.
450 B.C.	The Greek historian Herodotus describes the Scythians of central Asia throwing hemp onto heated stones under canvas: "as it burns, it smokes like incense and the smell of it makes them drunk."
100 B.C.	Chinese make paper from cannabis and mulberry.
45 A.D.	St. Mark establishes the Ethiopian Coptic Church. The Copts claim that marijuana as a sacrament has a lineage descending from the Jewish sect, the Essenes, who are considered to be responsible for the Dead Sea Scrolls.
70 A.D.	Roman Emperor Nero's surgeon, Dioscorides, praises cannabis for making "the stoutest cords" and for its medical properties.
400 A.D.	Cannabis cultivated for the first time in England at Old Buckeham Mare.
500 A.D.	First botanical drawing of cannabis appears in *Constantinopolitanus*.
600 A.D.	Germans, Franks, Vikings, etc. make paper from cannabis.
800 A.D.	Mohammed allows cannabis, but forbids alcohol use.
1000 A.D.	The English word *Hempe* first listed in a dictionary. Muslims produce hashish for medical and social use.
1150.	Muslims use cannabis to start Europe's first paper mill. Most paper is made from cannabis for the next 850 years.
1484	Pope Innocent VIII singles out cannabis as an unholy sacrament of the satanic mass.
1494	Hemp papermaking starts in England.
1545	Spanish bring cannabis cultivation to Chile.
1554	Spanish bring cannabis cultivation to Peru.
1563	Queen Elizabeth I decrees that landowners with 60 acres or more must grow cannabis else face a £5 fine.
1564	King Philip of Spain follows lead of Queen Elizabeth and orders cannabis to be grown throughout his Empire, from modern-day Argentina to Oregon.
1606	British take cannabis to Canada, to be cultivated mainly for maritime uses.

1611	British start cultivating cannabis in Virginia.
1619	Virginia colony makes cannabis cultivation mandatory, followed by most other colonies. Europe pays Hemp bounties.
1631	Cannabis used for bartering throughout American Colonies.
1632	Pilgrims bring cannabis to New England.
1753	Cannabis Sativa classified by Linneaus.
1776	Declaration of Independence drafted on cannabis paper.
1783	Cannabis Indica classified by Lamarck.
1791	President Washington sets duties on cannabis to encourage domestic industry. Jefferson calls cannabis "a necessity" and urges farmers to grow cannabis instead of tobacco.
1807	Napoleon signs the Treaty of Tilset with Czar Alexander of Russia; it cuts off all legal Russian trade with Britain. Britain blackmails and press-gangs American sailors into illegally trading in Russian Hemp.
1808	Napoleon wants to place French Troops at Russian ports to ensure the Treaty of Tilset is complied with. The Czar refuses and turns a blind eye to Britain's illegal trade in cannabis.
1812	On the 19th of June America declares war on Britain. On the 24th Napoleon invades Russia, aiming to put an end to Britain's main supply of cannabis. By the end of the year, the Russian winter and army had destroyed most of Napoleon's invading force.
1835	The Club des Hachischins, whose bohemian membership included the poet Baudelaire, is founded.
1839	The homeopathy journal *American Provers' Union* publishes first of many reports on the effects of cannabis.
1841	Dr. W.B. O'Shaughnessy of Scotland works in India and then introduces cannabis to Western medicine. In the following 50 years hundreds of medical papers are written on the medical benefits of cannabis.
1845	Psychologist and "inventor" of modern psychopharmacology and psychotomimetic drug treatment, Jacques-Joseph Moreau de Tours, documents physical and mental benefits of cannabis.
1857	*The Hasheesh Eater*, by Fitz Hugh Ludlow, is published. Smith Brothers of Edinburgh start to market a highly active extract of Cannabis Indica, which is used as a basis for innumerable tinctures.
1860	First government-commissioned study of cannabis and health conducted by Ohio State Medical society.
1870	Cannabis is listed in the U.S. Pharmacopoeia as a medicine for various ailments.

1876	Hashish served at American Centennial Exposition.
1890	Queen Victoria's personal physician, Sir Russell Reynolds, prescribes cannabis for menstrual cramps. He claims in the first issue of *The Lancet*, that cannabis, "When pure and administered carefully, is one of the of the most valuable medicines we possess."
1895	The Indian Hemp Drug Commission concludes that cannabis has some medical uses, no addictive properties, and a number of positive emotional and social benefits. First known use of the word "marijuana" for smoking, by Pancho Villa's supporters in Sonora. Mexico. (The song "La Cucaracha" tells the story of one of Villa's men looking for his stash of "marijuana por fumar.")
1910	African-American "reefer" use is reported in the jazz clubs of New Orleans, and is said to be influencing white people; Mexicans are reported to be smoking cannabis in Texas.
1911	Hindus reported to be using "gunjah" in San Francisco. South Africa starts to outlaw cannabis.
1912	The possibility of putting controls on the use of cannabis is raised at the first International Opium Conference.
1915	California outlaws cannabis.
1916	Recognizing that timber supplies are finite, USDA Bulletin 404 calls for a new program of expansion of cannabis to replace uses of timber by industry.
1919	Texas outlaws cannabis.
1923	The South African delegate to the League of Nations claims mine workers are not as productive after using "dagga" (cannabis) and calls for international controls. Britain insists on further research before any controls are imposed.
1924	At the second International Opiates Conference, the Egyptian delegate claims that serious problems are associated with hashish use and calls for immediate international controls. A sub-committee is formed and listens to the Egyptian and Turkish delegations while Britain abstains. The conference declares cannabis a narcotic and recommends strict international control.
1925	The Panama Canal Zone Report, conducted due to the level of cannabis use by soldiers in the area, concludes that there is no evidence that cannabis use is habit-forming or deleterious. The report recommends that no action be taken to prevent the use or sale of cannabis.
1928	September 28th: the Dangerous Drugs Act becomes law and cannabis is made illegal in Britain.

1930   Louis Armstrong is arrested in Los Angeles for possession of cannabis.

1931   The Federal Bureau of Narcotics is formed, with Anslinger appointed as its head.

1937   Following action by the Federal Bureau of Narcotics and a campaign by newspaper magnate William Randolph Hearst, a prohibitive tax is put on hemp in the USA, effectively destroying the industry. Anslinger testifies to congress that marijuana is the most violence-causing drug known to man. The objections by the American Medical Association (the AMA only realized that marijuana was in fact cannabis two days before the start of hearing) and the National Oil Seed Institute are rejected.

1938   The February edition of *Popular Mechanics* (written before the Marijuana Transfer Tax was passed) declares hemp the "new billion dollar crop."

1941   Cannabis dropped from the American Pharmacopoeia. *Popular Mechanics* reveal details of Henry Ford's plastic car made with and fueled by cannabis. Henry Ford continued to illegally grow cannabis for some years after the Federal ban, hoping to become independent of the petroleum industry.

1943   Both the U.S. and German governments urge their patriotic farmers to grow hemp for the war effort. The U.S. shows farmers a short film, *Hemp for Victory*, which the government later pretends never existed. The editor of *Military Journal* states that although some military personnel smoke cannabis, he does not view this as a problem.

1944   New York Mayor LaGuardia's marijuana commission reports that cannabis causes no violence at all and cites other positive results. Anslinger responds by denouncing LaGuardia and threatens doctors with prison sentences if they dare carry out independent research on cannabis.

1945   Newsweek reports that over 100,000 Americans use cannabis.

1948   Anslinger now declares that using cannabis causes the user to become peaceful and pacifistic. He also claims that the Communists would use cannabis to weaken the American troops' will to fight.

1951   UN bulletin of narcotic drugs estimates 200 million cannabis users worldwide.

1961   Anslinger heads U.S. delegation at UN Drugs Convention. New international restrictions are placed on cannabis, aiming to eliminate its use within 25 years.

1962   Anslinger is sacked by President Kennedy. Kennedy may well have smoked cannabis in the White House.

1964   The first head shop is opened, by the Thelin brothers, in the United States.

1966	The folk singer Donovan becomes the first celebrity hippy to fall foul of the law.

1967   In New York, on Valentines Day, Abbie Hoffman and the Yippies mail out 3,000 joints to addresses chosen at random from the phonebook. They offer people the chance to discover what all the fuss is about, but remind them that they are now criminals for possessing cannabis. The mail out was secretly funded by Jimi Hendrix, and attracts huge publicity.

1970   Canadian Le Dain report claims that the debate on the non-medical use of cannabis "has all too often been based on hearsay, myth and ill-informed opinion about the effects of the drug." Marijuana Transfer Tax declared unconstitutional by the U.S. Supreme Court.

1971   President Nixon declares drugs "America's public enemy No. 1."

1972   The White House passes a $1 billion anti-drug bill. The U.S. government Shafer report voices concern at the level of spending used to stop illicit drug use. From 1969–73 the level of spending rose over 1000%.

1973   President Nixon declares, "We have turned the corner on drug addiction in America." Oregon becomes the first state to take steps towards legalization.

1975   Hundreds of Doctors call on U.S. Government to instigate further research on cannabis. The Supreme Court of Alaska declares that "right of privacy" protects cannabis possession in the home. Limit for public possession is set at one ounce.

1976   Ford Administration bans government funding of medical research on cannabis. Pharmaceutical companies are allowed to carry out research on synthetic, manmade cannabis analogues. Holland adopts policy of tolerance to cannabis users. Robert Randal becomes first American to receive cannabis from Federal supplies under an Investigational New Drug (IND) program. Ford's chief advisor on drugs, Robert Dupont, declares that cannabis is less harmful than alcohol or tobacco and recommends its decriminalization.

1978   New Mexico becomes first U.S. state to make cannabis available for medical use.

1988   In Washington, DEA Judge Francis Young concludes at the end of a lengthy legal process that "Marijuana in its natural form is one of the safest therapeutically active substances known to man." He recommends that medical use of marijuana should be allowed, for certain life- or sense-threatening illnesses. The DEA administrator rejects the ruling. U.S. Senate adds $2.6 Billion to federal anti-drug efforts.

1989   Outgoing president Reagan declares victory in the War on Drugs as

From the origins of its cultivation 10,000 years ago, to the present day, growing Cannabis has always been an art. Here we see a modern, professional indoor grow operation that is the culmination of years of experimentation and study.

being a major achievement of his administration. Secretary of State James Baker reports that the global war on narcotics production "is clearly not being won."

1990   The discovery of THC receptors in the human brain is reported in *Nature*.

1995   588,964 people were arrested for marijuana offenses in the United States; 503,350 were for possession alone. This marks 10 million arrests for marijuana possession in the United States since 1965.

1996   Proposition 215 passes in California; it permits doctors to prescribe Medical Marijuana to patients and allows caregivers to cultivate legally at a local and state level.

2000   734,497 people were arrested for marijuana offenses in the United States; 646,042 were for possession alone.

2001   United States v. Oakland Cannabis Buyers Co-Op. The Supreme Court rules that medical use is not a defense, which marks the start of several dozen DEA raids on MMJ dispensaries.

2005   786,545 people were arrested for marijuana offenses in the United States; 696,074 were for possession alone.

2007   New Mexico becomes the 12th state to legalize medical marijuana use.

REFERENCES

Chris Conrad, *HEMP, Lifeline to the Future* (Creative Xpressions)
Ernest Abel, *Marijuana, The First 12,000 years* (Plenum Press)
Jack Herer, *The Emperor Wears No Clothes* (Quick)
Peter Stratford, *Psychedelics Encyclopaedia* (And/Or)

Thanks to the Cannabis Campaigners' Guide: http://www.ccguide.org and The Legalise Cannabis Alliance: http://www.lca-uk.org/ http://www.ccguide.org/chronol.php, as well as the cannabis law reform website www.ukcia.org , and Mr. Free Love Cannabis.

Chapter 2

Scientifically Speaking: A Glossary

Species

The modern scientific community only recognizes one species of cannabis, Cannabis Sativa. In fact, there are three different species: Cannabis Sativa, Cannabis Indica, and Cannabis Ruderalis. (There is also some debate about a fourth species, Cannabis Afghanica, which will be discussed.)

Cannabis Sativa

Cannabis Sativa is native to places such as Southeast Asia, including Thailand, China, and Vietnam, and so on; Africa, Mexico, and South America; typically, anywhere below the Tropic of Cancer (23° N). The plants are characterized by the following: a height range of seven to twenty feet, long internodes, and extensive branching. Most will grow in the classic conical, "Christmas tree" shape. Leaves are long and slender, "finger"-types. Sativa leaves generally have between nine and eleven blades; they are light to medium green in color and are heavily serrated and veined. Root systems are very extensive and

This is dried bud from a Cannabis Sativa plant. Sativa buds are light and airy.

spread out over a large area—taproots on Sativas can be over one foot long. Sativa buds are generally light and airy, with extensive spacing in between due to long internodes. The buds will develop into long, slender colas that will typically have much larger calyxes. Like the plant itself, Sativa pistils are longer and slimmer than those of Indicas. The same applies for trichomes, which will typically have longer stalks and slimmer heads than Indicas. The trichomes will primarily congregate on the calyxes—not like Indicas, where trichomes are commonplace on the fan leaves and leaflets.

Some words that are used to describe the effect of Cannabis Sativa are as follows: uplifting, inspiring, clear, motivational, creative, active, cerebral, electric, soaring. This means that when you smoke Sativa, you will feel like getting up and doing a task that needs doing; unlike the high of Indica, which will make you feel like sitting in the same spot and going to sleep shortly thereafter. This is why most people will refer to Cannabis Sativa as morning bud. (We credit the high of this strain to its high THC and low CBD (cannabidiol) content.

Cannabis Indica

Cannabis Indica is native to places such as the (greater) Middle East, including Pakistan, Afghanistan, and Lebanon; it is also found in India. Cannabis Indica is characterized by its short height of between 3 to 6 feet, its short internodes, and its comparatively little branching. Most grow into a short to medium bush in a wide semi-circular shape. Its leaves, five to seven blades per cluster, are generally broad and thick. They are generally of a medium to dark green color, loosely serrated, and with fewer veins than Cannabis Sativa. Indica root systems are denser and more compact than Sativas, with taproots usually extending less than 6 inches. Indica buds are generally short to medium in length and very thick, forming dense, solid, "rock hard" colas; its pistils are shorter and thicker than Sativas, too. Trichomes follow the pattern of being short and fat, with smaller stalks and much more bulbous heads. Also, the trichomes cover the calyxes, leaflets, and parts of the fan leaves, which makes them ideal for hash production.

The effects of Cannabis Indica are as follows: grogginess, tiredness, inertia, "couch lock," disorientation, hallucination, and red eye. Munchies are a must and are often followed by a nap. This high is caused by Cannabis Indica's higher concentration of CBD.

Cannabis Ruderalis

Cannabis Ruderalis is native to places such as Central Europe, Russia, and parts of Canada (and, in some cases, the extreme northern parts of the United States). Ruderalis mimics both Sativa and Indica species, depending on which part of the globe the plants are found. The only common trait shared by the Ruderalis is that they are

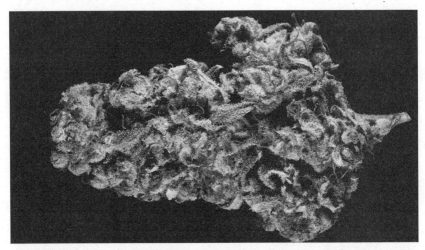

This is dried bud from a Cannabis Ruderalis plant. Very good trichome count.

This is dried bud from a Cannabis Afghanica plant. It is very similar to Cannabis Indica and is ideal for making hash. Note the fox tails which are typical calyx development with afghanica strains.

all auto-flowering. However, we might add another common trait: the only thing felt from smoking these plants is a headache. Ruderalis in its pure form will simply not get you high. This is partly because of the very low cannabinoid content; the cannabinoids that Ruderalis does posses are almost all CBD, with very minimal THC at best.

Cannabis Afghanica

There is some debate in the cannabis community over whether or not Cannabis Afghanica is a new species of cannabis or a variety of Indica. Until evidence proves that there is a definite distinction between Indica and Afghanica, we will be referring to Afghanica as a variety of Indica.

In any case, the Indica variant Afghanica is found only in parts of Afghanistan. Much like its Indica relative, it has broad, thick leaves, albeit larger, and more loosely serrated, and of a much darker color. It is common for Afghanica leaves to be twice the size of a grown man's hand. They seldom reach five feet in height, and typically peak between two to four at maturity. Afghanicas are the ideal Hashish plant; its trichomes grow much fatter than those of any other cannabis species. The effects of Cannabis Afghanica are like that of Indica, only more intense, because of an almost equal ratio of THC and CBD.

Cannabinoids

Cannabis is the only plant that produces the chemical compounds known as cannabinoids. There are at least 60 reoccurring cannabinoids that are known to affect your high. We'll start with the key cannabinoids.

Delta-9-Trans-Tetrahydrocannabinol

Most commonly known as THC. This is the main ingredient in cannabis that gets you, well . . . high as hell. Reports indicate that from 70 to 100% of the high from cannabis is from THC. It can be found in almost all cannabis varieties in amounts of 0.01% up to 95% of all cannabinoids present. Some strains have been tested as high as 37% THC. Hashish contains as much as 69% THC. Either of these percentages will have you playing on the moon in no time. This cannabinoid is responsible for the cerebral, up, motivational, "head high,"

Delta-8-Trans-Tetrahydrocannabinol

Think of this cannabinoid as the baby sister of Delta-9 THC. Nothing really to write home about: it doesn't contribute more than 1% to your high. Most people, when referring to THC, lump both 9 and 8 together, as we will do in the remainder of this book.

Tetrahydrocannabivarin

Also known as THCV. This is a very rare cannabinoid, found mostly in strains from Asia and Africa. Some prime examples are found in the Dalat strain from Vietnam, Swahili and the Zuluweed strain from South Africa. It is known as Super THC because this cannabinoid is associated with some of the most potent cannabis in the world.

11-OH-Delta-8-Tetrahydrocannabinol-dimethylheptyl

This is the cannabinoid that occurs when Delta-9 THC metabolizes in the liver. It is actually more potent than Delta-9 THC, due to the fact that when it metabolizes it acquires an extra Hydrogen3 carbon molecule, Choloride3 molecule, and Choloride2 Hydroxide molecule. This also accounts for that second high you may experience one to two hours after ingesting cannabis.

Cannabidiol

Also known as CBD. This is the cannabinoid responsible for that sleepy, groggy feeling strongly associated with Indicas. Like Delta-9 THC, this cannabinoid is found in most cannabis varieties in amounts of 0.01% up to 95% of all cannabinoids present. CBD is also responsible for the creeper effect, which refers to the notion that the effects of smoking cannabis do not fully take action until up to 15 minutes after smoking. It is not known whether CBD increases or decreases the intensity of the high, but what is certain is that it does prolong the high—or at least the coming down feeling.

Cannabinol

Also known as CBN, cannabinol is not made from the plant itself. It is a byproduct of THC. CBN occurs when THC is degraded, e.g., by exposure to oxygen, by mishandling, or by exposure to light. It is one-tenth as psychoactive as THC. Like THC and CBD, CBN contributes to certain aspects of the high. It is speculated that CBN gives you the general feeling of unawareness, poor coordination, and lack of togetherness. If your cannabis has been severely mishandled, CBN could account for 60 to 80% of the cannabinoids present.

Nabilone

This is a major psychoactive cannabinoid found only in female cannabis plants during the last weeks of budding. Not much is known about this cannabinoid. Like 11-OH-Delta-8, this cannabinoid has an extra Hydrogen3 Carbon and Choloride3 molecule—just one more reason to wait for the proper harvest time.

CP 55940

This is another major psychoactive cannabinoid controlled by temperature, released only by temperatures colder than 65°F. Again, there is an extra Hydrogen3 Carbon and Choloride3 molecule.

Anandamide 22:4, N-6

A naturally occurring chemical found in the human brain. This is the chemical that makes you feel happy; it is also one of 60 recurring cannabinoids in cannabis.

TAXONOMY

The scientific classifications of cannabis

Kingdom:	*Plantae*	(Plants)
Subkingdom:	*Tracheobionta*	(Vascular)
Super Division:	*Spermatophyta*	(Seed)
Division:	*Magnoliophyta*	(Flowering)
Class:	*Magnoliopsida*	(Dicotyledons)
Subclass:	*Hamamelidae*	(Pollinated by wind)
Order:	*Urticales*	(Single ovule, etc.)
Family:	*Canabaceae*	(Coarse, "hairy" leaves, etc.)
Scientific name:	*Cannabis Sativa*	
Authority:	*L* for *Latin*	

TERMINOLOGY

Asexual Propagation: method of propagation without involving seeds, i.e., cloning.

Axial Growth: side branching; branching coming from the nodes of the plants.

Bacteria: the most simple and widespread group of organisms. Bacteria will inhabit all environments where the temperature is below 275°F. Bacteria is one of the main decomposers of organic matter.

Bracts: single- and three-blade leaflets coming from buds.

Note the bracts on these seeds.

Calyx: calyxes are the plant matter that makes up buds or colas. A plant that has a higher number of calyxes to leaf ratio is considered a better, higher quality cannabis plant.

Chlorophyll: a green photosynthetic pigment found in most plants, algae, and cyanobacteria. Its name is derived from ancient Greek: *chloros*, green and *phyllon*, leaf. Chlorophyll absorbs most strongly in the blue and red but poorly in the green portions of the electromagnetic spectrum, hence the green color of chlorophyll.

Chlorosis: a condition in which plant foliage produces insufficient chlorophyll.

Chromosomes: a chromosome is a single, large macromolecule of DNA, and constitutes a physically organized form of DNA in a cell. It is a very long, continuous piece of DNA (a single DNA molecule), which contains many genes, regulatory elements, and other intervening nucleotide sequences.

Dioeceous: cannabis is a dioeceous species, in which there are both male and female plants (as well as hermaphrodites).

Embryo: part of a seed, consisting of precursor tissues for the leaves, stem (see hypocotyl), and root (see radicle), as well as one or more cotyledons. Once the embryo begins to germinate, it is called a seedling.

Enzyme: proteins that catalyze (or bring about) chemical reactions. In these reactions, the molecules at the beginning of the process are called substrates, and the enzyme converts them into different molecules—the products. Almost all processes in the cell need enzymes in order to occur at significant rates. Since enzymes are extremely selective for their substrates and speed up only a few reactions from among many possibilities, the set of enzymes made in a cell determines which metabolic pathways occur in that cell.

Filial Generation: offspring generation. F1 is the first offspring or filial generation; F2 is the second; and so on.

Fungi: one example of fungi is yeast and mycorrhizae. Fungi are the other leading decomposer of organic matter. Fungi can protect against disease and pathogens. 90% of the plants in the world have some dependence on mycorrhizae to survive.

Genes: a locatable region of genomic sequence, corresponding to a unit of inheritance, which is associated with regulatory regions, transcribed regions, and / or other functional sequence regions. Genes interact with each other to influence physical development and behavior. Genes consist of a long strand of DNA (RNA in some viruses) that contains a promoter, which controls the activity of a gene, and a coding sequence, which determines what the gene produces.

Genotype: the specific genetic genome of an individual in the form of DNA. It is basically the type of gene. Together with the environmental variation that influences the individual, it codes for the phenotype of that individual.

Heterozygous: an organism is a *heterozygote* or is *heterozygous* at a locus or gene

The leaves are where the miracle of photosynthesis occurs. Keep the leaves clean so that the stomatas are able to work at full efficiency.

when it has different alleles occupying the gene's position in each of the homologous chromosomes. In diploid organisms, the two different alleles were inherited from the organism's two parents. For example, a heterozygous individual would have the allele combination Pp. More on this in the breeding chapter.

Homozygous: an organism is referred to as being homozygous at a specific locus when it carries two identical copies of the gene affecting a given trait on the two corresponding homologous chromosomes (e.g., the genotype is PP or pp when P and p refer to different possible alleles of the same gene). Such a cell or such an organism is called a *homozygote.*

Hormones: are chemical messengers from one cell (or group of cells) to another. All multicellular organisms produce hormones. The function of hormones is to serve as a signal to the target cells; the action of hormones is determined by the pattern of secretion and the signal transduction of the receiving tissue

Internodes: the stem is normally divided into nodes and internodes; the nodes hold buds which grow into one or more leaves, inflorescence (flowers), cones, or other stems, etc. The internodes act as spaces that distance one node from another. The term *shoots* is often confused with stems: shoots generally refer to new, fresh plant growth and does include stems, but also to other structures like leaves or flowers.

This is the female pre-flower, also known as the pistillate. Females produce actual marijuana blooms, aka bud, and they contain more THC.

This is a male plant. Look at the pre-flower, also known as a staminate. You can determine the sex of a cannabis plant by looking for this on a seedling.

These are the female pre-flowers. You need to be able to identify these in order to sex your plants.

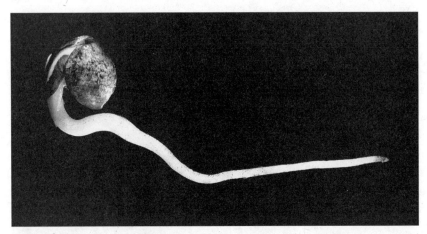

The taproot is just emerging from this cannabis seed.

All these roots come from that one original taproot that springs from the cannabis seed.

Microorganisms or Microbes: a broad category that describes microscopic organisms such as bacteria, fungi, archaea, and eukaryotes. These are generally simple, single-celled organisms.

Necrosis: the name given to accidental death of cells and living tissue.

Photosynthesis: the synthesis of glucose from sunlight, carbon dioxide, and water, with oxygen as a waste product. It is arguably the most important biochemical pathway known; nearly all life depends on it. It is an extremely complex fuckin' process, comprised of many coordinated biochemical reactions. It occurs in higher plants, algae, some bacteria, and some protists, organisms collectively referred to as photoautotrophs.

Petioles: the small stalk attaching the leaf blade to the stem. The petiole usually has the same internal structure as the stem.

Photoperiod: the physiological reaction of organisms to the length of day or night.

This prominent stamen lets us know loud and clear that this cannabis plant is a male.

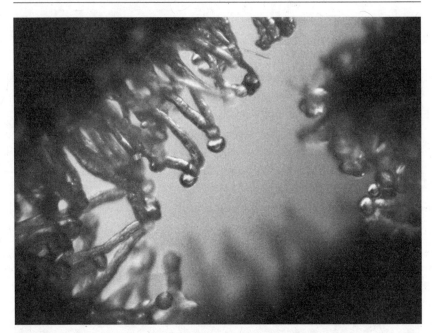

These are trichomes. The cannabinoids are developed and housed within them. You want lots and lots of these on your plants.

Phototropism: the directional plant growth in which the direction of growth is determined by the direction of the light source. It was formerly called heliotropism. Phototropism is one of the many plant tropisms or movements that respond to external stimuli. Growth towards a light source is a positive phototropism, while growth away from light is called negative phototropism.

Pistillate: the female pre-flower.

Phenotype: of an individual organism, either its total physical appearance and constitution or a specific manifestation of a trait, such as size, eye color, or behavior, that varies between individuals.

Phyllotaxy: the arrangement of leaves on the shoot of a plant. The basic patterns are alternate, opposite, whorled, or spiral.

Polyploids: the condition of some biological cells and organisms of containing more than two homologous sets of chromosomes. Polyploid types are termed according to the number of chromosome sets in the nucleus: triploid (three sets; 3x), tetraploid (four sets; 4x), pentaploid (five sets; 5x), hexaploid (six sets; 6x) and so on. Polyploidy is a mutation.

Sinsemilla: also known as sensi, this is the method of removing all males and hermaphrodites so your crop is seedless. Sinsemilla is regarded as the best, most potent cannabis.

Stamen: the male organ of a flower.

Staminate: the male pre-flower.

Stigmas: usually the terminal (end) portion that has no epidermis and is fitted to receive pollen (male gametes); it is commonly somewhat glutinous or viscid. Closely related to pistils.

Stipule: refers to outgrowths borne on either side of the base of a leafstalk (the petiole). A pair of stipules is considered part of the anatomy of the leaf of a typical flowering plant, although in many species the stipules are inconspicuous or entirely absent. On cannabis plants, the stipule is located on at the node and is sometimes confused with pre-flowers (primordia). It is just a wisp- or hair-like structure that serves no known purpose.

Stomata: a tiny opening or pore, found mostly on the under-surface (epidermis) of a plant leaf, and used for gas exchange. The pore is formed by a pair of specialized parenchyma cells known as guard cells, which are responsible for regulating the size of the opening.

Taproot: this is the main root that first appears when the seedling germinates. The taproot will continue to grow indefinitely until the plant enters the vegetative cycle. All other roots branch off from the taproot.

Tetraploid: has four homologous sets of chromosome.

Terpenes: a large and varied class of hydrocarbons, produced by a wide variety of plants. Terpenes are responsible for the different aromas and tastes in cannabis.

Trichomes: are the glands that develop and house the cannabinoids. Trichomes range in size and color depending on the strain but all develop the same way. There are three kinds you should know about. Bulbous: the bulbous type is the smallest. One to four cells make up the "foot" and "stalk," and one to four cells make up the "head" of the gland. Head cells secrete a resin—presumably cannabinoids and related compounds, which accumulate between the head cells and the cuticle. When the gland matures, a nipple-like protrusion may form on the membrane from the pressure of the accumulating resin. The bulbous glands are found scattered about the surfaces of the aboveground plant parts. Capitate-Sessile: the second type of gland is much larger and is more numerous than the bulbous glands. They are called capitate, which means having a globular-shaped head. The head is composed of usually eight, but up to 16 cells, that form a convex rosette. These cells secrete cannabinoids, and related compounds that accumulate between the rosette and its outer membrane. This gives it a spherical shape. Capitate-Stalked: cannabinoids are most abundant in the capitate-stalked gland, which consists of a tier of secretory disc cells subtending a large non-cellular secretory cavity. These capitate-stalked glands appear during flowering and form their densest cover on the female flower bracts. They are also highly concentrated on the small leaves that accompany the flowers. The male flowers have stalked glands on the sepals, but they are smaller and less concentrated than on the female bracts.

Some of this information was borrowed from wikipedia.com under the GNU Free Documentation License. Some of this information was informed through readings of articles on wikipedia.com under the GNU Free Documentation License, particularly the following article: Wikipedia contributors, "Cannabis (drug)," Wikipedia, The Free Encyclopedia, http://en.wikipedia.org/w/index.php?title=Cannabis_(drug)&oldid=349217943 (accessed March 11, 2010).

Chapter 3

Breeders, Seed Banks, and Cannabis Lore

Keeping the grow room clean and tidy is the first step to growing great bud.

Note: Because of the extensive list of seed companies, I will only be grading the most popular ones. You may notice that some are "not available to the public": this means you must purchase their seeds through a seed bank, as the company does not deal directly to the public.

AFROPIPS SEEDS
afropips.com
info@afropips.com

	Sells to Public	Price	Cannabis Cups	Feminized Seeds
	✓	$20-$100	0	✗

Afropips offers quality African strains at a reasonable price.

Cup Winning Strains: None

Currently Available Strains: Afropips Tribal Vision, Afropips Sweet White Malawi, Afropips Sweet Malawi, Afropips Swazi Red, Afropips Senegal Haze, Afropips Sangoma Seeds, Afropips Power Malawi Seeds, Afropips Nigerian x Afghan, Afropips Nigerian, Afropips Malberry, Afropips Malawi Mini, Afropips Malawi Gold, Afropips Malawi 99, Afropips Mabombe, Afropips Fast Blast

BARNEY'S FARM
barneysfarm.com
info@barneysfarm.com

	Sells to Public	Price	Cannabis Cups	Feminized Seeds
	✗	$37-$75	9	$130-$189

Barney's Farm is known for their respectable quality of product. Sold in packs of ten.

Cup Winning Strains: Vanilla Kush (2009 Cannabis Cup), Utopia Haze (2008 Cannabis Cup), G13 Haze (2006, 2007 Cannabis Cup), Crimea Blue (2007 Indica Cup), Night Shade (2006 Indica Cup), Willie Nelson (2005 Cannabis Cup), Amnesia Haze (2004 Cannabis Cup), Morning Glory (2002 Cannabis Cup), Sweet Tooth (2001 Cannabis Cup).

Currently Available Strains: Crimea Blue, LSD, Red Diesel, G13 Haze, Red Cherry Berry, Sweet Tooth, 8 Ball Kush, Morning Glory, Laughing Buddha, Violator Kush, Utopia Haze, Red Dragon, Blue Cheese, Phatt Fruity, Honey B, Top Dawg, Amnesia Lemon, Night Shade.

BIG BUDDHA SEEDS
bigbuddhaseeds.com
info@bigbuddhaseeds.com

	Sells to Public	Price	Cannabis Cups	Feminized Seeds
	✓	$62-$70	2	$60-$70

Big Buddha Seeds is known for a very respectable quality of product sold in packs of ten. He does stealth shipping and is easily reachable from his website and will do his best to make sure you receive the seeds you order.

Cup Winning Strains: Big Buddha Cheese (2006 Indica Cup), Blue Cheese (2006 Sativa Cup).

Currently Available Strains: Big Buddha Cheese, Blue Cheese, Chiesel, the Karli, G-Bomb, Buddha Haze, Cheesus, Bubble Cheese.

CHIMERA SEEDS
hempdepot.ca
6200672@hushmail.com

	Sells to Public	Price	Cannabis Cups	Feminized Seeds
	✓	$25–$60	0	✗

Very decent quality with some super potent strains, thanks in part to help from DJ Short. Good prices, sold in packs of twelve with stealth shipping. Generous with his seeds.

Cup Winning Strains: None as of yet – Chimera is a Canadian breeder still building his reputation.

Currently Available Strains: C4, C- Plus, Calizahr, Fighting Buddha, Mental Floss, Schnazzleberry#2, Sweetest Sative, Ultimix.

This delicious Mekong Haze bud from Delta 9 Labs is ready to roll.

DELTA 9 LABS
delta9labs.com
info@delta9labs.com

	Sells to Public	Price	Cannabis Cups	Feminized Seeds
	✗	$99–$127	0	✗

Delta 9 Labs are known for their very respectable quality of strains, as well as their medical marijuana-based organic and strictly "earth friendly" approach to seed breeding.

Cup Winning Strains: None – they are a relatively new company.

Currently Available Strains: CannaSutra, Southern Lights, Star Gazer, Mekong Haze, Brainstorm Haze, Brainstorm Haze G13, F.O.G. (Fruit of the Gods), Super Star, Double Kush, and Aiea.

DJ SHORT SEEDS
hempdepot.ca
6200672@hushmail.com

	Sells to Public	Price	Cannabis Cups	Feminized Seeds
	✗	$83–$170	4	✗

DJ Short is known worldwide as an excellent breeder with very good product

Star Gazer from Delta 9 Labs is a Sativa-dominant strain that offers a relaxing high with a peppermint aftertaste. A great cross of Warlock x AK-47 x Sensi Star. Enjoy!

quality. No rip offs with DJ Short seeds. Come in packs of ten.

Cup Winning Strains: Blueberry (2002-03 Toker's Bowl, 2000 Cannabis Cup – Best Indica), Flo (1996 Cannabis Cup).

Currently Available Strains: Blueberry, Flo, Blue Moonshine, F13, Vanilluna, Cocoa Kush, Old Time Moonshine, True Blueberry, and Grape Krush.

DNA GENETICS

	Sells to Public	Price	Cannabis Cups	Feminized Seeds
dnagenetics.com				
info@dnagenetics.com	✓	$109–$113	5	$62-$85

DNA Genetics offers a very respectable array of good strains with no rip-offs. Sold in packs of six or thirteen.

Cup Winning Strains: Martian Mean Green (2005 Sativa Cup, 2005 Breeder's Cup), L.A. Confidential (2005 Indica Cup, 2005 Breeder's Cup), Lemon Skunk (High Times Cup 2007).

Currently Available Strains: Martian Mean Green, L.A. Confidential, ReCON, Connie Chung, Cannalope Haze, C13 Haze, Cannadential, Cataract Kush, Chocolope (D-Line), Lemon Skunk, Pure Afghan, Rocklock, Sour Cream, Super Cannalope, Sweet Haze and Hashplant Haze.

DR. ATOMIC SEEDS
dratomicseedbank.com
dr.atomic@rocketmail.com

	Sells to Public	Price	Cannabis Cups	Feminized Seeds
	✕	$70-$90	0	✕

Respectable quality of genetics for a very reasonable price. Sold in packs of ten.
Cup Winning Strains: None.
Currently Available Strains: Atomic Haze, Atomic Northern Lights, Atomic NL, Atomic Haze, Atomic Shiva, Blueberry Jam and Thai Lights.

DR. GREENTHUMB
drgreenthumb.com
drgreenthumb@drgreenthumb.com

	Sells to Public	Price	Cannabis Cups	Feminized Seeds
	✓	$100-$200	0	$150-$225

Pretty respectable quality of strains from a great breeder. Sold in packs of ten, except for Sweet 105, which is in a pack of fifteen.
Cup Winning Strains: None.
Currently Available Strains: Endless Sky, Y2K, Sweet 105, Bubba Kush, OG Kush, 747, Big Laughing, Big Purps, Chumaluma, Columbian Skies, Endless Sky, Fire Hydrant, Iranian Short Season, Jazz, Kashmiri, Matanuska Thunderfuck, Millennium Bud, Niagara, Niagara x Shiva, Oh! Zone, Cindy 99, Chemdawg Kush, Chemdawg G13, Original Cheese, and Trainwreck.

Matanuska Thunderfuck from Dr. Greenthumb is so potent even experienced tokers need to beware. A great strain.

DUTCH PASSION
dutch-passion.nl

info@dutch-passion.nl

	Sells to Public	Price	Cannabis Cups	Feminized Seeds
	✕	$26-$90	6	$75-$183

Good genetics for an excellent price. They are the largest producer of moderately priced seeds.

Cup Winning Strains: Blueberry (2000-01 Indica Cup) Euforia (2000 Sativa Cup), Mazar (1999 Indica Cup), Super Haze (1992 Cannabis Cup), Skunk #1 (High Times Cannabis Cup).

Currently Available Strains: Mekong High, The Ultimate, Dutch Cheese, Ortega Indica, Jorge's Diamonds #1, Durban Poison, Khola, Skunk #1, Sacra Frasca, Skunk #11, Skunk Passion, Orange Bud, Ultra Skunk, Oasis, Green Spirit, Masterkush, Super Haze, Brainstorm, Isis, Californian Orange, Mazar, Dolce Vita, White Widow, Euforia, Skywalker, Blueberry, Original Flo, Blue Moonshine, Strawberry Cough, Power Plant, Tundra, Taiga, SnowStorm, PolarLight, Frisian Dew, Passion #1, Trance, Hollands Hope, Purple#1, Shaman, Twilight, Voodoo, Pamir Gold and Snow Bud.

FEDERATION SEEDS
seeds@cannabismarijuana.com

cannabismarijuana.com/federationseeds.html

	Sells to Public	Price	Cannabis Cups	Feminized Seeds
	✓	$65-$105	1	✕

Moderate quality of seeds with a good reputation for honesty and reliable strains.

Cup Winning Strains: Mikado (2005 Toker's Bowl).

Currently Available Strains: Big Mac, Crown Royal, Celestial Temple, Cotton Candy, Island Sweet Skunk, Mikado, Romulan and UBC Chemo.

THE FLYING DUTCHMEN
flyingdutchmen.com

info@flyingdutchmen.com

	Sells to Public	Price	Cannabis Cups	Feminized Seeds
	✕	$30-$95	1	$55-$145

A large producer of very respectable strains at a reasonable price.

Cup Winning Strains: Pot O' Gold (2003 Indica Cup).

Currently Available Strains: Pot O' Gold, Thai-tanic, The Real McCoy, Original Haze, The Pure, Dame Blanche Feminized, Early Durban, Edelweiss Feminized, Aurora B, Blueberry Skunk Feminized, Kerala Krush, G Force Feminized, Afghanica, Voyager Feminized, Dutchmen's Royal Orange, Skunk No.1 Feminized, Fuma Con Dios, White Widow Feminized, Flying Dragon Feminized, Haley's Comet, Power Skunk Feminized, Temple Haze Feminized, Skunk Classic Feminized, Pineapple Punch, Nepal Kush Feminized, Swazi Safari, Dutch Delight Feminized, Artic Sun, Amsterdam Mist Feminized, Haze Mist and Titan's Haze.

GREEN HOUSE SEED COMPANY
greenhouseseeds.nl

	Sells to Public	Price	Cannabis Cups	Feminized Seeds
Use website for contact information.	X	**$36-$110**	**32**	**$36-$110**

One of the largest and most successful cannabis seed producers in the world with a solid reputation for excellent genetics and strains. Sold in packs of five and ten. Huge selection of feminized seeds. In business since 1985.

Cup Winning Strains: Arjan's Ultra Haze (2005-06 Cannabis Cup), Great White Shark (2005 Highlife Cup), Hawaiian Snow (2003 Cannabis Cup), Super Silver Haze (2002 Sativa Cup), Super Kali Mist (2002 Cannabis Cup), Big Bang (2001 Cannabis Cup), Super Silver Haze (1998-99 Cannabis Cup), El Nino (1998 Cannabis Cup), Great White Shark (1997 Cannabis Cup), White Widow (1995 Cannabis Cup), and Citral Skunk (1994 Cannabis Cup).

Currently Available Strains: Big Bang, The Church, AMS, Lemon Skunk, Cheese, Himalaya Gold, TrainWreck, NL5 Haze Mist, Alaskan Ice, King's Kush, K-Train, Bubba Kush, White Widow, White Rhino, Great White Shark, El Niño, Arjan's Haze #3, Arjan's Haze #2, Arjan's Haze #1, Arjan's Ultra Haze #1, Arjan's Ultra Haze #2, Arjan's Strawberry Haze, Super Lemon Haze, Super Silver Haze, Neville's Haze, and Hawaiian Snow.

HOMEGROWN FANTASEEDS
homegrown-fantaseeds.com0

	Sells to Public	Price	Cannabis Cups	Feminized Seeds
orders@homegrown-fantaseeds.com	X	**$30-$80**	**3**	**$55-$8**

Very respectable quality of strains from this established Amsterdam seed company. Excellent price for good quality. Sold in packs of ten.

Cup Winning Strains: Blue Haze (2001 Sativa Cup), Homegrown 2000 (2000 Indica Cup) and Haze / Skunk (1992 Cannabis Cup).

Currently Available Strains: Blue Pearl, Afghani, Armageddon, Australian Blue, Big Bud, Blue Haze, Californian Orange, Caramella, Eclipse, Flashback, Early Girl, Fourway, Genie of the Lamp, Homegrown Haze, Cheese 100% female, Homegrown Purple, Jah Herrer, K2, Kamamist, Mango, Masterkush, Millennium, Northern Light, Original Misty, Shiva, Skunk #1, Super Crystal, The Fantasy, Top 44, Trainwreck 100% female, Amazing Haze, Parvatie, Homegrown Lowryder, Homegrown Cheese (feminized), Homegrown Trainwreck (feminized), Armageddon (feminized), Afghani (feminized), Skunk #1 (feminized), Haze (feminized), Diesel (feminized), Jah Herrer (feminized), White Widow (feminized), Northern Lights (feminized), Homegrown Lowryder (feminized).

Some delicious Northern Lights bud goes well with anything.

KC BRAINS SEEDS	Sells to Public	Price	Cannabis Cups	Feminized Seeds
kcbrains.com	✕	**$20**	**2**	✕

No email contact – buy from a seed wholesaler for KC Brains products.

An established Dutch breeder who tests his seeds regularly to ensure quality control. Interesting blends of Brazilian and Dutch strains. Sold in packs of ten for a very good price.

Cup Winning Strains: Mango (2002 Indica Cup) and Leda Uno (2001 Sativa Cup).

Currently Available Strains: KC 33, Leda, UNO, K.C. 36, Mango, Mind Bender, SWISS-xT, Spontanica, Brasil x K.C., T.N.R, Cyber Cristal, Afghani Special, California Special, Northern Light Special, Haze Special, Sweet Dreams, Cristal Paradise, White K.C., and Cristal Limit.

LEGENDS SEEDS
legendsseeds.com

info@legendsseeds.com

Sells to Public	Price	Cannabis Cups	Feminized Seeds
✓	$35-$100	1	$180

Reasonably high quality of strains from an established Vancouver breeder. No rip-offs here. Sold in packs of ten. He also sells other breeders' seeds on his website.
Cup Winning Strains: Fast Spear (2000 Indica Cup).
Currently Available Strains: Sweet Skunk Selfed (Feminized), Mountain Mix, Johnny Blaze, TIMEBOMB, Toe Jam, The Red Eyed Bride, Highend and Fast Spear.

MAGUS GENETICS
info@theattitudeseedbank.com

Sells to Public	Price	Cannabis Cups	Feminized Seeds
✗	$55-$95	3	$45-$100

cannabis-seeds-bank.co.uk/magus-genetics-seeds/cat_85.html

Magus Genetics is an independent breeder named Gerrit who is known for having a respectable quality of strains. The creator/breeder of the celebrated Warlock strain. Sold in packs of ten.
Cup Winning Strains: Zamal (2008 IC 420 Sativa Cup), Double Dutch (2007-08 IC 420 Indica Cup), Biddy's Bubble (2008 IC 420 Hash Cup), Double Dutch (2004 IC 420 Indica Cup), and Biddy Early (2003 Sativa Cup).
Currently Available Strains: Biddy Early, Biddy's Sister, Double Dutch, Exile, Motivation, Warlock, Motivation (Feminized), Exile (Feminized), Double Dutch (Feminized), Warlock (Feminized) and Biddy Early (Feminized).

MANDALA SEEDS
mandalaseeds.com

info@mandalaseeds.com

Sells to Public	Price	Cannabis Cups	Feminized Seeds
✗	$17-$52	0	✗

An earth-friendly, organic seed breeding company with an anti-capitalistic business ethic. They do not participate in cannabis marketing events and offer quality landrace genetics for a fair price.
Cup Winning Strains: None. Do not participate in events.
Currently Available Strains: 8 Miles High, Ganesh, Mandala #1, Hashberry, Speed Queen, Sadhu, Kalichakra, Satori, White Satin, and Krystalica.

MR. NICE SEEDS

mrnice.nl/dhtml/home.php

info@mrnice.nl

	Sells to Public	Price	Cannabis Cups	Feminized Seeds
	✕	$45-$23	0	✕

Respectable quality of strains from very experienced and renowned breeders, Shantibaba and Neville, as well as Howard Marks. Sold in packs of fifteen.

Cup Winning Strains: They do not enter their strains in competitions, so, none.

Currently Available Strains: Afghan Haze, Angel Heart, Black Widow, Angel's Breathe, Critical Mass, ASH, Devil, Critical Haze, Dreamtime, Early Haze, Early Queen, Master Kaze, Early Skunk, Neville's Haze Mango, Early Skunk Haze, Neville's Skunk, G13 Skunk, NHS-National Health Service, G13 Widow, La Nina, Mango Haze, Mango x Widow, Master Kush x Skunk, Medicine Man, Neville's Haze, Shark Shock, Shit, Spice, Super Silver Haze and Walkabout.

NIRVANA SEEDS

nirvana-shop.com/en/

info@nirvana-shop.com

	Sells to Public	Price	Cannabis Cups	Feminized Seeds
	✓	$15-$25	0	$94

Great seeds and strains for beginners at a very low price. Sold in packs of ten.

Cup Winning Strains: None.

Currently Available Strains: AK-48, Aurora Indica, Blackberry, BlackJack, Blue Mystic, Bubblelicious, Chrystal, Eldorado, Full Moon, Hawaii Maui Waui, Haze #1, Ice, Jock Horror, Master Kush, Medusa, New York Power Diesel, Northern Light, Papaya, PPP, Royal Flush, Short Rider, Snow White, Sterling Haze, Super Skunk, Swiss Cheese, Urban Poison, White Castle, White Rhino and White Widow. All strains are offered as feminized, as well.

PARADISE SEEDS

paradise-seeds.com

info@paradise-seeds.com

	Sells to Public	Price	Cannabis Cups	Feminized Seeds
	✕	$45-$145	6	$75-$140

Very respectable quality of genetics available from a great company. Sold in packs of five or ten (prices listed here are for packs of ten).

Cup Winning Strains: Opium (2006 Sativa Cup), Nebula (2005 Sativa Cup, 1999 Sativa Cup), and Sensi Star (2005, 2000, 1999 Indica Cups).

Currently Available Strains: Sensi Star, Swiss Bliss, Nebula, Sheherazade, Amsterdam Flame, Dutch Dragon, Sativa Spirit, Rox, Sugar Babe, Durga Mata, Magic Bud, Belladonna, Sweet Purple, Opium, Jacky White, Wappa, Ice Cream, White Berry, Spoetnik #1, and Delahaze, Automaria.

An incredible cross of two Super Shivas, Durga Mata from Paradise Seeds is so tasty it'll knock you to your knees.

REEFERMAN SEEDS
reefermanseeds.com

	Sells to Public	Price	Cannabis Cups	Feminized Seeds
info@reefermanseeds.com	✕	$75-$200	1	✕

Cup Winning Strains: Love Potion #1 (2004 Sativa Cup).

Currently Available Strains: Accidental Haze, Bazooka Joe Bubblegum, Black Seed, Cambodian (Phnom Phen), Cambodian x Haze, Cherry Bomb Indica, Cherry Haze, G13, G13 x Hash Plant 2, Hindu Kush x Haze, Love Potion #1, Love Potion #2, Original Haze, Panama Red, Super Silver Haze, William's Wonder, Burmese Delight, Nigerian Nightmare, Petrolia Headstash, John Sinclair, Thunderfuck Haze, and Willie Nelson.

RESERVOIR SEEDS
icmag.com

	Sells to Public	Price	Cannabis Cups	Feminized Seeds
icmag.com	✕	$45-$160	0	✕

Contact RezDog through the ICMag forums.

Reservoir Seeds offers a respectable quality of genetics to the public. Popular with experienced growers. RezDog is a very well-known breeder.

Cup Winning Strains: None.

Currently Available Strains: Apollo 11 G4, Apollo Mist, Basic Diesel, Bottle Rocket, D39, DSD v2, Firecracker, Gonzo #1, Kill Bill, Killer Apollo, Mindfuck, Omega Diesel, Orange Apollo, Petrol, Princess Diesel, Quick Mist, Quick Mist Diesel, Schroomy Deeze, Sour Diesel BX 1.5, Sour Diesel, BX 2.5, Sour Diesel v 3 aka ECSD v3, Sour Diesel IBL, Sour Mist, Sour Queen, Sour Queen II, Sour Wonder, Speedball, Super Silver Sour, Diesel Haze, Strawberry Diesel, Sweet Apollo, Thunderfuck Diesel, William's Wonder, BX#2, William's Wonder IX-1, William's Wonder Haze, Willy's Wonderful Cindy aka Wonderella, Wonder Diesel, and Wonder Fuck Aka ThunderFuckin'Wonder.

SAGARMATHA SEEDS
highestseeds.com
info@highestseeds.com

	Sells to Public	Price	Cannabis Cups	Feminized Seeds
	✕	$38-$133	3	$50-$130

Sagarmatha Seeds offers a very decent quality of product and their customers are always satisfied. Sold in packs of five or ten (prices listed here are for packs of ten).
Cup Winning Strains: Yumbolt (2001 Indica Cup), Western Winds (1999 Sativa Cup), and Stonehedge (1998 Sativa Cup).
Currently Available Strains: AK- 48, Double Diesel Ryder, Lowboldt, Solo Ryder, Star Ryder, Smurfberry, A-1 Haze, Blueberry Bud, Blue Thunder, Cal-train Wreck, Cheeze Wreck, Chunky Cheeze, DoubleBubbleBerry, Diamond Head, Hawaiian Punch, Indica XXL, Kwik Kali, Matanuska Tundra, Northern Lights no 9, Peak 19, Purple Pinecone, Strawberry D-Lite, Stonehedge, Western Winds / Kali Mist, Blueberry, BubbleBerry, Early Riser, Flow, Gardeners Choice, Mangolian Indica, Matanuska Mint, Northern Lights, Sanctuary, Slyder, Special K, Stupersonic, Thunderboldt, Wonderberry, and Yumbolt.

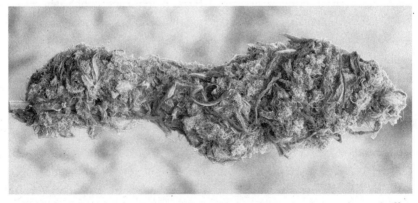

Yumbolt from Sagarmatha is a true beauty. She produces nice, large colas and offers a taste with hints of pine, lemon, mango and orange deliciousness.

SEEDSMAN SEEDS

seedsman.com	Sells to Public	Price	Cannabis Cups	Feminized Seeds
www.seedsman.com/contact.php	✕	$28-$57	1	$35-$80

Seedsman is a combination of two of the first seed companies, Sacred Seeds and Cultivators Choice. Seedsman Seeds doesn't breed seeds; they only market seeds bred by independent breeders. Good selection of solid genetics for a fair price.

Cup Winning Strains: Skunk #1 (1998 Cannabis Cup)

Currently Available Strains: Check out the website for a listing of the products they sell. Many great, independent breeders are featured on Seedsman Seeds' website. They do not ship to the USA, however, but Seedsman products can be purchased through other seedbanks. Do some research online. Generally, people looking for old school genetics go to Seedsman Seeds.

SENSI SEEDS

sensiseeds.com	Sells to Public	Price	Cannabis Cups	Feminized Seeds
Info@sensiseeds.com	✕	$28-$171	4	$50-$160

One of the largest and most successful cannabis seed breeding companies. They have quality strains and a huge variety of product. Sold in packs of five or ten.

Cup Winning Strains: Mother's Finest (2002 Sativa Cup), Jack Herer (1994, 1999 Sativa Cup), and Haze x Northern Lights #5 (1993 Cannabis Cup).

Currently Available Strains: Shiva Shanti, Hindu Kush, Afghani #1, Maple Leaf Indica, First Lady, Four-Way, Mother's Finest, Big Bud, Silver Haze, Black Domina, Jack Flash, Northern Lights, Hash Plant, Northern Lights #5 x Haze, Ed Rosenthal Super Bud, Mr. Nice G13 x Hash Plant and Jack Herer, Shiva Shanti II, Sensi Skunk, Skunk #1, Super Skunk, California Indica, Shiva Skunk, American Dream, Skunk Kush, Fruity Juice, Marley's Collie, Mexican Sativa, Ruderalis Indica, Guerrilla's Gusto, Jamaican Pearl, Early Pearl, Durban, Early Skunk, Early Girl, Ruderalis Skunk, White Skunk, Double Gum, Master Kush, Afghan Kush, Hollands Hope, White Label Rhino, White Widow, Cal Orange Bud, White Gold, Kali Haze, White Haze, White Label Jack Herer, Amnesia White, Super Skunk, White Ice, Big Bud (Feminized), Super Skunk (Feminized), Silver Haze #9 (Feminized), Jack Flash #5 (Feminized), Skunk #1 (Feminized), Shiva Skunk (Feminized), Early Skunk (Feminized), Northern Lights x Haze (Feminized), x HAZE (Feminized), Northern Lights (Feminized), White Widow (Feminized), Pure Power Plant (Feminized), Super Skunk (Feminized), White Ice (Feminized), White Gold (Feminized), Purple Haze (Feminized), White Diesel (Feminized), Snow Ryder (Feminized), and White Skunk (Feminized).

SERIOUS SEEDS

seriousseeds.com

info@seriousseeds.com

	Sells to Public	Price	Cannabis Cups	Feminized Seeds
	✕	$96-$106	4	$86

World-class genetics at very affordable prices. Sold in packs of eleven.

Cup Winning Strains: AK-47 (1999, 2003 Indica Cup), and Kali Mist (2000, 2002 Sativa Cup).

Currently Available Strains: AK-47, Bubble Gum, Chronic, Kali Mist and White Russian.

SOMA SEEDS

somaseeds.nl

soma@somaseeds.nl

	Sells to Public	Price	Cannabis Cups	Feminized Seeds
	✕	$94-$164	5	$145-$185

Very respectable quality of genetics with an organic, earth-friendly approach. Come in packs of ten.

Cup Winning Strains: Lavender (2005 Indica Cup), NYC Diesel (2001, 2002 Sativa Cup), Buddha's Sister (2002 Indica Cup), and Recycling Buddha (1999 Indica Cup).

Skunk is one of the most celebrated strains of all time, and for good reason.

Currently Available Strains: Reclining Buddha, Buddha's Sister, NYC Diesel, Kahuna, Big Kahuna, Amethyst Bud, Amnesia Haze, Haze Heaven, Lavender, Citralah, Somango, White Willow, Afghani Delight, Rockbud, White Light, Somativa, Kilimanjaro, Somanna, Free Tibet, Soma Salad, NYC Diesel (Feminized), Lavender (Feminized), Somango (Feminized), Somaui, Hash Heaven (Male), Somini, Sogouda, Kushadelic, Kushadelic (Feminized), Buddha's Sister (Feminized).

	Sells to Public	Price	Cannabis Cups	Feminized Seeds
SPICE OF LIFE SEEDS				
spiceoflifeseeds.net	✕	**$88**	1	✕

spiceoflifeseeds.com/contact-spice-of-life-seeds.php

Producers of some really excellent strains. SOL Seeds aims for quality, not quantity. Sold in packs of twelve.

Cup Winning Strains: Sweet Tooth (2000 Cannabis Cup).

Currently Available Strains: Sweet Tooth #3, BlockHead, LUI, Sweet Tooth #1.1, Sweet Blue, Blue Satellite #2.2, Blubonic, Donk, OG Kush x BS#2.2, GLO.

Satisfy your sweet tooth with this delicious Sweet Tooth plant.

SUBCOOL / TGA SEEDS	Sells to Public	Price	Cannabis Cups	Feminized Seeds
cannaseur.com	X	$86-$115	0	X

Check the forums at www.cannaseur.com, or www.breedbay.co.uk

Highly respected breeders with a very high quality of genetics. They are reachable through many of the online forums and are always helpful. One of the best in the business. Seeds come in packs of ten.

Cup Winning Strains: None

Currently Available Strains: Agent Orange, AstroQueen, Jack the Ripper, Jacks Cleaner #2, JillyBean, SpaceQueen, The Flav, Third Dimension and Vortex..

T.H. SEEDS	Sells to Public	Price	Cannabis Cups	Feminized Seeds
thseeds.com				
info@thseeds.com	X	$30-$145	10	$80-$115

One of the oldest seed companies in Holland with an established reputation for high quality genetics. Sold in packs of five and ten. All prices listed here are for packs of ten..

Cup Winning Strains: Kal-X (1995 Cannabis Cup), Bubblegum (1996 Cannabis Cup), S.A.G.E. (1998 Cannabis Cup: 3rd highest THC level with 21% THC), S.A.G.E. (2001 Sativa Cup), The HOG (2002 Cannabis Cup), MK Ultra (2003, 2004 Indica Cup), Sage 'n Sour (2004 Sativa Cup), Kushage (2005 Cannabis Cup), Wreckage (2009 Hash Cup).

Currently Available Strains: S.A.G.E. (Regular or Feminized), MK-Ultra (Regular or Feminized), Burmese Kush (Regular or Feminize), A-Train (Regular or Feminized), Kushage (Regular or Feminized), Chocolate Chunk, Mendocino Madness, Heavy Duty Fruity, Bubblegum, Skunk XXX, The Hog, Sage 'n Sour, Zero-Gravity, PG-13, Da Purps, Wreckage, Lambo, and Darkstar.

SEED BANKS

Seed banks are the wholesalers of cannabis seeds and they represent multiple seed breeders in one location. In this chapter, the most popular seed banks will be graded on six factors: number of companies, quality of the seeds, availability of products, prices, shipping, and customer satisfaction. For the most accurate and up-to-date information on seed banks, check out seedbankupdate.com, help Green Man out, and send your reports to him at admin@seedbankupdate.com. Like any other monetary transaction, ordering seeds can be somewhat risky. Please make sure that you trust the seed bank you choose to deal with. Check online forums and talk with people – discretely – in the cannabis community to find a reputable seed wholesaler.

Online Seed Banks

	# of Seed Companies	Quality	Availability	Prices	Shipping	Customer Satisfaction
CANNASEUR.COM admin@cannaseur.com	★	★★★★★	★★★★	★★★	★★★★★	★★★★★
CANNASEED.COM www.cannaseed.com	★★★	★★★	★★★★★	★★★★	★★★	★★★
DOPE-SEEDS.COM info@dope-seeds.com	★★★	★★★★★	★★★★	★★	★★★★	★★★
DRCHRONIC.COM mmiller@wwmail.co.uk www.hg420.com	★★★★★	★★★★★	★★★★★	★★★★★	★★★★★	★★★★★
GROWSHOPALIEN.COM/ ONLINESHOP/ online.alien@pandora.be	★★★★★	★★★★★	★★★★★	★★★★	★★★★★	★★★★★
HEMPDEPOT.CA 200672@hushmail.com	★★★	★★★★	★★★	★★	★★★	★★★
HIGH-LAND.CO.UK info@high-land.co.uk	★★★	★★★★★	★★★★★	★★★★	★ (no USA shipping)	★★★★
SEEDBOUTIQUE.COM www.seedboutique.com/store/contact_us.php	★★★★★	★★	★★★	★★★★★	★★★	★★★
SEEDSMAN.COM www.seedsman.com/contact.php	★	★★★★	★★★★★	★★★★★	★ (no USA shipping)	★★★★★

CANNABIS LORE: BREEDERS' HISTORIES AND CONTROVERSIES

Without a doubt, the cannabis seed business is an interesting world. Every company has a unique story as to how it was formed and where their strains originated. Likewise, there is a great deal of controversy surrounding many breeders and companies and the business ethics of breeding and selling cannabis seeds. Many of the prominent seed breeders and companies are listed here in alphabetical order.

Afropips Seeds

Afropips's owner worked his way through different regions of Africa collecting the seeds of the best smoke he could find in the late 70s. In 2000, he moved to England to create Afropips Seeds and his own F1 African hybrids based on his personal preferences. Afropips offers a number of excellent strains, such as Swazi Red, which is an African Landrace Sativa with red bud hairs, and Fastblast, a good beginner's Indica.

Brothers Grimm

The Brothers Grimm, comprised of Soul and Sly, are reputed to be the most mysterious figures in the cannabis world. No one (to my knowledge) has heard of them since shortly before the Overgrow online cannabis forum went down. These good brothers are responsible for many of the strains that we know and love today, and seed breeders around the world owe them the deepest respect. Neither breeders Team Green Avengers nor Reservoir Seeds' collections would be anywhere near what they are today without such Brothers Grimm classic strains as Apollo 13 and Cinderella 99. It is rumored that Brothers Grimm went on to become professionals in the field of plant horticulture; others say that they were busted for their involvement with Overgrow. It is perhaps best to think that they are doing what they have always done: making killer crosses for the cannabis community to enjoy for years to come. Every person that is a part of the cannabis community should light their next joint for the good brothers, Mr. Soul and Mr. Sly.

Dj Short

DJ Short may be one of the most famous breeders alive. He started his career during the late 70s and early 80s, collecting strains such as Highland Thai, Chocolate Thai, Oaxaca Gold, and Afghan Indica. These strains are responsible for Blueberry, Flo, and F13. The strains he has created have laid the foundation for many of the strains around today. Like most highly successful breeders, DJ Short is surrounded by hype. For example, on the one hand some people find that DJ Short's Blueberry plants are different than expected, but his Flo strain, on the other hand, is highly lauded and truly wonderful.

DNA Genetics

DNA Genetics got its start in the late 80s. They formed in Hollywood, California, collecting seeds from friends and family and, of course, rare bag seeds. In 2002, they moved to Amsterdam due to safety concerns in the U.S. Since the move, they have been able to expand their breeding operations and have larger numbers of plants, meaning better selection for their strains. DNA is known by many to practice good breeding techniques and superior selection standards to bring the best of So Cal genetics to the rest of the world. Try their Chocolope for a good beginner's Sativa; it is a cross of DNA's Original Chocolate Thai and their Cannalope strain.

Dr. Atomic

Dr. Atomic is an independent Canadian breeder who has traveled to the Middle East, Himalayas, and South Pacific collecting the best seeds he could come by. All of his strains have a very unique look and feel to them. His Atomic Haze and Nepal Baba are making Dr. Atomic a common name to growers and breeders everywhere. Dr. Atomic specializes in making F1 seeds of well-known hybrids, such as Northern Lights x landrace strains.

Dutch Passion

Established in 1987 in Holland by owner Henk, Dutch Passion is one of Holland's premier seed companies. Dutch Passion has built a good reputation with their genetics and is known for its outstanding customer service. Even though this is one of the most well-known and popular seed companies, Henk still finds the time to respond to every email and treats all customers with respect and integrity. Dutch Passion's debut strains were: Amstel Gold, Purple Star, PurpleWonder, and FourWay. The company was previously the only licensed distributor of DJ Short genetics, but due to some problems between DJ Short and Henk, DJ Short no longer supplies fresh seeds to Dutch Passion. However, Dutch Passion continues to inbreed and sell F2 and F3 generations of Blueberry and Flo, such as Blue Moonshine, a great Indica for potency, and Skywalker, a hybrid of Mazar and Blueberry.

Flying Dutchmen

The Flying Dutchmen is the oldest Amsterdam-based seed company still in existence. Founded by Eddie, one of the founders of Sacred Seeds, Flying Dutchmen was established in 1998 with their debut strain, Pot O' Gold. It is unclear if Flying Dutchmen kept the original haze and skunk #1 stocks, but they do offer The Pure, which is reportedly Skunk #1. Eddie's genetics, such as Thai-Tanic and Kerala Krush, are legendary in the world of seed breeding. Eddie also founded the Cannabis College, located across the street from the Flying Dutchmen shop in Amsterdam.

Green House Seed Company

Arjan, lead breeder for Green House Seed Comapny, is a figure shrouded in controversy and the owner/operator of one of the most successful seed companies in the business. Arjan opened the first Green House Coffeeshop in 1992, in Tolstraat, Amsterdam and since then has opened three other highly successful coffee shops and a celebrated seed company. He is the self-proclaimed "King of Cannabis" and is known to be a good friend of Steve Hager, editor-in-chief for *High Times* and founder of the Cannabis Cup. Green House Seed Company offers strains that consist mainly of three varieties: Brazilian, Super Silver Haze, and Laos. Most of his strains consist of different combinations of these stellar strains and a few other crosses. Some charge that Green House Seed Company's seeds are too hemp-like and lack sufficient trichome quantities, but the majority of Green House Seed Company's customers are consistently satisfied with the product they have purchased. Green House Seed Company has won over 30 Cannabis Cups with their excellent trademark crosses of Brazilian, Super Silver Haze, and Laos. There are reports of Arjan kiefing his entry buds in the Cannabis Cup in order to increase their THC content, but in the highly lucrative and competitive world of cannabis seed breeding, malicious rumors are a simple fact of life and one can never be sure of the truth. Green House Coffeeshops are well decorated and give off great vibes, and their seeds are consistent top sellers.

Joey Weed

Joey Weed is an independent breeder that collected some of the best strains, bred, and selected the best plants to make F2s and even F5s of some strains, such as AK-47, Blueberry, and White Widow. He also creates hybrids himself, such as his Blue Widow hybridization of White Widow and his own Blueberry male. Check out his Joey's Mix for a random mix of strains that Joey has actually created himself. Thanks to Joey Weed some of the best and most respected strains are still available in F2 and beyond for reasonable prices.

Magus Genetics

Magus Genetics, like many other scientific research companies, achieved its first success somewhat accidentally. In the late 80s, Gerrit, owner and breeder of Magus Genetics, started his very first crop with bag seeds from what was probably Skunk and Afghani. Since this was his first grow, he did not know the difference between male and female flowers. Reportedly, a male Afghani plant had pollinated a female Skunk. Gerrit then backcrossed these F1 seeds to another Skunk plant, but not as a backcross. This serendipitous error made his "Warlock" strain, which has been hugely popular ever since! Magus started to work for Bluebird coffee shops in Amsterdam, and they started selling his Warlock strain. Warlock is Magus Genetics' flagship strain and is used in most of their other crosses. The official seed shop, Magus Genetics, did not get started until 1998. Magus Genetics' success, like Fleming's accidental discovery of penicillin, is just one of those fortunate errors that lead to great things.

Mandala Seeds

Founders Mike and Jasmine formed Mandala Seeds in 2003. Mike and Jasmine traveled to such exotic locales as India, Africa, the Middle East, and South East Asia, searching for the most exotic landrace varieties. After 20 years they had accomplished their mission and began to cross these exotic varieties to make extreme F1 hybrids. Although most strains are of mysterious origins, as the exact location of the parents plant is not released, they produced extremely unique hybrids, such as Satori, a Sativa–Indica from Nepal, and Ganesh, an Afghani Indica–Sativa. They made the majority of their crosses in Spain, and then moved to England to set up shop. Mandala is known to be an extremely friendly and forthright company that is easily reachable for any and all questions. Mandala Seeds offer great genetics at even better prices.

Mr. Nice Seeds

Founder and lead breeder Shantibaba is a person of legend in the cannabis community, as is his seed company, Mr. Nice Seeds. Mr. Nice seeds is a collaboration of three great cannabis collectors: Shantibaba, seed breeder; Neville, founder of the Seed Bank; and Howard Marks, the most notorious cannabis smuggler in history. Mr. Nice Seeds acquired most of its parental stock from Neville via the Seed Bank. Shantibaba is one of the few breeders making his seeds from large warehouses full of plants to better increase his selection. Mr. Nice Seeds is a very well regarded seed company with consistently satisfied customers. They have produced such celebrated strains as Northern Lights No. 5, White Rhino, and White Shark.

Nirvana

The history of Nirvana Seeds is, like many seed companies, shrouded in mystery. The accepted story of Nirvana is that it was founded by one man seeking the best seeds from around the world. When he had around one hundred seeds from all over the world, he started his company. Some sources claim that he didn't know enough about selective breeding and how to stabilize traits to maintain a high quality of seed. Since most of his strains are from random pollination of a mix of these one hundred seeds, you can expect to get a wide variety of phenotypes from a pack of Nirvana or Sativa Seed Bank seeds. Sources claim that most plants grown from a Nirvana seed pack will not resemble any of the other plants in the pack. However, all of Nirvana's seeds can be purchased for about $20 USD, making Nirvana the first stop for many first time growers. Other first-timers just grow out bag seed from some of their best bud and find that they get fairly good plants and achieve better uniformity amongst their crop. Nevertheless, Nirvana offers seeds for the grower on a budget, and their AK-48 and B52 is definitely worth a try, not to mention their Blue Mystic strain, an Indica that many enjoy.

Paradise Seeds

After 12 years of selective breeding and experimenting, Paradise Seeds was established in 1994 in Switzerland. They hit the cannabis scene hard with Sensi

Sheherazade from Paradise Seeds is a very fine mix of Afghani and Kush that is pefect for sea of green growing. Guaranteed to please all smokers.

Star and many other well-known strains came later, such as Nebula. Luc, one of the owners / breeders for Paradise Seeds, is known by many as a great guy that offers very prompt customer service.

Reeferman Seeds

Reeferman discovered cannabis when he was around 20 years old, and it changed his life. Since then he has collected some of the most exotic cannabis varieties from around the world, including trying to make some elite clones available in seed form. Reeferman is also known to resurrect popular strains from the 70s, like Panama Red and Santa Marta, and create new strains from them. Prior to Reeferman, people thought that Panama Red and Santa Marta were extinct. Although his breeding practices are reportedly questionable because some of his strains herm extensively, he has many exotic varieties available—but they are notoriously expensive. It is important to note that the majority of Reeferman's stock comes from an associate breeder named Steve Tuck. Many claim that Tuck only sells his stock to Reeferman because he cannot sell it on his own due to a somewhat dubious reputation in the business for marketing Trainwreck x Skunk

#1 seeds as pure Trainwreck seeds. Regardless, Reeferman is a pioneer breeder that works hard to ensure that elite clones are available to the general public. Try out their Love Potion #1 strain for a great strain, and his other unique hybrid strains like Cambodian x Haze and Cherry Bomb Indica.

Reservoir Seeds

Rezdog is the man in charge of Reservoir Seeds. His main accomplishment is that he has stabilized and made available the offspring of Chemdog, meaning Sour Diesel, NYC Diesel, and other Diesel hybrids. Rezdog has made some very well respected and well-liked strains, such as Apollo 11 G4 and Firecracker, and the price reflects this. Reservoir Seeds and Team Green Avengers Seeds are bitter rivals. Several sources have suggested that Rezdog does not grow out and test the majority of his seeds before marketing them, but this is likely just conjecture as he is a very active member of the cannabis community.

Sacred Seeds

Sacred Seeds was the first cannabis seed company, established in the early 70s in California. Founded by Sam the Skunkman and Eddie from Flying Dutchmen Seeds, they made and offered renowned strains such as Skunk#1, Afghani#1, Hindu Kush, and Original Haze. Sacred Seeds is no longer operating, but most of the original stock can be purchased from Seedsman Seeds. Sam the Skunkman is still breeding as an independent breeder.

Sagarmatha Seeds

Tony from Cerebral Seeds founded Sagarmatha in 1994. They hit the scene with a strain called Yumbolt which made Sagarmatha Seeds into a celebrated seed company. Tony later introduced Matanuska Tundra, which brought him further recognition. Tony also sells AK-47 as Slyder, but no longer offers his Bubblegum. Sagarmatha offers 19 strains as of 2006, and appears to be going strong. The true identity of Sagarmatha him or herself is unknown and is subject to much conjecture.

Seed Bank

Seed Bank was founded by an Australian man named Neville in 1985. Neville traveled the world to obtain the best landrace genetics available, and his debut strain, Northern Lights, rocketed him into fame and fortune. He also released a celebrated strain known as Early Pearl, which is a cross of Early Girl. It is rumored that Neville was the first to ever amass a million dollars legally with cannabis and, in doing so, "retired" and sold the Seed Bank to Alan and Ben Dronkers in 1990.

Seedsman Seeds

Seedsman Seeds was founded at the end of summer in 2002. "The company's ethos and aims were to sell high quality cannabis seeds at good, honest prices. We also set out to provide genetic information on our varieties above and beyond most other companies." Seedsman, in fact, does not breed their own seeds: they only market seeds bred by independent breeders such as Afropip, Sensi Seeds, Paradise Seeds, and many others. Subsequently, some of the seeds are of great quality and others are of lesser quality, depending on what you order from them and who their supplier is. Essentially a seed company that markets and sells seeds from a variety of different breeders, Seedsman is a company that can provide you with excellent seeds—just make sure you know exactly what you are ordering from them.

Serious Seeds

Formally known as Cerebral Seeds, this was the collaboration of two well-known breeders, Simon and Tony. Simon majored in biology and was teaching biology to high school students in Amsterdam when Alan Dronkers, co-owner of Sensi Seeds, asked him to come work for him. Simon accepted the offer and he used his time at Sensi Seeds to learn about how to own and operate a seed company. He left Sensi and started Cerebral Seeds with his partner Tony. In 1994, their début year, they won several competitions with AK-47. In 1995, the duo split up. It is thought that this was because of different breeding practices. Simon wanted to stabilize the strains they already had, working towards a better product for his customers. Tony, on the other hand, thought that there was more money to be had in producing new, less stabilized strains each year. This is thought to have lead to the end of the partnership. That same year, Simon established Serious Seeds and Tony established Sagarmatha Seeds. It is rumored that in a recent bust, Serious lost their original AK-47 mother and AK-47 seeds are now very different than they used to be. This is likely just a malicious piece of gossip, however, as Simon undoubtedly had countless clones and seeds from the original plant.

Sensi Seeds

Founders Alan and Ben Dronkers bought Neville's company, Seed Bank, in late 1990. They retained all of the Seed Bank's original genetics. Sensi Seeds is most credited for the creation of Jack Herer, a strain named after the famous cannabis and hemp activist. Jack Herer is a three way cross of Northern Lights x Haze x Skunk #1. While Jack Herer isn't all that stable, it did lay the foundation for many Brothers Grimm crosses, like Cinderella 99. Sensi Seeds is one of the longest running and most successful seed companies in existence, and although some sources claim that customer service and seed quality has been lagging for the past few seasons, there is little verifiable proof of any problems with the company.

Soma Seeds

Previously known as Seeds of Courage, Soma Seeds was established in 1995. Soma started breeding in Florida but then moved their base of operations to Amsterdam. Soma's flagship strain, Afghani–Hawaiian, is used in most of their crosses. Soma specializes in Indica-dominant strains specialized for medical users, such as Somanna and Somativa, not to mention the excellent Afghani Delight.

Spice of Life Seeds ·

Breeder Steve is the founder and lead breeder for SOL Seeds. Steve founded SOL in 1994 and has been producing high quality seeds ever since. SOL has many good strains and works closely with DJ Short to produce some of the most well-known and well-liked strains in this day and age. Sweet Tooth #3 is a very good strain and has won Spice of Life much acclaim; it is most well known as a potent purple strain that is reasonably priced. It is my opinion that SOL produces some of the best strains around today that have actual breeding involved in their creation.

Super Sativa Seed Club

Commonly known as SSSC, this outfit was established in 1985 and many of their crosses are in the pedigree of some strains we love today. SSSC's flagship strain, Chitral Indica, was the first well-known and well-liked Indica dominant clone to hit the U.S. Rezdog / Reservoir Seeds uses many of the old SSSC strains such as M39 and DTC99. SSSC is also responsible for Williams Wonder and other well-known strains.

Team Green Avengers

TGA is the largest and most well-known seed company operating inside the United States and is a true pioneer of online cannabis culture. Team Green Avengers comprises five breeders: Subcool, the founding member and lead breeder; MzJill, Subcool's wife; Badboy; Homegrwn, TGA's Canadian counterpart; and ToB, the latest and second female member. Sunycheba, the breeder of Double Purple Doja and Sputnik 1.0, left TGA in 2007, reportedly due to breeding disputes. Subcool got his start 30 years ago in South Georgia, beginning, as many do, by experimenting with bag seeds and selective breeding. When personal computers and the internet became widespread, Subcool quickly became active in the online seed breeding community and learned much from people such as A/B Hyb, Nesta, and Vic High. Subcool was one of the first members of the Overgrow online marijuana forum, and his famous Jack's Cleaner hybrid parent came from a fellow member named Skoosh. Subcool also met MzJill on the Overgrow forum, and they were eventually married. Team Green Avengers is making some of the best hybrids commercially available and provides medicinal cannabis for many cancer patients. They are always breeding and coming up with new strains and documenting their work online, and are known for having good customer service. There have been reports that some TGA strains come from uncertain origins, but this is mostly just malicious speculation made by competitors. Regardless, TGA is a large, successful seed company with a celebrated history, consistently satisfied customers and a strong online presence. In a business as competitive as cannabis seed breeding, malicious rumors are a dime a dozen. Try Jilly Bean from MzJill for a good, euphoric strain with a great citrus taste that is good for medical users, and, of course, Subcool's Vortex, Jack's Cleaner, and Jack The Ripper are absolute classics for both medicinal and non-medicinal users alike.

Texas Resin Company
Lonestar is the founder and lead breeder for TRC and specializes in drought tolerant strains such as Double Karen, Blue 13, and the beloved Super Blue. Unfortunately, Lonestar was busted in 2008 and, at the time of writing, is still awaiting trial. An associate breeder by the name of Pistils has taken on the duty of preserving TRC lines.

T.H. Seeds
Formally known as C.I.A. (Cannabis in Amsterdam), T.H. Seeds was established in Holland in 1993. Doug and Adam are the owners and breeders for T.H. Seeds and were reportedly the first to bring the Original Bubblegum from Indiana to Europe. Adam, owner and breeder of T.H. Seeds, received the Indica pheno of Bubblegum and this is the version he stabilized. Following Bubblegum came the highly acclaimed flagship S.A.G.E. Other well-liked strains include: MK Ultra, Sage 'n Sour, and Heavy Duty Fruity. T.H. Seeds has also developed its own version of the west coast elite clone, the HOG. Check them out for quality seeds, particularly specialty strains.

Wally Duck
Wally Duck is an Australian breeder that is responsible for making Ducks Foot available worldwide. An Australian counterpart showed Wally a strain of cannabis called Aussie Bastard Cannabis (ABC) which resembled a wild weed. Wally then bred ABC with some mystery Aussie Sativa to produce some incredibly unique traits, such as the webbed trait in Ducks Foot. Not only did he stabilize the webbed leaves but he improved the potency and yield. Thank you, Wally Duck.

Chapter 4

Online Cannabis Forums

Use the forums to learn how to maximize your grow, whether it's making hash from your trim, or learning how to cook, the forums are a great way to connect with growers who have years of experience.

A great way to find information and get advice from the cannabis community is to participate in online forums. You can ask advice about which seed companies to buy from, how to grow specific strains, and interact with some really wonderful people. Below is a list, with descriptions, of some of the most popular cannabis forums on the Web. I have graded the following websites on the following qualities:

- attitude and experience of most members
- friendliness and helpfulness of the moderators
- location of servers
- censorship
- "infamous" users
- uniqueness; "what's different?"
- overall quality of the website

BREEDBAY.CO.UK

Members:	8,876 Registered Members; 2,230 Active Members. I can't say enough about the members of Breedbay. 95% of the members are very experienced, mature people. Experienced members outnumber inexperienced members about seven to one, which is incredible. The best part about the members is that, even with all the experienced members, they are still extremely humble and willing to help anyone in need.
Moderators:	The moderators here do their job well, and they are friendly people. Great stuff.
Server Location:	UK. Excellent.
Censorship:	Moderate to severe.
Infamous Members:	MzJill, Subcool, Sunycheba, Pistils, ToB, Rellikbuzz, Chemdog, Mizz Chemdog, Lonestar, Lonestar Kid, BakedAphrodite, bubbatail, doc bob, MsJones, farmermike1187, master420-chief, ITeachYourKids!, flying, Redwood-roots, h0meGRwN, SuperRY311, Gooeybreeder, Small Potatoes, Gene Bean, Mr. WYT, spliffmasta, Loran, Hammer, Pig&PotFarmer, smoky_Mcpot, Smokey, vaporedtrail, Weeds, The Pied-Eyed Piper, Cofi, and common.
Specialty:	A complete cannabis community devoted to breeding better cannabis. They feature a "Testbay" where all strains get tested before being sold on Cannaseur.co.uk which is a sister-site. There is also the "Breeders Community" section where TGA, Pistils, DNA, Mandala, and Dank Diary Seed companies are there for members to showcase their respective companies' genetics, and ask any questions of the breeders. There is a

"Breeders Library" and "Cannabis Alchemy" section. This is the only website that I know where you can chat with Grade A breeders about their work and see their "behind the scenes" photos. Breedbay also features a chat room where, most of the time, you can talk to MzJill and Subcool first hand.

Overall: Breedbay is the place to be for the experienced grower that's ready to take cannabis growing to the next level: breeding. Breedbay has all the information you need to learn how to breed your own killer genetics. If you run into any problems, Subcool, MzJill, Lonestar, and Mike are right there to answer your questions. The members are great and the moderators are even better. Even if you just want to learn how to perfect your growing, this is the place to do so. This is a tight-knit community, so close that they even raise money for those members that are unfortunate enough to get busted. Incredible website.

CANNABIS.COM

Members: 155,302 Registered Members; 6,618 Active Members. Users are mostly young, inexperienced growers with a few, experienced "teachers," as well.

Moderators: The male moderators have a reputation for being overly strict and not particularly helpful. However, the female moderators are known to be level-headed and un-biased.

Server Location: USA. Be careful of what information you post.

Censorship: Moderate amount of censorship.

Infamous Members: stinkyattic, the image reaper, a.k.a. roadcam, Organic Rasta, Orangeman, and stinkbudd.

Specialty: Regional sections: You can talk to people in your state, and there are sections for people in all the different parts of the world, including Canada, Africa, Central and South America, and Australia. There is no private messaging system, so you can't trade seeds/clones with other members.

Overall: This is probably the largest cannabis forum on the web with an excellent local section for people across the world; however, with size come certain problems...

FORUM.GRASSCITY.COM

Members: 229,916 Registered Members; 57,943 Active Members. Users

	range from second time growers to very experienced growers. Most users will have at least one grow under their belt.
Moderators:	Moderators are very nice and friendly, and always willing to lend a helping hand. They are open to various opinions.
Server Location:	The Netherlands. Excellent!
Censorship:	There is moderate censorship here but that is to be expected. Nothing out of the ordinary.
Infamous Members:	Dierwolf, unoit, GreenLantern420, DiAmOnD RaStA, and Indianatoker.
Specialty:	Offers a video section that has user videotapes of cannabis from around the world. The thread-deletion option is also great.
Overall:	This is a good cannabis forum featuring the basic grow information, good people, and a great moderating team. A solid website for beginners. The layout of Grasscity is really clean and refreshing, and you can buy cannabis accessories through the site, as well, although they claim not to ship the USA, Canada or Germany…

FREECANNABIS.CH

Members:	4045 Registered Members; 143 Active Members. Most users are fairly experienced with a reputation for snobbishness.
Moderators:	Nicer than the members.
Server Location:	Switzerland. Cool.
Censorship:	Moderate.
Infamous Members:	Mr.Mojo (R.I.P.), bigsur, Kread, saxby, and rockymtnbuds.
Specialty:	Good "shout box" feature and a chat option. The periodic competitions are great, too.
Overall:	A decent website with some experienced people, but due to a server wipe-down, they've become much smaller than they used to be. Much of the site is written in Italian.

GARDENSCURE.COM

Members:	40,796 Registered Members; 4,309 Active Members. Mix of first-time growers and highly experienced growers.

Moderators:	Polite and helpful, but they will correct you if they disagree with you.
Server Location:	USA. Be careful what you post.
Censorship:	Has a reputation for strict censorship due to US laws.
Infamous Members:	n d shadows, Old Phart, StOney, Higher Logic, mr.hyde, and Xjo.
Specialty:	Features most of the information recovered from Overgrow.com on their FAQ
Overall:	Pretty good cannabis site. Great starting place for amateurs and beginner growers, but be very careful logging in to this site from your personal computer, because it is located in the US and the webmasters reserve the right to disclose your activity to your ISP. Be careful out there.

ICMAG.COM

Members:	14,799 Registered Members; 633 Active Members. The website is comprised of mostly experienced members; some have been growing since the '60s. Most are friendly and welcoming, but don't believe in modesty.
Moderators:	Some are nice and civil, others are not. There have been reports of problems with the administration.
Server Location:	The Netherlands. Great!
Censorship:	Severe censorship.
Infamous Members:	guineapig, oldpink, 1tokeOverLine, Stoney Girl, Father Time, Dutch Grown, Gypsy Nirvana, I.M. Boggled, Rezdog, pontiac, jaykush, GreatLakes THC, BushyOldGrower aka BOG, bartender187, sunnyside aka kokua, wallyduck, zeppleindood, Sportster, sleepy, Growdocs, bounty29, jaws, hurricanefaniam, motaco, Mr. Nevermind, Harry Gypsna, Time2Unite, sproutco, Hempkat, grat3fulh3ad, resinryder, Canna Kid, Texas Kid, Coloradro, and fjällhöga.
Specialty:	Women's Forum section, Old Stoners Crash Pad section, and Worldwide Guide to Cannabis section, which features cannabis from different members' trips around the world. There is also a great section where you can submit articles you've written for publication in the International Cannabis magazine. Many Overgrow members are here, and the Vendor's Section is great because you can find rare seed companies through them. Multi-language section is useful, as well. Beware of posting here

because all information and photos you post become the property of Icmag, and you need the admins' permission to re-post it or else you are breaking copyright laws.

Overall:	Icmag has become the new Overgrow, and all the drama has followed it. There is a lot of good amidst the not-so-good, but it takes some digging to find it. Be careful of the copyright problems if you want to share your grow photos or stories.

PLANETGANJA.COM

Members:	4,448 Registered Members; 634 Active Members. This forum has a reputation for being somewhat unwelcoming to new members.
Moderators:	Better than the members in most respects. They moderate fairly.
Server Location:	Canada. It's not the US, but you still need to be careful.
Censorship:	Little to none. Excellent!
Infamous Members:	420_petchy_420, A Bloke Down The Pub, Agent Smith, Antique Hippy, Atom Heart, haxixe, BlazeOfGlory, JjonahJameson, Blkcat21, Brick Top, budslinger, dreamdancer, Fishhead, Gagabout, HellBoy, JohnGault, Prawn Connery, Kendo, and the notorious Plural of Mongoose (a.k.a. PoM).
Specialty:	Planet Ganja features a "seed and weed scams" section and a "shark tank" section where anything goes – a place to talk about everything you're not allowed to talk about at other forums! Also, they feature a Subcool and Paradise seed help desk.
Overall:	I would advise growers to register at Planet Ganja; unlike most forums, "drama" isn't frowned upon here. They realize that unpleasant things happen that need to be talked about. However, things get out of hand rather quickly and there is always someone flaming someone…

UK420.COM

Members:	38,102 Registered Members; 5,492 Active Members. Even mix of experienced and inexperienced growers. Very welcoming to new members.
Moderators:	Fair but tough. They don't act nice; they just answer your queries.
Server Location:	UK
Censorship:	Moderate
Infamous Members:	Oldtimer1, Lazlo Woodbine, Bish, sittingrelaxing, The Head Gardener, Smokey_McPot, Joolz, Lawless, and Bend it like Beck.

Specialty: Primarily for UK growers; great breeders forum where you can find A.C.E., Canna Biogen, DNA Genetics, Mandala, Mr. Nice, and Tiki Seeds.

Overall: Great European site with huge following, but American growers tend to be out of the loop because they use UK products and terminology that we, as Americans, don't know or cannot access easily. One great thing about UK420 is that the legendary OldTimer1 posts there.

WEEDFARMER.COM

Members: 6,196 Registered Members; Users range from inexperienced to very experienced, although the majority are inexperienced. A good place to learn.

Moderators: Most moderators are very friendly, willing to help, and open to others' opinions.

Server Location: The Netherlands. Excellent!

Censorship: Severe censorship, which can be a problem.

Infamous Members: jd2769, blueberryyumyum, funnyfarmer73, younggrower, angelsoffspring, and DankBudZ.

Specialty: A good learning environment for young growers; the minimum age requirement for membership is quite low.

Overall: A very nice, closely knit community with great competitions and community events, and a positive learning atmosphere.

420GENETICS.COM

Members: 1,126 Registered Members; 228 Active Members. Many experienced growers, but less experienced breeders.

Moderators: The moderators aren't the greatest. They tend to be younger and less experienced than you'd expect, although there are a few really excellent moderators here, as well.

Server Location: The Netherlands. Good.

Censorship: Moderate.

Infamous Members: bongrip420, Captu4ik, Grassmaster, Heath Bogenreif, herbgrower, Herbman, hushpuppy420, Mary Jane, Mermaid, mistical, Mr.Wakenbake, Scorpion King, Stash, straightdope, Tiberon, trillions of atoms, web420.

Specialty: They have a strain guide and seed bank / breeder rating system with very useful information, as well as the Overgrow FAQ. Nice.

Overall: This is a place for those that are good at growing but don't get into breeding. If the moderators were a little less biased and a little more responsible, this forum would be much nicer.

420MAGAZINE.COM

Members: 100,000 Registered Members; 57,607 Active Members. Most members are very kind and helpful and there is a good mix of both experienced and beginner growers on the forums.

Moderators: Tough but fair, and always willing to help.

Server Location: Canada. Servers are located in Canada to protect their members in the U.S.

Censorship: Understandably strict but always fair. Foul language is frowned upon.

Infamous Members: Medifreddie, Keysman, ChicagoJoe, Stonas, wildmanmaxx, proliferation, gunjababy, TheCriMsonK20, bizz, Tortured Soul, Lump, Sungoddess, honestone, bongtastic, Harry Red, 420, User, Boss, Jimbo, 420 Girl, Soniq420, Steven, Be Irie, McBudz, Setting Sun, BayAreaStoner, CocoJoe, Southern Weed, The Weed, Wingman 580, Propa Gator, Cozmo, HappyKitty, Ganjarden, Weedpipe.

Specialty: International cannabis news and medical cannabis awareness and information resources. They also run the 420 Girls site, which features female models smoking weed – always a plus!

Overall: This site has been in operation since 1993 and is reportedly the largest and most comprehensive resource for cannabis in the world with over 100,000 members. They do great videos and cannabis information pieces, and the founder, Rob Griffin, is a tireless campaigner for the legalization of cannabis. Check out the 420 Girls, as well, and their book Naked Girls Smoking Weed: Best of 420 Girls by Rob Griffin.

Chapter 5

Strains

The first record of human intervention with cannabis breeding was in India around 2,000 years ago. Certain families in India inbred select cannabis strains for increased potency. The Indians brought their inbred cannabis varieties with them when they became British slaves. When the British colonized parts of the Caribbean, Central and South America around 1834, they brought their Indian servants and with their servants came their cannabis.

Fast forward to the 1970s on the West Coast. It was there that such infamous Indicas as Afghani #1, Mazar-i-sharif, and Hindu Kush were bred with Colombian, Mexican (Acapulco Gold and Oaxaca), and Thai Sativas. Thus were such hybrids as Skunk #1 created, which is a three-way cross between Colombian Sativa, Acapulco Gold, and Afghani #1. Northern Lights, which is a cross between Afghani#1 and Thai Sativa, was created using the same hybrid breeding techniques. Original Haze, which is a four-way cross of Colombian, Mexican, and Thai Sativas and a South Indian Indica, is yet another celebrated example of West Coast breeding. These hybrids were then inbred numerous times, but only Skunk #1 was ever truly stabilized.

Modern breeding began with groups of cannabis cultivators in the West Coast working together and experimenting in order to create great cannabis strains that they could enjoy, and share with their friends. However, due to the criminalization of cannabis in the US, many breeders and their genetics found their way to Holland, where cannabis had been de-criminalized. And thus the modern business of cannabis seed breeding began, from its grassroots on the West Coast, to today's lucrative Dutch market.

Collected here is a list of the most well-known cannabis strains from the world's top breeders. Enjoy!

Choosing a strain will often come down to your personal preferences – something functional and heady, something narcotic and pain relieving, or a mixture of the two.

123

3D from Subcool / TGA
Originated in the United States
This is a cross of Apollo 13 x Jack the Ripper. Personally, this is not one of my favorite TGA offerings but others can't say enough about her. Some phenos produce the amount of trichomes you would expect from these two great strains, but not all. The taste is obviously lemony with spicy after tones. The most impressive trait of this cross is the quick finishing time of around 50 days.

A

Acapulco Gold from Dr. Greenthumb
Originated in Mexico
The real Acapulco Gold is a famous 70s strain that most old tokers still rave about. The high is extremely cerebral, even described as "mind numbing" by some. Others have reported hallucinations from it. Taste is somewhat spicy for a Sativa.

Afghan Delight from Soma
Originated in Afghanistan
This is an Indica dominant plant. Classic Indica hash with a spicy smell and flavor to it.

Afghani #1 from Sacred Seeds
Originated in Afghanistan
The godmother of all Indicas, if not the first true breeding Indica in the world. This is the Indica you want for your breeding ventures. Offers a good body stone. Also great for medicinal purposes. No longer available from Sacred Seeds but you can still get the same genetics from Seedsman.

Afghanica from Flying Dutchmen
Originated in Holland
A hybrid with a touch of Sativa in it. Typical Indica dominant plant. Some phenotypes have a sweet taste.

AK-47 from Serious Seeds
Originated in Holland
Mostly sativa hybrid, this one is sure to impress. When smoking a normal amount you feel up and creative. Smoke a bit more and you'll be falling asleep in no time. Look out for the cherry pheno AK-47: very potent and an excellent taste. Note: there are rumors that Serious Seeds has lost the original AK-47 mother, but their bud still tastes good and is pretty potent, so the truth of this rumor is uncertain.

Amethyst Bud from Soma
Originated in Holland
Mostly Indica hybrid, this is one of the famous Lavender crosses. The Lavender parent comes through in the plant's coloring and taste. Some phenotypes have more of a sweet, flowery kind of taste, but the Lavender phenotypes taste like "purple" (weird, I know, but when you smoke it you'll see what I mean).

Amsterdam Flame from Paradise
Seeds
Originated in Holland
Mostly Indica hybrid, this plant is all
the rave in Eastern Europe. Popular for
its gentle, relaxing body high and its
sweet, fruity aftertastes.

Amnesia Haze from Soma
Originated in Holland
Mostly Sativa hybrid, this is another
award-winning creation from Soma
making its way through "cannaseur"
circles around the world. Favored for
its inspirational, motivational high and
its citrus undertones.

Apollo 11 from Brothers Grimm
Originated in the United States
Mostly Sativa hybrid, this is a variant of
the much loved Apollo 13. Created
using a lemon phenotype Genius mom
crossed with an especially frosty
Cinderella 99. The high is much like a
Sativa and tastes a bit like peppered
green apples. No longer available from
Brothers Grimm; some later generations are available through Joey Weed
and Dr. Chronic, but the reliability of
these I cannot comment on.

Apollo 13 from Brothers Grimm
Originated in the United States
Mostly Sativa hybrid, this may be
regarded as the "Holy Grail" of
cannabis strains. Only 500 of these
babies were ever made and it exists
only as a clone now. She was created

using the same lemon phenotype
Genius mom x the Princess 75 (prede-
cessor to Cinderella 99). Tastes and
smells just like lemons. One of the
most horded strains around.

Apollo Mist from Rezdog / Reservoir
Seeds
Originated in the United States
Mostly Sativa hybrid created from
Apollo 11 x Kali Mist. This is a very popular strain because of its respectable
yield and incredible flavor. She does well
both indoors and outdoors; also favorable for SOG (sea of green) or ScrOG
(screen of green) setups.

Apple Pie from Reeferman
Originated in Canada
A supposedly 100% landrace hybrid
known as a super sativa. Created with
Acapulco Gold x Nepalese; grows well
in southern climates like Texas.

Arjan's Strawberry Haze from
Greenhouse Seeds
Originated in Holland
Created Swiss Sativa, Haze Mist, and
Northern Lights #5. Consistently pop-
ular strain which tastes like Mexican
brick when smoked.

Arjan's Ultra Haze #1 from
Greenhouse Seeds
Originated in Holland
Award-winning strain. Created Neville's
Haze, Cambodian, and Laos plants.
This is a mostly Sativa hybrid that cre-

Arjan's Ultra Haze #1 from Greenhouse Seeds is an award-winning strain that offers an uplifting, racy high. Be careful though, it is very strong.

---

ates a very uplifting, racy high. Not for the inexperienced toker.

Asia Girl from Reeferman
Originated in Canada
A three way cross of Thai x Nepalese x Northern Lights #6. This Sativa-dominant plant behaves almost like a pure Sativa. Tendency to herm because of Thai background. Finishes in around 9 weeks.

Astroboy from Subcool / TGA Seeds
Originated in the United States
A cross of the infamous A-13 x Ortega x C99. A nice resin machine. This one takes even the most experienced tokers back to their schoolyard days. The taste is reminiscent of A-13 but with a hint of cherries. The Ortega adds a bit of color to her as well. This is a nice Sativa smoke.

Aussie Bastard Cannabis from Australia
Originated in Australia
ABC, as it is commonly known, is a very unique landrace variety of cannabis that resembles a wild weed much more than any species of cannabis. Some have claimed that ABC is a colchicines (a plant regulator) experiment gone wrong, but I have been provided proof that is untrue. ABC is a wild landrace variety of cannabis native only to Australia. ABC is not potent, nor does it offer good yields, but it does have the possibility of being used in crosses like Duck's Foot, in order to camouflage plants.

B

Basic Diesel from Rezdog / Reservoir Seeds
Originated in the United States
This is an old Super Sativa Seed Company strain, M39 (known for its fat yields), crossed with ESCD. If you pick the right pheno you can get the high, taste, and smell of ESCD and the yield of M39.

Belladonna from Paradise Seeds
Originated in Holland
A nice Sativa-dominant plant with an Indica finishing time. A nice hybrid with

Belladonna from Paradise Seeds is a Sativa-dominant plant that gives a trippy, somewhat hallucinogenic high.

some beautiful colors, valued for her wide variety of growing climates and trippy, somewhat hallucinogenic high.

Biddy Early from Magus Genetics
Originated in Holland
Was created using Warlock x Early Skunk for outdoor growing in short season climates such as Holland. She displays nice red and purple colors when exposed to cooler temperatures. Despite her Sativa-dominant genetics, the high is more Indica.

Big Buddha Cheese from Big Buddha
Originated in the United Kingdom
Created using an "Original Cheese" x Afghani, this is a plant that perfectly encapsulates the "long greasy cola."

Very clear high with no ceiling. You know if you have the real cheese by the smell.

Black Cherry from Sunycheba / TGA Seeds
Originated in the United States
Created by using a cherry phenotype Dannyboy x Black Russian, giving her nice coloring and cranberry-scented buds. She is a quick finisher, as well: between 7–8 weeks.

Black Domina from Sensi Seeds
Originated in Holland
Reputedly a 100% Indica hybrid. In fact, with Northern Lights in its genetic makeup, it cannot be. Smells spicy.

Black Russian from Nebu
Originated in the United States
A very respected strain developed by Nebu using the legendary Blackberry x a special cherry phenotype of AK-47. This strain is legendary in its own right. No other purple strain has coloring like Black Russian. The strain tends to be horded.

Blackberry from Som-A-Blaze / Nebu
Originated in the United States
Another "Holy Grail" of cannabis strains. No words quite describe the exotic taste of Blackberry. She's definitely a Sativa though. Nebu has horded Blackberry but there is another unique phenotype from Mullaway Seeds that doesn't carry the same exact traits as the American Blackberry but is very special nonetheless.

Blockhead from Spice of Life
Originated in the United States
This is another bagseed mystery surprise, and a wonderful one at that. The female mystery clone was pollinated from the same male that made Sweet Tooth #3. This plant displays many vibrant, beautiful colors, somewhat like ST#3. The best part of her is her potency—she really levels you with her Indica-like high, although some buds have a more Sativa feel to them.

Blue Cheese from Big Buddha
Originated in the United Kingdom
Created using a different breeder's version of Blueberry Cheese x Original Cheese. This strain offers the same uplifting, "no-ceiling" high popular with the original Cheese, combined with subtle Blueberry undertones.

Blue Moonshine from DJ Short
Originated in the United States
Created by crossing a unique Blueberry phenotype x Hash Plant. This is a welcome change to the run-of-the-mill Indicas. You get the overwhelming Indica narcotic high but without Indica's spicy, hashy taste.

Blue Satellite from Legends Seeds
(DJ Short x Spice of Life)
Originated in Switzerland
A cross of Blueberry mom x F2 Shiskaberry male. This is a nice, tasty Indica-dominant hybrid with a lot of potency and an above average yield.

Blueberry from DJ Short
Originated in Canada
This is a 3-way Sativa-dominant hybrid created using Highland Thai x Purple Thai x Afghani #1. Blueberry has a cult following amongst many growers, and lots of people rave about certain phenotypes, but I'm not a fan of Blueberry because I've never been fortunate enough to find and grow out one of the good phenotypes.

Bubbleberry from Sagarmatha
Originated in Holland
A crowd pleaser. Created using two favorite strains, Bubblegum and Blueberry,

Bubbleberry from Sagarmatha is a crowd pleaser that offers a cerebral head high that quickly becomes an evenly balanced body high as well.

she definitely pleases the palate of the most experienced tokers, producing amazing colors, including golds, reds, purples, and maroons. The high doesn't disappoint either: at first it's a cerebral head high but it quickly becomes an evenly balanced body high as well.

Bubblegum from T.H. Seeds, Serious Seeds, and Sagarmatha.
Originated in the United States
Bubblegum is an original strain from Indiana. The creator of this strain sold it first to T.H. Seeds who were the first to get Bubblegum. Then, as the creator tweaked his strain, he sold different cuts to Serious Seeds and Sagarmatha. Serious Seeds' Bubblegum is more sativa and Sagarmatha's is more Indica. Both are killer.

Burmese Pure from Reeferman
Originated in Burma
Supposedly a true breeding Sativa. This is good breeding stock for other potential lines. The high is reputedly anti-anxiety.

Butterscotch Hawaiian from Reeferman
Originated in Canada
This is a strain favored by medical and commercial growers for her big, greasy colas and ease of growing. Has a great butterscotch aftertaste, but not all phenos possess this trait.

CannaSutra is the flagship strain of Delta 9 Labs, and for good reason. What a great strain.

C

Canna Sutra from Delta 9
Originated in Holland
Canna Sutra is the flagship strain of Delta 9 labs, and for good reason. Created from a Reclining Buddha x Sensi Star, this strain gives a stupefying high that is equally head and body. It is said to function as an aphrodisiac, as well as a bronchodilator. She was bred for indoor use but also performs well in warmer outdoor climates. Has a very sweet smell and taste to it.

Cannalope Haze from DNA Genetics
Originated in Holland

This mostly Sativa hybrid will leave you begging for more. Renowned for its sweet melon flavor and trippy head high, this strain was created using Hazebro Bagseed x Mexican Bagseed.

Carmella from Homegrown Fantaseeds
Originated in Holland
An evenly mixed hybrid with long running colas that sport a caramel smell and flavor.

Champagne from Reeferman
Originated in Canada
This is Reeferman's version of the widely popular Champagne clone. This is a Champagne clone x Burmese Pure.

Chemdog from Rezdog / Reservoir Seeds
Originated in the United States
This is what started all of Rezdog's Diesel crosses and many other famous strains, such as OG Kush. Twelve seeds of what eventually became known as Chemdog were found in a pound of delicious herb. When it made its way to NYC, someone changed the name to Diesel but it is the same strain. Chemdog tastes amazing—very chemically—no matter how it's grown. I can honestly say that I have never tasted herb that was so peculiar.

Chocolate Chunk from T.H. Seeds
Originated in Holland
Supposedly a pure Indica, but it was created from an Afghan x S.A.G.E, and the latter has Sativa in it. I've heard that some phenos have an interesting taste, but it's not a chocolate taste, as the name would imply.

Chronic from Serious Seeds
Originated in Holland
Supposedly created from Northern Lights x Afghan, but there's definitely something else in there to get these huge quality colas that Chronic delivers. Chronic is known to be the commercial grower's dream, as quality and quantity are certainly present with these beauties. Has a slight smell and taste of blooming flowers.

Cinderella 99 from Brothers Grimm
Originated in the United States
Created from a special lemon phenotype Jack Herer F2 x Shiva Skunk, which created "Princess." Princess was then backcrossed four times, creating P.50, P.75, P.88, a.k.a. Cinderella 88 (which was the first line of Cinderella released to the public), and lastly Cinderella 99. This is another "Holy Grail" of cannabis strains.

Citralah from Soma
Originated in Holland
This is Soma's version of Citral, a hash plant variety from the Citral Valley in Pakistan. The strain is great for hash and has a lemony citrus smell and taste, too, with spicy undertones.

Critical Mass from Mr. Nice Seeds
Originated in Holland
This is the modern day Big Bud, using beefed-up genetics, Afghani x Skunk #1. This is a large producer—maybe more product per plant than Chronic—but the quality isn't as good as Chronic. Still, great for the commercial or cash crop grower.

D
Dannyboy from Subcool / TGA
Originated in the United States
Created in memory of a fallen brother, the lineage is Killer Queen x Ortega x C99. With a 50-day season, it is a truly fast finisher. (It benefits from extra time in the vegetative state to produce a great yield.)

Double Purple Doja from Sunycheba / TGA
Originated in the United States
A cross of Apollo 13 x Black Russian (a.k.a. Sputnik 1.0), backcrossed to its Black Russian mother. This potent, deep purple strain is the new standard to judge all purple strains. Balancing beautiful colors and mind-boggling highs, it is sure to impress any grower.

Duck's Foot from Wally Duck
Originated in Australia
This is a miraculous plant—a true breeding mutant. It was created from a native mutant "ABC" plant x Australian Sativa, then backcrossed five times. A stealth plant, the leaves look nothing like cannabis; in fact, they are webbed together. This is one of my favorite strains and Wally has certainly outdone himself with her.

Durban Poison from Dutch Passion
Originated in South Africa
This is a great strain for both growing and breeding purposes. One hundred percent Sativa, this is the head high you're looking for—reminiscent of Thai. Breeding-wise, it's great for shortening the finishing time of any late-finishing strains.

Durga Mata from Paradise Seeds
Originated in Holland
Created by crossing two Super Shivas. A popular white Indica hybrid, but I'm not a big fan – I find that most white Indica hybrids taste the same to me.

E
Early California from Kulu Seeds
Originated in the United States
One of the best early-maturing plants on the market. This strain was another one of the most popular hybrids "made in America" in the early 80s. She's very easy to grow, as are most early strains, but this one yields nicely as well.

Early Durban from Flying Dutchmen
Originated in Holland
A faster finishing version of Durban Poison.

Early Girl from Sensi Seeds

Originated in the United States
Early Girl was one of the first hybrids made on the West Coast. Although not known as a particularly potent strain, it has one of the quickest finishing times around.

Early Misty from Nirvana
Originated in Holland
Early Misty is an early-maturing White Widow x Early Skunk. Expect the same from her as White Widow, except on a slightly smaller frame.

Early Pearl from Sensi Seeds
Originated in the United States
A very popular strain for its Sativa growth pattern and high and Indica yield and finishing time. As well as being easy to grow, it is very mold resistant and can take a lot of abuse. As an added bonus, it has a sweet, fruity fragrance.

Early Queen from Mr. Nice Seeds
Originated in Holland
A three-way hybrid featuring Early Pearl x Early Girl x Super Skunk. Nothing fancy here, just a quickly maturing (6–8 weeks) hybrid.

Early Riser from Sagarmatha
Originated in Holland
Nothing exciting here: just a quickly maturing hybrid.

Early Skunk from Sensi Seeds
Originated in Holland
Created from an Early Pearl x (an espe-cially early maturing) Skunk #1. This gives all the benefits of Skunk #1 with a quicker finishing time.

El Nino is an Indica-dominant strain from Greenhouse Seeds that is popular for a reason. One of the greatest plants ever for hash making and head stash.

El Nino from Greenhouse Seeds
Originated in Holland
A very popular Indica-dominant hybrid. Talk about a resin machine! This baby is great head stash; it will also make great hash. You can't go wrong with this potent, award-winning baby.

F

F-13 from DJ Short
Originated in Canada
Flo backcrossed five times. Reported to be the fastest Sativa cross that DJ Short has, finishing in just 7–9 weeks. Also reported to taste like vanilla, but tastes vary.

Fighting Buddha from Chimera
Originated in Holland
This was a crossbreeding project from Chimera and DJ Short. Chimera's heritage is Burmese female x Blueberry male. She takes a bit long to finish because of her Sativa dominants, but offers a limey, citrus taste and smell.

Flo from DJ Short
Originated in Canada
A highly regarded hybrid from DJ Short. Popular for its purple phenotypes; great for outdoor production. Created by using the same Purple Thai x Afghani #1 that was used to create Blueberry.

Four Way from Sensi Seeds
Originated in Holland
Created by crossing four different Indicas. Unstabilized, so you will find a variety of phenos in each pack.

Free Tibet from Soma
Originated in Holland
Another Indica-dominant hybrid offered by Soma. This is the original Free Tibet, so beware of cheap imitations. Created using a Nepalese Hash Plant x Afghani-Hawaiian.

Fuma Con Dios from Flying Dutchmen
Originated in Holland
Created using a "Skunk #1 father" x Original Haze mother. The Haze part may be true but the Skunk #1 father part is probably not because Skunk#1 was a female clone brought to Holland in the 70s. Because of its Haze mother, Fuma Con Dios does posses the Haze high and taste, along with a quicker finishing time of 9–12 weeks.

G

G-SUS from Reeferman
Originated in Canada
G13 x God makes this Indica-dominant plant. Popular for its taste and rock-hard, dense colas, some of which feature pink pistils.

Genius from Brothers Grimm
Originated in the United States
The godmother of most Brothers Grimm strains. Genius was the original Jack Herer pheno found in that legendary coffee shop gram. Genius is responsible for Apollo 11, Apollo 13, Princess, Cinderella 99, and other, less noted Brothers Grimm strains. Good luck trying to get your hands on this girl.

Grape Krush from DJ Short
Originated in Canada
A suspected hybrid of either Flo or Blueberry. Taste is something along the lines of grape candy. Also reported to have unusual leaf formations.

Great Garberville from Reeferman
Originated in Canada
An Afghani–Hawaiian x Thai. Considered to be a Californian strain. Supposedly a pure breeding IBL (inbred line); finishing time 7-8 weeks.

Some growers choose strains based solely on yield.

Great White Shark from Greenhouse Seeds
Originated in Holland
A cross of two well-known strains, Super Skunk x White Widow. I find it bland, but you'll have to try it for yourself.

Green Giant from Spice Brothers
Originated in Holland
This commercial strain was created from Big Bud x Shiva Skunk. The taste won't amaze you, but the yield will. Another great point is the finishing time (mid-October).

H

Hash Heaven from Soma
Originated in Holland
I don't understand why this one is called Hash Heaven, as it is one of the few Soma strains that is Sativa-dominant. Supposedly HP13 (Hash Plant 13) x G13 Haze. Great outdoor strain.

Hash Plant from Seedsman
Originated in the United States
Lebanese x Thai x Northern Lights #1. Created in the 70s, this Indica-dominant plant was cloned and made its way to Holland. It is now one of the most popular Indicas to date. Finishes in 6–7 weeks and, thanks to its Sativa parentage, has a sweet taste.

Hashberry from Mandala
Originated in India
Quickly becoming a popular strain. Even though it's an Indica and does get quite tall, it is thought that South Indian Sativas were bred with this variety, resulting in big, fat colas that smell a bit fruity and musky. The high is said to relieve anxiety, and as the name suggests, it's great for making hash. Also a valuable breeding stock.

Haze (Original) from Seedsman
Originated in the United States
This is a four way landrace cross: Thai x Mexican x Colombian x India. Renowned world over for its racy, psychedelic, and sometimes panic-induced high. It also offers a sweet and sour flavor. Takes up to 14 weeks to finish.

Hempstar from Dutch Passion
Originated in Holland
Created using Northern Lights #5 x Original Haze. This plant has sturdy branching and nice yields, but I find it somewhat boring.

Herijuana from Reeferman
Originated in the United States
Originally bred in Kentucky, this is a cross of Killer Newhaven x Petrolia Headstash. Reeferman backcrossed the Sativa pheno x Indica pheno. Great growing plant with great taste to match.

Highend from Legends Seeds
Originated in Canada
Created from Rene x Blueberry. Said to have very complex flavors and aromas ranging from funky and fruity to spicy and citrusy.

Himalayan Gold from Greenhouse Seeds is a wonderful strain. Fruity with an after-kick you'll love.

Himalayan Gold from Greenhouse Seeds
Originated in Holland
A three-way cross of landrace varieties from Nepal, India, and Vietnam. Fruity, with a little after-kick.

Hindu Kush from Sensi Seeds
Originated in India
Another infamous strain. This extremely stinky Indica is perfect for medical users or breeding stock. Typical Indica structure, but the high and taste are a bit different from other Indica hybrids on the market.

Holland's Hope from Dutch Passion
Originated in Holland
Developed for the moldy, cold climate

in Holland and bred since the 80s. This strain has a tendency to produce loose buds that mature rather quickly. Potency is average and taste is reminiscent of many other popular Dutch strains.

HOG from T.H. Seeds
Originated in Holland
Created from Afghani x Skunk #1. It is an Indica-dominant strain.

I

Ice Princess from Brothers Grimm
Originated in the United States
Created from Cinderella 88, a.k.a. Princess 88 x White Widow. Nice resin production and reasonably fast finishing time. Depending on the phenotype, some have a more spicy / skunky taste because of the White Widow parent.

Indian Haze from Sacred Seeds
Originated in Holland
Much like its cousin Indian Skunk. Created from India Kerala x Original Haze. This is a pure Sativa hybrid.

Indian Skunk from Sacred Seeds
Originated in Holland
Created in the 70s from India Kerala x Skunk #1. Reported to have the taste of Kerala with the yield and early maturation of Skunk #1.

Island Sweet Skunk from Federation Seeds
Originated in Canada

An inbred Skunk from Hawaii gives this baby her exotic flavor. This award-winner has many complex tropical flavors and aromas. She is a mostly-Sativa hybrid that can really reach for the sky.

J

Jack Flash from Sensi Seeds
Originated in Holland
This is a three-way cross featuring Jack Herer x Super Skunk x "Original Haze." All three of the parent plants are incredible strains, and thus Jack Flash is a popular one as well. I'm not a fan of it personally because I feel the hybrid lacks the best qualities of the parents.

Jack Herer from Sensi Seeds
Originated in Holland
Without Jack Herer we wouldn't have many of the great strains such as Genius, Apollo 11, Apollo 13, Princess, Cinderella 99, and their resulting hybrids. This is a three way cross of Skunk #1, Original Haze, and Northern Lights #5. The pheno you get will depend on which year the cross was made. It is suspected that the Genius and Princess plants of Brothers Grimm were from the Original Haze mother. Personally, this isn't one of my favorite strains: it's a decent plant, but nothing that I find extraordinary. That said, Genius and Princess and their hybrids are extraordinary, so kudos to Brothers Grimm and Sensi Seeds.

Jack the Ripper from Subcool / TGA
Originated in the United States

Created from Jacks Cleaner x Space Queen, a.k.a. "Space Dude." Space Queen added increased resin production and better taste, although the lemon pledge scent is still evident. I've found that JTR (as it is commonly known) sometimes produces mutant offspring. There are triploid and twinning mutations – triploid is fine because then you get three branches per node, but twinning is less desirable and is discussed in my chapter on breeding.

Jacks Cleaner from Subcool / TGA
Originated in the United States
Created from a rare phenotype of Skoosh x Jack Herer. This is the flagship strain of TGA genetics. Noted for its lemon pledge scent and resin production. Only available in F2s to the public.

Jamaican Pearl from Sensi Seeds
Originated in Holland
Created from the same Jamaican landrace used to create Marley's Collie and Early Pearl. This is actually a very good cross; the flavor is very sweet— a friend compared it to Granny Smith apples—but during growing it reportedly smells peculiar: a mix of cheese, detergent, and skunk. Even though she was crossed with Early Pearl she's a good 10-week finisher.

Jillybean from MzJill / TGA
Originated in the United States
Created using Orange Velvet x Space Queen, a.k.a. "Space Dude." Jillybean

Trifoliate plant, a sometimes useful mutation that grows three shoots every node.

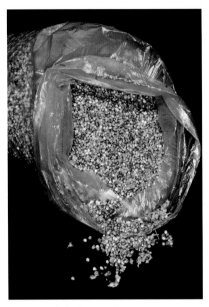 

Seeds and shake. Seeds come in a variety of patterns and textures.

Seeds can be brown, grey, tan with black motts or stripes that can be vertical or horizontal in direction.

The direct plant method. Just pop your seeds in the dirt and water. It doesn't get much easier than that!

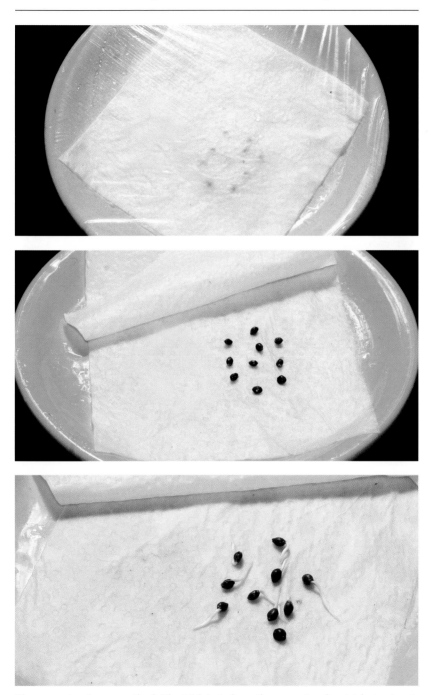

The paper towel germ method. The trick is to keep the paper towel moist but not saturated. These babies are ready to go to the dirt!

This is the improper way to germinate seedlings – too many plants per Jiffy pellet. I don't recommend Jiffy pellets as a medium.

These seedlings will need to be thinned out so that only one remains.

The husk is going to fall off naturally.

This is the proper way to plant your seedlings, one seed per container. These seedlings are stretching for the light, though.

An example of an un-useful mutation. This plant should be culled to make room for other, healthier plants that will produce more bud.

This mutant seedling never developed its first true set of cannabis leaves.

When a whole batch of seedlings are mutants it can mean a few things; the soil is toxic; the strain is toxic; or you have used a chemical on your seedlings like colchicine.

A trifoliate seedling, newly emerged. We should wait to see if this mutation will be beneficial or not.

A fully rooted clone ready to be transplanted.

Clones should have healthy white roots like these.

A tray of healthy clones ready to be transplanted.

A perpetual garden showing newest clones on the left and older plants on the right.

A 150w CFL grow. The CFL's low heat allows it to be placed very close to the plants.

Female preflower. Notice the white pistils.

The male preflower will develop a claw like hook with a "ball."

The male pollen sacs are releasing pollen into the air. These tiny specks contain years of genetic research conducted by Alpine Seeds' head breeder, MoD.

This plant has had too much fertilizer and should be flushed immediately.

Magnesium and calcium deficiencies are common in flower. Correct with Cal-Mag.

Nitrogen deficiency coupled with excess salt build up causing nitrogen to be "locked out" of the plant.

Potassium deficiency. Note the dark green interior color and the yellow tips starting with the serrated edges.

Powdery mildew affecting a plant in late flower. Remove all affected areas and add a dehumidifier to try and save your crop!

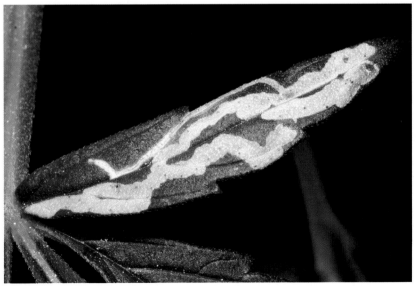

Pests leaf mining fly copyr by GBI 2009 – Leaf Miners are harmless if they only attack the leaves but once in the stalk they wreak havoc. Crush them between fingers or remove affected portions of the plant.

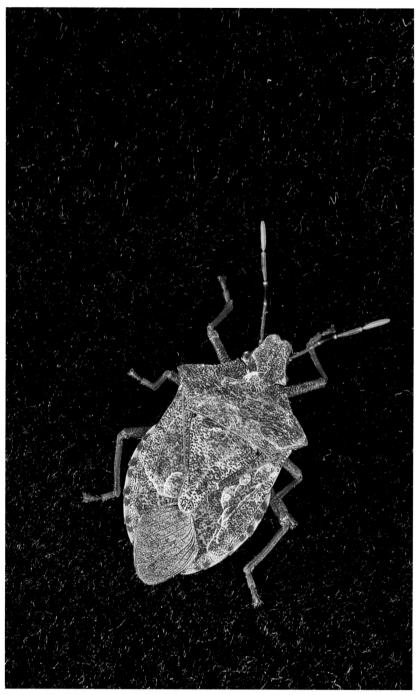

Stink bugs are just as harmful as grasshoppers. More prevalent in the Southern US.

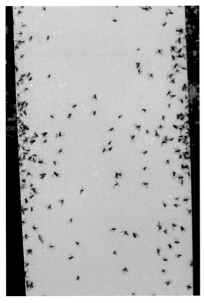 

Yellow sticky traps are effective for combating many flying pests including white flies and gnats.

Thrips are a major pain but there are a variety of ways to destroy them.

Spider mites, the arch-nemesis of the Cannabis grower, have ruined this healthy grow.

Natural pest control. Cannabis grew well before we ever knew it existed.

produces beautiful hues of burgundy—certainly a pretty lady. You're sure to find a keeper in one of these packs. Jillybean has an orange–pineapple sweetness to it. Look out for the candy store" phenotype, which is the tastiest.

Johnny Blaze from Legends Seeds
Originated in Canada
Created with an Original Neville's Haze x Blueberry. This is a great, predominantly Sativa hybrid; nowhere near stable, but you can usually find a keeper in each pack. A green citrus / blueberry scent.

K

Kahuna from Soma
Originated in Holland
This baby is a four-way cross featuring Super Skunk x Big Skunk Korean x Jack Herer x AfghanHawaiian. Soma says this is an Indica-dominant hybrid, but I would have to disagree. It definitely grows like an Indica, with super-thick, hardy buds that have a sweet and spicy scent to them, but the high is cerebral, indicating Sativa dominance. So if you would like a Sativa high with an Indica pattern of growth, this is the plant for you.

Kali Mist from Serious Seeds
Originated in Holland
Serious Seeds won't release the pedigree of this amazing strain but it is assumed that one part is a landrace Sativa, most likely from Asia, and the other is an exotic Sativa-dominant hybrid. This strain has a very unique taste, almost indescribable. Perfect for outdoors, this award-winning strain is mold resistant, has a moderate maturing time, and a fat yield. Serious Seeds revamped her in 2000 to make even fatter yields without compromising flavor or potency. Most cash croppers or commercial growers are pleased with this strain's yield as well as potency. (Also reported to ease menstrual cramps.)

Kalichakra from Mandala
Originated in Holland
This is a landrace hybrid featuring an Indian Indica x Asian Sativa. This hybrid performs well indoors thanks to its Indian Indica momma. Reports have indicated that it smells a bit like fruity incense when flowering. She also performs very well outdoors and finishes in just over nine weeks.

Kerala Krush from Flying Dutchmen
Originated in Holland
Created from the Indian Sativa, Kerala, and Skunk #1. This is a very nice Sativa cross that is responsible for several other great strains. The Skunk #1 father adds speed and fattens up yields, while the Kerala provides a sweet smooth exotic taste and aroma. Kerala Krush finishes in around 10 weeks.

Kill Bill from Rezdog / Reservoir Seeds
Originated in the United States
Created from Killer Queen x William's Wonder. The Killer Queen does more for

this cross than the William's Wonder, but in my opinion this strain doesn't do either justice.

Killer Apollo from Rezdog / Reservoir Seeds
Originated in the United States
Created from Killer Queen x Apollo 11. This strain really likes to stretch and doesn't produce solid colas because of her Sativa-dominant heritage. Though not very stable, she is a good strain: you're likely to find some keepers. Very frosty and fast finishing (7–8 weeks).

Killer Queen from Motarebel
Originated in the United States / Canada.
Created from "Airborne" G13 x Cinderella 99, this is an F5 cross of the British Colombia Growers Association (BCGA). This trichome machine is great medication for those in need; it has an overwhelming head and body high.

King's Kross from Reeferman
Originated in Canada
Reeferman's version of a Vancouver Island clone which was King x Charles Kush, backcrossed to King. This is an Indica-dominant hybrid that finishes in 8–9 weeks.

Krowberry from Sierra Seeds
Originated in the United Kingdom
My favorite purple strain, this is a third degree purple; not only is it purple, it's potent as well. Reportedly Blackberry x

Grand Daddy Purple, these are feminized seeds but so far I have seen no ill side effects. Beautiful plum-colored buds with orange hairs!

Krystalica from Mandala
Originated in Holland
This is probably the only strain offered by Mandala Mike that's not a pure landrace. Some type of Indian Indica cross, this girl is favored for her great outdoor growth and recessed, large calyxes. She is a mostly Sativa-dominant plant that finishes in around 10 weeks.

Kushage from T.H.Seeds
Originated in Holland
Created fromO.G. Kush x S.A.G.E. This is a great Indica-dominant hybrid that packs an interestingly different flavor with Indica structure and high. Definitely the Indica for you if you're tired of the typical bland Indica flavor.

L

L.A. Confidential from DNA Genetics
Originated in the United States / Holland
Created from L.A. Affie x Afghani, this pure Indica hybrid is one of my personal favorites. She produces dense, beautiful buds that finish in about eight weeks. This award-winning strain is a favorite for indoor sea / screen of green gardens.

La Nina from Mr. Nice Seeds
Originated in Holland

Created from Haze x White Widow, this is Mr. Nice's version of El Nino. While La Nina is a nice hybrid she has nowhere near the taste or trichome production that made El Nino famous. A decent hybrid nonetheless.

Lambsbread Skunk from Dutch
Passion
Originated in Holland
Supposedly a "Lambsbread" mother x Skunk #1 father, there are several reason why this is doubtful, but this strain nonetheless does perform well outside. She is definitely Sativa-dominant, taking 11+ weeks to finish, with an interesting taste and a classic Sativa high.

Lavender from Soma Seeds
Originated in Holland
This is some of my all time favorite smoke. Reportedly a three-way cross of Super Skunk x Big Skunk Korean x Purple Afghani Hawaiian, Soma chose the most potent and colorful of each parent, creating this wonderfully beautiful and potent strain. Lavender actually tastes "purple," with spicy after tones. For an Indica-dominant plant she can get quite tall—highly recommended for SOG gardens. She also does very well outdoors, but indoors or out, she'll produce some of the prettiest buds around.

Leda Uno from KC Brains
Originated in Holland
Most likely the best offering from KC

Brains. Reportedly a four-way cross featuring a "secret" Brazilian landrace x KC 33 x Leda x KC 606. This is a pretty even hybrid, slightly favoring Sativa. The taste is piney with strange after tones. Most phenos will produce fat, thick buds.

Legends Ultimate Indica from
Legends Seeds
Originated in the United States / Canada
Created from an unreleased Ortega mother x Sweet Tooth father, this F1 was then backcrossed to the Sweet Tooth father. This is a favorite of many Indica lovers, and with the yield of Ortega and the taste of Sweet Tooth, what's not to like? However, the strain is not very stable, despite the first backcross. LUI, as it is commonly known, is prone to mutants as well.

Love Potion #1 from Reeferman
Originated in Canada
Created from G13 x Santa Marta Colombian Gold backcrossed to SM Colombian Gold. There's a lot of hype surrounding this strain in terms of its herm ratio, some positive and some negative. At the end of the day, LP #1 is some tasty smoke, vaguely reminiscent of old school Mexican.

Love Potion 1.1 from Reeferman
Originated in Holland
A cross from the Indica-dominant Love Potion #1, with reportedly denser "G13-tasting" buds.

Love Potion #2 from Reeferman
Originated in Holland
Yup, you guessed it: a cross from the Sativa-dominant Love Potion #1, reportedly tasting like "lemon pledge." It is my opinion that LP #2 is a Love Potion #1 father x Jacks Cleaner mother, and not a Colombian Gold, as some people suggest, because Colombian Gold tastes nothing like lemons.

Lowryder from Joint Doctors
Originated in Holland
Ah, the infamous Lowryder plant. Supposedly a three-way hybrid of Northern Lights x Williams Wonder x landrace dwarf Ruderalis, there are many pros and cons to this strain. Of course, Ruderalis is a THCless, headache-causing cannabis species that auto-flowers regardless of photoperiod, and Lowryder was largely overlooked by breeders because of this. It is not quite clear what strain Joint Doctors crossed the Ruderalis with to create Lowryder; whichever it was, they found the phenotype they desired in the F1 cross, then repeatedly back-crossed to the "mystery" parent, creating the relatively stable Lowryder. Lowryder can be planted any time of year and in a wide variety of climates that normally could not grow cannabis. Because you can flower Lowryder under 24 hours of light, a greater yield per square foot than any other strain may be grown, making it perfect for SOG grows; correspondingly, there is no need to separate into vegetative and budding rooms, and no need to worry about light leaks. The entire life cycle of Lowryder is 8–9 weeks. Now, the downsides are that you cannot clone or reveg your plant, requiring you to sow new seeds every time. Although Lowryder is certainly lacking in potency and taste, many crosses have been made to improve the quality. Moreover, Lowryder is perfect for concealing your grows (hardly ever reaching 12 inches tall), allowing you to plant in flower beds and even window sills.

Lowryder #2 from Joint Doctors
Originated in Holland
Reportedly Lowryder x Santa Maria from Brazil. A cross to improve yield, taste, and potency. Taste is a little better, but potency is still lacking. Finishing time is a bit longer as well.

M

Malawi Gold from Afropips
Originated in Africa
This is a great strain for the Sativa lover and also for the breeder wishing to incorporate a pure Sativa into their crosses. Malawi Gold is regarded by some as the most powerful landrace Sativa from Africa. Because of her landrace status, she is very spicy in flavor but provides a very uplifting cerebral high. There is also an indoor version available with a quicker finishing time, but it doesn't hold a candle to the real Malawi Gold.

"Mangolian" Indica from Sagarmatha
Originated in Holland
This is a three-way cross featuring Afghani Skunk x Afghani x Northern Lights. If you like powerful Indicas, this is the strain for you. Although I have never tasted any mango or fruit of any kind with this strain. Sagarmatha says this is his favorite strain.

Marley's Collie from Sensi Seeds
Originated in Holland
Reportedly a cross of Jamaican Lambsbread x Maple Leaf Indica. Don't let the tag fool you: this is most definitely an outdoor strain. Indoors she gets too tall and leggy to manage without extensive training. The taste is very appealing—somewhat fruity—and the high is a nice balance of both Sativa and Indica, although the Sativa phenotype typically dominates.

Martian Mean Green from DNA Genetics
Originated in the United States / Holland
This is a Sharks Breath x G13 Haze hybrid. Not a very stable strain, but almost every phenotype is a keeper. Not only are they potent, but these are also some of the most beautiful buds you will ever see. A nice Indica stone with a Haze taste.

Master Kush from Dutch Passion
Originated in Holland
Reportedly a cross between two differ-

ent Hindu Kush plants. It is thought that the cross is Hindu Kush x Black Label's Master Kush (which in turn is Hindu Kush x Skunk #1). So, that would make Dutch Passion's Master Kush a cross of Hindu Kush x Hindu Kush x Skunk #1. Master Kush is one of the fastest finishers I've seen, but I find the taste to be a little boring.

Matanuska Tundra from Sagarmatha Seeds
Originated in Holland
This is Sagarmatha's version of Alaskan Thunderfuck (ATF). Some say this is true ATF, but that is a clone-only strain, so I theorize that Matanuska Tundra is probably ATF x Mongolian Indica. ATF comes from the Matanuska Valley, Alaska, where ATF is legendary. It is thought that ATF is a landrace Ruderalis x Indica. Matanuska Tundra is a nice smoke with a quick finishing time, and a taste that is somewhat chocolaty. Sagarmatha has also crossed this in a number of other strains.

Mazar from Dutch Passion
Originated in Holland
Reportedly a Mazar-I-Sharif female crossed with a Skunk #1 male. I find that critics are divided about this strain because there are so many phenos in each pack. If you choose the right pheno, it's a very potent strain, but if you don't then the plant can be bland and unappealing.

Medicine Man from Mr. Nice Seeds
Originated in Holland
This is a three-way cross featuring Brazilian x South Indian x Afghani. Also known as White Rhino, this strain is rumored to be incredibly potent and great for medical users. Medicine Man is reasonably stable. Not all plants will have the same vegetative characteristics, but they will all produce copious amounts of resin.

Mendocino Madness from T.H. Seeds
Originated in Holland
This is a cross of the Northern Californian Clone called Madness x the male parent of Kwiksilver. This plant is a heavy yielder, especially outdoors, which it favors. She is also mold-and-pest resistant, which makes her even better for outdoor growing.

Mexican Sativa from Sensi Seeds
Originated in Holland
A three-way cross featuring Oaxaca x Pakistani x Durban. This strain is pretty nice for the outdoor grower, producing nice yields in a short amount of time. Most phenos are Sativa-dominant, but a few Indica-dominant phenos persist.

MK Ultra from T.H. Seeds
Originated in Holland
Reportedly a "G13" x OG Kush. The OG Kush taste is definitely there, as well as the crystal production, and whatever "G13" he used definitely beefed up the yield. Very nice work from T.H. Seeds on this one.

Morning Glory from Barney's Farm
Originated in Holland
Sweet Tooth x Super Silver Haze (SSH). Award-winning strain with SSH providing the dominant taste, but I'm not a huge fan because I prefer the taste of Sweet Tooth over SSH.

Mother's Finest from Sensi Seeds
Originated in Holland
A three way cross featuring Jack Herer (JH) x Haze x an unknown Indica. This is a new creation from Sensi. There are three common phenotypes—a JH, Haze, and Indica pheno—in my opinion, the JH pheno is the best, but all are very tasty and potent.

Mountain Jam from Chimera
Originated in Canada
This is a cross between SoulShine, a well known Indica-dominant Canadian clone, x DJ Short's Blueberry. This cross created a very colorful, beautiful, potent hybrid. There are two main phenotypes—Soulshine pheno and Blueberry pheno. The Soulshine pheno is the one to look for, as it has superior potency as well as yield (although the Blueberry pheno might be a bit more tasty).

N

Nebula from Paradise Seeds
Originated in Holland

Paradise Seeds won't divulge the lineage of Nebula, but it is most likely a descendent of a Dutch version of Skunk #1. Has some interesting after tones. In particular, a hint of tropical lime taste can be found on the more Sativa-dominant phenos.

Neon Super Skunk from TGA / Subcool Seeds
Originated in the United States
A Super Skunk x Black Russian cross, with a nice yield and amazing colors— a mostly Skunky taste, too.

Neville's Haze from Greenhouse Seeds
Originated in Holland
Reportedly 75% Haze x 25% Northern Lights. This is a great strain if you like the spicy Haze taste and racy Haze high. Although many hardcore Haze fans prefer the original haze strains.

New York City Diesel from Soma Seeds
Originated in Holland
This is supposedly an F1 cross of the famous Diesel, a.k.a. OG Kush, a.k.a. Chemdog. Whether or not it's true is debatable, but the strain is very potent, nonetheless.

Nigerian from Afropips
Originated in Africa
This landrace Sativa is a surprisingly fast finisher, noted for is spiciness and hash taste.

Nigerian Nightmare from Reeferman
Originated in Canada
This is a three-way cross featuring Nigerian x Afghani x Brazilian; a pretty nice twist on an old classic. The high from Nigerian Nightmare is reportedly very nice, a balance of both body and mind, slightly leaning to the mind side. The taste is somewhat like orange, but there is definitely a touch of floral to some phenos. Most phenos will turn different shades of brilliant purple colors. Though yields are small, they are sure to please all your senses.

NLX from Grow Shop Alien
Originated in Holland
This is a freebie that GSA was providing with some orders; made up of Northern Lights x White Widow, it is a very nice, easy to grow strain—not very stable but better than most freebies. The taste is not spectacular, not unlike most members of the "White" family, but the high is definitely a knock out.

Northern Lights from Seedsman Seeds
Originated in the United States
This may be the most notorious of all cannabis strains. The original Northern Lights was developed in the United States and was comprised of three different kinds of Indicas, with a Sativa mixed in. This plant never became stable and when it was sent to Europe as

a clone-only strain it was then crossed with Dutch Skunk #1 and Haze varieties. There are several different types of Northern Lights, the most remarkable of which is Northern Lights #5, commonly known as NL5. NL5 is NL x Thai, and is much better than NL, in my opinion. The high from Northern Lights is typically Indica-dominant, but the taste isn't my favorite. Commonly used as a breeding partner to produce copious trichomes.

O

OG Kush

Originated in the United States

When Chemdog, a.k.a. Diesel was crossed with Super Skunk the resulting cross was Sour Diesel. Sour Diesel made its way to the West Coast as a clone only strain, which in turn became known as OG Kush, a.k.a. Original Gangster Kush, or L.A. Kush. This clone is highly sought after but is fairly common in SoCal (Southern California). A pound usually runs more than $8,000 dollars and it is not unheard of them going for $10,000 dollars or more. Talk about supply and demand.

Omega Diesel from Rezdog / Reservoir Seeds

Originated in the United States

All that Rez will say about this strain is that it is a great Diesel cross. As such, it is not suitable for breeding purposes, but is a solid strain nonetheless and consistently popular with growers.

It is not one of my favorite Diesels – I prefer ESCD and Sour Diesel, but everyone's taste is different.

Orange Apollo from Rezdog / Reservoir Seeds

Originated in the United States

This is reportedly a cross of an Aeric Californian Clone x Apollo 11 (A11), backcrossed to A11. This cross provides the mind-bending high of A11 with a hint of orange flavor: as appealing to your THC receptors as it is to your palate.

Orange Velvet from MzJill / TGA Seeds

This was gifted to MzJill by a local grower and she did some work selecting phenos, so, although TGA made the strain publicly available, it is not truly a TGA strain. Orange Velvet produces amazing colors—deep purple / burgundy hues—early into budding. She is not very potent, but her taste is certainly amazing: like Dreamsicles (vanilla ice cream coated with orange sherbet). This is where Jillybean gets her amazing colors.

Original Haze from Seedsman Seeds

Originated in the United States

This is reportedly the old school Haze of Mexican x Colombian x Thai x South Indian. This powerful combination of Sativas from around the globe will surely send you soaring. This taste is incredibly spicy and people have reported hallucinations when smoking this strain. Not for the inexperienced toker.

P

Pandora's Box from Subcool / TGA
Originated in the United States
Reportedly a Jack the Ripper female x Space Queen, a.k.a. Space Dude, male. This is one of the newest offerings from TGA. Not much is known at this time about Pandora's box, but if its parents indicate anything, she promises to be dank.

Petrol from Reservoir Seeds
Originated in the United States
An inbred cross of two Sour Diesel plants. Good high and flavor are what you would expect from Sour Diesel, with an added boost in yield.

Petrolia Headstash from Reeferman
Originated in the United States / Canada
This is an elite clone that has been passed around the "Emerald Triangle" since the late 70s. Petrolia Headstash is valued for its pain-relieving effects and amazing colors. Reeferman's Petrolia Headstash is the clone-only Petrolia Headstash mother x a mystery Afghani.

PG-13 from T.H. Seeds
Originated in Holland
Supposedly a cross of the legendary HP-13 x G13. Sources have told me that it could very well be a cross of the infamous HP-13, which was Hash Plant inbred thirteen times to form one of the most potent, tastiest strains around. G13 doesn't do anything for this cross, but it does make HP-13 available to the masses.

Pot of Gold from Flying Dutchmen
Originated in Holland
Reportedly a combination of (the Dutch versions of) Hindu Kush x Skunk #1. This strain is easy to grow and a nice yielder, with a mild resistance to mold, as well. Some examples of the plant have a sweet and spicy taste to them, too.

Power Plant from Dutch Passion
Originated in Holland
This is a hybrid of South African Sativas combined with an Indica plant, most likely a Dutch version of Northern Lights or White Widow. There are rumors of stress-induced herming, and I find that she lacks on the high.

Princess from Brothers Grimm
Originated in the United States
Reportedly a rare pheno of Jack Herer x a semi-rare pheno of Shiva Skunk. This plant was cubed to bring us the legendary Cinderella 99.

Princess Diesel from Reservoir Seeds
Originated in the United States
This is one of my favorite offerings from Rezdog. Both of these strains (Princess and Sour Diesel) cross extremely well

with one another, and the favorable traits of each are expressed in most of the F1s. Combines Princess' resin production and structure with Sour Diesel's extraordinary taste.

Puna Budder from T.H. Seeds
Originated in Holland
Supposedly a mystery "Hawaiian" x Afghani. There is no telling what this strain really is, because experts agree that no landrace strains are indigenous to Hawaii. Although the lineage is not known, the high is very Indica with a nice tropical taste. If you're looking for a good Indica high for pain relief, but hate that boring Indica taste, this is the strain for you.

Purple Star from Dutch Passion
Originated in Holland
Purple Star comes from an unknown cross of two Indicas. Most phenos will turn a deep, dark, rich purple color, but, sadly, like most purple pot, Purple Star isn't particularly potent.

Q

Quick Mist from Reservoir Seeds
Originated in the United States
Reportedly Kali Mist x Mighty Mite. I would have preferred for the exotic taste of Kali Mist to prevail, but Mighty Mite is more dominant in the cross. So, it has a fast finishing time, which is Mighty Mite's specialty, but, again, I would have preferred the taste of Kali Mist to be dominant.

Quick Mist Diesel from Reservoir Seeds
Originated in the United States
Reportedly Quick Mist x Sour Diesel. Reservoir Seeds attempted to improve on the taste and effect of Quick Mist, and they have succeeded. The finishing time is longer, but this strain is worth the wait.

Querkle from Subcool / TGA
Originated in the United States
Supposedly a Purple Urkle clone x Space Dude male. Can't be sure if the clone was really Purple Urkle or not, as there has been some debate on the issue. This is Subcool's effort to speed up vegetation and flowering times for Purple Urkle by pollinating it with Space Dude.

R

Real McCoy from Flying Dutchmen
Originated in Holland
No one is quite sure about the lineage of this strain; it is most likely a Dutch Skunk #1 x a mystery "Hawaiian." Think of this plant as Skunk #1 with a tropical citrus taste to it. This is a very nice, easy strain for a beginner to grow if they want a taste of something out of the ordinary.

Reclining Buddha from Soma
Originated in Holland
Reportedly a four-way cross featuring a Holland's Hope base x Jack Herer x Super Skunk x Big Skunk Korean. One

of the few Soma offerings for the outdoors, this plant is mold-resistant
thanks to its Holland's Hope parent.

ReCON from DNA Genetics
Originated in Holland
Supposedly a "mutant" L.A. Confidential
x Cannadential, this strain is fairly popular, but I'm not a fan. This is actually
the only DNA strain that I don't recommend, but give the ReCON strain
some more time to be tested and
developed and it may become a strain
I can recommend.

Rock Bud from Soma
Originated in Holland
Reportedly a four-way cross featuring
Super Skunk x Big Skunk Korean x
Afghani x Afghani Hawaiian. It is hard
to come across an Indica lover that
hasn't grown and loved Rock Bud. As
the name suggests, when properly
grown, colas develop into rock hard,
dense buds that are full of hues of
red, burgundy, and purple. She is a
truly knockout smoke and a great
plant for SOG.

Rocklock from DNA Genetics
Originated in Holland
Reportedly a Magus Genetics Warlock
x Rockstar. This is a very nice, heavy
yielding Indica hybrid, perfect for the
cash-cropper or Indica-lover. I find the
taste a bit bland, but the huge, trichome-covered buds make up for that.
The best part is: she finishes in just

over eight weeks. That Rocks!

Romulan from Federation Seeds
Originated in Canada
Supposedly some sort of White Widow x
White Rhino cross, but there is definitely
something Hazy about Romulan. For a
member of the "White" family, she has a
lot of color to her. It has been inbred
repeatedly, increasing the intensity of
the high each time. Any "cannaseur"
should add this to their collection.

S

Sadhu from Mandala Seeds
Originated in Spain
Reportedly a Himalayan Male x unknown
Sativa x Indica landrace hybrid. Sadhu
is a Sativa dominant and has a rare
candy-like aroma / flavor. Sadhu is also
heat resistant and easy to grow. She
does tend to get bigger than Satori,
though.

SAGE from T.H. Seeds
Originated in Holland
Reportedly an unknown Haze hybrid x
random Afghani. SAGE stands for
Sativa Afghani Genetic Equilibrium.
SAGE has created a great deal of buzz
in recent years. Although it is supposed to be an equal cross of Sativa
and Afghani, it leans more to the Sativa
side, which is a good thing. Meanwhile,
the Afghani increases the yield and
makes this a very nice plant to grow
outdoors.

SAGE 'n Sour from T.H. Seeds
Originated in Holland
Reportedly a SAGE male x Sour Diesel female. Phenos of this cross differ, but if you can find the rare "deez" (Diesel) phenotype this plant is definitely a keeper. The "deez" pheno combines the unique taste of Sour Diesel with the yield of SAGE.

Satori from Mandala Seeds
Originated in Spain
This is some sort of Nepalese landrace hybrid. What is known for certain is that she is a very potent, easy-to-manage, Sativa-dominant hybrid. Satori has a pungent citrus aroma that is sure to please even the pickiest pot snobs. Like most of Mandala's strains, Satori is heat resistant.

Scarlet Queen from Homegrown and Badboy / TGA
Originated in Canada
This is probably my favorite TGA offering. This is a Killer Queen mango pheno female x Space Queen (a.k.a. Space Dude) male. These F1s were grown out in large numbers, picking the best seeds to continue the line. The results are very uniform, extremely potent, beautiful buds. These plants stretch a good bit, but form solid colas that take you to the moon. This plant begins to pack on trichomes very early, and at an astounding rate. This strain is very colorful with beautiful red / pink tents to the buds. The taste is also very cherry-like. All in all, this strain appeals to all senses.

Schnazzleberry from Chimera
Originated in Holland
Reportedly a Blue Domino female x Shiskaberry male. The father Shiskaberry from Spice of Life adds weight to the yield, an increased color spectrum, and makes the flavor more appealing. If you can find a Shiskaberry pheno of this strain, it is definitely the keeper.

Schnazzleberry #2 from Chimera
Originated in Holland
This is Schnazzleberry x a DJ Short creation. It is unknown exactly which strain was used in this cross, but it did add color, whatever it was. I found the potency to be lacking compared to the original Schnazzleberry, but the color is incredible.

Schroomy Deez from Rezdog / Reservoir Seeds
Originated in the United States
Reportedly Schrom x Sour Diesel. Schrom is a unique clone from a grower named Schroomy. Schrom has a very unique, somewhat velvety taste to it, and Rezdog has crossed it with his trademark Sour Diesel. In my opinion the Sour Diesel is too overpowering in this strain; I would have preferred if the Schrom taste was dominant.

Shaman from Dutch Passion
Originated in Holland

Reportedly a Purple #1 x Early Skunk, I like this strain from Dutch Passion. Although not very potent, she does have a good daytime high and nice bag appeal (for the buyer), with most of the phenos turning some hue of purple.

Sharks Breath from DNA Genetics
Originated in Holland
Supposedly a Great White Shark x Jamaican Lambsbread. Since Lambsbread refers to a broad range of good quality Jamaican cannabis, the specific Jamaican strain used is unclear. One thing is certain, though, and that is that there is very little Lambsbread influence; she is a mostly Indica hybrid that is short and stout and really packs on the resin glands.

Shiva from Dr. Atomic
Originated in Canada
This is reportedly a three-way cross between Afghani x Atomic Northern Lights x Super Crystal. These three plants come together to create a heavily Indica-dominant plant that is great for pain relief. This girl yields ounces upon ounces of beautiful dank buds that have a spicy, exotic aroma that I cannot describe.

Shiva Shanti #1 from Sensi Seeds
Originated in Holland
An unknown three-way hybrid heavily consisting of an Afghani known as "Garlic Bud." I think Shiva Skunk is part of its make up because it tends to be a rather leafy strain. Shiva Shanti is more potent than you expect.

Shiva Shanti from Sensi Seeds has heavy characteristics from its Afghani parentage, the infamous "Garlic Bud." A potent strain.

Shiva Skunk from Sensi Seeds
Originated in Holland
This is a Dutch version of two of the world's most celebrated strains: Skunk #1 and Northern Lights #5. Shiva Skunk is incredibly leafy but lacks somewhat in potency. There are two known phenos of Shiva Skunk, a green (white) pheno and the ultra-rare purple pheno. The purple pheno is one of the most rare clones on the planet, and is rumored to be insanely potent and beautiful.

Shiva Skunk #2 from Sensi Seeds
Originated in Holland
This is a three-way hybrid consisting of Garlic Bud x Skunk x Afghani. This strain works quite well, and I feel that it improves on Shiva Skunk. Shiva Skunk #2 is a much better strain overall, with improved yield and potency.

Silver Haze from Sensi Seeds
Originated in Holland
Supposedly Haze x an unknown Indica. This is an interesting cross that beefs up the yield of the typical Haze. The buds are, for the most part, still light and airy, but they begin to become dense around day 60. If you're looking for a Haze variety that finishes in less than 100 days, this is for you: most phenos finish between 70–80 days.

Silver Pearl from Sensi Seeds
Originated in Holland
This is a three-way hybrid that consists of Early Pearl x Skunk #1 x Northern Lights. The Skunk #1 pheno is the best one, and the Early Pearl adds a quick finishing time to most phenos. I don't know where the "silver" part came from, though. Silver Pearl is very easy to grow, especially outdoors.

Skunk #1 from Seedsman Seeds
Originated in the United States
Reportedly a three-way cross featuring landrace Afghani x Colombian Gold x Mexican Gold. This was the first ever stabilized hybrid made specifically for indoor use. It was also the first strain to combine the heavy yields and quick finishing time of Indica with the high and structure of Sativa. Even after all this time, this is still one of my favorite plants. Unlike Northern Lights, Skunk #1 was stabilized, which means you can pretty much expect a uniform bunch of plants from a pack of seeds.

Skunk #1 is also remarkably easy to grow and can tolerate much abuse. While she was bred for indoor cultivation, she does do remarkably well outdoors. Skunk #1 has been used in more crosses than Northern Lights and Haze; in fact, she's present in over 60% of today's strains. The original is still available through Seedsman Seeds thanks to Sam the Skunkman.

Skunk Passion from Dutch Passion
Originated in Holland
Supposedly an inbred line of Dutch Passion's version of their Skunk #1. This is a good, Sativa-dominant hybrid that will be sure to please you. The buds are long and lanky, rarely connecting to form a whole cola.

Skywalker from Dutch Passion
Originated in Holland
Reportedly a cross between DJ Short's Blueberry male x Mazar female. If you pick the right pheno this is a truly beautiful, not to mention potent, plant. The Mazar was lacking flavor, but was potent; the Blueberry gave a nice flavor; together, they form Skywalker: one of the most popular and potent offerings from Dutch Passion.

Somango from Soma Seeds
Originated in Holland
This is a three-way cross featuring: Super Skunk x Big Skunk Korean x Jack Herer. Like all of Soma's offerings, this plant really is a knockout; not only

through the high, but visually as well. When grown properly, Somango showcases many of the colors of the rainbow, including orange (which is a very uncommon color in cannabis). As the name indicates, most phenos have a tropical, somewhat mango-like flavor. All the phenos that I grew of this plant were keepers.

Somanna from Soma Seeds
Originated in Holland
This is a four-way cross featuring: Super Skunk x Big Skunk Korean x C. Chinensis x Afghani–Hawaiian. The most interesting thing about this strain is the C. Chinensis, which is a landrace variety from China. Some phenos will display a unique mutation because of this. Like most of Soma's offerings, Somanna does not display much color, but it does get exceptionally crystalline.

Somaui from Soma Seeds
Originated in Holland
Reportedly Hawaiian Sativa x G13 Haze. This is one of the few Sativa-dominant hybrids that Soma offers. This strain behaves like a typical Sativa, with most phenos taking longer than 100 days. She does get leggy, but the high is definitely something that Sativa lovers are looking for. A very interesting tropical taste, too.

Sour Cream from DNA Genetics
Originated in Holland
Reportedly Sour Diesel x G13 Haze. This is a very nice cross. The flavor of Haze

and Sour Diesel together is extraordinary! This is one of my all time favorite smokes. Although she is a bit difficult for the rookie grower, experienced growers will love her and clone her over and over again. Best when grown outdoors.

Sour Diesel IBL from Rezdog / Reservoir Seeds
Originated in the United States
This is the final step in several backcrosses, Sour Diesel (SD) backcrossed (bx) 1.5, SD bx 2.5, and SD v3. That brings you an inbred line (IBL) of SD, which supposedly gives you the SD clone in seed form.

Sour Mist from Rezdog / Reservoir Seeds
Originated in the United States
Reportedly a Sour Diesel x Kali Mist. A great Sour Sativa that is sure to please both Sour Diesel and Sativa lovers. Expect a long finishing time with this beauty—80 days plus.

Sour Queen from Rezdog / Reservoir Seeds
Originated in the United States
Reportedly Killer Queen x Sour Diesel bx 1.5. This is a very unique offering in which both strains are equally expressed. Killer Queen provides a better yield and a lemon / cherry flavor to the Sour Diesel. It's a shame Rezdog discontinued this strain, as it was probably my favorite offering from Reservoir Seeds.

Sour Queen #2 from Rezdog / Reservoir Seeds

Originated in the United States

This is Sour Queen backcrossed to Sour Diesel. A very popular strain, but in my opinion, they should have gone the other way, backcrossing to Killer Queen, because Sour Diesel overpowers almost anything it is crossed with. It would be nice, for once, to have Sour Diesel as an aftertaste.

Southern Lights #1 from Delta 9

Originated in the United States

This strain has been making a lot of noise in certain circles. Created from Paradise Seeds' Sensi Star x Soma NYC Diesel, Southern Lights #1 is very stable— the plants look like clones. Unlike Northern Lights, Southern Lights balances the Sativa–Indica effects and leaves you able to walk after smoking, but it can be used as a night cap, as well. This plant gets covered in milky, white, glistening trichomes, and has a very unique taste.

Speed Queen from Mandala Seeds

Originated in Spain

This is some sort of Indica dominant landrace hybrid from the Northern regions of India. Speed Queen boasts a fast finishing time, some phenos finish in less than 50 days. Speed Queen is extremely resinous and has a sort of Nag Champa Incense taste to it.

Sputnik 1.0 from Subcool / TGA

Originated in the United States

Reportedly an Apollo 13 x Black Russian hybrid. This strain, nicknamed "Pinky," was one of my favorites. Made to increase the potency of Black Russian while retaining its color, Sputnik 1.0 did a pretty good job of it. The color wasn't quite like Black Russian, but amazing nonetheless, with beautiful hues of pink and light purple.

Sputnik 2.0 from Subcool / TGA

Originated in the United States

Reportedly a Sputnik 1.0 bx (backcrossed to) Apollo 13. This was an effort to stabilize the A13 genetics in Sputnik 1.0, which worked out well, but most phenos lost their unique color. The strain was later scrapped, but was well-liked in its heyday.

Stonehedge is a great Sativa strain from Sagarmatha. This is by far the heaviest yielding Sativa ever. Incredible.

Stonehedge from Sagarmatha
Originated in Holland
Some sort of Cambodian x Western Winds. This is by far the heaviest yielding Sativa. Known to have common foxtails, this plant is very easy to manage for a Sativa and performs well both indoors and out.

Strawberry Diesel from Rezdog / Reservoir Seeds
Originated in the United States
That's right: yet another Sour Diesel cross. This is reportedly Kyle Kushman's Strawberry Cough x Sour Diesel. In limited release, the piney–strawberry flavor had growers begging for more; sadly, none were ever made.

Super Cannalope from DNA Genetics
Originated in Holland
Reportedly Cannalope x G13 Haze. It has a longer flowering time than Cannalope and a hint of spiciness on the palate. I prefer Cannalope, but both are popular with growers.

Super Haze from Dutch Passion
Originated in Holland
Reportedly Dutch versions of Haze x Skunk #1. This is a nice hybrid that actually reminds me of Haze! It has a beefed up yield with the addition of Skunk #1. Typical Haze-ish taste, with a long finishing time.

Super Silver Haze from Mr. Nice Seeds

Super Haze from Dutch Passion is a really nice hybrid with an excellent yield because of its Skunk #1 parentage and a good Haze taste.

Originated in Holland
This is a three-way hybrid featuring Skunk #1 x Haze x Northern Lights. This strain's effect and taste lean more to Haze, while it has the structure of Skunk #1 and the yield of Northern Lights. This plant has won several awards and is a favorite of many. If you're looking for something hazy with a faster finishing time and heavier yield, this is the plant for you.

Super Skunk from Sensi Seeds
Originated in Holland
Supposedly Skunk #1 x "its original Afghani parents. The yield is a bit fatter than original Skunk #1 and the taste and effect are more Indica, but those are the only noticeable differences.

Swazi Skunk from Seedsman Seeds
Originated in Holland
This is Swazi, an African landrace variety, x Skunk #1. This is a truly unique plant that performs well outdoors, but, depending on the phenotype, can be managed indoors. The Swazi pheno gives you that psychedelic high that African cannabis is famous for, and the plant also has the improved yield of the Skunk #1. There's a spicy, skunky taste and aroma to this plant.

Swazi Red Beard from Afropips
Originated in Africa
This is a unique variation of Swazi—the red beard—wherein the pistils, as they wither, become blood red. Swazi is not a heavy yielder, but it is a 100% landrace Sativa, which makes this plant ideal for incorporating some African landrace genetics into your gene pool or if you're just looking for a pure Sativa smoke.

Sweet Haze from DNA Genetics
Originated in Holland
Reportedly a Skunk Haze x Cannalope Haze, this is one of my favorite Haze crosses and that says a lot because I am not a Haze fan. For a Haze-dominant hybrid, she is not airy but forms a long, solid cola. The colors are amazing and the yield is immense, both due to Cannalope's presence. The taste is something like spiced rum over mangos. If you do grow it, be sure you have a lot of headroom in your garden or are well versed in training techniques. Best grown outdoors for maximum taste and effect.

Sweet Tooth 1.1 from Steve (SOL) and DJ Short
Originated in Canada
Reportedly a Sweet Pink Grapefruit mother x Blueberry male. This strain is popular and has many attributes, but I prefer the colors and stability of Sweet Tooth #3.

Sweet Tooth #3 from Breeder Steve / Spice of Life Seeds
Originated in Canada
This amazing plant is a descendent of Sweet Pink Grapefruit. Backcrossed for many generations, Sweet Tooth #3 is most famous for her amazing colors—she is very potent, to boot. What caps this plant off is the taste: very sweet, as the name suggests, with hints of citrus fruit and a tart aftertaste, as well. This is my all time favorite purple pot—even over the purple haze of the 70s. She is mostly Indica, but Sativa phenos do exist and are much better: watch for them, and when you find some, clone the hell out of them. An added bonus with this plant is that it produces beautiful hues of purple. You are practically guaranteed to get at least one purple pheno out of a pack.

T

Thai Lights from Dr. Atomic
Originated in Canada
This is a landrace Thai x Dr. Atomic's

Northern Lights. Like most of Dr. Atomic's strains, this one is very unique and exotic tasting. There are several phenos existing within this strain, but in my opinion the Thai dominant pheno is the best. Takes up to 12 weeks to finish.

Thai-tanic from Flying Dutchmen
Originated in Holland
Reportedly Skunk #1 x Thai, this plant has a wide variety of phenotypes. Some plants act like Skunk #1, others behave like Thai strains (including herm traits), and still others are nicely balanced, and these are the plants to keep. The balanced plants have the exotic taste and effect of Thai strains with the yield and finishing time of Skunk #1.

Titans Haze from Flying Dutchmen
Originated in Holland
This is supposed to be Skunk #1 x Original Haze, but I've also heard that there is some Fuma Con Diablos in there, bred with itself. Give it a taste and see.

Top 44 from Homegrown Fantaseeds
Originated in Holland
Supposedly Skunk x Viking. Most of these plants mature extremely fast—they say 44 days, but I never heard of one finishing that early. These plants are ideal for people that are impatient or have a short growing cycle. However, they do not produce much because they finish so quickly.

Trainwreck
Originated in the United States
This baby was born in Humboldt County, California. It is rumored to be a combination of the Mexican x Colombian x Afghani hybrids that were passed around the Emerald Triangle for years. Trainwreck has become a clone only strain, but other versions of Trainwreck appear in seed form, such Arcata Trainwreck. The original Trainwreck is a resin freak that finishes early and produces moderate yields. Trainwreck is valued highly for its medicinal uses. The only drawback of the plant is that I have yet to see a Trainwreck clone that did not herm, which makes me think that there is some heavy Thai in its genetics.

Trance from Dutch Passion
Originated in Holland
This is Skunk #1 x Indica bx Indica. Just a faster version of Skunk #1, acclimatized for a European outdoor climate. Very nice yield.

U

Ultra Skunk from Dutch Passion
Originated in Holland
Reportedly Swiss Skunk x Skunk #1. This was a Dutch Skunk variety that never got much recognition. Most varieties displayed hot pink pistils, but the phenos could vary in strength, some stronger than others.

V

Valencia from Badboy / TGA
Originated in the United States
Reportedly Orange Velvet x Grimm. Valencia takes the orange flavored Orange Velvet mom and crosses her with a Brothers Grimm male. This is an attempt to improve the potency of Orange Velvet while retaining her unique flavor and coloring. This worked very well and most phenotypes are uniform in flavor and potency.

Viper from Reeferman
Originated in Canada
Reportedly Burmese landrace x Blackseed. This was one of my favorite offerings from Reeferman, despite the hermaphrodite tendencies. The color and high from this plant were nothing short of mind blowing. A very exotic taste—something like tart cherries mixed with Nag Champa Incense— added to a high that sometimes caused hallucinations. This strain also displayed beautiful color, with deep hues of purple and (sometimes) shades of red. Sadly, Reeferman scrapped this strain due to its her-maphrodite traits.

Voodoo from Dutch Passion
Originated in Holland
This is most likely Thai x Northern Lights (or some other Indica-dominant hybrid). Voodoo has been a strong choice for European growers looking to incorporate Thai into their gardens.

Voodoo from Dutch Passion is a good choice if you want to get some Thai in your garden. The high is strongly cerebral. One of the most popular strains in Europe.

Voodoo does have nice after tones, and the high, which leans more to Indica, gives a strong cerebral sensation.

Vortex from Subcool / TGA
Originated in the United States
This is a high-potency strain that is not for lightweights. It combines two extraordinary strains, Brothers Grimm Apollo 13 x BCGA's Space Queen (which is Romulan x Cinderella 99). Every pheno of Vortex is just as good as the next. While the Apollo 13 pheno is more dominant, a Space Queen pheno does exist (but is a little bit smaller than the A13 pheno). Each

plant is covered in an extraordinary amount of trichomes. The taste is the only thing that could use improving, as it has a bit bland lemon / pine flavor.

W

Warlock from Magus Genetics
Originated in the United States
Reportedly Skunk bx Skunk x Afghani, though no one knows for sure. This is one of the most popular strains on the market, but I find the taste and high to be somewhat boring. Most phenos will get quite large, so be careful where you grow it and be ready for a decent harvest.

White Rhino from Greenhouse Seeds
Originated in Holland
Reportedly White Widow x Afghan. This is one of two strains by Arjan that have become famous. I often hear kids on the street trying to sell dime sacks purported to be White Rhino because it is such a well-known and popular strain. White Rhino is a pretty nice strain if you get a rare pheno, and when left out in cooler temperatures, she can become quite colorful. I find the taste a little boring, though.

White Russian from Serious Seeds
Originated in Holland
Reportedly a rare AK-47 pheno x White Widow. The AK-47 supplies a cherry flavor, which improves the taste of White Widow. Together the strains combine to provide extraordinary yields. If you can get a hold of seeds from before Serious lost their cherry AK-47 mother, then you will love this plant as well. Ideal for the cash cropper.

White Satin from Mandala Seeds
Originated in Spain
This is a hybrid of an Indica from the Punjab region of India. White Satin is a remarkably easy strain to grow, and produces nice, dense colas that are remarkably resinous. White Satin also matures quite early, which is ideal for the impatient or short-seasoned grower.

White Widow from Greenhouse Seeds
Originated in Holland
This is the combination of two strains, Brazilian x South Indian. This is the other one of Arjan's strains that has become globally famous. I'm not a huge fan of this strain from the "White" family, but she does have the promising ability to increase resin production for personal breeding projects.

William's Wonder Haze from Rezdog / Reservoir Seeds
Originated in the United States
Reportedly Super Silver Haze x William's Wonder. Super Silver Haze is the most dominant plant. Basically just Super Silver Haze with a quicker finishing time.

Willie Nelson from either Barney's Farm or Reeferman

Originated in either Holland or Canada Reportedly a landrace Vietnamese x Highland Nepalese. The story goes that Willie Nelson (the musician) smoked a bit of this herb and bought all he could. For being the combination of two landrace Sativas, the strain's leaves are pretty wide and the buds get pretty fat. No one knows who is the original breeder of this strain, but Reeferman made it famous with his '05 Cannabis Cup victory.

Wonder Diesel from Rezdog / Reservoir Seeds
Originated in the United States
You guessed it, William's Wonder x East Coast Sour Diesel. This is a variation of Sour Wonder using different fathers.

Y

Yumbold from Sagarmatha
Originated in Holland
Supposedly Afghani x Himalayan lan-
draces combined to form this amazing strain. Many phenos exist within this strain, but almost all are incredibly tasty. Hints of pine, lemon, mango, and orange all lie within this unique and tasty strain. She also produces large colas when grown properly.

Z

Zorro from Badboy and Homegrown / TGA
Originated in the United States
This is one of the newest offerings from TGA seeds. Reportedly Hash Plant x a Grimm male. This is a close relative of Conquistador, and although it will not replace Conquistador it does produce some frosty buds. For the complete Overgrow Strain Guide—another helpful reader—in zip file format, visit www.marijuana-passion.com/strainbase/OG_Straingu ide_win.zip

The Process

Do not let pets in your grow room. They will probably have pests on their fur, and, if so, those pests will soon be on your plants. Bad kitty.

Chapter 6

First Time Growers

There are some basic lessons that apply to first time growers that experienced growers most likely already know. These rules will be listed here for reference; refer to them often.

GENERAL RULES

Don't scrimp on your plants' nutrients, lighting, etc. You will get out what you put in. Also, don't start growing until you have all your supplies, including proper lighting, nutrients, and a pH meter and PPM (Parts Per Million) or EC (Electrical Conductivity) meter. You will need these throughout your grow and it's better to have them at the beginning.

For every foot of vertical growth, you want at least one gallon of soil, meaning that a five-foot plant goes well with a five-gallon container, but a three-foot tall plant in a two-gallon container is not sufficient space.

Have only one plant per container. Plants will compete with each other for water, nutrients, and space, and if you have two in a pot, neither plant will grow to their full potential.

This should go without saying, but make sure your containers have plenty of holes in the bottom for drainage; otherwise, the plant's roots will rot and your plant(s) will die.

For your first time growing, don't invest a lot of money in your supplies. Your first grow is to understand cannabis plants and how they grow. I don't advise you go out and buy the full line of Advanced Nutrients and a 1,000-watt light for your first grow. At the same time, you will not get long, dense colas from incandescent and fluorescent light fixtures.

It is important to remove your expensive light bulbs before attempting to move your fixtures around.

It is recommended that you should not use any hydrogen peroxide other than 35% (food grade). This is because other percentages—3% is most common—may contain contaminates that are bad for your plants. I can neither confirm nor deny this, but why risk it? Also, always wear gloves when dealing with 35% H2O2.

Do not rush the budding cycle. You spent so much time and money in the germination, seedling, and vegetation stages, you don't want to throw all that away because you were impatient. When you start to see recessed calyx and about 80% withered pistils, this is a pretty good way of determining that bud is nearing the end of its life span. For the newest growers, I would recommend picking up a handheld microscope such as the $10 ones Radio Shack carries.

Removing the protective grill from *plastic* fans will increase their efficiency and life. (Don't remove the grills from metal fans.)

Do not follow the budding times set forth on breeder's packets or websites. I have found that 90% of the time these "guidelines" are untrue and are just a marketing ruse.

Make sure to have adequate space between plants (unless growing sea of green), and remember that when plants are crowded they stretch to outgrow the competition. Also, make sure your plants/branches are not crowding / shading each other in the budding cycle, or they will yield less.

Always make sure to put sticky traps in your grow room. They can prevent many pests from becoming a problem. Some traps hang on your plants' branches, others sit on the floor; remember, yellow traps for fungus gnats, white flies, aphids, and other flying insects; blue traps for thrips, leaf miners, and other crawling insects.

Stay away from clear containers. Roots need darkness to function properly, *period*!

The number of blades per leaf does not indicate that your plant will be more potent or that it is of a later generation. The number of blades per leaf only indicate the influence of Sativa / Indica genetics or the lack thereof.

You must have air circulating through your plants to change out the oxygen and CO_2.

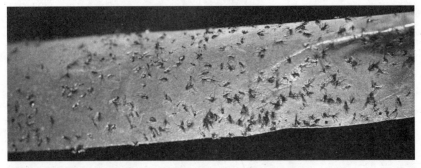

You should always hang sticky traps in your grow room. They catch the pests before they can cause any problems.

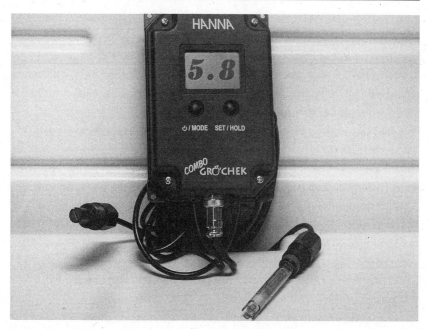

Be sure to check the pH of the water and soil your plants will be feeding from. Imbalances in pH can ruin an otherwise perfect grow.

Anything above 90°F is going to impact your plants in a very negative way, causing leggy growth, possible males, or hermaphrodites, as well as airy buds and slowed growth.

Anything above 1,800 PPM is going to completely fry your plants. Personally, I don't recommend going above the 1,500 PPM mark. Cannabis does not require much fertilizer to grow vigorously.

Soil pH kits, strips, etc., are a very inaccurate way to measure pH. Instead, pour a cup of water, pH it to 7.0, and add in 1 tbsp of soil. Stir well, and let it sit; then measure pH and PPM: this will give you a good account of the soil's pH and available nutrients.

Inspect your grow room when the room is dark by going inside, letting your eyes adjust, and looking everywhere for light leaks going on inside your room. Light leaks inside are not a problem in vegetation, but in budding they wreak havoc, causing hermaphrodites and loose bud structure. If outside security is a threat when the lights are on in the room, get the area outside your grow room as dark as possible and look for where the light is coming from.

Keep a grow journal and write down major events such as when you fed, how much you fed, what you fed with, when you placed the plant in vegetation and budding cycle, any signs of deficiencies that you see, etc. No need to write down the height and dimensions of your plant or useless facts like that, unless you're breeding about height. Be forewarned that this journal, if found, will incriminate you.

Always pay for your growing supplies or anything relating to cannabis in cash or money orders. Money orders are available from Wal-Mart as well as most convenience stores. Money leaves no trails and tells no tales.

If possible, stock up on your growing supplies during the off-season (winter). You will find that most gardening supplies are more than 50% off at this time. Likewise, try to avoid buying your growing supplies during the spring, as they will be marked up a considerable amount.

Watch for pre-flowers before switching your plants into the budding cycle. Pre-flowers signal that your plant is ready to begin budding. If you do place your plants in a 12 on / 12 off light schedule before the pre-flowers emerge, it will cause a longer waiting period from the switch and will hamper bud development.

Kill or remove all males from your grow as soon as pre-flowers are spotted, unless you are using them for breeding purposes.

Using bong water or coffee will not improve the speed of growth or quality of your plants.

Do not believe everything you hear. On most cannabis forums you will have to search through much misinformation to find anything of merit. This is also true about so called "authorities" on cannabis cultivation.

Never think you know all there is to know; read and research all you can: knowledge is power.

DEFICIENCIES

Before you try to correct any deficiencies, check your pH first; if you have not checked your pH, there is a great possibility that a pH imbalance is your problem. Gradually lower your pH to the desired range.

Find the PPM of your plain water before calculating your PPM with fertilizer. Deduct the number of PPM of the plain water from the PPM of the fertilizer water. This will give you a true reading of the amount of fertilizer you're dosing your plant with.

When you have ruled out pH as a problem, only adjust one thing at a time. This means you shouldn't feed with PBP Grow and Cal Mag at the same time to correct a deficiency. The reason for this is that you will not know what caused the problem to get better or, likewise, what made it get worse.

INFESTATIONS

Keep your grow room as clean as possible. This means wiping down all areas with a disinfectant and bleach weekly. Standing water is the greatest cause of grow room problems. Sweep out any debris on your floor ASAP.

Keep your plants from touching if at all possible. This will keep bugs and mold from spreading quickly to other plants, if one plant should become infested.

Do not let pets in your grow room. They will probably be carrying insects on their fur. Also, don't take a walk through your yard and then into your grow room; doing so might result in you bringing insects into your garden.

If one plant is infested, it is best to remove that one plant instead of losing your entire crop.

LIGHTING

Do not use mirrors or glossy paint to reflect light. Light must pass through a mirror before being reflected back, and light is lost in this process.

Do not try to use a HPS (High Pressure Sodium) bulb in an MH (Metal Halide) ballast, or vice versa. It will not work and could result in an explosion or fire. It will also shorten the life of the bulb and / or ballast.

Periodically wipe down your reflector, glass, and Mylar. This will give you as much reflection as possible.

NUTRIENTS AND FERTILIZER

Cannabis will not grow better or faster with an abundance of nutrients. It will cause excess salt buildup and nutrient lockout / toxicity which will stunt and eventually kill your plants. I suggest you purchase an EC / PPM meter to ensure that you are not feeding your plants too much.

The recommended dosage on a bottle of nutrients is usually much higher than you would want to feed your plant; a good rule is to cut this amount by half for a full-strength feeding.

Do not use fertilizer that contains anything with ammonium in it—the most common is ammonium nitrate. Ammonium hurts plant roots and kills young tender roots, such as roots from a clone or seedling.

WATERING AND HUMIDITY

"Don't apply until they're dry." A common mistake that first time growers will make is to over-water their plants. Don't apply until they're dry is a catchy little phrase to remember not to over-water. Put your finger two or more inches into the soil—if it is still moist, or when you withdraw your finger there is soil stuck to it, don't water the plant. You may also water your plant thoroughly and then lift the pot to get an idea of the weight of a watered pot; do this every day until you need to water again. After this, you will have an

Remove any bud that has been affected by mold. Do not smoke it – you could get a lung infection. It is not worth it.

idea of how much a plant should weigh at each stage of watering.

When you water, water thoroughly; do not stop until you see water coming out of the holes in the bottom of the container. If possible, water along the edges instead of dousing the stalk and center of the container. Watering along the edges will make your roots spread out and grow quicker in search of water.

When in the flowering cycle, lower your humidity to about the 35–40% mark. This will cause your buds to grow bigger and denser. It also greatly lowers your chance of developing mold and fungus. If you do see signs of mold or fungus, remove all of the infected bud, stem, leaves, etc., as well as any and ALL areas that moldy bud, stem, and leaves touched (or even might have touched). Trust me, it is better to remove too much that *might* have been touched than to lose your whole plant to mold or fungus. Monitor the rest of your plant closely throughout budding. THROW MOLDY BUD AWAY!! I cannot stress this enough. Also, do not smoke moldy bud, as it will cause many health problems such as severe lung infections.

Do not spray anything on your buds! This is extremely important, especially if you have dense buds; water, i.e., moisture will get into the buds and will not be able to escape; this creates mold. If you *must* spray some sort of insecticide, make sure you do so at least a week before harvest, and rinse off the residue left by the pesticides with clean water before harvest. If it can be avoided, don't leave the residue to sit overnight. Also, don't ever spray anything on your plants with the lights on—especially under HID lights. The water droplets will magnify the light and create burn spots on your plant.

Moisture meters don't work. Don't waste your money.

Chapter 7

Security

KNOW YOUR RIGHTS

This section will deal with laws, politics, and law enforcement officials, as they interact with various aspects of your life.

You may have noticed that I refer to the plant under discussion as cannabis instead of marijuana. This is because U.S. propaganda wants cannabis to be known as marijuana because marijuana sounds foreign, harmful, and dangerous, whereas cannabis sounds scientific and familiar. It's not just a personal preference: there has been a study done into this subject. I urge you to start calling cannabis by its proper name instead of a name given to it by the U.S. government, especially when talking with someone who views cannabis as a negative thing.

Before deciding to grow cannabis, you must be aware of the laws you might be breaking. For the most up-to-date information on the laws in your state, visit NORML.com. NORML will show you interesting facts about each state and will help you determine the number of plants you want to grow at a given time. I strongly advise you to visit this site and know how severe the penalties could be if you get busted.

States to avoid include those states that impose a "Mandatory Minimum Sentence," or MMS for short. A MMS is a minimum term of imprisonment that the court is required to impose on a defendant depending on his or her "crime." This tactic was first introduced in 1986 as part of the "war on drugs." This is a truly unjust way to sentence "criminals". There is a certain amount of time you must serve regardless of what the individual judge may want to give you. Your case is decided by the congress, which has never heard of you or your case. The judge cannot deliberate based on the information and special circumstances that each case presents. MMS shackles the judge's hands and is ruining our judicial system even more than it already is. With the enormous salary that judges are paid, they should at least be allowed to do their job. Since 1986, MMS has increased prison overcrowding by 80%; a pathetic response to the "war on drugs." Along with racial injustice, which increased from 11% of African Americans jailed to 49% four years after Mandatory Minimum Sentences were instituted. Do your part to repeal MMS and write your state representatives. Some of the worst states for cannabis growing would include those in the Southeast and Central United States—especially Texas, Nebraska, and Alabama.

States that should be considered for growing are, obviously, those states that have decriminalized cannabis to some degree. These states include California, Washington, Oregon, Alaska, Maine, Nevada, Colorado, Hawaii, Maryland, Montana, Vermont, and Rhode Island in 2006. Of these states, Alaska is the most decriminalized, but California is the heart of the cannabis scene in America—in recent years, however, Oregon has become a hot spot as well.

If you are a medicinal user and live in a medicinal-cannabis-approved state, you should get a doctor's prescription for your ailment. This will pretty much grant you immunity to your local and state law enforcement. However, if you are a caregiver and you get too well known, local or state law enforcement could alert federal agencies and the next thing you know you have the DEA kicking in your door with a "no-knock search warrant." Just ask Eddy Lepp, the famous medicinal grower who was raided in 2004. The root of this threat is that cannabis is only decriminalized on a local or state level; federal government does not recognize these laws. Only seven people in the country are recognized as medicinal cannabis patients by the federal government. These seven people receive their meds directly from the United States government every month, and are not permitted to grow their own.

DEALING WITH LEOS

I strongly urge you to memorize your Constitutional rights, specifically the Fourth and Fifth Amendments.

The Fourth Amendment states:

The right of the people to be secure in their persons, houses, papers, and effects, against unreasonable searches and seizures, shall not be violated, and no Warrants shall issue, but upon probable cause, supported by Oath or affirmation, and particularly describing the place to be searched, and the persons or things to be seized.

This means that a LEO cannot search you or your property without probable cause unless you consent to a search.

A common example:

During a traffic stop. . .

Officer: "You don't have an illegal contraband do you? You don't mind if I search your car then?"

Driver: "No"

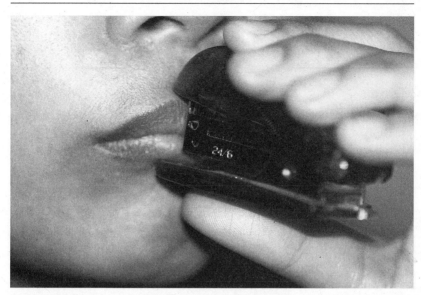

The Fifth Amendment states that you cannot testify against yourself or indict yourself. So, if your lawyer is not there, shut your mouth.

The officer used a compound question to fool you into granting him permission to search your car.

The Fifth Amendment states:

No person shall be held to answer for a capital, or otherwise infamous crime, unless on a presentment or indictment of a Grand Jury, except in cases arising in the land or naval forces, or in the Militia, when in actual service in time of War or public danger; nor shall any person be subject for the same offence to be twice put in jeopardy of life or limb; nor shall be compelled in any criminal case to be a witness against himself, nor be deprived of life, liberty, or property, without due process of law; nor shall private property be taken for public use, without just compensation.

This means that you cannot testify against yourself or indict yourself.

A common example:

During a traffic stop. . .

Officer: "Do you know why I pulled you over?"

Driver: "I guess I was speeding"

You just waved your Fifth Amendment right not to incriminate yourself. You do not have to admit to breaking any law to a LEO.

There are some key things you should always do when dealing with LEOs, regardless of where you are.

1. *NEVER PHYSICALLY RESIST!* This may be the single most important thing you do.

Law Enforcement Officers cannot search you or your property without probable cause unless you consent to a search.

Even touching a LEO can result in you being charged with "assaulting an officer" and "resisting arrest," which is a felony offense punishable by three to ten years and a five thousand dollar fine. You can only state your refusal to a search; if the LEO still searches you, there is nothing more you can do.

2. *Remain polite and respectful.* It is not always safe to say "officer" when addressing an LEO—they may be a captain or lieutenant. If this is the case, then you are insulting them, which will make any encounter all the less pleasant. If you do not know how to distinguish the difference, always address them as "sir" or "ma'am."

3. *Don't consent to any searches.* This is self-explanatory. Even if you do not have anything to hide, do not consent to a search. This accomplishes two things. First, it prepares you for the scare tactics and bullying that LEOs use to get you to consent to a search. Second, it teaches the LEO that not all people who refuse a search have something to hide when / if they decide to illegally search your car.

4. *Remain calm.* Sweating, acting nervous, stumbling over your words, or changing your story can be viewed as probable cause in some states / cases.

5. *Always keep illegal items out of plain view.* If a LEO sees a roach or rolling papers out in the open, this is probable cause; because of the "plain view rule," they then have all the evidence they need to search you and your property.

6. *Have a kempt appearance.* Do not wear tie-dye clothing or anything with Bob Marley or the Grateful Dead on it. Have nicely trimmed hair and no foul body odor. Most LEOs will also notice your fingernails; although they are not allowed to, an LEO not only profiles based on race but on character, too. This means that if you fit the

description of a "pothead," the more likely you are to be subject to a search. In some cases your description may also serve as probably cause.

A Hispanic, African American or other non-Caucasian is more than twice as likely to be subject to an illegal search than a Caucasian. A man is also three times more likely to be subject to an illegal search than a woman. If you're a non-Caucasian male you're five times more likely to be subject to an illegal search than a Caucasian female. It's sad but it's true.

7. *Don't keep a lighter on you if you do not smoke tobacco products.* This is the single most over-looked thing that people do; not only does it make for an awkward moment, but it may constitute as probable cause.

8. *Never lie to a LEO.* If you are asked a question that, were you to answer it, would raise suspicion or incriminate you, you do not have to answer. Remember your Fifth Amendment. Don't answer any questions that may be used against you without your attorney present. You have nothing to lose by refusing to answer any questions.

Remember that in most cases a LEO is only asking you if they can search you or your property because they do not have sufficient evidence to search you without your consent.

ON THE ROAD

Before driving with illegal items, check all the lights of the vehicle; this includes head-lights, brake lights, parking lights, and turn signals. Make sure any auxiliary lights are working; if not, then turn them off. While you cannot get pulled over for a burnt out auxiliary light, it will disrupt the chameleon-like appearance you are trying to achieve.

Search your car thoroughly for a "secret stash spot" that almost every car has. Out of the six vehicles I have owned and countless vehicles I've ridden in, all of them had such a hiding place. If you cannot find a secret stash spot for your vehicle, an airtight stash jar, such as the fix-a-flat, is perfect camouflage.

Always keep illegal items out of view and especially don't place them in your glove box, center console, or anywhere else where you keep your registration and proof of insurance. Have your registration and proof of insurance in a sure spot clear of clutter, such as your side door compartment. Every second you spend fumbling around looking for these items the LEO is taking a thorough inventory of all the items they see in your vehicle. If you're riding with a friend, LEO may sometimes ask him to get the registration and proof of insurance because your friend probably does not know where it is and will open more compartments and spend longer stumbling around, letting him see the contents of them.

Sadly, all those NORML and "no victim no crime" bumper stickers do constitute probable cause. Don't ride with illegal contraband in vehicles that have these stickers.

Always make sure you know who is riding in your vehicle and what they are carrying. Make sure that all of your alibis match in case of a traffic stop. Keep the inside of your vehicle as clean as possible. Having a lot of clutter and fast food wrappers in your backseat places you in the "drug user" category.

Don't dispute a traffic ticket; just accept it and leave. If you have any dispute you can handle it in traffic court and traffic court is much better to be in than criminal court. Over 50% of LEO encounters happen over traffic stops so it's extremely important to follow the following steps.

Pull over immediately. The longer it takes you to pull over after being flagged by an LEO the more they think you have something to hide. Pull over as soon as it is safe to do so.

Turn off your car and place your keys on your roof. This will reassure the LEO that you are not going to speed off.

Leave your window cracked. Do not roll your window completely down and do not leave it all the way up. Leave enough space to communicate with the LEO and pass them your license, registration, and proof of insurance. The reason for this is so the LEO cannot get a good smell of the inside of your car. (Do this after placing your keys on the roof)

Keep your hands in plain view. On top of the steering wheel is usually best. A LEO wants to ensure that they are safe and in order to do so they must be able to see your hands at all times.

Do not reach for anything. This is very important, unless you feel like getting shot. Always ask the LEO's permission before reaching for anything, including your license, registration, and proof of insurance.

Keep all illegal or incriminating items out of sight. This cannot be stressed enough. The trunk is usually the best place. Do not smoke in your vehicle!

Remember the three Cs. Be calm, courteous, and careful. Don't lose your personality and become legal robots; this is one of the telltale signs that you are up to no good. Remain respectful always, but if given the opportunity don't hesitate to make a joke or laugh at theirs. You might have an officer ask if you are carrying any, "knives, guns, bombs, or grenades"—responding with a straight "no, sir" would probably gave him reason to suspect you were in possession of something you shouldn't be.

Don't get caught in "gotcha games." LEOs will often play "gotcha games," asking you a question or a series of questions in a confusing or illusive manner. These are not random questions; these are questions they teach LEOs to use in order to get you to admit you have broken the law. I have yet to be pulled over and have the LEO not ask me, "Do you know why I pulled you over?" You can respond one of two ways: you can say, "No, sir, I do not," or you can say nothing. This second option I do not recommend as it can cause tension between you and the LEO.

Ask the LEO if you're free to go. Make up an excuse that you have somewhere to be—an appointment, or dinner waiting. Never stay any longer than you have to.

On Your Person

This applies to walking or riding a bicycle.

If you are being detained by an LEO, they have the right, without your permission, to perform a "pat down." This is for the LEO's safety—it gives them a chance to feel for weapons. If they happen to feel or hear a bag crunch while doing a "pat down," this constitutes probable cause and you will then be searched.

You can pass a "pat down" while carrying illegal items if those items are in your shoe or hat; and, of course, if you "crotch" it. Also, if you are carrying a bag and you place the items in the bag, they cannot search the bag unless you give them consent or they have probable cause.

Determine why you have been stopped. Calmly ask the LEO why you have been stopped and if you are free to go. Say you have to catch a bus or make up a similar excuse; just make sure your story is airtight. If they say you are suspected of criminal activity, you are being detained and may be placed in hand cuffs "for their safety." At this point, the LEO is trying to gather probable cause in order to arrest you. It is very important not to consent to a search at this point and to keep asking if you are free to go; once again, if you aren't comfortable with answering a question, DON'T!

Determine if you can leave. If this is a casual stop you can terminate your encounter at any time. If you are being detained you can repeatedly ask the LEO if you are free to go, insert excuse. If the LEO does not answer your questions continue to ask until you receive an answer.

On the Subway

After the London tube attacks, LEOs are now conducting random searches on subway users, although they are not racially or character profiling, of course. If you are walking through a random search area and are stopped, you can refuse the search and leave the subway, unless you are past the turnstiles. Doing so does not legally constitute probable cause. You do not have to show ID. Contrary to popular belief, you do not have to present ID or immigration papers to LEOs on the subway unless, again, you're past the turnstiles.

At Your Residence

This is it, folks: a screw-up here could result in you spending a quarter or more of your life behind bars and spending a hefty chunk of change trying to stay out of a federal penitentiary. A 9-1-1 hang-up or an alarm going off automatically enables LEO to enter your home without your consent.

It would be nice to have a dog that barks when visitors are around so you will know if anyone shows up on your property. Most often, an LEO agent will take a thorough look around the premises, trying to look for probable cause or anything out of the ordinary, before letting you know that they are there. If you have a dog to alert you of their presence, you can meet them outside before they get a chance to snoop and discover any potential smells or light leaks.

Other key rules:

Never throw parties, especially loud parties, at your residence while you are growing. This is an open invitation for trouble.

Avoid toking outdoors if you can help it. If you do have the urge to do so, make sure you do so in your backyard or other secluded part of your property.

Have all odors eliminated with a carbon scrubber. It may smell good to you because it lets you know you have accomplished a successful grow, but it smells good to LEOs too, because it lets them know a big bust is about to be under way.

Keep your residence looking like your neighbors'—or better. Mow your lawn, plant some flowers and shrubs. Re-paint your house if necessary. The better your house's "curb appeal," the less likely an LEO is to think anything suspicious is going on. Also, adding an American flag to a flagpole is an inexpensive way to prevent an LEO thinking of you as a "drug user."

When having a heavy session at your residence, only do it in a back bedroom or garage area and air it out while doing so. You don't want to open your door and have a billow of smoke come out with you.

Have a nice secret stash spot where you keep the bulk of your stash at any given time. No, I'm not referring to a stash box. A good low odor spot is under the icemaker in the freezer. You can always make the outlet safe for a good, cheap stash spot. Between $4.99 –9.99 each, this makes for a very affordable option. These are available at most head shops or online through a variety of places. You can install them by either removing an existing electrical outlet, leaving only the junction box. Be sure to off the power to the area you are working in prior to removal of the outlet plate. The other option is to trace a typical outlet plate where you would like to install your wall safe, use a drywall cutter to cut along the lines, install the junction box, and then mount your wall safe into the junction box.

Don't keep paraphernalia out in the open. This falls under the plain view rule. If something is in plain view that's all the probable cause they need to search your residence. Another thing you don't want is to be scrambling to put away bongs and bowls when the police come knocking at your door.

Answer your doors as soon as possible. This rule is the same as the pull-over-ASAP rule; the longer they have to wait, the more they're going to suspect you of having something to hide.

Do not let LEOs enter your residence. Without a search warrant or probable cause, LEOs cannot legally enter your residence. When you open your door to an LEO, step outside and close the door behind you. Do this as quickly as possible so as not to let any "odors" out. If an LEO indicates that they wish to enter your residence, this means you have become a criminal suspect. This is no time to panic; you must assert your constitutional rights now more than ever. Of course, do not consent to having an LEO enter or search your residence. They have to ask, "may I come in?" just like any other visitor. If you leave your door open, LEOs may view this as you inviting them in.

Determine why an LEO is paying you a visit. In most cases, this will not have anything to do with you. They may want to ask you questions about a crime committed nearby, to let you know of a suspicious person, or to warn you of someone they're looking for. They may also be asking you take your barking dog inside or lower the volume of your music (which shouldn't be turned up anyway). Simply agree to these requests and answer any question not dealing with you personally.

Terminate the encounter as quickly as possible. Do this so you can go inside and breathe a sigh of relief—in most cases, you'll also need to change your pants! A good excuse is "Sir, I was in the middle of cooking a meal—is there anything else?"

Illegal Searches

We all know that LEOs do not always follow the law they are supposed to be enforcing. Countless times LEOs have performed illegal search and seizures, and if you're one of the millions of people this has happened to, that's OK—you did all you could do. You asserted your constitutional rights and you gave your lawyers a fighting chance.

If illegal contraband was found during an illegal search and seizure, your lawyer can file for a "motion to suppress," which, if the judge allows, will result in the evidence being thrown out and your case dismissed.

If you are the victim of an illegal search and seizure, or if you feel you or your rights have been violated, don't argue or physically resist the LEO. State again clearly that you do not consent to what the LEO is doing.

As soon as possible, get the names and contact information of all the witnesses possible. Get the LEO's name and badge number—they must give you this information if asked. Write the whole event down as soon as possible, so you will not forget anything. It would be ideal if you had a way to record either audio or video (or both) of your encounter with LEO. With many of today's cell phones this is possible. Contact your lawyer or local ACLU office to determine your next course of action. Remember that if you pay your taxes, you are paying their salary, and it is your duty to report unprofessional police officers.

Of course, when traveling to a different country, none of these rules apply. You should check into the laws of that country before venturing to score any cannabis or hash. If you think the United States is bad, some countries in the Middle East and South Pacific have much harsher penalties, including DEATH!

ONLINE BASICS

In this day and age, one can never be too cautious. This section will provide you with information that will aid in avoiding problems with security online. By educating your-self and taking a few precautions, you can surf the Internet on the subject of cannabis with confidence. Sorry, Mac users: the majority of this section will apply only to PC users.

First, find out what laws you're going to be breaking by checking NORML.com and their state guide to marijuana laws. It is an up-to-date directory of each state's mar-ijuana laws. While you're there, print out your NORML foundation Freedom Card.

Alternately, you can look in the back of *High Times* for an experienced lawyer in your state; to check the qualifications of these or any potential lawyers, I advise you visit the Martindale-Hubble database at martindale.com

Call and make an appointment with one of these lawyers so that you can intro-duce yourself and possibly your situation, as well as the fact that you might be in need of their services in the future. Trust me when I say that you'll both appreciate not meeting them for the first time behind bars. If you're doing a large-scale com-mercial grow, I suggest moving to a state that has decriminalized marijuana, such as California or Alaska. Now, let's start with Internet security.

There are many useful tools that can help protect your identity while surfing online. An IP address is, in computer terms, your street address: it's a mark of your presence online. Obtaining a ghost IP will log a false IP / proxy address with a web-site's memory instead of your actual IP. Websites store IP addresses for a number of reasons. Should a search warrant be issued and your computer seized, having a ghost IP can help protect you against others knowing exactly where you've been on the Internet. The easiest way of doing this is as follows:

First visit mozilla.com and download the latest version of Firefox. This is going to be your new Internet Explorer (if that's the browser you're accustomed to, and chances are it is.) Now go to whatismyip.com. This website will tell you your IP address. This will be your new, "naked" IP address. Make sure you write it down to use as a reference later on; we'll return to it.

Once Firefox has been downloaded, you can remove Internet Explorer from your computer. You may, however, choose to keep it as your regular browser for everyday web surfing, and use Firefox when visiting cannabis-related websites.

To uninstall Internet Explorer, click *Start*, choose *Control panel*, then select *Add and remove programs*. Scroll down the list of currently installed programs and click on the program you want to remove. Internet Explorer should be down at the bottom of the list. To remove the program, click *Remove*.

Your computer will guide you through the rest of the process. After Internet Explorer is uninstalled, you will need to restart your computer.

Now go to http://tor.eff.org/download.html.en and download the TOR / Privoxy Bundle. Once this is complete, you should see some new icons both on your home background and in your tool tray in the bottom right hand corner.

Find the TOR icon in the tool tray, right click on it, and turn it on.

Now use your Firefox browser to navigate to https://addons.mozilla.org/firefox/2275/. This will give you the option of adding a button that turns TOR on and off to your Firefox browser. Install the TOR button by following the simple setup instructions.

In the notification area of the task bar of Firefox, which is located at the bottom right-hand corner of your screen, you'll notice a small TOR icon. When pointing the cursor at this icon, you will find that it says *TOR Disabled* in red letters. To enable this program, simply click on the icon and it should change to *TOR Enabled* in green lettering.

Right-click on the TOR icon again, and click *View network*. This will open another window. In the top left-hand corner you'll see the *New identity* button. Click this and yet another window will open, revealing the message, "All subsequent connections will appear to be different than your old connections." Congratulations: you have just masked your IP address. Your IP address will remain concealed as long as TOR is enabled.

To verify that your IP is indeed masked, go back to whatismyip.com and compare the old number with the current number. They should be drastically different.

You may change your IP address as often as you like. If at any time you wish to change this fake IP address to a different, equally bogus IP address, simply click on the TOR icon in your taskbar, select *View network*, and click *New identity* again. Your IP address will change again.

WARNING: Some functions may not perform properly because Internet Explorer was deleted. When TOR is enabled, it will drastically slow the speed at which your page loads because now it is being re-routed through TOR to develop the fake IP address / proxy and mask your real one. Dial-up users will find that their connections are slowed to a crawl.

As an extra safeguard to ensure that your identity remains a secret, there are a few extra steps you can take. Open your Firefox web browser and click the *Tools* button located above the address bar. Click *Options*, then *Privacy*. Uncheck all of the boxes except *Cookies*, and select *Keep until I close Firefox*. Now go to *Security,* uncheck both boxes referring to passwords, and click *OK*.

While you're in *Options,* select *Main* and check the box that says *Always check to see if Firefox is the default browser on start* up. This will be located at the bottom of this screen. Click *Check now.* A new window will open, revealing the message *Firefox is not the default browser. Would you like to make it one now?* Click *Okay.* This is an extra step, but it will make your life easier.

The next thing you'll need to do is get a secure email address that uses PGP (Pretty Good Privacy) software. While free email accounts are available, it's worth it in the long run to pay the yearly fee of $29.95 USD and get all the bells and whistles. PGP software works by using Java to encrypt your incoming and out going emails. It's 99% secure—a far more secure way of communicating than regular email or telephone. Go to hushmail.com to get yours today.

Important Note: Since the time of writing, Hushmail, a Canadian company, has turned over its encryption keys to the DEA. This follows the investigation of an anabolic steroid manufacturer, but it is highly probable that they are using the keys to look into other emails as well.

Stealthmessage.com is a lesser-known alternative to Hushmail, but it will likely have the same drawbacks. Do not use Gmail as an alternative: every incoming and outgoing message is scanned, as well as any compressed or protected attachments, and that data is saved in their servers. Gmail, as well as Google, keeps, tracks, and records IP addresses both to and from, meaning that if someone sends you an email using Gmail they have recorded your IP. Google keeps archives full of everything that any and all IP addresses search for and has yet to permanently delete any of this data. Surprisingly, AOL's search engine is actually the best to use, as they do not store IP searches and purge their database on a regular basis once a month.

In addition to browser settings and secure email accounts, there's a handy little device called the Stealth Surfer II that you might want to consider. This device plugs into any USB port and allows users to hide URLs, downloaded files, cookies, and history by storing the information on the apparatus itself instead of your computer. It also provides a ghost IP. Starting at $99 for 128MB of memory, it's relatively affordable. For complete product information, go to stealthsurfer.biz.

Buying Online

So, is that it? We've covered many helpful tools that will assist in protecting your identity online. Not so fast. Plenty can go still go wrong if you don't protect your *purchasing* identity.

Anonymous credit cards are the most recent, innovative way to protect your identity with online purchases. This resource allows you to purchase all your gardening supplies, seeds, books, and anything else cannabis-related, without having to divulge any personal information (such as your social security number). It's similar to a pre-paid phone card, in that you choose the amount to load on the card. You then have your own predetermined amount set up to spend however you wish. The amounts range from $20.00–500.00. Please be aware that there is a fee for this service. You can go to websecretcard.com for more information. Another option would be to order an American Express gift card or the Visa "Green Dot" credit card for yourself and do your shopping with that.

CARDINAL RULES

The above information lists the major ways to protect your identity online. Here is a fundamental list of the basic ways to keep your identity secret:

1. Never put photographs of yourself, or your residence, on cannabis-related websites.
2. Never make your street address public.
3. Never have anything cannabis-related sent to the growing site. Set up a P.O. Box or have the packages shipped to a close friend or relative's house (with their permission, of course).
4. Delete all browsing history daily.
5. Do not allow your PC to store user names and passwords.
6. Never check *Remember me* boxes on websites. Regardless of what the administrator says, any site that contains a *Remember me* option logs IP addresses and installs cookies on your computer.
7. Have anti-virus software installed on your computer to protect against spyware. Norton and McAfee are the best and most popular.
8. Never have cannabis graphs, photos, or information stored on your computer.
9. Use a wireless router. If it comes down to it, one could argue that someone else was stealing the Internet connection to visit those websites.
10. Add a disclaimer to your signature on cannabis forums, such as: *I am not currently, nor have I ever, grown, smoked, or even seen real cannabis. None of the photographs posted here are mine (though I did post them myself). Any and all information is strictly for education and entertainment purposes.*

STAY SAFE
Indoor Gardening Safety

Now that we've covered Internet safety, let's move on to general indoor gardening safety.

Forward Looking Infrared Radar (FLIR) captures heat escaping your home, whether it's through a window, wall, vent, or door. This is the next topic we need to discuss. The Supreme Court ruled that FLIR is not an invasion of privacy. This means that Law Enforcement Officials (LEO) can take as many photos of your residence as they want, as often as they want, using FLIR.

It would be advisable to stay away from attic growing. If this is your only option, make sure that you put up a couple of fresh layers of polyshield insulation. Polyshield is a black and white poly infused with metals to block those outgoing heat signals. It's also 92% reflective. Go to polyshield.ca for more information on this product.

As an alternative to attic growing, an interior closet, or, my personal favorite, the basement, might be worth considering. For numerous reasons, the basement is the best location for growing. It's the most secluded place in most homes, and it stays cool and its exterior walls are made up of thick concrete blocks, making FLIR less of a concern. For added protection, construct the growing room near the hot water heater.

If your basement has windows, be careful not to board them up or cover them with other objects. Sadly, search warrants have been issued solely on this basis. Instead, begin approximately one or two feet out from the window and seal all around it with black plastic. This will make the room appear dark at all times.

Electricity usage is a valid concern for growers. As a general rule of thumb, keep in mind that for every bedroom in your home, you may have one 1,000-watt HID (High Intensity Discharge) light without triggering any suspicions from your electric energy provider. If the meter reader questions you about increased electricity, you can tell him that you attribute the increase to additional occupants living in your home. Perhaps that new big screen TV, or the electric hot water heater you've purchased could be a contributing factor. Seldom will a representative from your electric company call and ask if you are aware of an increase in your power consumption; if they do, give them the same story and thank them for their prompt service and looking out for your best interests and all. . .

I've never heard about a search warrant being issued solely on increased electrical usage, but just to be on the safe side, keep track of how much your electricity has increased. Usually, electric bills will come with a graph showing your past monthly electrical use. Whatever you decide to do, NEVER STEAL ELECTRICITY! This is a felony offence and the number one, sure-fire way to get you busted.

Installing a security device in your grow space is a must. This may seem like common sense, but it is essential that you take the necessary precautions to keep unwanted intruders out of this space. If at all possible, put a lock on the grow space, or at the very least, the door leading to it. *Always* use a dead bolt. Never use padlocks or combination locks as they can easily be removed with bolt cutters.

Keep your outdoor plants in pots or grow bags for easy mobility.

Grow bags are a great option for keeping your plants mobile. Just pick it up and move it to where it is safe, or where there is more sun.

Outdoor Gardening Safety

Outdoor safety for backyard growers is a fundamental principle that should not be taken lightly. Keep your plants in pots or grow bags for easy mobility. Not only is this critical for security reasons, but the amount of sunlight an area receives will change throughout the season and you'll want to move them to the area that gets the most sunlight. Place your plants in an obscure location, as far away from neighbors and the street as possible. In addition, make certain no artificial light is shining on your plants! Also make sure you plant with some good cover plants such as hibiscus or tomato. (This topic is covered in depth in the outdoor chapter of this book.)

Again, make sure your cover plants bear no resemblance to cannabis as this could potentially draw spectators in for a closer look. Even a quick investigation could reveal that you are in fact growing cannabis! If part of your property is a wood lot, clear a spot in the woods where you could claim that someone was trespassing on your property illegally and you didn't have any idea about it. Of course, this is only a valid excuse if there isn't any physical evidence linking you to the plot; also be fore-warned that if push comes to shove they can still forfeit your property.

Do not plant near a source of water. Law Enforcement Officers (LEOs) understand that this is a common practice and they often pay special attention to these areas. Take special precautions when planting on a hill—this is another target area for LEOs. Have all plants mobile. Grow bags would be the best option. To minimize the

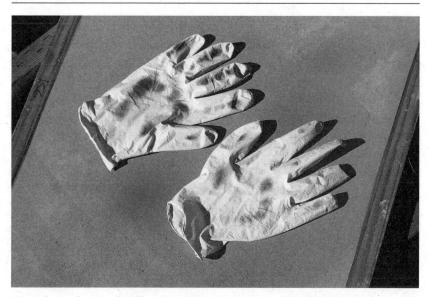

Wear gloves when you handle equipment and containers. Your fingerprints can be used against you in a court of law. And dispose of the gloves carefully, too.

plants' profile, dig a hole for each plant so the bag is out of sight completely. Cover with surrounding leaves and sticks to camouflage any evidence of a dig. It is imperative that the site be made to appear natural. The plants should blend in with the surrounding vegetation.

I am sure you have heard the expression, "don't put all your eggs in one basket." This is especially prudent for guerilla growing. Scatter the plantings. Again, take caution in plant placement, making sure the surrounding plants are of similar color and resemble cannabis in some way. Additionally, never leave grow supplies at the site and make an effort to take different paths to your plants each time you stop by.

One of the clearest distinctions of cannabis, from an aerial view, is its overall circular shape. To resolve this dilemma, alter the plants' profile. Train the plants to grow along the ground by manipulating the growing stalks. Using a stake and string, carefully bend the stalks down while they are still pliable. By training the stalks to grow horizontally instead of vertically, you will change the circular appearance of this plant, thus reducing the risk of detection.

It would be wise to use vinyl or latex gloves (with double thickness) when handling containers and supplies in remote areas. Leaving fingerprints behind could make your identity traceable.

A tip for both backyard and guerilla growers is to affix plastic flowers from artificial flower arrangements to the leaves of the plant to help disguise it. Be careful not to get anything too bright or colorful. This could potentially draw someone's attention enough to make them want to smell it. Cedar produces a strong pleasant odor and also repels certain insects.

TELEPHONE SECURITY

Don't talk about anything illegal on the phone, ever. If you have to, use a public phone, but don't use the same payphone every time. Code words aren't fooling anyone. They just make you look like a jackass.

If you do have to use a personal phone, your choices aren't very good. It's hard to say which method is the most insecure. Landlines are easily tapped and cell phone signals can easily be intercepted, letting anyone hear your conversations.

Landlines are easily tapped, and from a variety of different ways. If you hear weird clicking noises or an echo in your phone, relax (to some degree): you're not being tapped. The tapping that LEOs use are through the phone company's switching station, so you'll never know about them. In fact, in 1999, a total of 1,350 wiretaps were authorized by federal and state courts.

- 72.4% for drug investigations
- 10% for racketeering
- 4.6% for homicide or assault
- 4.4% for gambling
- 0.5% for kidnapping

These statistics are from before the so-called USA Patriot Act, since which the number of wiretaps has more than doubled.

Modern cell phones contain GPS that is accessible only to phone companies and (with a warrant) law enforcement. This GPS even triangulates your position when it's off.

The interaction with your cell phone provider's network allows them to bring up when and where you had conversations. All numbers, both incoming and outgoing, are stored and ready to be viewed by the LEOs. If you must use a cell phone, use a pre-paid.

GENERAL SAFETY RULES

ALWAYS PURCHASE ANY GROWING SUPPLIES IN CASH OR MONEY ORDER!

Double up on your latex gloves: a single layer of latex will still show your fingerprints. Vinyl gloves are usually thicker, but this is not always the case, and they may need to be doubled as well.

LEOs can and will give you or sell you illegal substances.

LEOs can and will try to start the transaction of you purchasing illegal substances.

LEOs don't under any circumstances have to tell you they're undercover—nope, not even if you ask. It is almost impossible to win a case based on entrapment.

Time to stop throwing those killer parties you're known for.

Make sure your property blends in with the neighbors; you don't want anything to draw suspicion to you or your property. This means freshly cut grass, a little landscaping, upkeep of the house itself, etc.

Place cedar shavings or mulch in flowerbeds and around your property—or grow cedar itself—as the plant disguises odors.

Don't use your burglar alarm when growing; when the alarm is tripped police are permitted to enter your residence with or without your consent.

Don't leave your trash at the curb; the Supreme Court ruled that police snooping through your trash when it's at the curb isn't an invasion of privacy and doesn't constitute the need for a search warrant. Keep your trash in the back of your house until the day of trash pickup.

Be extra careful if you're receiving government aid to pay for college; if you're caught in possession of illegal substances, say *goodbye* to that government aid!

Each firearm that is in the residence of the grow house is a MANDATORY MINIMUM OF 5 YEARS!

The law cites that an officer has the same right to intrude on our privacy as a "reasonably respectable neighbor." Only "No Trespassing" signs, with or without fences, will give your lawyer the argument that the officer should not have come to your door.

The fewer people that know about your grow the better—avoid the temptations of showing off your grow (which can get very hard when everything is looking mighty fine), and don't tell anyone unnecessary about your grow—that means the people you live with. You'll be surprised at how fast word of mouth gets around. It happens like this:

Officer: "Where did you get this stuff from?"

Friend of a friend whom you've never met before: "Uh...some guy off the street sold it to me."

Officer: "That's bullshit, punk, where'd you get it!?"

Friend of a friend: "I told you, sir, from a guy off the street."

Officer: "Look, if you give up they guy we'll drop your charge and you're free to go—or at least you'll get off with a few hours community service."

Friend of a friend: "OK. I got it from this guy that grows weed. . ."

It's all downhill from there, even though you don't even know this person exists. What matters is that he knows *you* exist. He's not going to narc on the person that actually sold it to him. You'll also be surprised at how quickly an ex-lover or "best friend" will roll over on you as well.

If at all possible, avoid going to a hydro shop; I would estimate that *at least* 30% of all busts have originated from hydro shops. Ordering online and having it shipped to your door is *much* safer, but avoid companies that have the words "hydroponics," "hydro," "grow," and so forth in their names. It doesn't get much worse than having the UPS delivery person hand you a package that has "east coast hydroponics" plastered all over it.

ORDERING SAFETY

Getting beans (seeds) in the mail is a great delight, either by ordering them from a seed company or by trading with a very well known e-friend. Most people get really paranoid when ordering seeds but really it's not a big deal at all. Hundreds of thousands of these packages are being sent all around the world each day! If by chance your parcel is intercepted, you'll merely get a letter from customs saying that having cannabis seeds in the U.S. is illegal. Just as how you don't solicit telemarketers to call your house—you can't help who sends you random packages of seeds in the mail! I assume you get put on a "watch list," but you didn't get those seeds shipped to your grow address anyway, right? Most seed companies have elaborate stealth shipping techniques. The only seed company that I know that actually guarantees that your order will get to you is cannaseur.com.

Do not have your cannabis seeds shipped to the same address you grow at. Be smart with your beans.

A word about trading seeds online. Make sure you know who you are trading with. I recommend that they be an established member of the website you're visiting, and that they have built up a good reputation for themselves there as well. Make sure their stories about their strains check out, as well. Don't be afraid to ask other respected members about the member in question. If they bred the seeds themselves, have them review how they made them. Compare that to the breeding section of this book to see if everything adds up. Now, remember: there is no guarantee that you will receive the package. I would say that, from personal experience, you'll get maybe 1 of 3 packages. Just because you don't receive the package, don't think the other person was pulling one over on you. If you follow the guidelines above, it might be that the package just got lost in the mail. It happens...

SENDING SEEDS AND CLONES SAFELY

Now it's time for you to send your seeds, possibly even clones! Just remember to wear gloves during the whole process. Most people choose to send the seeds in button baggies (if you do so, make sure you label each seed bag). The seeds have traditionally been sent in CD cases, and the CD case is then inserted inside of a plain 6 x 9-inch bubble wrap manila mailer. It ordinarily takes 4 stamps to make sure it gets there, but you will see many variations in how people send their seeds over the years; maybe you will come across something that works better for you, but in the meantime just stick to this standard.

Sending clones is a lot riskier. The old standard for sending clones is as follows:

You'll need a standard black VHS case. Your clones will have to be rooted in rapid rooters or (God forbid) rockwool cubes in order for this to work. They should be fully established, healthy rooted clones in order for them to make the move successfully. Lay them lengthwise in the VHS case; you can fit about three to a case, so choose wisely. Make sure to saran wrap the VHS completely a few times to make sure no smell leaks out. Send the case in a 10 x 11-inch bubble wrap manila mailer; it will take many more stamps than the seeds so it's best to get it weighed and paid for at the post office and wipe it down with alcohol wipe to get your prints off.

Make sure you drop any packages off at a random drop box located a couple towns over. Always send your packages USPS; I know it might sound dumb, but all other parcel services (UPS, FedEx, etc.) reserve the right to open any package, but it's a felony offence with the United States Postal Service. Always wear gloves when packaging and preparing your packages. Drop them in a drop box a few towns over. *Never* include your real return address even if it's just a PO Box. Oh, and always send your clones overnight express.

Rellikbuzz has this to say about trading clones:

It would be naive of us to think that, while it is against many growing websites' rules to do so, the shipping of clones doesn't occur all of the time in all parts of the world. But what is the best way to do this? There are certainly many ways to ship clones. Some ship the fresh cuttings in water. Some simply wrap the base stem of a fresh cutting with a damp paper towel after applying a rooting compound to the cut. (This procedure deals with already-rooted cuttings exclusively.) Although it would probably work as well with Jiffy Pellets, since they are similar in size, I've found greater success with rooting clones in Rapid Rooters, as they provide a bit of food for the cutting and hold moisture better than Jiffy Pellets.

Step One: Starting with a tray of freshly rooted clones, you will need paper towels, empty toilet paper rolls, properly pH'd water, masking tape, two large zip lock freezer bags, and a box large enough to hold the clones for shipping.

Step Two: Take a single white paper towel (no colored flowers or inks) and wet it with the pH'd water solution. (In my case, my solution also had a little Superthrive, 1 ml of Advanced Nutrients Fulvic Acid, 1 ml of AN's Voodoo Juice, and a drop or two of dishwashing liquid in one gallon of distilled water pH'd to 6.3.) After wetting the paper towel, ring out the excess water and fold it in half, and in half again, until you have it shaped into a rectangle of approximately 3 x 8 inches.

Step Three: Take your clone and spray with the Rapid Rooter lightly, but don't wet the leaves as this could cause mold. Take the folded wet paper towel and wrap it around the Rapid Rooter.

Step Four: Take a piece of masking tape long enough to wrap around the Rapid Rooter more than once (as the tape won't want to stick to the wet paper towel, and you will need to overlap onto the tape so it will stick.) Be sure to first fold the excess paper towel at the bottom against the Rapid Rooter and tape it securely to keep it from unfolding. This should protect the bottom of the roots and also keep excess paper towel from hanging out of the bottom of its shipping container.

Step Five: Insert the now-bundled clone into the top of an empty toilet paper roll. This is a bit of a chore as it is a rather tight fit. Be gentle, as you don't want to damage any of your vulnerable roots. This serves to hold the Rapid Rooter securely and helps protect the clone during shipment. Push the wrapped base of the clone all the way down to the bottom of the empty roll.

Step Six: With the clone now inserted into the empty toilet paper roll, gently tuck the leaves and foliage into the top of the roll, being careful not to crush or break the meristem. For this reason, it is certainly best to take clones that are 2–3 inches tall so that they will fit inside the roll.

Step Seven: Take another single paper towel and cut it into six even pieces. This will give you a piece that is about 3 x 4 inches; place this piece over the top of the roll with the clone inside, and tape it all the way around. This will protect the clone and still let it breathe.

Step Eight: Take another piece of masking tape and place it across the bottom of the roll to keep the clone from sliding out the bottom.

Step Nine: Now that you have got your clones into the empty toilet paper rolls and secured them, it's time to put them into the first zip lock freezer bag. You'll want to make sure that the rolls didn't roll around inside the bag, so put three or four in the zip lock, centered in the bag, and tape the first four securely to the inside of the bag. Once the first four are secure, stack the rest in there neatly and tape them to the first four—they don't all have to be taped to the inside.

Step Ten: Now that all the clones are secured inside the bag, exhale into the baggie to partially fill it up with CO_2, and then seal it. This should also help them survive the two or three day journey.

Step Eleven: Take the now semi-inflated bag of clones and insert it into a second zip lock bag. This is the reason you don't want to fully inflate the first bag as it is a bitch to get the first bag into the second one as it is, let alone if it were totally full. I choose to insert the zipped end first into the second baggie. You can do whatever you want.

Step Twelve: Now all that's left is to pack your securely wrapped baggie of clones into your box of choice for shipping. Sometimes the box is a bit bigger than the baggie, so fill in the open spots with packing peanuts.

MAIL ORDER MARIJUANA

A word about MOM (mail order marijuana). I strongly advise against ordering buds through the mail, as doing so has different consequences than seeds: if your package gets intercepted, you'll get more than just a letter in the mail! I wouldn't trust the companies that advertise MOM in cannabis publications, either. If you have some killer buds that you want to send to a friend across the country or across the globe, it's still risky business, but if you follow these steps you can increases your chances of it arriving safely.

First of all, don't send more than an ounce, and put the bag of buds into another quart double zip lock bag. Wrap saran wrap around this bag 3 or 4 times, and for added security tape up the whole package with packaging tape. Now vacuum seal that puppy at least two times. Go to your local exotic market and purchase the darkest, strongest Columbian coffee. Empty the coffee out, leaving only an inch or two at the bottom, put your package in the coffee container, and then fill around the sides and over the top of the pot with coffee beans. While the coffee beans won't mask the smell to dogs, all the packaging should prevent the smell from leaking out. Prepare your parcel right when you are going to send it—this will give less time for

These look like real soda cans, but in fact they are stealth stash cans with hidden compartments for storing your bud. A great way to remain inconspicuous.

the smell to permeate through the packaging. Make sure to pack it in tight, just like when you first purchased it. Now either saran wrap the whole package or place it in a Tupperware container. Add a cheesy little note like, "saw this at the store and thought you would enjoy it, seeing how you like Columbian coffee so much," or something to similar effect. Then overnight it to wherever you are sending it.

It is a good idea, if possible, to send your cannabis parcels around the Holiday time of year, because of the sheer volume of packages.

TRAVELING SAFETY

First of all, only break one law at a time. Don't have unpaid tickets, don't have warrants out for your arrest, don't carry a firearm when driving with illegal substances (especially if the firearm isn't registered), don't make any traffic violations, don't have anything hanging from your rear view mirror. A cop with a chip on his shoulder can pull you over and write you a citation for obstruction of view. Don't have any cracked or busted lights or windows, make sure all your headlights, taillights, brake lights, and turn signals are working fine. Don't have your music blaring. I would strongly suggest having a police monitor in your car, but make sure it's not the kind that you have to hang in your window. Try to tuck it out of sight so that if an officer approaches your car from the driver's side door it cannot be easily seen. You want to be a chameleon and blend in as well as possible to the surrounding traffic. Don't be conspicuous by staying right on the speed limit; go with the flow of traffic. However, if there is an officer behind you, I recommend obeying all the rules of the road religiously. It should be noted that if a police officer really wants to pull you over, he can easily do so—even if you have not violated any laws—just by saying you failed to maintain your lane. Keep all your registration and proof of insurance easily accessible and make sure you're not hiding your stash in the same place. Besides those little secret spots that most cars have, you can stash some weed under the carpet or by lifting up the center console and hiding something under it—none of these spots will help you if they have a dog. Cops once made a friend's teenage son dissemble his subwoofer to check it for illegal substances even though he did not have to; they just used their power against his lack of knowledge of his rights.

When riding with large quantities, *resist the urge to light one up*! Always have Visine, some strong chewing gum or breath mints, and Ozium (the strongest air sanitizer / deodorizer available) accessible, should an "emergency" arise. Also: the sunglasses aren't fooling anyone, especially Johnny Law. My favorite stash spot is investing in the "Fix A Flat" airtight stash safe. An added bonus is that it actually works! And it can hold up to two ounces if you really cram it in there. For just $20.00–30.00, it is the ultimate traveling stash safe. Another recent option for traveling safety is TightPac containers. They come in a variety of sizes and vacuum seal each time they are closed; however, they are difficult to conceal because of their bulkiness and flashy colors.

If you do get pulled over, remain calm and courteous. Have your license, registration, and proof of insurance ready. Turn your radio off and roll down your window. Always say "no" to searches without a search warrant. The reason they're asking is because they don't have any evidence to get a search warrant or to conduct a search without your consent. Just say, "Officer, I know you're trying to do your job but I would like to invoke my Fourth Amendment right to not consent to any search of my private property." The officer may say that he's going to get a warrant anyway, so you might as well save time, or he may just go ahead and search you anyway. Just remain peaceful and non-confrontational. There is nothing more you can do at this point. If the latter doesn't happen and he just says OK, ask whether you are being detained; make up some story that explains why you have to leave as soon as possible. You don't want to have to wait around any longer than is absolutely necessary. You don't have to answer any question the officer asks you. Of course, you don't answer any questions without your attorney present, but it is best not to come right out and say this about simple questions. Visit flexyourrights.org for more information.

To stay current on all the latest DEA news and their up-to-date drug searching techniques, look at the DEA's monthly newsletter at http://www.dea.gov/programs/forensicsci/microgram/index.html

Chapter 8

Building Your
Grow Room

Find an obscure part of the house and consider the following: available power (or the ability to run power to the area easily), drainage (i.e., the potential for leaks), standing water must be eliminated, noise control (fans and ballasts), the ability to circulate air, odor control, and the ability to secure your grow room.

BASEMENT GROWING

As I mentioned earlier, I've always been a big fan of basement grow rooms. You don't have to worry as much about escaping heat; thick concrete walls protect your heat signatures and hot air rises, which means your upstairs will always be warmer than your basement and if somehow they do notice something, it can be your hot water heater. This means not having to spend hundreds of dollars on insulation or polyshield. Most of the time, the basement has no external access, and is accessible only from inside the house; or, even if they have external access, there's a deadbolt on the door—or there should be. It is relatively easy to ventilate a basement by the house vents, window, or sewer. It is also relatively easy to run power. The floor will better insulate noise—better than the attic, say—as you have more layers to go through: carpet, flooring, and the layers of flooring are built with thicker wood and insulation. An attic, meanwhile, will just have insulation, thinner wood, and drywall. Most of the time, basements are inconspicuous places where few people go, especially to that nasty, dark, creepy corner that every basement has. One of the drawbacks of basement growing is humidity, which is usually an issue, but a $99–140 dehumidifier can easily solve this problem.

Find a spot close to one of those house vents; most are usually 12x5 inches, have a screen, and allow you to open or close them manually by moving the metal grate to the left or right. The reason you want to grow close to these vents is because ducting and tubing—which you would need more of if you grow at a distance from a vent—is more expensive and harder to work with than electric cable. Remember that if making a corner grow room you only have to worry about constructing two walls, but that there is more risk of escaping heat signatures.

Now that you've found where you want your room to be, you have two convenient options for how to construct your room, either by wood or PVC pipe. Of course, wood is stronger and sturdier than PVC pipe, but is also more difficult to work with and more expensive in most cases. You also must have an electric screwdriver and screws in various lengths to build your room out of wood. PVC pipe, on the other hand, is inexpensive and only requires either Y, T, or X connectors. If you are going the wood route, 2x4s and ¾-inch marine-grade plywood are usually all that is needed for most home growers; however, for larger commercial applications you might want to upgrade to 4x4s and 1-inch marine grade plywood. For the PVC route, 3–3½ inches is fine for most home growers, but for bigger applications you might want to consider between 4-6 inches.

All you need to do is make a square or rectangular frame for the bottom according to the size of the desired room. A matching size frame for the top, four pieces at least 6 feet tall to mount into the corners of the frames (7 feet is much better, but this size will vary according to the room you have to work with), and four pieces the same size to mount in the middle of the four corners to add sturdiness should do it. Mind you this is only an option for wood.

Depending on the length of your room, you may want to add supports in the middle of your pieces. For most PVC applications you will need only eight T connectors to complete your frame. I would also recommend running the appropriate length heavy-duty galvanized screw (a nut and bolt is best) through each joint where your pipes join the T connectors. Voila! You have your completed frame.

For PVC users, you'll have to attach your ballasts to the rafters of your basement or make a shelf outside of your grow room out of sturdy wood at least ¾-inch thick. For wood users, you can add a sturdy shelf in an out of the way part of the top of your grow

A decent dehumidifier can turn your basement into the perfect grow area.

room, or you can miter a reinforced beam double 2x4 into the frame. Having the ballasts in the center of the room with the hoods on either side works well. If you attaching your ballasts to your center beam, here's the easy way: cut a plate out of either a ³⁄₄–1-inch piece of wood or a ³⁄₄-inch (7–8mm) piece of steel. Now drill a ⁷⁄₈-inch hole in the four corners of the wood where the slots are in the ballast. You'll need four screws at least one inch long and two sets of four washers— small ones that fit the head of the screw and larger ones that the smaller washer fits, too. The reason for this is because the washers displace more weight. You'll also need four lock washers and four nuts. Now bolt your plate to your ballast; not too tight, though—just about five or six threads up the screw should do it. Drill a pilot hole for your ¹⁄₄-inch hook. Now mark the spot where the ballast will hang, drill your pilot hole, and screw in the hook: you're ready to hang your ballast. You can hang up to four 30-pound ballasts. This is a great method because you can mount a fan in front of the row of ballasts, pointing in the direction of the outtake, and keep all of them cool.

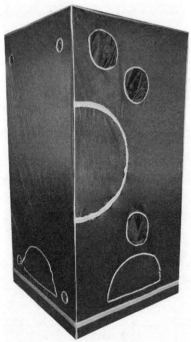

HydroHut instant grow rooms are ingenious products that assemble in under an hour. This 4x4 edition is seven feet tall and costs about $275.

Add styrofoam insulation for added noise dampening and to keep the heat from escaping, especially if you're doing a corner room. Use zip ties to attach insulation to PVC pipe, and a staple gun if you're using wood.

Whichever you choose, use this as a guideline to determine the size of your space. For optimum results, you'll want to have at least 45-watts of light, or at least 4,500-lumens per square foot. To calculate square footage, multiply the length x width of your space. Sea of green growers usually have at least three plants per square foot—up to nine plants. For normal growers not opting for ScrOG or SOG, it's one plant per 2–3 sq ft. If you're not growing SOG you do not want your plants competing with each other for space and light.

After you've decided on the size of your room and constructed your frame, you need to cover it. Go to your

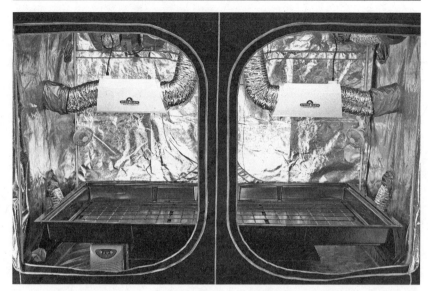

The HydroHut Silver Edition is the instant grow room of the future. Notice the light placement and fans in the corners to circulate the air. Perfection for the small-scale grower.

local home improvement store and purchase a roll of black "construction" heavy-duty plastic for $35–50. One roll covers 10,000 square feet, so you should have enough to do your room at a double thickness. While you're there, pick up the Velcro strips needed to make a sealed door. Now you have a few choices for the inside of your room. Of course, you don't want black walls sucking up all that light, so you can either paint your walls with flat white paint, which is a pain, or go with my personal choice: go to a party supply store and purchase two rolls of those white plastic table cloths. At eight bucks a pop you can't beat it. The only down side to this stuff is how thin it is, but that's why you get two rolls. Then, of course, there's Mylar, which is the most reflective surface you can have next to Foylon, which is even more reflective and much stronger. Both will cost you a pretty penny though.

REFLECTIVITY

Foylon	94–97% light reflected
Mylar	93–95% light reflected
Flat White Paint	84–93% light reflected
Semi Gloss White Paint	75–80% light reflected
Aluminum Foil	70–75% light reflected
Black Plastic	<10% light reflected

If money is not a factor, save yourself the hassle and purchase a HydroHut instant grow room. This is a rather ingenious product that is constructed of steel tubing, black plastic on the outside, and white plastic on this inside. The HydroHut instant grow room comes in two sizes, 4x4 and 4x8, and both are seven feet tall. They have intake and exhaust holes and Velcro flaps for cables to pass through without causing light leaks. Also, three of the sides unzip to allow easy access and the floor is four inches thick to prevent water leaks. The 4x4 is around $275 and the 4x8 is around $475 and assembles in less than an hour.

VENTILATION

Now it is time to run your ventilation. Ventilation is an extremely important aspect of the grow room that is often overlooked. Plants need to have the air changed around their stomatas at least once every minute. If this does not take place, the plants will start to suffocate (to a degree) and growth will slow drastically, if it doesn't cease completely. All that is needed is to set up an outtake fan that can move your entire volume of air in your room two to three times a minute. Calculate your volume by multiplying length x width x height. So, for example if you're using the HydroHut, 4 x 4 x 7 would be 112 cubic feet. You need a fan that is rated at least 224 CFM (cubic feet per minute). To give you an idea about the size of fan needed, a computer fan is around 26–45 CFM and a 20-inch Box Fan is around 10,000+ CFM. If you have a fan that is at least two times the size of your space you will not need an intake fan. You just need an opening slightly larger than the size of your outtake. This is known as a passive intake, active out-take system; the outtake is in the upper portion of the grow room, preferably in the opposite corner from the intake. This is the most common type of ventilation.

Now that you have your fan set up, it's time to run your ducting to the outdoors. There are several ways to do this, the easiest of which would be just to vent through the basement vent we talked about earlier. You'll need to purchase either a 4- or 6-inch flexible duct connector and insert the front of the fan. Then use duct sealer, a.k.a. caulk, and duct tape, making sure both surfaces are clean so that the tape sticks cleanly. Use as much as is needed to make sure there are no leaks. I find that 2-inch masking tape works better than duct tape. Now you need to insert your connector into your tubing or ducting; you will need a tight fit, so use hose clamps and sealer. About midway through, you want to insert your carbon scrubber. A carbon scrubber uses activated carbon to purify the air passing through it; you will periodically have to replace the carbon to keep your operation stealthy.

Warning: Use only fish safe silicone, sealer, or chalk to prevent toxic fumes poisoning your plants.

There are several good DIY carbon scrubber instructions on online forums—hg420 has a good one, as well as breedbay.

Attach your hose to the carbon scrubber and clamp it, seal it, or tape it. Use a vinyl hanger strap to suspend your carbon scrubber in the air. With a carbon scrubber there is no real need to vent to the outside as the air is being "scrubbed" and the odor removed. Most types of DIY carbon scrubbers do not allow you to continue your ductwork out the other end; however, other professional models do.

If you're not using a carbon scrubber and are going straight to your basement vent, make sure that your ducting has at least one 90-degree bend so light doesn't escape into the outdoors. Additionally, be sure that the basement vent you are venting to is not close to any entrance into the home and is far away from any part of your home where visitors will be.

This Phat filter is designed to keep the air fresh in your grow area. It can filter about 224 cubic feet, or a grow space that is 4 x 8 x 7, like the Silver Edition Hydro Hut.

Remove your basement vent screen, attach a Master Flow click starter collar (these are used to transition from lined or ductboard pipes to round pipes; either the 7- or 8-inch one will do), and seal the collar to the vent. For added insurance, tape it as well. After your sealer is dry, attach your hose to the collar with a hose clamp and then seal it.

Fire up your fan and check all the joints for leaks and feel the outside extraction to make sure you're pumping all the air through that you should be. Hold a lighter to all the joints and see if the flame is blown outwards from the ducting. Do this for every joint.

You may also vent through your chimney or sewer, but I don't recommend the chimney because it is very easy for the smell to seep into your living room or wherever the fireplace is.

To vent into your sewer, find the pipes running from the upstairs toilets. Follow the pipes until you see a Y connector. Depending on where and when your house was built, this will either be a metal pipe or, if you're lucky, a PVC pipe. You'll need a pipe wrench to remove the cap at the Y connector. Note: Some plumbers will glue the PVC cap in place; use extreme caution before force to prevent serious damage.

I warn you: make sure you have completed all the duct work ahead of time before removing this cap. Sewers are filled with poisonous gases, namely methane, which is flammable and toxic. Make sure you're doing this away from your water heater pilot light. So have all your tubing down ahead of time and make sure you preformed all your checks and everything is in perfect working order. I also suggest that you add a smaller centrifugal inline fan to make sure the air is being pumped out of your room and doesn't back up into your house. When you remove this cap you'll usually find a 4-inch hole. Most hoses will be 6 inches; this is no problem, just use a 4-inch reducer and then attach it to the hole. Again, make sure that all your hose clamps are tight and sealed well. This method, while hazardous, is the most secure way of venting your smells. It is impossible to determine where the smell is coming from, and the heat signature is undetectable.

Warning: this should be performed only by a licensed plumber. The author and publisher of this book assume no responsibility for unlicensed plumbing.

You will have to purchase a thermometer and hydrometer. These measure the ambient air temperature and relative humidity in your room. I recommend getting a cheap meter from your local home improvement store. You can get a combo meter for less than $10. Mount this meter in a vertical position somewhere that is not receiving direct light. I also recommend getting a remote thermometer / hydrometer. This is a handy tool, as it allows you to place the sensor in your grow room and the receiver somewhere in your house, where you can monitor the temperature and humidity at any time without having to go into your room and look at the thermometer / hydrometer. This is especially useful if your grow room is in the basement, and at night. These can also be purchased relatively inexpensively, depending on which model you choose. Prices range from $25–40 dollars.

OTHER GROWS
Attic Growing
Certainly the most risky form of indoor growing. While it does have its advantages, such as easy ventilation and the option of available natural sunlight, its drawbacks include the difficulty of controlling the temperature, the fact that escaping heat signatures show easily and are expensive to conceal, the trouble of running power, the need for increased insulation to dampen noise, the conspicuous requirement of adding a lock to your attic door, and, finally, the awkward ceiling pitch which means your plants will be clustered in the center. Unless your attic roof is above 8 feet tall, you'll have to construct your grow room in a rectangle down the middle of the attic.

Generally, your attic grow room will only be 2–4 feet wide, depending on the angle of roof pitch. Start your room at the end of the attic near one of those big gable vents. You'll construct your room the same as above, with a few minor exceptions.

You should double up on insulation and add the polyshield to the inside of the grow room, then cover it with either Mylar or white plastic table cloths. You'll definitely need the polyshield, and expect to drop a shiny dime for it, too. It doesn't matter if your space is either rectangular or square. It's the square footage that matters. Your room will probably be either (6 x 3 =) 18 square feet or (8 x 3 = 24) square feet. So, a combination of one 600-watt Hortilux HPS and one 1,000-watt HPS will be perfect for a 6x3 space and a combination of two 1,000-watt Hortilux HPS and one 400 watt HPS will be perfect for an 8x3 space. It's best to use Mylar for your attic rooms so the light is reflected more evenly. Drop some 42-watt CFLs to make up for the diminishing light at the ends of the grow; also, some 48-inch fluorescent fixtures, hung vertically, will add some side lighting. You'll need at least a 144 CFM outtake fan for the typical attic ceiling being 6 feet high (8 x 3 x 6 = 144). Vent your exhaust to one of those gable vents. This will typically require very little ductwork, but again, make sure you add one 90-degree bend so light doesn't escape. Generally, no carbon scrubber is needed. Just follow the same duct guidelines as above, but instead of sealing the collar to the vent you can just wedge it in between the vent flaps.

One great modern invention for attic growing is Veluxusa. It comes in either a 22-inch diameter, which is $299.95, or a 14-inch diameter for $257.95. It is basically a skylight that doesn't lose its intensity. Mount this on the side of your roof that receives the most sunlight and the sun funnels right into your grow space. You can use this product even if you're growing in a closet or basement; it will just require much more ductwork. It doesn't give off hot spots, so heat isn't an issue. If the sun isn't working to your advantage, you can simply cover the skylight with black plastic and Velcro strips. It is a truly great way to provide adequate natural sunlight to your room.

Visit veluxusa.com for more information.

Closet Growing

Closet growing is one of the safest and easiest ways to grow cannabis indoors. After all, everyone has a closet. They're great for dampening noise. An interior closet is safe from prying FLIR radars. One of their drawbacks, though, is the build up of heat due to lack of space. You must make sure that your ventilation is in perfect working order or your plants will suffer greatly. I suggest venting into your attic. Since hot air rises, and so do aromas, you can either let it sit up there and escape naturally or you can add a carbon scrubber when you vent it into the attic (since your closet won't have space for a carbon scrubber).

Walk-in closets are the best. You should set it up similarly to the attic grow room. If your closet is one that's wide instead of narrow you could partition it, half and half. My personal opinion though, is to have one closet for vegetation and one for budding. It makes life a lot simpler and you don't have to worry about light leaks. You can't trust your closet door to seal them up. Usually one 400-watt Hortilux HPS with two 48-inch fluorescent fixtures hung in opposite corners will do a great job for full-sized budding closets. One 400-watt Hortilux MH with two 48-inch fluorescent fixtures will do well for full-sized vegetation closets, as well. Max Yields dual stage closet setup is a great design.

Bedroom Growing

I would advise against bedroom growing for two main reasons: one, because it is not safe from FLIR radars and heat can easily escape, and two, because how would it look if one bedroom of your house was always shut and dead bolted? Very suspicious is what it would look like. People might even assume something worse than growing cannabis. You can correct the FLIR problem with enough polyshield and insulation, but you will spend a small fortune doing so. There's still that remaining problem about the lock—say a friend is too wasted to drive home and he needs to stay the night or relatives come in and you put them up on the sleeper sofa. The question will arise: "Why can't we sleep in that spare bedroom?"

However, some very nice factors of bedroom growing are the AC and heating vents, and the fact that power is already available, although you may have to upgrade to a heavier duty circuit breaker. Also, somewhat easy ventilation into the attic is an added bonus. Don't attempt to ventilate through the window. Speaking of windows, don't be obvious and board up your window; instead, make sure you use the matching blind or curtains that are in the other windows of the house and hang them in the window as normal. Now cut out a piece of plywood (card board is too thin) the exact size of the window, staple polyshield to one side and insulation to the other, and place the side with the polyshield facing out. Fill up the remaining space with thick pink insulation. Once you have the space filled with that pink insulation, seal off the entire window opening with another sheet of polyshield. The reason you need so much polyshield and insulation at the window is because this is a FLIR hotspot, if you will. Very easy to detect. You'll need to repeat this plywood, polyshield, and styrofoam insulation on all the exterior walls if you plan on growing in the whole room or doing a corner grow. If you plan on constructing your own grow room in the middle of the bedroom, which is safest, follow the same plans as in the basement. You'll most likely use PVC pipe, so anchor the ballasts to the rafters in the ceiling. A typical bedroom is 12 x 12 x 7.5, so to grow in this entire bedroom you'll need three 1,000-watt Hortilux HPS lights, a 2,160 CFM fan, plus you'll have to leave the door open for intake. I also suggest pulling the carpet up because it will harbor moisture, bacteria and fungus.

Shed Growing

I strongly advise against growing in a shed or building detached from your house. LEOs tend to think that "exploring" these areas isn't against the law. They are easy to break into, and you will spend a fortune trying to protect against FLIR. Not to mention that you will have to run extension cords or go through a great deal of trouble to create its own power supply—which is another dead give away that that shed is doing more than housing garden supplies. Also, bugs are extremely hard to keep out. Stick with the closet or bedroom.

Perpetual Harvest

This is a technique where you implement two or more grow rooms, one or more vegetative rooms, and a bud room. Your rooms can be as small as a 3x2-foot cab or as big as a warehouse. They need to be separated completely and free of light leaks, especially your budding chamber. In order to implement the perpetual harvest technique you will need to be an expert cloner. You must have clones so as not to waste time with slow-growing seedlings that have unknown sexes. Additionally, some of you may want to have a separate mother room to house the moms that you will continue to take your clones from. If this is not an option you will want to make extra space for your moms in your vegetative room, but this is not recommended because if an insect infestation or disease runs rampant in your vegetative room you are at risk of losing your mothers as well. It is a good idea to implement the Bonsai Mom technique if you have limited space, details of which can be found in the advanced techniques chapter. You may also want to set up a small room for your newly rooted clones or a separate section in your vegetation room.

For perpetual harvest you construct your grow room as described in the methods above, although you may want to link up the exhaust ducts to one another before you vent. Your vegetation room can be lit with "daylight" fluoros or a 250 or 400-watt Metal Halide. Just remember to have 50 watts per square foot. Mothers should be lit with a 250 or 400-watt Metal Halide to develop an abundance of healthy branches, i.e. potential clones. Your budding room should consist of sufficient wattage HPS light for the size of the room (see lighting) or, ideally, one HPS and one MH.

Most perpetual gardens implement the SOG technique, although you can grow regular gardens if you have a large enough grow space. Let's say that you are using a 3x2-foot area that's six square feet, and you're doing a SOG setup. That's six plants per square foot. Find a suitable mother and take six clones (see the cloning chapter). After these clones have rooted and begun their vegetative cycle, place them in the vegetative room.

Now you have two options. About two weeks before you move your plants into the budding cycle you can start your new batch of clones. The two-week period is to allow them to root and be ready to move into the vegetative room as soon as you free up that room (you must have a separate cloning room for this option). If you do not have a separate cloning room or would prefer to stagger your harvests, you can wait until you move your plants to the budding room, and then make your new clones.

You should get from clone to bud in 45–90 days time. You can repeat this every 45–90 days, which will allow you 4–6 harvests each year. This, of course, depends on the type of clone (Indica or Sativa) and how long you let them veg for.

V-Garden

This is a system of gardening where you stack the plants on shelves in a "V" shape. You place bare bulbs in the center of the V, which illuminates both sides of the V. There are normally just two shelves on each side of a V garden setup. This can be constructed with cinder blocks, for soil growers. On the lower shelves, place the cinder blocks on their sides and place a 1-inch thick board across the blocks for the containers. For the higher shelves, the cinder blocks are stood on end and the board is placed between them.

That said, V gardening has many disadvantages and I do not recommend growing with this design. Only one side of the plant receives light at a given time, unless other lights are added to each side of the V. When plants on the lower shelves grow up, they shade the plants on the higher shelf. When plants on the higher shelf grow up, you must raise the lights so they are not growing up in the dimly lit areas. Adjusting your light will cause the plants on the lower shelves to receive inadequate lighting.

ELECTRICITY

WARNING: ALL ELECTICAL WORK SHOULD BE DONE BY A LICENSED ELECTRI-CIAN! The author and the publisher cannot be held accountable for faulty wiring or wiring not installed by a licensed electrician.

Depending on where you're constructing your grow room, it will require either the switching of circuit breakers and outlets or the installation of circuit breakers, wiring, and outlets to the location of your room.

WARNING: Always shut off the power before performing electrical work.

US NATIONAL ELECTRICAL CODE
Maximum Amperage

AWG Wire Size	Two Current Carrying Conductors (Ampere)	Three Current Carrying Conductors (Ampere)
18	7	10
16	10	13
14	15	18
12	20	25
10	25	30
8	35	40
6	45	55
4	60	70
2	80	95

The above chart shows you what gauge wire you will need to suit your application.

COMMON CONVERSIONS
for North America and other 110-volt countries
Lights:
1,000-watt / 110-volt = 9.1 amps
600-watt / 110-volt = 5.4 amps
400-watt / 110-volt = 3.6 amps
250-watt / 110-volt = 2.3 amps

Circuits:
10a x 110-volt = 1,100-watt and 80% safe usage is 880-watt.
15a x 110-volt = 1,650-watt and 80% safe usage is 1,320-watt.
25a x 110-volt = 2,750-watt and 80% safe usage is 2,200-watt.
30a x 110-volt = 3,300-watt and 80% safe usage is 2,640-watt.

COMMON CONVERSIONS
for the UK and other 240-volt countries.
Lights:
1,000-watt / 240-volt = 4.1 amps
600-watt / 240-volt = 2.5 amps
400-watt / 240-volt = 1.7 amps
250-watt / 240-volt = 1.1 amps

Circuits:

10a x 240-volt = 2,400-watt and 80% safe usage is 1,920-watt.

15a x 240-volt = 3,600-watt and 80% safe usage is 2,880-watt.

25a x 240-volt = 6,000-watt and 80% safe usage is 4,800-watt.

30a x 240-volt = 7,200-watt and 80% safe usage is 5,760-watt.

For safety reasons you should only use **80%** of the circuit breaker's capacity.

For example, a 1,000-watt grow light divided by 120 volts (the common house hold volt) = 9.1 amps. On a 15-amp circuit breaker you are using 68% of that circuit breaker's capacity. Only one 1,000-watt light can be run on a 15-amp circuit breaker. For each 1,000-watt light you should have 15 amps, i.e., two 1,000-watt lights should have a 30-amp circuit breaker, four 1,000-watt lights should have a 60-amp circuit breaker, etc. You can get away with running a 1,000-watt and 400w light on a 15-amp circuit breaker which is 12 amps; in doing so you're using 82% of that circuit breaker's capacity, which is fine—but adding fans and side lighting will overload the circuit breaker.

When preparing to supply electricity to your grow room / greenhouse, the following information will be helpful. This particular guide focuses on utilizing a subsidiary breaker panel in addition to the main breaker panel. Regardless if you're working with a 200 amp breaker panel, or smaller, the same safety precautions should be taken.

INSTALLING CIRCUIT BREAKERS

The first step is cutting off the power in whatever section of the house you are working on. The circuit breaker that feeds this subsidiary panel can often be shut off at the main breaker panel. The use of a voltage meter will be helpful in determining if the power has been shut off. Don't forget to set up your drop light via extension cord, powered by a separate circuit, before you shut off the power.

Organize your circuit breaker in the following way:

1 & 2 Incoming Hot Wires (from main breaker panel)

3 Neutral Wire

4 Ground Wire

5 Ground Bus Bar

6 Neutral Bus Bar

7 Circuit Breakers

8 Outgoing wire (to grow room)

9 Circuit Breaker (slotted) Anchor Point

10 Power Supply Bus Bar

Use the appropriate method for running the Romex cable most suitable for the application. This depends on the distance from the circuit breaker to the outlet, the size of circuit breaker, and the amount of current running through the cable. For this demonstration 14/2 Romex with ground was the appropriate cable.

Apply conduit, cable clamps, and/or insulated staples where required.

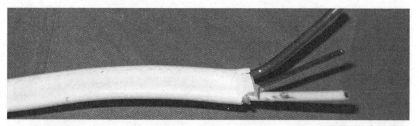

14/2 with a ground, Romex wire, showing neutral (white), positive (black) and ground (un-insulated copper).

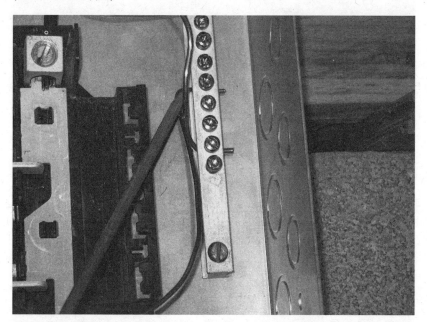

This is showing the ground block within the fuse panel. This is the attaching location for the ground wire.

Step 1

Begin by connecting the ground wire to the ground bus bar. Be sure to make the appropriate bends in the wire so it will lie in an orderly fashion inside the panel. To install the ground wire, loosen a screw in the ground bus bar and insert the wire through the ground bus bar, exposing the ground wire on the opposite side. Be sure

This is the neutral buss bar within the fuse panel. It is the attaching location for the neutral wire.

Neutral wire installed in the neutral buss bar.

to firmly tighten the screw. Refer to panel manufacturer for the proper torque specifications. Be advised that loose connections overheat, and overheating can lead to fires. Be certain that all connections are tight.

Step 2

Connect the neutral (white) wire to the neutral bus bar after removing the appropriate amount of insulation. Do not expose too much wire, just enough wire to pass through the neutral bus bar and be seen on the opposite side. Make sure to route the wire neatly to the neutral bus bar. To install the neutral wire, loosen a screw in the neutral bus bar and insert the wire through the neutral bus bar, exposing the neutral wire on the opposite side. Be sure to firmly tighten the screw. Refer to panel manufacturer for the proper torque specifications. Be advised that loose connections over heat can lead to fires. Be certain that all connections are tight

Step 3

Connecting the hot wire will be done through the circuit breaker. A 15-amp breaker is being used in this application. Be sure to install the appropriate circuit breaker(s) for your growing needs. For example, this 15-amp circuit breaker is appropriate for two 600-watt HIDs and possibly some side lighting and exhaust and oscillation fans, making sure not to exceed 1,320w.

Up to two hot wires can be attached to the connection terminal for the circuit breaker.

Remove enough insulation from the hot wire to provide a clean connection, typically $5/8$ of an inch. Loosen screw and insert stripped hot wire into connection terminal. Tighten screw securely.

The circuit breaker is now ready to be installed.

Step 4

To install the circuit breaker you will first need to insert the plastic locking tabs into the slotted anchor point. Only then may the U-clips be attached to the power bus bar. There are no fasteners to secure this style of circuit breaker to the panel; only the interference fit between the metal U-clips and the power bus bar hold the circuit breaker in place. Only after the front of the panel has been installed are the circuit breakers secured.

Be sure to firmly seat the circuit breaker, making sure that it is completely parallel to the panel and other circuit breakers. Remember what we said about loose connections.

You can now reattach the front of the panel after you remove the metal knockout tab for your newly added circuit breaker.

15 amp circuit breaker ready to be installed.

You are now done with this stage of the electrical process: congratulations, the hardest part is behind you. You should now make an opening into your grow room for the Romex cable so we can begin our next step. You will want to caulk (for dry wall) or tape (for plastic) to make sure this opening is sealed after the Romex wire is through.

INSTALLING OUTLETS

Now we will be working inside the grow room. Once again, make sure you have all the power disconnected in the area that you are working in, and again, don't forget to set up your drop light from a different circuit ahead of time.

The first step is choosing where you want to mount your first outlet. All your outlets need to be GCFI (Ground Circuit Fault Interrupter) outlets that are required for areas with high humidity. GCFI outlets are more expensive than regular outlets but are well worth it and are actually easier to install.

Now, the first step is installing the junction box, which, depending on the model, requires just a few screws or nails. Most have two nails that are placed on the sides and are simply hammered into a wall stud. Mount this first junction box where it is most accessible for your grow room's electrical needs. You have the option of wiring several outlets in series or to separate circuit breakers for each additional outlet. This decision is dependant on the required application and amount of equipment, so as

This is the inside of a junction box. The two holes on the side are for nails to hold it on the wall.

Here is the junction box with the cover installed. Before you mount the junction box, be sure to remove the knockout tabs for the Romex wire to pass through. They've been punched out in this photo, so it's ready to go.

not to overload the circuits.

Before you have your junction box mounted, remove the knockout tabs for the Romex wire to pass through and secure the box in the chosen location. *Ideally,* install cable clamps to secure the Romex wire in the box. Pull about 12 inches of wire through—you want to have enough wire to work with comfortably. It is a real pain trying to stretch wires to your outlet after the fact.

The images below display two Romex cables already trimmed to fit this outlet application. Start with about 12 inches of wire pulled through your junction box and trimmed, after all connections have been measured and reached. Notice that two Romex wires are used in this junction box because the outlets are run in series. If you are only wiring one outlet per circuit breaker, you will only have the one to connect.

On a ground fault circuit interrupter (GFCI) outlet, your ground is a screw at the bottom. Your hot wire goes to the left side and the neutral (white) goes to the right side, as shown in as shown in the images below.

If you're running one circuit breaker per outlet, you will use only the connection 1 on the system. If you are running your outlets in series, you will connect the incoming hot wire to connection 1 and your series hot wire to connection 2. Incoming neutral wire connects to the neutral side of connection 1, and series neutral wire on the neutral side of connection 2. The reader should note that brass screws are for hot wires and steel screws for the neutral wires.

Step 1

Like the circuit breaker, connect the ground wires first to the ground screw. With needle nose pliers, create a Shepherd's hook in the ground wire(s). You want to bend this wire so that when the screw is tightened the wires will be twisted securely onto the screw, as shown in the images. Remember: righty tighty.

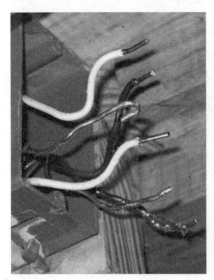 

Ground wire bent and ready for the ground screw.

Ground wire with ground screw in position and ready to attach.

Attaching the ground wire.

*Attaching positive (black) wire and neutral (white) wire. *Positive wire always goes to the copper connection, neutral wire always goes to the silver connection.*

Step 2

Now that we have our ground wire(s) secure, we can connect our neutral (white) wires. Strip the wire(s) about ⅝ of an inch and, for GFCI outlets, you simply insert the neutral wires straight into the connection and tighten the screws. This is shown in the images; for photographic purposes we loosened the ground wires.

Step 3

Now we can connect our hot wires. These are the last wires we have to connect before securing our outlet into our junction box. Just like with the neutral wires, strip ⅝ of an inch off the hot wires (black wires in this application), insert, and tighten them one at the time.

Step 4

Now that we have all our wires connected we can mount the outlet to the junction box. Begin by trying to neatly bend the wires into the junction box—which is no easy feat. Now you will basically have to muscle the outlet into the junction box while simultaneously pulling the slack in the wires out of the back of the junction box. Do this until the outlet's mounting bracket is flush with the junction box. Line up the holes and secure with screws.

Now attach your protective / decorative plate and you're all finished. Obviously, you will have to repeat this step for every outlet you plan to install.

SAMPLE GROW ROOM SPECS

Below are examples of optimum grow rooms and how many plants each can grow for the best results.

250-watt HPS (High Pressure Sodium), 28,000 lumens, 2 x 2 foot area, 7,000 lumens per square foot, and 62.5 watts. Either four SOG (sea of green) plants or two regular plants, max. Have the bulb 8–16 inches above plant canopy, depending on circulation

400-watt Hortilux HPS, 55,000 lumens, 3 x 3 foot area, 6,111 lumens per square foot, and 44.4 watts. Either nine SOG plants or five regular plants, max. Have bulb 12–18 inches above canopy depending on circulation

600-watt Hortilux HPS, 87,000 lumens, 4 x 4 foot area, 5,437 lumens per square foot, and 37.5 watts. Either sixteen SOG plants or eight regular plants, max. Have bulb 16–24 inches above canopy depending on circulation

1,000-watt Hortilux HPS, 145,000 lumens, 5 x 5 foot area, 5,800 lumens per square foot, and 40 watts. Twenty-five SOG plants or twelve regular plants, max. Have bulb 24 or more inches above canopy depending on circulation

I use Hortilux HPS lights because they provide the most lumens and have 25% more blue spectrum, so they are a suitable light for both vegetation and budding cycle. The best lighting though is a mixture of both Metal Halide and High Pressure Sodium. For more information on lighting refer to the lighting chapter.

A quick way to find out how many watts you need in your grow room is to visit http://www.hydromall.com/info/formula.html

Chapter 9

Lighting

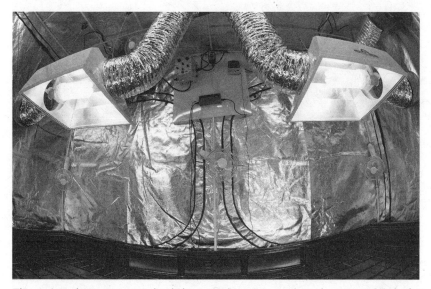

This 4x8 HydroHut uses two big lights to make sure your plants have enough light for photosynthesis, and three rotating fans to keep the air moving so things don't get too hot and clammy.

Lighting may very well be the most important aspect of indoor growing. After all, without light, plants cannot perform photosynthesis (gather energy) and most importantly, they can't grow! If you have inferior lighting in vegetation, your plants will have elongated internodes—even if they're Indica dominant—and if you have inferior lighting in bud your plants will just develop little popcorn buds. While they'll be potent, you'll be fortunate to yield a half-ounce from one 2-foot tall plant. This is why lighting is such a crucial aspect of indoor growing.

This is a good balance of plants to light sources. There are six 1,000w air cooled lights with two ebb and flow tables in an SOG grow.

Here are some terms you need to be familiar with for measuring light

Foot Candle: Standard measurement of light intensity. A foot-candle is how bright the light is one foot away from the source.

Lumen: Measure of light output. A lumen is equal to one foot-candle falling on one square foot of area.

Lux: Standard of luminance. One lux is equal to one lumen per square meter.

Watt: Measure of strength of light. A 120-watt light emits more lumens than a 60-watt, etc. Measures how many joules of energy per second are passed through the light.

All of the above are measures of light to the human eye, what we see.

CRI: Color Rendering Index is the measure of the ability of a light source to reproduce the colors of various objects being lit by the source.

KELVIN TEMPERATURE

Another accurate way to measure the actual amount of light that plants are receiving. Bulbs are measured in Kelvin temperature. Kelvin charts range from 1,800K, which is nothing but red photons, to 28,000K, which is nothing but blue photons. 2,000K–3,200K is considered warm; 3,400K–4,400K is considered neutral; 5,000K–6,500K is considered cool.

PAR: Photosynthetically Active Radiation, a specific portion of nanometers between 400–700 that plants use to grow.

PAR watts: Actual amount of specific protons a plant needs to grow. PAR can only be calculated using a PAR light meter.

Radiant heat: Heat that is emitted from your floors, walls, etc. "Hot spots," when in reference to reflectors and hoods, is radiant heat reflected from your lights. You should think about radiant heat before moving your HID lights too close to your plants. Even if your lights are far enough away that they don't burn the back of your hand, radiant heat may still adversely affect your plants.

THE COLOR SPECTRUM

Blue spectrum lighting promotes bushy, dense growth with short internodes that are ideal for the vegetative cycle. Blue spectrum lighting has also been linked to increasing the number of females in the vegetative cycle.

Red spectrum lighting promotes plentiful, beautiful blooms that are ideal for the budding cycle. Red spectrum lighting has been linked to increasing the number of males in the vegetative cycle.

White spectrum is considered neutral on both parts. As such, it aids both vegetative and budding cycles.

A balanced spectrum with both blue and red are best for plants. The sun uses both spectrums, and it is what plants are used to. Neither an MH (Metal Halide) or an HPS (High Pressure Sodium) is the ideal grow light for either phase—plants grow best with a mixed spectrum of both MH and HPS.

There are several ways to measure the amount of light in your grow space. Almost all of them require that you calculate your square footage (length x width of your space) and your total lumens, watts, etc. Divide your square footage into your total of lumens or watts. For example, take a space that is (5-foot x 5-foot =) 25 square feet. Say you have two 400-watt Hortilux HPS lights and two dual 48-inch fluoros (fluorescent lights) with 6,500K daylight bulbs. The two Hortilux bulbs are 55,000 a piece, so they total 110,000 lumens, and four daylight flours are about 2,500 lumens a piece, totaling 10,000. Your grand total is 120,000 lumens. Now, divide 25 (square feet) into 120,000 (lumens) = 4,800 lumens per square foot. Even 4,800 lumens per square foot are not sufficient for our purposes; optimum conditions require at least 7,500 lumens.

However, lux, lumen, watts, and foot-candles are only human measures of light. The human eye can only see a very small portion of light—500–600 nanometers. For an accurate measure of what the plants are actually "seeing," you will have to purchase a PAR light meter, and these can be quite expensive—in the neighborhood of $250–300.

An important rule to remember is that 150,000 lumens are 150,000 lumens regardless if they come from one 1,000-watt HPS light or from four 400-watt HPS lights. It is actually better to have a greater number of smaller lights than to have one big light. This is because you can place your lights closer to your plants and have multiple light points instead of one, which results in more even light distribution. More sources of light are better for plants as they get the same* amount of light from 2 or more different angles. It would be ideal to have six or seven 250-watt lights to replace one 1,000-watt. This is probably not an option because this would cost much more than one 1,000-watt system, but if money is no object then maximize your yields with many smaller lights instead of a few big ones.

You want at least 40-watts per square foot, albeit 50-watts is optimum in your grow room to sustain rapid, healthy growth. To calculate the number of watts in your grow room, divide your total square footage into your total watts, i.e., 1,000 watts divided by 12 square feet equals 83 watts per square foot.

Lumens aren't everything, however. Most growers will opt to get an HPS because they produce more lumens than MHs, but it's the spectrum that matters most. Standard HPS lights produce only red / orange waves, and plants need both red and blue waves to grow to their full potential. While more red / orange waves increase budding weight, they will not do it by themselves and should be used in addition to MH lights. Also, 20K MH lights will not produce good results on their own, either, as they contain only deep blue / purple waves. A 4K or 6K would be better suited for overall growth if you cannot afford both a HPS and MH light.

INCANDESCENT LIGHTS

Incandescent lights consist of a glass enclosure that houses an inert gas, typically nitrogen, argon, or krypton; this gas helps to reduce the need for stronger glass and ensures that the filament has a prolonged life. The glass enclosure also seals out the oxygen in the surrounding atmosphere from combusting. The filament, typically made of tungsten, is where the electrical current is passed and what, when heated to between 2,000–3,000°F, provides light, because the tungsten metal glows white-hot at those temperatures. Most growers start out with "Grow Lux" or "Spot Grow":

These low wattage Metal Halide HID lights can be raised or lowered via the support wires as the seedlings grow. They are air cooled with the tubes.

incandescent lights coupled with a few fluoro fixtures. While they do allow plant growth, your plants will be tall and skinny with long internodes and little branching.

Incandescent lights are suitable for your mom's orchids during the winter, but not suitable for our needs. Incandescent lights range from 2,600K–3,100K, which also contributes to the "leggyness" of your plants. Incandescents burn too hot to get close to your plants; closer than one foot and you may start burning your plants.

HALOGEN LIGHTS

Think of halogen lights as a concentrated or super incandescent light. However, instead of a big glass enclosure, halogen lights use a small quartz enclosure, also known as an envelope. Quartz is used instead of glass because glass would melt under the extreme temperatures that halogen lights produce. The gas inside the enclosure is also different, and when reacting to the close proximity of the tungsten filament, through a complex process, it super heats the tungsten filament and prolongs its life. These gases are known as Halogen group, typically either Fluorine or Chlorine gas. Halogen lights are worse than incandescent lights in regard to cannabis growing for the fact that they generate so much heat. However, the spectrum is decent for growing cannabis. Halogen lights are very bright; they are on the neutral part of the spectrum chart similar to a 4,400-watt MH. Like with incandescents, the

This Badboy T5 fluorescent lighting grid is ideal for clones and seedlings.

heat they generate disables you from placing them close to your plants, rendering them useless for some of your needs.

FLUORESCENT LIGHTS

Fluorescent lights are a bit more complicated in terms of chemical reactions that take place to emit light. Obviously, the main physical aspect is the long sealed glass tube. Inside the tube is a small amount of liquid mercury, and phosphor powder, which coats the inside of the glass tube. The tube contains two electrodes, one at each end of the tube, and both are wired to an electric circuit. When the light is turned on, a simple explanation is that enough voltage comes through the electrodes to force electrons to migrate from one end of the tube to the other. The voltage converts some of the liquid mercury to gas, creating gaseous mercury atoms. The electrons collide with the mercury atoms, creating light photons. These photons collide with the phosphor atoms from the phosphor powder, which creates light. The different shades of light emitted from fluorescent lights result from the variations of phosphors.

Fluorescent lights are like the wood bat of baseball. They are a tradition—a pastime, if you will. There are a few different types of fluorescent lights available. There are standard fluorescents, High Output (HO) fluorescents, and Very High Output (VHO) fluorescents. HO and VHO are most commonly used for aquarium tanks. Standard fluorescents are known as T-12s; they come in a variety of sizes—24, 36 and 48 inches are the most common. They also come in 25-, 30- and 40-watts, the 40-watt being the most prevalent. T-12s are the biggest fluoros lights available. T-8s are one size down. They are the most efficient fluoros available. They are most common in smaller sizes than T-12s: 12- and 24-inches. T-5s are the smallest fluorescents available. I do not recommend them for growing.

HO Fluorescents usually come in T-12s and T-5s. They are typically 36 to 48 inches in length. The wattages ranch from 54 to 80-watts. HO fixtures hold 2, 5, or 6 tubes each. The fixtures that hold 2 are around $170; fixtures that hold 5 are around $250–299. HO tubes are between $15–20 each.

VHO fluorescents usually come in T-12s and T-5s. They are typically 60–72 inches in length, and the wattages range from 96–120-watts. VHO fixtures hold 2, 5, or 6 tubes each. Fixtures that hold two bulbs are around $250, fixtures that hold five bulbs are in the neighborhood of $350, and fixtures that hold six bulbs are around $400. They also make VHO fixtures that have two bulbs on the outside and can hold two MH bulbs on either end; these fixtures will set you back around $650–700.

Fluoro bulbs come in a variety of spectrums. "Daylight" will usually be in the cool end of the spectrum, between 5,000–6,500K. "Sunlight" is typically neutral, around 3,000–4,000K. Bathroom or kitchen fluoros will typically be in the warm spectrum, 2,500–3,000K. You can also tell what kind of bulb you have when you plug it in. Cool (blue) will glow blue—the bluer the color, the bluer the spectrum. Warm will glow yellowish. Plant / aquarium lights will glow purple, as they are designed to combine red and blue spectrums of light. If you do not plan on switching out your fluorescent lights according to your cycle, you should use plant / aquarium lights, the only downside of which is their lack of lumens: they typically have 1,000 lumens less than other fluoros.

Fluorescent lights are perfect for starting table batches of seeds or clones. You should know that the strongest source of light is in the center of the tubes; it tapers off as it goes to the ends. Fluorescents also provide great side lighting if you mount them vertically in the corners of your grow space. You must keep fluorescents less than an inch away from your plants so that the light is effective. They're virtually just decoration further than five inches away.

I don't recommend using fluorescents after 2–3 weeks of seedling growth, because you have to raise them up almost daily and they lack the intensity to penetrate the canopy.

COMPACT FLUORESCENT LIGHTS

Most commonly known as CFLs, these were first created in the late 1970s but did not become a major commercial product until the mid 90s. The use of advanced technology allowed manufacturers to introduce a different combination of inert gases and, once the electrons from the electric ballast passed through them, they would collide with different types of phosphor powder to produce light. Critics of CFL growing say that it is not possible to grow dense buds with them, but many growers have proved them wrong. However, it is easier to get dense buds using HID lights and CFLs primarily for seedlings, clones, mothers, and vegetative plants.

With CFLs you can create a more even cage of light around your plants. CFLs can be especially convenient for mothers; four 42-watt CFLs will suffice for each mother

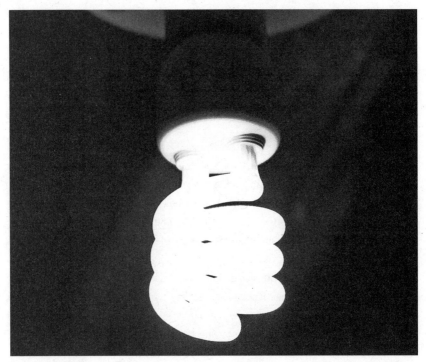

A compact fluorescent light (CFL) like this one is perfect for seedlings, clones, mothers and vegetative plants.

plant. Use two over the top and two on the sides.

Like fluorescents, CFLs come in a wonder of varieties and spectrums. You can find 22–42 watters at Lowes, Home Depot, etc., and they are usually around $10 for the 42-watt. I wouldn't get anything lower than 42 for growing. For higher wattages, you'll have to order online; I've seen them as high as 150-watt for $80. These also work well to be dropped down vertically in between plants to provide side lighting for large gardens. 42-watt CFLs lose their effectiveness further than a foot away, and 150 watts can be efficient up to three feet away.

Note: for maximum light, CFLs should be hung horizontally; this allows a greater surface area of the bulb to shine on the plants—unless the bare bulbs are going to be dropped down in between plants.

HID LIGHTS

High Intensity Discharge lights. HID is a broad classification for several specific types of HID lights. HID lights in general produce the kind of intensity and foliage penetration that is needed when growing cannabis, especially if you are seeking plants with tight internodes and long, dense buds. Make sure you do not plant young seedlings and clones under HID systems if you have to place them around the perimeter of the light.

When handling your HID bulbs, make sure to wipe your greasy fingerprints off of them; as with halogen lights, they may burn so hot that the grease may cause them to explode.

MERCURY VAPOR

Mercury vapor lights are the precursor to metal halide lights. Mercury Vapor (or MV for short) was created circa 1948. The arc tube contains mainly mercury gases, which the electric current passes through to create light. Some manufactures will coat the inside of the protective glass casing to improve light rendition. These lights give off a blue / green glow when viewed from a distance. These are also the cheapest HID lights available. MV contains only mercury in the bulbs, giving them their name.

Contrary to popular belief, MV lights do not produce green spectrum of light. They are high on blue and white spectrums. Modern MV lights have a phosphor coating to make red spectrum available as well. One of the biggest flaws with using MV lights for indoor growing is they are not as efficient as their metal halide counterparts, in terms of lumen to watt ratio. I would not advise purchasing a MV light for your indoor grow, but if you have one lying around and you're low on lumens or balanced spectrum, it wouldn't hurt to add it to your room. MV also produces ultraviolet waves, which is one ingredient for increased trichomes. A 175-watt MV produces around 8,725 lumens.

METAL HALIDE

Metal halides were first created in the 1960s for industrial lighting usage. They operate by passing the electric current (arc) through the arc tube made of quartz because of the intense heat. This arc tube contains a variety of gases: argon, mercury, and a number of metal halides. As with incandescent lights, metal halides (commonly known as MH lights) are protected by an airtight glass container that prevents oxygen from disrupting the arcing process and causing combustion. An upgrade from the MV light, MHs are best for vegetative growth for indoor cannabis growing. MHs come in spectrums ranging from 3K, which is neutral, and 20K, which is very blue in spectrum. The blue spectrum would be the preferred ones for vegetative growth. Metal halide bulbs contain argon, mercury, and metal halides, which give it its name. They give a blue glow when viewed at a distance, as well as up close.

The amount of these gases, as well as the types of halides, control the spectrum of light emitted from different MHs. MHs are less efficient than HPS lights, however, so if you're low on cash and can only afford one type of light fixture, go for the HPS with the Hortilux bulb. Hortilux bulbs have 25–30% increased blue spectrum, making them better for all cycles of growth. MH lights produce a little bit of ultraviolet light due to the mercury in their bulbs, but not enough to matter. MH lights are generally more expensive than HPS lights, ranging from $125–450 dollars.

HIGH PRESSURE SODIUM

High pressure sodium, commonly known as HPS lights, were invented a little bit later than metal halide lights—the 1970s. HPS lights operate similarly to all HID lights. Inside of their arc tube is a mixture comprised primarily of sodium and a bit of mercury. Instead of the arc tube being comprised of quartz, it is made of translucent aluminum oxide. The high level of chemical activity causes pressure—hence the name high-*pressure* sodium. With their spectrum full of red and orange waves, these lights are mistakenly preferred for budding. Buds are bigger than with using an MH, but nowhere close to as big they would be if they had a mixed spectrum.

HPS lights are the most efficient of the HID family. This is why if you're low on cash you should purchase an HPS light, which can grow successful crops from vegetation to budding, especially with a Hortilux bulb. The 600-watt HPS light is the most efficient HPS light of all. 1,000-watt HPS lights are used to light highways and streets, and smaller, 400-watt HPS lights are used to light parking lots and security lights. HPS lights range from $100–400 dollars.

CONVERSION LIGHTS

Conversion bulbs come either as HPS conversion to MH or MH conversion to HPS. Conversion bulbs combine the best of MH and HPS spectrums. This is ideal for people on a limited budget who are wanting to get more blue spectrum for vegetation; this way, they can get a conversion bulb for their HPS fixture and vice versa. However, the conversion bulbs do have their drawbacks, such as lowered efficiency. They produce lower lumens than either a single HPS or MH bulb, but once again, lumens aren't everything.

LED LIGHTS

Short for Light Emitting Diode, these are the futuristic way to grow cannabis. The makers and users of these lights argue that instead of intense wattage, it is simply the right light spectrum that plants use to grow; that you can leave out the enormous number of watts. The advantages of using these lights include: the longest life for any grow light, a decreased power bill, and a cool temperature, so you can put them as close to the plants as fluorescent lights. Personally, I have not seen any conclusive reports of their use for growing cannabis and I'm not completely sold on the idea. They are avail-

These LED lights are the futuristic way to grow cannabis, using the right light spectrum instead of just intense wattage to grow dense bud.

able in only red or blue lights. You had better take out a second loan on your house if you want to grow with these babies. Prices range from $100 to $150 for a single 20-watt light, and for a complete system between $795 to $995! Not to mention that they can only be used on track lighting rails, which will cost an additional $18.00 each.

LIGHT CYCLES

Light cycles play just as an important role in plant growth as the type of light itself. The amount of light Cannabis plants receive on a daily basis directly determines whether they remain in the vegetative growth cycle or start the flowering cycle. The plant interprets a higher number of light hours as a signal to keep on growing vegetatively because it is still summer. When the amount of light decreases from, say, 20/4 or 18/6 to 12/12, this signals to the plant that winter is approaching and it needs to flower. By manipulating light cycles we can control how long the plant remains in vegetation, thereby controlling how big the plant will get before flowering. We can also control how quickly we want the plant to mature, thereby speeding up the growing process from a yearlong process to one that can be finished in four months or less.

Vegetative cycles are basically any light cycle where the amount of hours on is greater than hours off. The most common ones are 24/0 or 18/6. However, I cannot stress enough not to use 24/0. Plants need darkness to function properly—the simple version is that plants gathers energy via photosynthesis in the daytime to use this energy to grow at night. Personally, I have achieved great results using 20/4.

Flowering cycles are a bit more limited. 12/12 is the firm standard for flowering, albeit some growers that would like to sacrifice yield in place of a quicker finishing time will use the 12/12 light cycle for a month or so into flowering and then switch to 11/13 or 10/14.

Light cycles are always measured with the light on being the first number and the light off being the second number. 12/12 is twelve hours on / twelve hours off; 24/0 is 24 hours on / 0 hours off—although most commonly known as 24/7.

WAVELENGTHS

Light wavelength nanometers (nm) and their effect on cannabis.

200–280 nm: UV-C ultraviolet range is extremely toxic to cannabis plants as well as humans.

280–315 nm: Includes UV-B ultraviolet light that is beneficial to cannabis plants.

315–380 nm: Includes UV-A ultraviolet that is neither beneficial nor harmful to cannabis plants.

380–400 nm: The beginning of the visible light spectrum. Chlorophyll production begins.

400–520 nm: Includes violet, blue, and green spectrum waves. Peak absorptions for chlorophyll. Has great influence for photosynthesis.

520–610 nm: Includes green, yellow, and orange spectrum waves. This range is neither bad nor good for cannabis growth.

610–720 nm: Includes orange and red spectrum waves. This range is ideal for photosynthesis.

720–1,000 nm: Little absorption by chlorophyll. Supposedly greatly affects budding and germination.

1000+ nm: Contains only infrared waves (heat).

By this chart we can determine that the majority of light used by cannabis is between 400–700 nanometers.

These custom box hoods are directing all the light straight down, which is good for this style of grow.

LIGHT MOVERS AND HOODS

Moving the lights in your grow room will allow you to reduce the number of lights needed to light a particular area. However, light movers are not all they're cracked up to be. Just remember that when using a light mover, half of the area that is not being lit is going to be in the shadows or receiving indirect lighting. This means that less is more when using light movers. You want to have your light moving as little as possible to still be effective. You want to have your plants to be still receiving a good bit of direct light when using a light mover. This will usually mean moving your light 1–1½ feet at the most. Another important aspect of light movers are that it allows you to place your lamp closer to your plant tops, since the heat does not build up in one spot; however, radiant heat is still an issue, so adjust with caution. One advantage of light movers is that they deliver lighting from different angles, which results in even lighting.

I would advise *against* using circular light movers, except in the use of spinners.

Of course, having the right hood is also important to get the widest footprint while still maintaining the most intensity. Horizontal hoods are more efficient for HID growers than vertical hoods. Horizontal hoods hold the bulb parallel to the canopy; this results in only half of the light having to be reflected by the hood, which is good because reflected light is diffused, loses intensity, and, it is speculated, shortens the life of the bulb. With vertical hoods all of the light emitted from the bulb must strike the hood before being reflected to the canopy below. Vertical hoods also waste light by letting it escape out from the sides.

Most hoods that come with Hydrofarm systems (for example) focus their light over a very small area and do not disperse heat evenly, creating hot spots. These hoods are similar to boxes. Enclosed hoods like the Hydrofarm hoods must be placed further away because the heat builds—unless you are using air-cooled lights.

For spreading light evenly over a wider area, parabolic hoods are best, it should be noted that these are vertical hoods and, for reasons mentioned above, are only sufficient for the vegetative phase of growth. These hoods are similar to a circle where the bulb usually faces downwards. Batwing reflectors are an example of an open reflector which dissipates heat fairly well because it is not enclosed; they spread light well east to west, but poorly north to south. It is usually easy to modify your hood to perfectly suit your needs; to do this you will need some tin snips and Mylar. You can then shape your hood / reflector to what suits your area best.

A good quality hood will have dimpled aluminum instead of slick chrome surface. The dimpled aluminum surface diffuses light so that few or no hot spots are created. This means they can be placed closer to the plants without harming them.

Having air-cooled hoods allows you to place your light closer to your plants, say less than 8 inches. You must hook up your air-cooled hoods to your outtake system via ductwork, which can be a pain but it's worth it if your grow room temperature is getting too hot to sustain good growth.

Light movers with air-cooled hoods are an even bigger pain because you have to account for the slack in the ductwork.

It is a good idea to measure out a piece of string and attach it to your hood, say 1 ½ feet long for a 1,000-watt light. You want the end of the string to be at the top of your plants. As the plants grow, you will know how much to raise the hood.

To utilize all the available light in your grow room you should consider installing a shelf around the bottom perimeter of your room. This allows you to have smaller plants at the same level as your taller, more mature plants. Another option is to stack the smaller plants onto empty five gallon buckets turned upside down or cinder blocks until the desired height has been reached.

In order for all plants and all parts of the plant to receive the same amount of light, you should manually rotate them every day or every couple of days. Rotate not only the container, but also the plants' places in the grow room.

This complex rope and pulley system allows you to raise and lower your lights, which helps ensure your grow system always has the right light distance.

LIGHT DISTANCE

The distance between the light and the plants is just as important as the intensity of the light itself. For example, a 1,000-watt Hortilux HPS emits 145,000 initially. One foot away is roughly 140,000 lumens; two feet away is roughly 36,000 lumens; three feet away is roughly 18,000 lumens; four feet away is roughly 12,000 lumens; and five feet away is roughly 8,000 lumens, based on the Inverse Square Law. So, as you can see, a 1,000-watt Hortilux HPS is a great fit for a 4x4-foot area; it provides just over 9,000 watts per square foot, but in a 5x5-foot area that is just 5,800 watts per square feet. Light intensity pretty much doubles when the light is moved within 6 inches of the canopy, this is true for all wattages of light. This also demonstrates why an even canopy is so important: so that the light is the same intensity all across the tops of the colas / plants. Plants that are spaced too close together will compete with each other for light, growing tall and skinny.

SPINNING LIGHT TECHNOLOGY
Contributed by The_Seed
At first glance, you might think that Life Light Technologies (LLT) spinning lights are actually some kind of science fiction type of lighting. In reality, spinning the lights give you layers of benefits that we'll go into here in this chapter.

Traditional lighting systems for growing have pretty much been the same for decades now: same shapes and styles, air-cooled and not. The ballasts that run the lights are pretty much the same as always: 60 Hz magnetic ballast with a transformer, a capacitor, and an igniter, depending on if it was MH or HPS.

People have no idea how messed up traditional lighting systems are. Horizontal reflectors are destroying your light, HPS light is killing your photosynthesis, and the 60 Hz ballast is wasting most of your energy.

Life Light makes 4-arm and 6-arm lighting arrays that spin at 30 RPM. There's a dual lamp rotator as well that holds two lamps opposite each other, and that one spins at a speedy 60 RPM. The system that you're going to want to get is going to depend on how much space you have, and how tall your plants are going to get.

There is a lot of science and physics that go into why the systems do everything they do, and it would probably glaze you all over like a sugary donut to try to absorb it all. The most important thing about this new technology is that it actually works, and does everything you would want a plant light to do.

LIGHT DELIVERY
Spinning the light sends light everywhere into the garden so you can get more photosynthesis and more yield because of it. The light can penetrate into the canopy and give you growth in the places you've been stripping away because of the limitations of using a horizontal light that just sits there and shines down like a flashlight.

Another huge feature is that you can keep the lights closer to the plants than ever before, and not burn them because the system is spinning. This means more light energy to the plants for them to benefit from. For those of you who know inverse square law, you know that at one foot you get full output from the light, and at two feet you get ¼ of that light. Now you can keep the light as close as possible, allowing you to get more light energy, because you're closer than a foot.

As the system spins, it makes a convection current that sucks heat away from the plants before it can build up on them. Every grow room should have a basic temperature and humidity controller and exhaust fans to dump the excess heat. Heat is pulled away from the plants, the hood itself, and keeps it from building up on trays, containers, and everything else in the room.

A FEW THINGS THEY DIDN'T TEACH YOU AT THE GROW SHOPS

Photosynthesis has been overlooked as one of the most important elements of the grow room. When you're getting a lot of photosynthesis and chlorophyll, you also get more sugars and more vigorous growth.

Photosynthesis stops on the leaf surface at 5,500 footcandles. That's huge for every one of you that's running a 1,000-watt system thinking that it's helping you. The truth is that 1,000-watt lights are shutting down your photosynthesis and making your growing life a lot more trouble. Most books like these would advise you to run 10,000 footcandles at the canopy. Anything over 5,500 footcandles shuts down photosynthesis and is converted to heat by the plant, so you don't get all the photosynthesis that you could have gotten.

HPS light is the wrong color for plants. It only has 22% of the sun's quality and clarity, and has the least amount of energy of all the colors of the spectrum. Don't use it! Plants and living things have evolved with all the colors of visible light, not just the reddish ones. The hydroponic industry didn't reinvent evolution and what makes plants photosynthesize. For best results, you should mix your spectrum with both a MH and a HPS light. Another option is to use a conversion bulb.

FREQUENCY

Frequency is something important to know about, but only a very few are actually talking about it. If you didn't know already, the electricity that cycles off of your wall does so at 60 Hz, one hertz equaling one cycle per second. Europe cycles at 50 Hz. It's very different, and that's why you can't plug your U.S. made products into a European outlet. Every street light, every outlet, and most lighting have always been at 60 Hz. All the lamps for all those ballasts were made for 60 Hz ballasts: they're 60 Hz lamps!

Enter the electronic ballasts, little companies that saw an opportunity in China and took advantage of it. These electronic ballasts operate at 30,000–45,000 Hz. A radio station operates at 600 watts at 30,000 Hz—now imagine the guy who has

These control panels allow easy access to the six ballasts, timer and CO2 control.

10 of them: he has a big radio station. Electromagnetic interference (EMI) can disrupt radio, broadband, plasma screens, CB's, ham radios, and the list goes on. Make sure the electronic ballast you buy is FCC compliant; if it's not, keep on looking.

The sun that shines on the earth—the visible spectrum—hits the Earth at a whopping 400,000 to 800,000 Hz. Now, if we want light to behave like sunlight, we better give it some power! The Sun is massive, shining, and beats down on to the earth with cosmic rays and such. A traditional lighting system runs at 60 Hz and, as we learned, that's nowhere near the 800 KHz the sun shines on the earth. Life Light offers a ballast that operates at up to 300,000 Hz. That's half of the Sun's usable energy on the visible spectrum! That's like cranking the light power onto the maximum setting.

Another huge thing they didn't tell you at the grow shop is that it takes red light and blue light to make photosynthesis. If you only use HPS light, you're only getting half of all the photosynthesis and chlorophyll that you could. You must have a fuller spectrum light to get all the benefits you can. Basically, plants want light like the sun offers, like the kind they evolved with for eons.

SPECTRUM

PAR (Parabolic Aluminized Reflector) light is visible light—the light that shines on the earth. That's what plants use and want; they just don't need all of the energy that the sun delivers. We can't pick and choose what colors we want to use. Plants use all the colors. Photobiologists have learned that plants do absorb green light and use it for photosynthesis along with the other colors of the spectrum. The old myth that plants reflect green light is only partially true—it does reflect green light when the plants are making chlorophyll. The world is changing all around us. What we know and thought we knew is always shifting.

Spectrum plays a key factor in the spinning lights. Now that you have the light delivery device, you want to have the right quality of light delivered. On Life Light's Star Mixer 4-arm systems, you use lamps with 4 different color temperatures (the Kelvin Scale). They offer a 3K, 4K, 6.4K, and 10K lamp that between them are like the spectrum in four pieces. When you spin the light, all four colors get blended together and are delivered in a pulse of light to the plants with the entire spectrum. The sun pulses light, so it's the most natural way to deliver the light without destroying it in a reflector.

So let's recap. The Life Light delivery systems have three main features that together make it an amazing photosynthesis machine.

Distribution of light to the plants.

The frequency or power of that light.

The spectral quality of the light

Put these three things together into the Life Light systems, and watch the fun begin.

A FEW QUICK TIPS ON USING THE GEAR

Use a light meter! At 5,500 FC, photosynthesis stops, so if you want them to grow you might want to set the canopy FCs at 4,000–5,500 FC or so.

Use a temperature gun! Every degree of leaf temperature over 76 °F, you lose 10% photosynthesis. That means at 86 degrees of leaf temperature, that leaf is done photosynthesizing, and the leaf is now a little radiator trying to stay alive. Get the temperature gun right down onto the leaf; don't try beaming it from 8 feet away or something, unless you like calculating the math for the distance.

Don't use so many chemicals, additives and unnecessary enhancers! Now that you can get more photosynthesis, you don't need so much plant food and extra products. The only reason growers need most of those enhancements anyway is because they aren't getting enough light energy. You still want to have something going in the fertilizer when you hit those trigger points, and those are easy to find in the marketplace.

Quit using HPS light! It's the worst thing you can do for your plants, and kills half of your photosynthesis and chlorophyll production. How, you ask? Photobiology proved in 1950 that it takes red light and blue light to fire the light harvesting complexes in the thylakoid membranes in the leaf surface. Does that sound like a mouthful? Well, it is, but it just proves that your HPS light is worthless for plants, by itself. But my plants look so good under my sodiums! I can hear you saying now. Well, there was a time when typewriters, 8-tracks, and cassettes were considered the best, too. Think about it, 8-track was once state of the art technology. Until you heard a CD you wouldn't know how good it was. Plants will adapt to whatever environment you put them into; it doesn't mean that it was the optimal environment. In the best grow op you've seen the grower was lucky to be getting 25% photosynthesis; now imagine getting much more.

BARE BULBS

There is something to be said for bare bulb growing. There is some controversy regarding that of hoods and reflectors. When using hoods and reflectors, the heat builds up which diminishes the life of the bulb and creates more heat for the plants.

Using bare bulbs, all the light is emitted in a 360° pattern around the bulb. The heat rises away from the bulb and plants, going upwards, and is not trapped in by reflectors. This is ideal for dropping down the bulb in between plants to create side lighting. However, for mounting the bulb above the plants, a hood / reflector that holds the bulb horizontally is best used for this purpose. It is a good idea to drill between 10 to 12 quarter inch holes in your reflector to let heat that has built up escape.

If you are noticing that your light seems dimmer than usual, or that your buds are not as full, and yet all growing conditions are being met, it is likely because your bulb needs to be replaced. HID bulbs need to be replaced every 5,000 hours, or every 10 months, whichever comes first; common CFLs need to be replaced every 3,000 hours, or every year, whichever comes first; and common fluorescent lights will need to be replaced every 1,000–2,000 hours, or every 6 months. These times will vary depending on the condition of your grow room—mainly moisture and the quality of the manufacturing.

This cola is starting to pack on weight. Cannabis is a beautiful plant when it is in flower.

A nice, clean carbon scrubber air filtration system. Great for blocking smells and keeping the air clean.

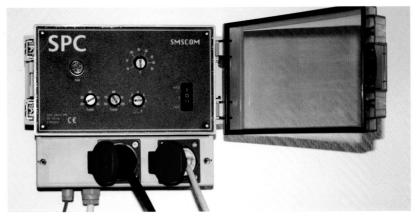

SPC environmental control panel. This is vital for a well-organized grow.

Hanna pH/EC Pen. A must have for all growers.

Here we can see eight LED panels wired together.

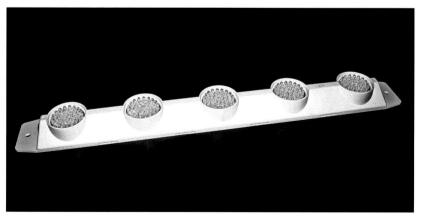

A single pre-made LED panel. Some believe that LED is the future of growing.

This grower is taking the time to build their room correctly, and will reap the rewards later on.

The rewards! This grower is wise to stake his maturing plants.

This grower is using CFL's to keep down the heat in the small room.

A small, make shift grow room with a light that can be raised and lowered.

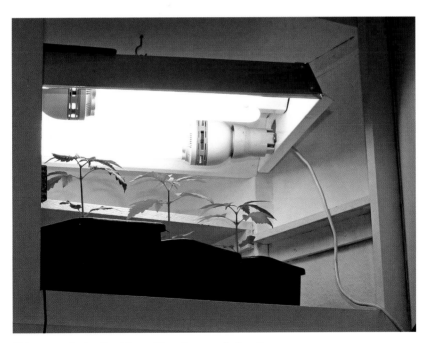

This grower is starting his seedlings in a small closet!

Over 500 clones in this walk in closet!

A great idea for clones is to have a clone box. The basic design should allow as much light as possible to enter the box while maintaining high humidity levels. Be aware of dampening off though.

DWC hydroponic system in a bathroom. Note the fan for air circulation and the support stakes.

Ebb and Flow table in a SOG grow. The organization is perfect so the harvest should be great.

The Perfect Attic Grow! Over 8K in lighting! The fans are necessary to circulate the air in such an enclosed space.

Basement growing often offers inconspicuous places for your plants to grow. Be aware of plant location if you have visitors, though.

Yes, like the hanging gardens of Ancient Babylon. This technique is more popular with hydroponic gardeners but this grower is doing it old school in dirt!

Here we see an inline fan mounted in between the carbon scrubber and 6" duct. This will ensure that the air is being replenished at least 3 times a minute.

A control panel with two industrial timers. Planning and organization are key to large scale operations.

This grower is mixing a ton-o-soil and adding in his special blend of amendments and additives.

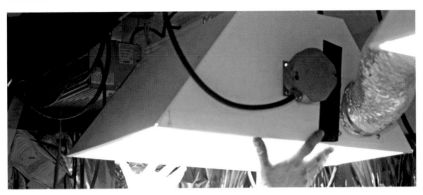

Box hood with air extraction will prevent over heating, but it is cumbersome to move.

Here we see a CO_2 generator. The thin, metallic piece is a pilot light, and the brass one is actually the burner. This unit can have up to 4 burners, but this generator only has one going.

Two fresh carbon scrubbers, ready to be installed.

Overview of seedlings on the right and clones on the left.

When this door closes it looks like a typical bedroom.

But when you walk inside, it's a completely different story.

SOG grow with two gallon pots. These plants are easy to move and care for because of the appropriate containers.

Overhead view of the same SOG garden. It's important to remember that you need to be able to access all of your plants, so plan accordingly.

An ebb and flow table before plant placement. Good ventilation is needed to keep the heat down.

After a few weeks of growth. This is how clean your grow room should be.

A few weeks later. Notice the rapid growth.

The grower has trimmed all the sucker growth from the bottom of the plants. Some growers refer to this as "lollipopping."

These lights have the ballasts attached directly to the hood. Popular with European growers.

Air filtration, control panel and water leads all neatly laid out. No doubt this grower has had some experience.

This girl is ready to be transplanted. Note that the sucker growth has been removed.

ENERGY USAGE

There are several things you can do to decrease the amount of energy used in your home. If your hot water heater is electric, replace it with a high efficiency water heater or switch to gas. Set your hot water temperature for 130 °F. Upgrade your central heating and air to a more efficient unit. Convert your electric stove to gas. Of course, these are drastic and costly ways to decrease your energy usage. Below are some easier options.

You can also replace your common household incandescent bulbs with lower wattage CFL lights. This will save around ten dollars per month on your electricity bill. Avoid using halogen floodlights, as these are major electricity consumers.

Use a laptop computer instead of a desktop; desktop units use much more power than laptops.

Try to use a smaller T.V. instead of turning on that big screen, or listen to the radio instead.

Use battery-operated appliances if possible.

Try to do fewer loads of laundry.

Try to use your microwave less and your oven more, if it is gas; if not, you can use a propane grill.

Follow those rules that your mom always griped at you about: turn the lights off when you leave a room, etc.

The same amount of power required to turn on a standard T-12 48-inch fluorescent light is the same amount of power needed to run that light for three hours. Meaning that if you are going to turn on a fluorescent light, you can use it for three hours without it using any more additional energy.

You may also run a generator (a 4,000-watt generator is just under $1,000), but with the increasing cost of gasoline this is not an effective alternative anymore. Not to mention the amount of noise that most generators produce.

Without drawing suspicion, you can operate one 1,000-watt HID light per bedroom in your home, meaning that you can have up to three 1,000-watt HID lights in a three-bedroom house.

Just remember that growers are the electric company's best friends. They are the customers that use the highest amount of electricity, and it doesn't benefit the company if you go to jail. If you are a good customer and pay your bills on time, they are not going to be ratting you out to the police without a court order.

If you or a family member is not home during the day and the meter reader stops by and sees your meter whizzing around with nobody home, this will raise a few eyebrows.

So if you or a family member are not usually home during the day, you should set

This big HID with a good reflector hood is the crowning glory of a well-organized grow room. The fluorescent lights in the corner are set at different light distances for young plants at different stages of growth. This is known as the perpetual grow system.

your room to be off during the day and on at night. This, however, is a double edged sword, because if a curious neighbor or police officer wants to take an illegal midnight visit to your premises while you and your family are sleeping and sees your meter whizzing by with every light in the house off, this will raise a few eyebrows as well, and when these eyebrows get raised it will more than likely to lead to your loss of freedom. So, pick your poison.

| COST PER kWh | 12 HOUR DAYS | | 18 HOUR DAYS | | AVG. GROW |
	day	month	day	month	*3.5-months
$0.02	$0.24	$7.20	$0.36	$10.80	$29.70
$0.03	$0.36	$10.80	$0.54	$16.20	$44.55
$0.04	$0.48	$14.40	$0.72	$21.60	$59.40
$0.05	$0.60	$18.00	$0.90	$27.00	$74.25
$0.06	$0.72	$21.60	$1.08	$32.40	$89.10
$0.07	$0.84	$25.20	$1.26	$37.80	$103.95
$0.08	$0.96	$28.80	$1.44	$43.20	$118.80
$0.09	$1.08	$32.40	$1.62	$48.60	$133.65
$0.10	$1.20	$36.00	$1.80	$54.00	148.50

*Based on 14 weeks total: 5 weeks of 18/6 and 9 weeks of 12/12.

The above chart is an example of how much you're spending on your electricity for your grow room.

Whatever you do, *do not steal electricity*!

I know it may be tempting after seeing these numbers, but just think about how much money you're saving without having to go out and buy your own supply. Not to mention how much better the quality is. Speaking in terms of money, it is worth it in the long run.

This rainwater was collected outside my house in a bucket. The pH and TDS levels checked out, so it was ready to use on my plants.

Chapter 10

Water

Water is one of the essentials for life. Water accounts for up to 95% of the weight of some plants. Water supplies oxygen to roots, and without oxygen the plant's roots would suffocate and the entire plant would die. In order for a plant to grow properly, the roots must be thoroughly saturated and then allowed to dry before watering again. How quickly it takes for your medium to dry will depend on your medium's composition, the amount watered, the size of your containers, and the size of the plant.

TAP WATER
This is most freely available and widely used water source for growers. The amount of pH and the kinds of minerals and pollutants in your water will differ from county to county and state to state. Most counties will provide a yearly assessment of the quality of the tap water; if not you can call your county water department and ask for a Drinking Water Analysis. This report will tell you the TDS/ PPM of your tap water and also what kind of nutrients / minerals are floating around in it. Before using tap water for your plants, you should first run the water out of the tap for about 30 seconds before adding the water to a bucket—this will stop the heavy metal build up from your pipes going into the water you are feeding your plants. The reason you want the water in a bucket is to let the chlorine evaporate before using. Chlorine will evaporate in 24 to 48 hours of sitting in an open air environment without a lid. Using an air stone works best. Some government water supplies are using a new chemical that can only be evaporated by sitting in the sun for several hours, so beware. Organic growers should take extra precautions to ensure that the chlorine has been evaporated from their water supply—just one watering with chlorinated water can destroy the soil ecology that you have worked so hard to create and that your plants are thriving in. If you can, add an air stone to your bucket, or if not make sure you enrich your water with oxygen prior to watering.

You can easily do this by transferring the water from one bucket to another; two or three times will be sufficient.

If you're lucky, your county will send you a yearly report without you having to ask, and if you do have to request one, then be discrete about it.

DISTILLED WATER

This is the water you want to use for starting seedlings and clones because it is free from any nutrients, impurities, and minerals, meaning it has zero TDS (Total Dissolved Solids) / PPM (Parts Per Million) and EC (Electrical Conductivity). Distillation is simply boiling the water and re-condensing the steam in a clean container, which leaves behind all the impurities. You will still have to pH your distilled water before using it and enrich it with oxygen.

MINERAL WATER

This is water taken directly from a natural source, such as a mountain stream. Mineral water contains a large amount of micronutrients; calcium, sodium, magnesium, and iron are the most abundant. Mineral water is not commonly used for growing because of its high TDS / PPM and its unknown nutrient amounts and content. There have been cases of growers using mineral water with great success, but I cannot advise you to do the same because of the unknown sources of the water. Technically speaking, tap water could also be classified as mineral water.

REVERSE OSMOSIS WATER

This is the purest form of water available. Reverse osmosis (RO) is used to remove all the impurities, dissolved solids, viruses, bacteria, etc, and it is accomplished by passing the water through a semi permeable membrane under pressure. This is the hardest and most expensive water to come by. RO water will still have to be pH balanced, but usually not as much as other types of water.

RAINWATER

Ideally, rainwater is the most natural form of water available and will not have to be pH'd. However, because of pollution from industrial factories, forest fires, vehicles, and so on, your rain may be acidic. Rain from rural or secluded areas will be the cleanest. To check the acidity of your rainwater, gather it in a bucket or other container and test with a pH meter and TDS / EC / PPM meter.

All raw or naked water should contain less than 50 PPM. If your reading is higher than this you should filter your water before using. There is a good chance that there are heavy metals present which will adversely affect your plants.

Check the pH and chlorine levels in your water, especially tap water, before you use it.

pH

The best range for your pH is between 6.3–6.8 in soil and 6.0–6.4 in hydro; this will allow for uptake of all the nutrients needed for cannabis to develop properly.

pH is the logarithmic measure of hydrogen ion concentration. Danish biochemist Soren Peter Lauritz coined the term in 1909. The "p" stands for the German word *potenz*, meaning that pH is the abbreviation for "power of Hydrogen." A pH of 7 is considered neutral because the concentration of hydrogen ions is exactly equal to the concentration of hydroxide ions produced by dissociation of the water. Increasing the concentration of hydrogen ions higher than $1.0 \times 10\text{-}7$ M lowers the pH of the water; decreasing the hydrogen ions lower than $1.0 \times 10\text{-}7$ M increases the pH of the water.

The best way to control your pH is by using store bought pH up and pH down. No brand of pH solution is really better than any other, so just get what whatever is cheapest. Use an eyedropper and add roughly half a dropper per gallon of water. Some will require more or less, depending on the brand and pH of the water. The water will show a slight change in the pH a minute or so after applying. For correct results however, check 20 minutes later. This is true for every time you want to lower or raise your pH. You should apply what you think is the right dose of pH solution, stir, and then leave to sit for an hour or so. Always rinse your pH meter in some clean water—I prefer to use distilled—and make sure you dry the probe before using again. This is very important to get an accurate reading.

The first few times you add pH up or pH down to your water, do it a couple drops at a time, stir, and let it adjust for 20 minutes. Write down how many drops you add each time and repeat this process until you come to your desired pH. This way, you'll know more or less how many drops to add each time instead of using a lot of pH up or down to compensate for adding too much or too little.

When checking your pH, place the meter in the water up to the maximum height indicated by the line on the meter. Stir the water with the meter and then return the meter to the center of the container. Wait a minute or however long it takes for the reading to stabilize and you will have the true reading of your pH.

I strongly suggest that you use the store bought pH solutions, but you can make your own.

To raise the pH, make the water more alkaline: use lye or sodium hydroxide. The most available source of sodium hydroxide is Crystal Drain Cleaner, which is 100% sodium hydroxide, and which is available at your local home improvement store.

To lower the pH, make the water more acidic: use sulfuric acid, a.k.a. battery acid or muriatic acid. Sulfuric acid is available at auto parts stores and muriatic acid is available at some hardware stores. You can also use white vinegar from the grocery store but it will require a much higher amount.

The above methods are neutral so they will not change the amount of nitrogen, potassium, or any other nutrient.

Use extreme caution when employing these methods: always apply the acid to the water and not the water to the acid, as this can cause the acid to splatter. Always wear eye protection, or a full mask if you have it, and of course thick rubber gloves.

If you find that your pH is unbalanced you should slowly adjust .1 –.3 notches at a time. If you adjust more than this, the shock has a great chance of turning your plants hermaphroditic.

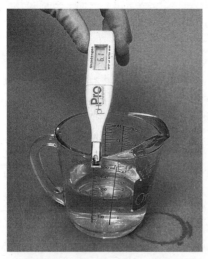

Use a good pH tester to make sure your water is good to use. Here we've got a pH of 6.1 which should be good for my hydro plants.

EC AND PPM / TDS

EC Electrical Conductivity is a measurement of electrically-charged nutrient ions in a solution. Pure water will not conduct electricity. Water usually conducts electricity because it is full of impurities—in our case, electrically charged nutrient ions. The two black dots on the end of a nutrient probe are called electrodes. When these are placed in a solution, an electrical current passes from one electrode, through the water, to the other electrode, and in so doing it counts the number of electrically charged ions present. This represents the units measured. EC is sometimes referred to as Conductivity Factor, or CF.

MS / CM2 Millisiemen per square centimeter; this is the common unit used to measure EC.

TDS Total Dissolved Solids is a measurement of the dissolved solids floating around in your water, meaning all the nutrients and minerals in the water.

The best way to control pH is by using store bought pH up and pH down.

PPM Parts Per Million is a form of measuring TDS. TDS and PPM are basically one and the same. PPM measures the TDS in the form of parts per million.

Now you can either purchase an EC meter or a TDS meter. EC meters only tell the measurements in EC, which, through a little backwards math, you can convert to PPM / TDS. Or, you can purchase a TDS meter that will give its readings in PPM, and then easily convert to EC.

I prefer a TDS meter to an EC meter because PPM is really what you're after, not EC. Plus, it is easier to convert PPM to EC than EC to PPM.

For seedlings, a feeding of 350–550 PPM (U.S.) is optimum. Typically, though, seedlings should not need any nutrients other than what's in the medium but for soilless growers the aforementioned PPM is ideal.

For vegetation a mild feeding is 550–700 PPM, and a heavy feeding is 750–1,000 PPM.

For budding, a mild feeding is 600–800 PPM, and a heavy feeding is 850–1,300 PPM.

The highest feeding I would do is 1,500 PPM; anything above 1,800 PPM is going to burn your plants.

Meter Maintenance

Periodic maintenance is necessary to ensure that your meter remains accurate. When testing water that contains nutrients, a film remains on the glass bulb; over time, this film will develop more layers and you will not be able to remove it easily. It will distort your readings and ruin your meter.

Parts Per Million (PPM) Conversions

EC	U.S.	Europe	Australia	CF
ms/cm	0.5 PPM	0.64 PPM	0.70 PPM	0
0.1	50 PPM	64 PPM	70 PPM	1
0.2	100 PPM	128 PPM	140 PPM	2
0.3	150 PPM	192 PPM	210 PPM	3
0.4	200 PPM	256 PPM	280 PPM	4
0.5	250 PPM	320 PPM	350 PPM	5
0.6	300 PPM	384 PPM	420 PPM	6
0.7	350 PPM	448 PPM	490 PPM	7
0.8	400 PPM	512 PPM	560 PPM	8
0.9	450 PPM	576 PPM	630 PPM	9
1.0	500 PPM	640 PPM	700 PPM	10
1.1	550 PPM	704 PPM	770 PPM	11
1.2	600 PPM	768 PPM	840 PPM	12
1.3	650 PPM	832 PPM	910 PPM	13
1.4	700 PPM	896 PPM	980 PPM	14
1.5	750 PPM	960 PPM	1050 PPM	15
1.6	800 PPM	1024 PPM	1120 PPM	16
1.7	850 PPM	1088 PPM	1190 PPM	17
1.8	900 PPM	1152 PPM	1260 PPM	18
1.9	950 PPM	1216 PPM	1330 PPM	19
2.0	1000 PPM	1280 PPM	1400 PPM	20
2.1	1050 PPM	1334 PPM	1470 PPM	21
2.2	1100 PPM	1408 PPM	1540 PPM	22
2.3	1150 PPM	1472 PPM	1610 PPM	23
2.4	1200 PPM	1536 PPM	1680 PPM	24
2.5	1250 PPM	1600 PPM	1750 PPM	25
2.6	1300 PPM	1664 PPM	1820 PPM	26
2.7	1350 PPM	1728 PPM	1890 PPM	27
2.8	1400 PPM	1792 PPM	1960 PPM	28
2.9	1450 PPM	1856 PPM	2030 PPM	29
3.0	1500 PPM	1920 PPM	2100 PPM	30
3.1	1550 PPM	1984 PPM	2170 PPM	31
3.2	1600 PPM	2048 PPM	2240 PPM	32

Note: there are three different scales for measuring PPM. In America—500 PPM scale—Hanna or Milwaukee; In Europe—640 PPM scale—Eutech; In Australia—700 PPM scale—Truncheon.

After each time you use your meter, you should swirl it around in a cup of distilled water. Dry with a paper towel as best as possible, making sure to clean the glass bulb well. Then place the protective cap back in place to store.

If you notice your meter is jumping around when giving the readings, you should clean your glass bulb. To do this, soak a Q-tip with isoprene alcohol (rubbing alcohol), and clean the bulb as much as possible. Again, swirl it around in a fresh cup of distilled water and dry thoroughly.

After this period, calibrate your meter and your readings should stabilize quickly, instead of, for example, going from 3.2 to 6.8 and bouncing around in between.

This method can be applied to both pH and TDS / EC / PPM meters.

FLUSHING

Flushing, also known as leaching, is a process that attempts to leach out the nutrients / salt deposits left in your soil from feeding your plants—although salt deposits should be next to nothing because we have been using organic nutrients. Flushing is a vital part of any grow, and if you do not ever flush your plants, heavy salts will accumulate, especially with chemical grows, affecting the pH of your medium as well as locking out nutrients from your plants. The plants will not be able to absorb any nutrients and will begin to show deficiencies, in which case you will probably increase your feeding, which will only worsen your problem. "When in doubt, flush it out": this is especially true with growers that use chemicals to feed their plants.

Contrary to popular belief, you should not just flush your medium days before harvest. You should be flushing every four weeks or after every third feeding. Meaning that you water, water, feed (one), water, water, feed (two), water, water, feed (three), *flush*.

This leaches out any accumulated salts from past feedings and keeps your grow operating smoothly. Flushing is an attempt to separate the nutrient ions from the grow medium / roots.

Incorporating flushing into your water cycle will also allow you to feed at a higher PPM, or more often than you would otherwise. Just remember to adjust your flushing to accommodate for the increased level of nutrients.

Now there are different levels / amounts of flushing. For your periodic flushing throughout your plant's life cycle, you should do a "light" flushing with twice the amount of properly pH'd water as your container. This means that if you're growing in a 5-gallon container you should flush with 10 gallons of pH'd water, or if you're growing in a 2-gallon container you should flush with 4 gallons of pH'd water, and so on.

If a problem should arise in your grow, you should flush with three times the amount of water per container. This is a "normal" flushing. If you're growing in a

Flushing is a vital part of any grow. Be sure to flush your plants regularly in order to get rid of excess nutrient / salt deposits in the soil.

5-gallon container, you should flush with 15 gallons of pH'd water.

For your final flush before harvest you should perform a "heavy" flush. This is done by using four or five times the amount of water per container, and is an extensive process that should be performed at least 7 days (ideally 10 days) before your intended harvest. In a 5-gallon container you will be flushing with at least 20 gallons of properly pH'd water. Most growers and "experts" will say to only flush with two or three times the container amount, but smart growers know that the more flushes the better the final product will be.

Because of this extensive flushing, your plant will begin to use all of its stored nutrients, which will result in a much better, cleaner, and tastier smoke.

Hints and Tips for Flushing

It is a good idea to add one tsp of food grade hydrogen peroxide (35%) to each gallon of water that you use to flush. This will help sterilize the growing medium and give a fresh start if any bad microbes or insect larva are present in your medium. It is speculated that the hydrogen peroxide will help to separate the ionic bond between the nutrients and growing medium.

There are several products on the market that reportedly help to separate the bond between nutrients and grow mediums by attaching to the nutrient and separating it from the medium, which then allows you to leach it easily from the medium. One such product is Clearex, from Botanicare. However, note that some growers have used this product and, frankly, could not find a discernable difference in the taste of their buds.

I am flushing this soil with water and food grade hydrogen peroxide (35%) to get rid of any harmful bacteria or nutrient / salt buildups.

Some people like to flush their plants by submerging the entire container in a larger container with pH'd water until air bubbles stop rising from the container that houses their plant. Once the air bubbles stop rising, they remove their plant and let it drain. This proves to be a very effective method of performing a light–moderate flushing, however, it is not appropriate for a final flush.

Recently, there has been some debate online whether or not flushing does anything at all. For those growers that think that flushing is a useless gimmick, I implore you to do the following.

Take clones of the same plant, mix the same medium for both plants and mix them *thoroughly*. Plant both clones in the same size container and water with the same batch of nutrients at the same time. Now, in the last two weeks of growth, flush clone A properly and do not flush clone B. Apply nutrients as needed for clone B. Harvest both plants and once the buds are dry, take one bud from clone A and one from clone B and water cure them for one day in separate containers (or all the way through if you would like). Don't forget to keep everything labeled. Be sure to note the PPM of the water before placing the bud in the container full of water. After 24 hours, remove the buds and take the PPM of both containers, making sure to clean your meter in between testing. Your results should indicate that the flushed bud is much lower in PPMs than that of the unflushed. Which means that there are fewer solids in your buds, which means the smoke is "healthier" for you because you are not smoking heavy metals. This test is much more responsive if done by chemical growers versus organic growers, but you will certainly see a difference either way.

Chapter 11

Seeds and Seedlings

In recent years, the cannabis scene has expanded triple fold. Cannabis, commonly known as marijuana, has become a mainstream pop-icon while retaining its dubious illegality. However, there have been some enlightened strides towards legalizing, or at least decriminalizing, cannabis in places such as the Netherlands, Spain, England, Canada, and Holland, as well as the West Coast of the United States. With the noose around the neck of cannabis slowly being loosened since the Reagan Administration, many seed breeders have emerged and are now openly selling seeds to the masses. These breeders sell seeds that are generally crosses between C. Sativa, C. Indica, C. Indica variant Afghanica, and occasionally C. Ruderalis for its auto-flowering gene. Very few breeders still sell pure landrace varieties.

The parentage of the seed is the sole factor in determining the potential quality of the seed. The male gamete and the female gamete (haploid) will combine to form a diploid zygote (a new individual). These genes will determine the size, root production, floral pattern, leaf structure, stem size, and cannabinoid content, as well as many other traits, such as flavor.

Healthy seeds come in all colors and sizes, from light to dark brown, grey, tan, even black, and all of these seeds may have stripes or mottled spots on their outer shell. They can have only a few stripes (light striping) or many stripes (heavy striping); the same is true for mottled spots. Seeds that are pitch black are overripe and the embryo is dead. Immature seeds range in color from a light green to white. These seeds were not allowed to fully mature and the outer shell as well as the embryo are not completely developed. These seeds can be easily crushed between two fingers. Such seeds have poor germination rates and as such should be overlooked. Space Queen is one of the few exceptions to this rule. Space Queen seeds will always be white, no matter how long they are allowed to stay within the seed bract.

The Johnny Blaze seed is a small seed which is characteristic of the F2 generation

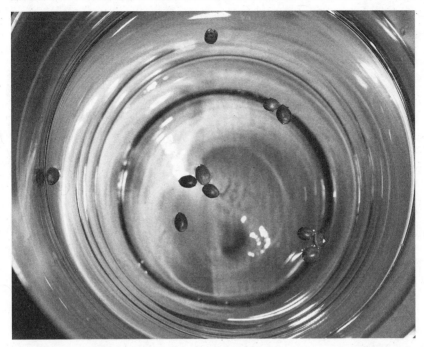

Use the sink or float method to check the vitality and likely germination rates of your seeds.

or later. Since the plant has lost hybrid vigor, the calyx sizes decrease, which dictate the size of the seed. The JTR seed is an example of a normal medium sized F1 seed. The landrace seed is the largest because it has the largest calyxes. A good rule of thumb is that the seed size will determine the size of the calyx. Bigger calyxes equal a better plant because they hold more trichomes and generally contain more THC. Large seeds are also an indication of a potential landrace Sativa. Remember, small seed equals small calyxes, large seed equals large calyxes.

However, this is not always the case, and some great plants / strains have come from the smallest of seeds.

Seeds have the highest germination rates when they are planted two to three weeks from their initial harvest. After that the germination rates fall 3–10% depending on storage techniques each subsequent year that the seeds are left unused.

A good method for finding out the vitality of seeds is to drop them in a jar of water. Hold the seed about five to six inches above the water and release the seed. The seeds that fall immediately down to the bottom or falls soon after are the best seeds. These seeds have full embryos that take up all the space inside the shell. There is no room for air pockets to develop which would keep the seeds on the surface of the water.

Always research the strain of cannabis that you purchase to be sure it has the qualities you want.

BUYING SEEDS

The rise of the cannabis seed breeder has given the grower a wider variety than ever before to choose from for their desired plant. These breeders have given their seeds catchy names such as Pure Power Plant, Nebula, Chronic, etc., in an attempt to market them. Do not be swayed by such names; look at the breeders' descriptions and do your own research on the plant, such as looking up grow logs and smoke reports, to see if you like what you see. Also, be sure that you can replicate or come close to the same growing conditions that your researched plant was grown in, because the plants that you grow may look nothing like the plants the other grower grew. Buy seeds that *you* want to grow! Not what's popular. Remember, you will be the person enjoying the bud produced so be sure to pick out what you like, not what everyone else likes.

You may also notice that many breeders sell some of the same product such as Durban Poison, Skunk#1, Hash Plant, and so on. These are not all the same plant! A side by side grow comparison will point out certain noticeable characteristics that differ per the breeder's variety. The original versions of some of these varieties still exist but it may take a little research and lie-sifting to discover who offers the original. Even then, you may like another breeder's version of that variety. Just remember that the name of a seed / plant has no effect whatsoever upon the quality of the plant. Bagseed, a common name for seeds pulled from commercial bud, may be just as, if not more potent than, a strain you paid top dollar for.

Bagseed grows can prove to be extremely valuable. These grows provide hands-on knowledge that can only be gained through practical means. The best thing about these grows is the seeds are free (if you don't count the cost of the bud that contained them). Some growers find that the bud they grew from bagseed is some of the best they may ever grow. Some of the most well known hybrids and elite clones came from some random bagseed.

GERMINATION

In nature, the passing of winter and the moisture and warmth of spring create activity in the dormant embryo. Water is absorbed and the embryo begins to swell until it splits the suture. The taproot appears first, and burrows as far into the soil as is possible. This will serve as the plant's anchor; all other roots will branch off from the taproot or radical.

During this time, the seed is being lifted upward by the division and growth of cells, which are busy forming the seedling's stem. With the roots forming, being able to provide water and nutrients, the cotyledons unfold and start gathering energy via photosynthesis. The germination process is usually complete within 7–10 days.

Seeds only need three key elements to germinate: water, air, and heat. Contrary to popular belief, you do not need light to germinate cannabis. As a matter of fact, cannabis prefers a dark environment in which to germinate. Fresh, healthy seeds germinate anywhere from 24 hours to four days after all germination requirements are met. Seeds germinate in temperatures that range from 70–85°F (21–32°C), with 78°F being optimal. Temperatures above 90°F and below 70°F will impair germination.

You should plant your seeds in 1 x 1 x 4-inch plastic nursery containers or 16 ounce "beer cups," although the latter is a little too big. Your soil mix should be comprised of one part Pro Mix (BX is preferred), one part sand, and one part humus; experimenting with sand, Pro Mix, humus, and worm castings along with additional Perlite has proved successful. Rapid Rooters are also a good medium, just make sure you soak them in pH'd water beforehand and give them a good squeeze when you dunk them. You might also consider adding a root stimulator, such as mycorrhizae powder, or pre-soaking with House and Garden Root Stimulator several days prior to placing your seeds in the mix.

It has been speculated that when seeds are exposed to ethylene, a naturally occurring gaseous hormone, they produce a greater number of females. Banana peels produce ethylene as a result of the ripening process. Placing your seeds in a zip lock bag for 14 days with banana peels could increase the number of females. There is nothing to lose by trying the process, so go ahead and give it a shot.

The towel method is an excellent way to germinate your seeds. Keep the towel moist, but not soaking.

Towel Method

This is the most common method of germination this day and age. You will need a plain white napkin or paper towel, fold it four times into a square, and label it with a water proof marker or pen. Place your seeds in the middle of this paper towel / napkin. Be sure the paper towel stays moist, but not soaking. In two to four days time you will see taproots emerge from the shell. Carefully pick up the seed and place it, taproot facing down, into your growing medium. Some growers wait until the taproot is 3 or more inches before placing it in the growing medium, but a good practice is to do it 1½ inch. Be sure that you do this transfer as quickly as possible. The taproot is not meant to see light.

Scuffing

Some seeds have an outer shell that is too dense to allow water to penetrate. To scuff the seeds you will need a matchbox, sandpaper, and seeds. Place the sandpaper on the bottom of the empty matchbox and then insert seeds. Shake the box for approximately 30 seconds. Remove seeds and check for scuff marks. Once properly scuffed you can either soak the seeds in water overnight or plant them directly into your growing medium. Scuffing allows the taproot to easily penetrate the outer shell, speeding up the germination rate. Scuffing is a good practice for all seeds.

Scraping

This method is used as a substitute for scuffing. This method is a trickier one than scuffing and requires a bit of know-how. You will also need a sharp razor blade in order to complete this task. (I also must warn you before hand that if you are of a clumsy nature, then scuffing is the safer route for you) Where the seed comes to a point or oval shape, the suture, you want to cut away this edge until you see a thin black line. Do this all along the point of the seed. Doing so will let the taproot easily emerge instead of having to pass through the shell.

Pre-Soaking

Put distilled water in a glass and soak your seeds overnight. Soaking them longer than 24 hours could cause the embryo to suffer from oxygen deprivation and, eventually, rot. Now remove your seeds. You may notice that some of the shells have opened a bit. These will be the first to emerge from the soil. Plant these seeds as you would when direct planting, and they should emerge between two to five days. Make sure to keep the soil moist. This is basically a quicker way of direct planting.

Direct Planting

Going back to the roots, so to speak. Place seeds twice as deep as their width into your growing medium—roughly a ¼ inch. Keep your medium moist, but not waterlogged. You can put saran wrap over your container to keep moisture in. Once the seed breaks through the surface, you will need to remove this cover so that oxygen can reach the little seedling. For best results, keep the soil temperature at 78°F and the air temperature between 72–75°F. Avoid using peat pellets, jiffy pots, and rockwool cubes at all costs!

For best results, plant your seeds gently into the growing medium, and keep the medium moist but not waterlogged.

I am not a fan of these Jiffy pellet containers, but if you do choose to use them, remember to keep them really moist.

RAPID ROOTERS
by Rellikbuzz

Well, let me join the Rapid Rooter Lovers Club! I've used them for both seeds and clones with outstanding results. Yes, the key is to keep them really moist. I pre-soak the RR's in a mixture of H_2O_2 (35% horticultural grade at a rate of one tbsp per gallon of water), Superthrive (2 drops maximum per gallon of water), and Advanced Nutrients Voodoo Juice (1½ teaspoons per gallon of water). The H_2O_2 will kill off any bacteria that might attack the tender seedling or cutting and will oxygenate the root zone and promote rapid, healthy root development.

Once pre-soaked, I wring out the Rooters a bit to get excess water out, plant the seed or clone (if a clone, the clone is scarified and dipped in Clonex), and place it in a humidity dome that has been well-misted with about a quarter-inch of water in the bottom of the tray. For those that think the quarter-inch in the tray keeps the RR's moist: *it will not rehydrate a dry Rooter.* Water in the tray mainly keeps the humidity levels up in the dome. You cannot avoid hand watering the Rooters. I usually use a mist bottle with the above-mentioned mix in it, and spray the tops of the Rooters until they are sufficiently moistened. If a Rooter gets dry, you can tell, as it turns a lighter brown than when they are wet (which is a really dark brown).

I also trim about ⅓ of each leaf on each clone completely off. This slows down the photosynthesis process so the plant's energy can be focused on root growth. I have quarter-sized holes in the ends of my humidity dome to allow some fresh air in at all times. Humidity levels stay plenty high and the plants can breathe a bit of fresh air while they're rooting. This also helps to "harden-off" the cutting / seedling so that they won't wilt when you remove them from the dome.

During the first three days in the humidity dome, I will mist the underside of the dome and cuts once a day. Before I do this, I leave the dome off for 15–30 minutes and use the dome to wave back and forth, creating a breeze on the cuttings. This helps them to build stronger stems early on. On the fourth day, assuming the cuts are nice and green, I will stop spraying them and only spray the underside of the dome. This will force the plant to push out roots in search of moisture. It is imperative to keep the Rooters good and moist at this time. I continue this process until the clones are rooted. Daily, I take off the humidity dome to let the cuts breathe and I wave the dome at them for two or three minutes to give them their daily workout. I have never had wilt from my seedlings / cuttings after transplant with this method, and cuts root consistently in 7–10 days—I have even had them root in 6 days!

Using the Rapid Rooters with the H202 mix and this process, I have had close to 100% success over a three-year period. That's my experience, anyway.

Tip for germinating seeds in Rapid Rooters: plant the seed about an ⅛-inch into the hole of a Rooter and pinch off a small piece of the Rooter's bottom side. *Gently* wedge the bottom piece into the hole on top of the seed. Wedge it in, but not so tight that the seedling will have trouble pushing it out of the way. This blocks the light and keeps the area in contact with the seed husk moist. This should help to germinate your beans, but be sure to scarify the seed husks and soak them in water (or, my preference, a black tea pre-soak) beforehand and this will greatly improve your results! Also: *don't forget to keep everything labeled!*

*When your seedlings first emerge from the soil they will grow rapidly in search of light. If lighting is not adequate or the lights are too far away, the seedlings' stalks will stretch until they reach the adequate light. I have seen growers that had stalks longer than 8 inches between the cotyledons and the base of the plant! These seedlings quickly topple over and make weak plants later on; they are also subject to higher rates of dampening off. Keep those lights low to your seedlings and prevent this easily avoidable problem. Fluorescent lights should be no further than 2 inches from the tops of the seedlings, but 1-inch or less is ideal, and low watt CFLs should be no further than 4 inches, but I prefer 2–3 inches. During the seedling cycle your lights should be on a 20/4 cycle, meaning 20 on and 4 off. To prevent stretching, keep the top 1–1½ inches of your container free of soil, and as the seedling stretches place the same soil mixture around the base of the seedling until you're about ¼-inch underneath the lip of the container. Dampening off will not be a concern if your grow room has proper ventilation and your medium does not stay soggy.

DAMPENING OFF

This is a type of fungus that mainly affects seedlings (especially weak seedlings), also known as Pyrethrum Wilt. You can prevent dampening off by making sure that you have adequate lighting, proper temperature and humidity. Not over-watering your plants is key. Also: be sure the medium drains properly. Dampening off targets the vulnerable stalks of young seedlings, the stalks wither just above the soil line, and the plant topples over. Once dampening off has occurred there is no effective way to keep that seedling alive and even if there was, that seedling should be thinned out for breeding purposes. Some growers spray their plant's stalk with a fungicide as a preemptive strike against dampening off. However, a proper climate should have no problems with dampening off.

FEMALE SEEDS

Many seed breeders are now offering feminized seeds of their most popular strains. These seeds come at a higher price than your regular seed pack but are "guaranteed" to produce female plants. Be forewarned, these seeds have a higher hermaphroditic rate and or mutation rate due to the method of their creation. Female seeds are created when a female plant develops male sex organs by either "natural" stress or chemical stress. These sex organs are commonly known as nanners, thus becoming a hermaphrodite. Occasionally, breeders will use plants that turn naturally hermaphroditic such as Thais. Doing so will result in hermaphroditic tendencies being passed down in the genes of your seeds, this means that many of your "female" seeds will become hermaphrodites as well. The male pollen sacs release their pollen and pollinate the female parts of that plant. Depending on the breeder of the female seeds, they will either pollinate the hermaphrodite plant itself (selfing) or pollinate another female plant of the same strain. Pollinating another female plant with a naturally stress induced hermaphrodite creates the best female seeds. These seeds will have a greater chance of being female without much chance of turning hermaphroditic. Using properly bred female seeds are good for Guerilla growers that cannot constantly watch their plants to remove the males. I strongly advise against the use of female seeds for future breeding purposes.

SEEDLINGS

When your little cannabis plant first breaks through the soil it will have a set of small, oval-shaped leaves called cotyledons. These first leaves gather the first light that aids the plant through photosynthesis. When your seed hatches, inside the cotyledons you will see a pair of tiny little wisps. These wisps are the first set of true leaves. After a few days of these "wisps" being growing, they will begin forming the easily recog-

The small, oval-shaped leaves are called cotyledons, and the two leaves with serrated edges are your plant's first set of true leaves.

nizable cannabis leaves. These leaves are characterized by their serrated edges and trademark shape. When your first sets of leaves are fully developed and your second set start forming, you have entered the seedling stage.

These seedlings are ready to be transplanted into 16-ounce beer cups. At this time if you germinated in Rapid Rooters or (God forbid) rockwool cubes, you should transplant into one-gallon containers and have your medium comprised of ¼ Pro Mix, ¼ sand, ¼ humus, and ¼ worm castings, with some chunky perlite mixed in for added flavor.

If you are using a completely inert, soilless soil medium such as Pro Mix or Coco Coir alone, you will need to fertilize with 350–550 PPM of a product like Botanicare PBP Grow. Temperature should be in the mid 70s. Humidity should be in the 50%–60% range.

Once your baby plant enters the seedling stage, transplant it to one-gallon containers with a good growing medium.

At this time you should have a fan blowing on your tender plants to strengthen their stalks. They will want to topple over, especially if your lights are too far from your plants and the stalk starts to stretch. Your stalk should never get longer than 2 inches from the base to the cotyledons. You should begin to thin out your plants at this time for breeding purposes, removing the ones that don't stand up on their own or do not produce any scent. This is hard to do with an expensive pack of ten seeds. You may want to use toothpicks and twist ties to keep your young seedlings from toppling over if you are not seeking these for breeding purposes.

Gently playing with the stalk for a minute or so each day will strengthen up the stalks as well. In order to do this, simply bounce the stalk left to right between your index and middle finger.

During the seedling stage, you should have your lights positioned close to your plants. You may become frustrated with your plant during this stage due to the seeming lack of growth. Don't be. The seedling stage is the time that a plant establishes its root system so it can effectively take up the nutrients and water for vigorous vegetative growth. You may accelerate this process by using organic root accelerators and by decreasing the hours of light your seedlings receive. Plants grow their roots when it is nighttime.

Don't be tempted to give your plants any fertilizers in an attempt to accelerate their growth—you will end up doing more harm than good and could possibly kill the young plant. Also, be careful when you water in that you don't pour a stream at the base of the seedling. Use a watering can with a drip spout so you don't risk this unwanted and easily avoidable problem.

The third and fourth week of your plant's life is a crucial time in determining the sex of that plant. At this time, your plant is highly susceptible to stress. This stress will determine the sex of your plant. The owner of Dutch Passion, Henk, was the first to document this phenomenon, and he proposed the following method for increasing the number of females in your batch. Henk states that you should start this process when the first set of three-bladed leaflets appear and continue it through to the fifth week of the plant's life.

1. Increase the level of nitrogen while decreasing the level of potassium feed with a 3-0-0 or 15-1-3. Use something with a much higher dose of nitrogen than potassium or phosphorus. (Tip: avoid using fertilizers containing ammonium nitrate, as this will burn roots. Also, you do not need a large number of nitrogen: a 3-0-0 would be the ideal choice.)

2. Increase the humidity to around 75%, and decrease the temperature to between 60–65 °F. Tests have been performed with temperatures as low as 32 °F, and out of six plants all six were female from regular seeds.

3. Increase the light spectrum to the high end—anything above 5,000K will do nicely. This means more blue, i.e., Metal Halide, Hortilux Blue Bulb, "daylight" CFL, or fluoros, etc. At the same time, decrease the amount of light per day. During the seed / seedling stage you should set your light cycle for 15/9 or 14/10, on/off. This will provide all the hours needed for the little ones to gather light for photosynthesis. If you're below the Mason Dixon line, that is typically more light than plants receive outside. This also does the job of decreasing the amount of light so as to increase the number of females. After the 5th week has passed, you should increase to 18/6 to support the rapid rate of growth the plants are capable of.

4. When your plant has established its fourth node (which marks the beginning of the vegetative cycle), you can start to LST, Top or FIM if you so choose. See the advanced techniques chapter for more information on this.

Note: If you are seeing one or two blades per leaflet past the second node your plant is not receiving adequate lighting and may suffer from retardation because of this. You can improve the situation by increasing the number of lights, increasing the intensity (wattage), and/or moving the lights closer to your plants. You should avoid transplanting your plant through this stage; it's better to transplant into one-liter / one-gallon pots before entering this time period.

If planting multiple seeds in one container – cull the weakest so that only one seedling per container remains.

Some growers plant multiple seeds, up to four, spaced evenly in a 6-inch pot. Mark and compare growth between seedlings until the second set of true leaves have developed. Then thin out the weakest-looking seedlings; do not pull up the seedling but cut off the stalk below the soil line. Save only the two best seedlings, wait a week, and then thin out the weakest seedling again, leaving only one seedling per container. This is a good breeding practice, starting with large numbers and then thinning out the weakest plants throughout the growing process.

FROM SEED OR CLONE?
Growing from clones and from seed both have their advantages and disadvantages. If growing from clones, you can bypass the abovementioned process and proceed directly to the vegetative cycle (if you're working with fully established clones, that is).

Advantages for Clones
• Clones are much faster to veg and flower than starting from seed, resulting in a quick harvest and a much shorter turnaround time.
• Rooted clones can be flowered immediately if space or time is a problem.

- Clones provide exact genetic copies of a special plant, resulting in even growth and uniform ripening. They will all have the same growth characteristics.
- Clones grow faster and are usually hardier than seeds.
- No need to worry about having males from female clones.
- With clones you know exactly what you're getting, unlike seeds, which are a gamble.

Disadvantages of Clones

- Clones can be difficult to find, as opposed to seeds, which are available from seed banks. Clones from unknown sources are of suspect quality.
- Growers run a high risk of inheriting problems from the last grower: root rot, spider mites, powdery mildew, etc. If these problems are not identified and treated, they can quickly spread to an entire crop.
- Unhealthy clones may die or remain in shock for an extended period
- Shipped clones may be in shock and take weeks of TLC to recover. There are many stories of medical clones shipped with protection that arrived flattened!
- If an insect attack or disease infects your crop, it will spread to all of your plants more quickly than if the plants were of different strains.
- You must have a separate grow room and preserve the clones by keeping them alive, as seeds can be stored in the freezer with little maintenance.
- The cost of clones is often much higher than that of seeds.
- It is harder to ship clones than seeds.
- The greatest disadvantage is that you do not have both males and females to perform any breeding endeavors, without the use of chemicals.

Advantages of Seeds

- Seeds obtained from reputable seed banks are of known lineage and genetics. You should have a reasonable idea of what the strain will do in terms of yield, quality, and flowering time.
- Breeding and crossing options are possible without using chemicals.
- F1 seeds contain hybrid vigor, which grow bigger and faster than clones.

Disadvantages of Seeds

- Seeds not giving plants as advertised.
- Unstable hybrid strains.
- Not all seeds germinate every time, which results in wasted money.
- It may take many seed packs to discover a good mother.
- Seeds take longer to reach maturity and harvest.
- Must wait longer to make a mother from seeds.

HARDENING OFF

Hardening off is a process that smart growers will implement when they want to move their indoor seedlings, clones, or plants outside. The inside environment is stable and predictable; you have complete control of everything that affects your plants. Outdoors, this is far from the case, and while HID lighting is the best lighting for plants indoors it cannot compare to that big HID in the sky, the sun.

The sun on average emits 6,840,000,000,000,000,000,000,000,000 lumens. That's a tremendous amount, much more than your plants are used to. However, it is not necessarily the amount of light emitted, as it is the heat. Obviously, you would not want to just throw your plants outdoors and let them attempt to adjust all at once, you want to "harden them off" to this intense new environment.

Hardening off is accomplished by setting your plants outdoors, starting with about an hour a day. Set them right in the middle of the hot sun and then move them back in. Gradually repeat this process and lengthen it by an hour each time you do. Ideally, you want to harden off for two weeks, but you could call it quits at about the one-week mark. There is some confusion about what you are "hardening off." In fact, you are hardening off the roots, the most sensitive part of the plant. Some people think you are hardening off the leaves of the plant, but this is not the case—the leaves will absorb and store all the light they receive: they're loving this new environment. It's the roots that are having a hard time adjusting.

Chapter 12

Cloning

Using the proper equipment for the cloning procedure ensures a smooth, successful operation.

Growers use cloning as a form of preserving their favorite plants for years to come, and to pass on an exact genetic copy of their favorite plant to their friends and family. Clones are best if taken from mothers, as opposed to clones of clones, as we will discuss below. Taking the following cloning precautions / procedures will dramatically lower the chances of your clones mutating from the original. Every serious grower / breeder must incorporate cloning to find "keeper" plants and preserve identical copies of that plant for later use. Successful cloning is one of a grower / breeder's best tools.

This section offers a step-by-step tutorial of how to make successful clones.

You will need:

- Small, sharp scissors
- Rubbing alcohol
- Small plastic cup with water
- Cloning solution
- Rapid rooters or an appropriate cloning medium.
- Labels
- Humidity Dome
- Cheap plastic (Bic) pen
- Spray bottle
- Dual blue "daylight" fluorescent, 36 inches or bigger, or 2–3 small, blue CFLs (Compact Fluorescent Lamps), 42 watts or less.

Optional Items:

- Mycorrhizae powder or tablets
- Heat mat

Turn your rapid rooters upside down so they will be freestanding, and insert the pen in the rapid rooter to make a hole for the cutting. Only insert the pen between $\frac{1}{2}$ to $1\frac{1}{2}$ inches into the rapid rooter. Do this ahead of time, so all you have to do is insert the cutting's stalk when ready. Make sure that you have already dunked your rapid rooters into a bucket of pH'd water (6.5). Organic rooting enhancer is optional but recommended.

Make a hole in your rapid rooter that you can insert the stalk of your clone into.

When taking clones, the lower the branch is to the bottom of the plant, the better.

The first step in cloning is preparing your mother or donor plant for taking clones. This is done at least one week prior to the actual taking of the clones. You want your plant to be at least one month old and have an abundance of branches. Any plant that has developed lateral growth longer than 2 inches can be cloned. This is done by stopping feeding at least one week prior to taking clones, and giving a good flush with at least double the amount of water for that container. You will also want to reverse-foliar feed, meaning spraying plain, pH'd water on your plants leaves every-day for a week before the day before you clone. Doing so will remove the stored nitrogen from the leaves, an abundance of which increases the difficulty of cloning, while building the amount of carbohydrates in the leaves, which makes it easier and faster for the clone to develop roots.

Prepare your supplies ahead of time. This means cleaning your scissors with rubbing alcohol and letting them dry, mixing the cloning solution, if needed, and having everything laid out so you don't have to waste any time.

You want to select branches considered "sucker growth" if possible; sucker growth is defined as growth on the lower, inner part of your plant, growth that is smaller and generally weaker-looking than other branches. Selecting sucker growth not only provides you with clones, but will remove growth that does not receive sufficient light-ing, so energy and nutrients can be concentrated on the main shoots. While it is true that the best clones come from the best looking branches, the strongest and health-iest sucker growth should be used—branches that are firm and ridged, with a stalk no smaller than 2mm in diameter, and leaves that are healthy and not sickly.

When taking clones, the lower the branch is to the bottom of the plant, the better. Older branches have the oldest hormones, which make them easier to root. The closer you get to the top of the plant, the longer it will take to root and the more problematic it will be.

You want your branches to have three nodes, ideally. Two nodes go below the soil line, and one goes above. If your internodes are too long, you will have to settle with just one node below the soil line. Branches smaller than 2 inches will make poor clones.

Use your scissors to cut the branch right on the node coming from the stalk. Don't leave a stub because the plant could get a mold or fungus infection.

Take your scissors and cut the branch right on the node coming from the stalk. You want to leave no stub for mold and fungus to attack.

Note: Some people like to use a single edged razor; if you choose to go the razor route, use extra caution not to cut your hands and fingers.

As soon as you remove the branch from the plant, making it a "cut," immediately place that cut in a fresh cup of water. This will prevent an air bubble from developing in the stem, which will eventually kill the cut.

Once you have taken all your cuts (making sure to label separate cups for different plants), go back to your "cloning station" to prepare them. While your cuts are still in the cup(s) you should carefully inspect them—all leaves, nodes, branches, and, especially, the undersides of the leaves.

Inspect all of your cuts to make sure they are healthy. Check the leaves, nodes, branches, and most importantly, the undersides of the leaves.

Remove all the petioles coming from the nodes that will be under the soil level.

You will want to remove all the petioles coming from the node(s) that will be under the soil level.

After you remove the petioles, cut in between them at a 45-degree angle.

This is also the time to "scrape" your cutting's stem, if you want. This removes the outer layer and exposes the cambium layer, which allows for quicker rooting. To scrape a stem, take a razor blade and scrape each side of the stalk. You may also split the stalk in two, exposing the inner cambium layer. This technique exposes more area for roots to develop. Splitting the stalk will cause a greater shock and recovery time, but eventually a greater number of roots develop.

Remove the petioles using scissors or a razor blade, and then scrape the stem to expose the cambium layer which will allow for better rooting.

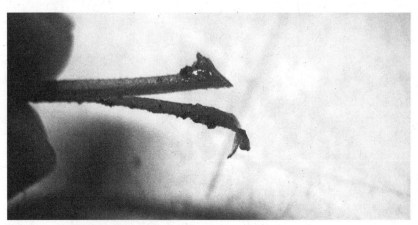

Another method to promote better rooting is to split the stalk, which exposes the inner cambium layer. The shock to the plant is larger and the recovery time is longer, but you eventually get a greater number of roots. Your choice.

Now dip your stalk in your cloning solution—in this case, we are using Olivia's cloning gel.

Make sure you have a generous amount of the cloning solution on the stalk

Carefully insert your cutting into the rapid rooter, or whatever medium you have chosen.

Close off the rapid rooter's hole as much as possible by pinching it closed.

Once you have your cutting in the medium, you should remove about 60% of the fan leaves to lower the transpiration (evaporation) rate and improve the health of the clone. Most clones do well with only one cut fan leaf, along with a growing tip. This will also cause the clone to grow faster, generating more leaves to gather energy.

This is also when you want to label your cuts; in this case, they were all of the same plant, so we just needed one label.

Repeat this process and make as many clones as you want. Once you have all the cuts you're going to use, you may place them back in the rapid rooter tray. Now mist the humidity dome heavily and cover the tray. The humidity dome keeps the relative

After scraping or splitting the stalk, dip it in the cloning gel. We used Olivia's Cloning Gel, here.

Make sure there is a generous amount of cloning gel on the stalk of your clone.

Carefully insert the cutting into the rapid rooter. Make sure that you have already dunked your rapid rooters in water pH'd to 6.5 before you put the clone in.

humidity high which will lower the transpiration rate of the clones, allowing them to retain a higher amount of water than if they were left un-covered. Having a humidity dome will decrease the turnaround time and ease the stress of cloning.

If your humidity dome has vent holes, open them only half way.

Put the lights near the top of the humidity dome; as the water droplets evaporate, spray again. Repeat this process as necessary.

For the first few days—and up to a week—you will see the clones wilting and looking pretty rough. Don't worry: this is normal; they just went through an incredibly stressful process and will need time to recuperate. Within a weeks' time, you should be seeing a good amount of healthy white roots growing out from the rapid rooter. You may notice yellowing or fading of green on the lower leaves; this is normal and nothing to worry about. Once you see roots, your cut has now become a clone. It is important not to let your growing medium dry out, but not to keep it too soggy either. Too dry and tender roots will dry up and die; too soggy and roots will not be able to grow.

When transplanting into the 4 or 6-inch nursery pot, you may feed them with a mild dose of vegetative nutrients after they have been acclimatized to their new environment. At this time, before transplanting, you may incorporate a technique known as "root topping," wherein you snip or pinch the visible roots, a procedure which branches them into two (just like topping or pinching does above ground).

Set your light cycle for 18 on / 6 off; this will enable a good balance of the leaves

Once you have your cutting in the medium (rapid rooter), then you should remove about 60% of the fan leaves.

Cutting the fan leaves lowers the transpiration (evaporation) rate of the plant and causes the clone to grow faster, generating more leaves to gather energy.

gathering energy during the day for the roots to use during the night. Avoid 24 on / 7 off, as this will result in roots / clones growing slower.

You want your temperature to remain above 70°F during the entire process, with humidity up to 85–90%.

When you start seeing vertical growth on the cuttings, the cloning process is

Once you've done all the clones, put them in the humidity dome because it eases the stress of cloning and decreases the turnaround time.

complete. Congratulations—you have just made clones!

For the 5 to 20 days it will take your cuttings to fully root, they should be treated like seedlings—they are very tender and fragile, especially to intense light, nutrients, and temperatures. After they are fully rooted and ready for transplant, you can treat them as vegetative plants. Refer to my chapter on the Vegetative Cycle, for more information.

OTHER CLONING METHODS
There is always more than one way to skin a cat, and the same is true for cloning. Here are some different methods used by different cultures.

Outdoor Cloning or Serpentine Layering
This is done by using branches that are closest to the ground and cannot be performed if the branches will not touch the ground.

In order to perform outdoor cloning you will need to have a plant with long side shoots.

Take a branch and, ever so gently, place it on the ground and mark the ground where the branch touches.

Make sure there is one node above each bend; once you have marked where the branch reaches on the ground you need to make a small V shaped incision in the branch where it touches the ground.

Cut into the branch by slicing a small V shape into it. Apply cloning solution to the V incision.

Bury the cut portion of the branch under ground in fertile soil. Place a rock of medium weight on top so as the branch does not rise out of the soil.

Repeat this until you have reached the end of the branch. In two – three weeks time, they should have been thoroughly rooted. Now cut the branch at each bend, you now have 2 or 3 plants (one for every incision you made).

Jamaican Cloning

The Jamaicans have developed an ingenious method of making clones on the plant. To implement this method of cloning, you will need a balance of Pro Mix BX and Worm Castings; any mycorrhizae powder that you would like to add would also be very beneficial. You will also need coffee filters, string, cloning solution, and a fresh single-edged razor blade.

Make your V shaped incision at any node around the top of any branch, just as long as the branch does not sag under the weight of the soil. The reason we are using the top instead of the bottom is because you will cut below the rooted node and you can't have a two-foot clone.

Coat this incision with your cloning solution.

Now tie the moist bag of soil onto the branch, making sure that the soil is firmly seated into the incision. Keep the bag moist but not soaking, and you should see roots growing through in about a week and a half.

At this time you should cut just below the node, where the incision is made. You now have your finished clone using the Jamaican cloning technique.

GENETIC MUTATION AND GENETIC DRIFT

Do clones change genetically? This has been a question that has plagued the cannabis community for some time. The general outlook on this topic during the early years of cloning was that clones did not change and were consistent in all ways, no matter how many times they were cloned. However, recent research has shown this assumption to be false.

Typically, the change in the clone's appearance is caused by environmental factors such as the plant's diet, temperature, and so on. The plant keeps its ability to combat these environmental factors encoded in its DNA, unlike other, "higher" organisms. When a certain stressor is activated, a previously unused section of that plant's DNA will respond and this response can be tracked throughout the generations. The change in the genetics is more prominent in clones taken from clones, rather than clones taken from the original mother plant. Even more important is how the clones were taken and if all safety precautions (for the clones) were taken as outlined above. However, mother plants that are poorly maintained will also produce clones that show mutations. Some clones will herm and others may not resemble the original mother in any form. One such strain that this is evident in is Cinderella 99; it will show genetic mutation most prominently around the 5th generation, and may become quite undesirable. When a cell in a plant is exposed to viruses, bacteria, or some other pathogen (usually in the cloning process) that alters the DNA in that particular part of the plant, any cut taken from that part of the plant will have a different DNA sequence than the original mother plant, thus making that cut a different cut than the mother.

Genetic drift is also a proven factor in cannabis. Genetic drift is the term used in population genetics to refer to the statistical drift over time of gene frequencies in a population due to random sampling effects in the formation of successive generations. For a whole organism's DNA to drift would require it to shift or change at approximately the same rate and in response to all the cuts taken from the original mother plant. Genetic drift is, in essence, a widespread and common genetic mutation that occurs naturally because of a plant's attempt to adjust to its environment and survive for an indefinite period. While some growers may say they are experiencing genetic drift, they are more than likely experiencing the clone's reaction (evolution) to their own personal growing environment. Occasionally, some growers can experience clone mutation, but typically only if the clones were poorly cloned / taken care of.

HINTS AND TIPS FOR CLONING

Most growers prefer cloning gel. Their second favorite is a liquid, such as Vita Grow, which also does well. The worst product to use for cloning is a powder. Powders are available at most garden supply centers, but are obsolete. It is difficult to get the powders to remain on the stalk and you must wear a mask so you do not breathe in harmful particles.

When you're mixing your liquid cloning solution together, try adding a couple drops of natural honey to the mix. This will protect against pathogens (i.e., disease) from infecting your vulnerable cuttings.

You may also dip your cuttings directly into honey and just use that as your cloning solution. I do not recommend this as it takes much longer—almost a week longer—to see the same results.

Turn your rapid rooters upside down so they will stand freely by themselves.

If rapid rooters are not an option for you, you may use thin plastic seed pots that come attached in packs of six. They taper from wide at the top to narrow at the bottom, forming a sort of point. I have found that a 60:40 ratio of Pro Mix BX and sand works well as a medium. Then place your clones in a clear shoe bin, mist everything and place another clear shoe bin over it. Drill about ten half-inch holes in the top shoe for ventilation, and place a fluorescent fixture directly on top of the top shoe bin.

You will see a dramatic increase in the speed of root development with the addition of a heat mat. Your household heat mat that you use for your aching back will not work; you will need one on which you can control the temperature exactly. Set the mat for 80–85°F and place it under the rapid rooter tray.

If possible, take your clones at night, ideally an hour or so before the room lights come on. This will result in all the auxins and other plant hormones remaining in the donor plant, which studies have shown to retreat to the roots at night. This is better for both the clones and the mother / donor plant.

Un-rooted clones (cuts) can be stored in the refrigerator in a zip lock bag for a short amount of time. Wrap the cuts with a damp (but not soaking; you don't want any mold), plain paper towel; place the towel with the cuttings inside the zip lock bag and inject CO_2, or simply breathe in the zip lock bag to blow it up; then seal it. Place the bag in the vegetable crisper section of your refrigerator, and your cuts will last as long as four weeks if prepared properly. Periodically check to make sure the paper towel is still damp and to inject fresh CO_2 (breath) into the bag.

When the clones start showing deficiencies, fertilize them with a mild solution of vegetative plant food with trace elements (between 250–400 PPM will suffice). Do *not* use any fertilizer that contains ammonium nitrate (or ammonium period, for that matter); it will fry the roots.

Chapter 13

Transplanting

You will need to transplant a plant around five times in its life cycle. From Rapid Rooters, rockwool, or Jiffy Pots; to a 4 or 6-inch nursery pot; to a 1-gallon container; to a 2-gallon container; and, finally, to a 5-gallon container, or whatever size you choose for your final container. It is time to transplant your plant when you see an abundance of root tips coming out of the majority of the holes in the bottom of the container.

SOME RULES

When transplanting, you will want to have the same consistency medium that you're transplanting from to what you're transplanting to. Meaning that if you have a sandy, loamy medium in your six-inch nursery pot, you will want to have a sandy, loamy medium in your two-gallon pot, and so on. The reason for this is so an air pocket doesn't develop between the pockets of different soil media. The roots will stop short of the new medium, and never grow past the already-defined root ball.

Don't transplant a plant in a 6-inch container directly into a 2-gallon or 5-gallon container. The same applies for a plant in a 5-gallon container into a 15-gallon. The reason for this is that a plant in a 6-inch container will not grow as fast or develop as healthily when transplanted directly into a 2 or 5-gallon container. The plant will not be able to take advantage of the container size, and when watered the pot will stay soggy because the plant will not have enough roots to absorb all of the available water. Plants will likely suffer from a lack of oxygen, meaning they are over-watered.

Growers' views on transplanting differ. Some will not pack the soil at all, so the roots can grow easily throughout the soil. Some add a bit of soil, water it, and repeat this process until they reach the top of the container. Others will just add all their soil and "flush" it with the desired pH water.

Just like with the cloning procedure, transplanting your plants goes best when you have the right equipment and it is organized for easy use.

STEP-BY-STEP

First, have all your supplies together: soil, amendments, containers, pH'd water, labels, marker, and, obviously, the plants.

Take your soil and fill up your container, leaving about 1–2 inches at the top.

Optional step:

Flush with pH (6.5) water. This does pack the soil down, but the plants will not suffer from improper pH; if you have the adequate amount of humus and lime or gypsum in your soil you can bypass this step, but you will have to wait about a week for your soil pH to adjust.

Optional step:

Flush until you see the water coming from the containers. You will notice that the

Fill your containers up with soil, and leave about 1-2 inches at the top.

Flush the containers with water pH'd to 6.5 to ensure good soil conditions. This packs the soil down, so you'll have to add a little to the top once you're done to fill up the container again.

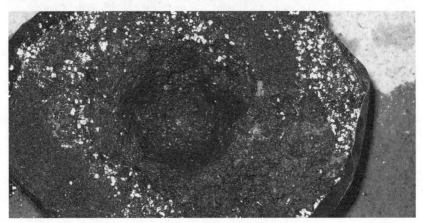

Use your spade to make a hole in the center of the container that your plant and its original container can fit into.

soil has been packed down, so you will need to add a bit of soil to fill up the container, leaving (again) about 2 inches of space at the top.

Take your spade and remove the soil in the center of the container; do this until you can place your plant, with its container, in the hole.

Now, if your plant is level with the soil, you're golden; but if it protrudes from the soil, you must remove more soil to make it level.

To remove your plant, first warp the container a bit—squeeze the sides of the container until they warp. Place the stalk of your plant between your ring and middle fingers. Turn it upside down and try to stop as much as the topsoil from falling as possible with your hand. This is quite a feat with 5-gallon pots!

Your plant should come out with no resistance if you warped your container prop-

Make sure that the plant is level with the soil. Keep trying and add or remove soil from the bottom of the hole each time to make sure it goes in perfectly.

Don't be afraid to move the soil in the container around your plant to make sure it fits in tight. You really do not want air around its roots.

erly. If your plant does not come out all the way, gently tap the bottom of the container, twist the container again, and she should come right out. If not, then you must set your plant and container back down and re-warp your container or separate the roots and soil from the inside of the container by sliding a very narrow piece of metal, wood, or plastic, such as a ruler, down the sides. This method should only be used in extreme circumstances as you can easily damage roots.

Slowly and carefully place your root ball into your new container. Some growers will squeeze the bottom of the root ball to break up the root-bound roots—they claim that this speeds up the root growing process—but in my experience it stunts growth.

Fill in around the sides of your plant, carefully leaning your plant on its stalk in the

To remove your plant from its original container, squeeze the sides to loosen the roots, and then take the stalk gently in your hands and flip the container over.

opposite direction of the side where you are filling in. It is best to use a garden spade to fill in with soil, and a ruler to press down the soil to make sure no air pockets remain. Be careful to not damage any roots. Warning: this can be a messy process, so put down plastic ahead of time, if needed.

Now top-dress the soil with your choice of rock, so that roots can take advantage of all the soil in the container instead of only ⅔ of it. The rocks must be heavy enough to displace water. Don't forget to add the label identifying the strain!

Water your plant with the pH'd water. You may also add Superthrive or a root stimulator to this water.

Now you're all done. Congratulations, you just transplanted your plants and they will have no transplant shock if you did this correctly.

DOUBLE POTTING

This technique was first documented by a grower known as BushyOldGrower, a.k.a. BOG. Double potting is perfect if you do not feel like transplanting the entire plant, and it is much easier to do than regular transplanting. Of course, it is not without its drawbacks: double potting uses much more vertical space, and roots do not develop as quickly or efficiently as with regular transplanting. Also, if you are growing in a 5-gallon bucket, you will not be able to cut through the bottom of the bucket without damaging the root ball in the process; your container is destroyed, too. It also takes

Put the plant gently into its new home. Make sure you fill in all around the plant's roots because air pockets can cause problems. Then water your plant with pH'd water.

much more water to reach all of the roots. ¾

If you wish to implement this technique you will need a larger container than the one the plant is presently growing in, and a sharp, heavy duty pair of scissors (tin snips work better). It is much easier to double pot using grow bags than with buckets.

Fill your new container ¾ of the way full of soil. Draw a line around the perimeter of your container one-inch from the bottom. Use your scissors to cut around the line you just traced, and remove the bottom that you just separated from the rest of the container. Place your open-bottomed container into the bigger container; you will want your smaller container to be half way down into the bigger container. Water the top thoroughly until you see all of the container's visible soil wet on top, and until water runs off through the bottom. This is not to be confused with up-potting, which is the same basic process as outlined above except for the fact that the container is removed, but each time you transplant the root ball you stack up, creating a tier effect from smallest on top to biggest on the bottom.

If you treat your plant well during the vegetative cycle, you'll end up with some potent bud, like this Cream Caramel from Sweet Seeds.

Chapter 14

Vegetative Cycle

You enter the vegetative cycle when the plant's stalk exceeds 4–6mm in thickness and rapid growth begins. This is generally after the fourth node is established. In the vegetative cycle, the plant's transpiration rate becomes much higher because the plant is adding new leaves, which increases the photosynthesis rate, which in turn increases the transpiration rate. The increased photosynthesis rate is key because this increases the speed at which new cells form, and new cells equal plant growth. Because of the higher transpiration rate, your plant will require more water to support this increase in growth. Your plant will also be developing increased amounts of auxins, cytokinins, and gibberellins, which are all natural growth hormones. Arguably the most important of these hormones are auxins; indeed, Robert Clarke says that auxins are directly responsible for "stem growth, root formation, lateral bud inhibition, floral maturation, fruit development, and determination of sex." Auxins are discussed in greater detail in the Advanced Techniques chapter.

The light cycle in the vegetative cycle should be between 16–20 hours. I do not recommend using anything above 20 hours, because plant growth will be stunted and plants will become problematic: it's simple, plants need darkness! Plants gather and store their energy during the day and use this stored energy at night. The standard is to use 18 on / 6 off, however I have seen a substantial increase in growth with some strains using 20 on / 4 off.

Note: when moving your plants outdoors, it is best to reduce the hours of light until you get to two hours more than the light cycle outside. Occasionally, when your plants move from, say, 24 or 18 hours of light indoors, and then are placed outdoors where there are only 14 or 15 hours of light, it can shock the plants into flowering even if there are no auto-flowering tendencies.

There should be ample lighting during the vegetative period, following the guideline of at least 50-watts per square foot.

These young pot plants are entering the vegetative state. Fluorescent lights are being used to maintain the on/off cycle and prevent burn spots.

Increasing the amount of CO_2 to between 800–1,000 PPM will increase the growth rate substantially. This is not necessary unless you're a speed grower looking to turn over the biggest harvest in the shortest amount of time.

In the vegetative cycle your plant will need higher doses of vegetative plant food, and at a greater frequency in order to sustain this rapid growth. Ample nitrogen is key to fast plant development. If you're using a high NPK ratio such as 30-15-15—which you shouldn't be as that's a chemical fertilizer—you will not need to feed as much as (say) if you were using a 5-1-1. Top growers agree that using a lower NPK more frequently is better for the plants than using a high NPK once in awhile. Don't forget to flush regularly, perhaps every four weeks, to get rid of any accumulated salts and to keep your plant happy. The amount you will need to fertilize and how often will depend on the make-up of your medium. Some growers will only need to fertilize once, if at all, because of all the additives in the soil (refer to the soil chapter).

You should fertilize only when your plant is showing signs of slow growth, paling leaves, or some other deficiency. For more information on deficiencies refer to chapter 18. When this happens, fertilize your plants with a nutrient solution no higher than 1,000 PPM. It is also a good idea to foliar feed weekly with 1 tbsp of liquid kelp (Maxi crop) per gallon of water. This will provide auxins, gibberellins, and trace elements that will increase growth rate and boost plants' immune systems.

FOLIAR FEEDING INSTRUCTIONS

• You can use any organic vegetative nutrient to foliar feed your plants. To avoid nutrient burn, your nutrient solution strength should be no more than ⅓ of the manufacturers recommended dosage.

• The best ambient air temperature is about 72°F (when stomata on the underside of the leaves are open); at over 80°F, they may not be open at all. So, find the cooler part of the day if it is hot outside and the warmer part of the day if it is cold out.

• Use a good quality sprayer; have your sprayer set for the finest mist possible.

• Always be sure your HID lights are off and cool before foliar feeding! For extra safety, wipe your bulb with a dry cloth after spraying. After spraying is when fluoros and CFLs become extremely handy: use them so your plants aren't sitting in the dark and disrupting your on/off cycle. CFLs and fluoros are not intense enough to cause burn spots.

• Make sure the pH of your foliar feed solution is between 6.3–6.8.

• Spray leaf surface on the tops and the undersides until the liquid begins to drip off the leaves.

• Homemade fertilizer sprays will be fine for about two weeks.

• Foliar feed as needed. Foliar feeding with Maxicrop seaweed extract provides many helpful plant hormones (such as auxins), stimulates cell elongation and cytokinins, promotes cell division (plant growth), and promotes lateral branching as well as plant enzymes, sugars, and trace elements. These will aid in plant growth and help protect the plant against possible bacterial and viral infections. Seaweed extract also contains a bit of nitrogen but is normally not enough to make a noticeable difference in plant foliage.

BENEFITS OF FOLIAR SPRAYING

• To provide a quick nutrient fix for root-zone nutrient problems or deficiencies; this allows more time to solve the problem(s).

• To prevent excess yellowing on clones.

• Instantly provide nutrients via the leaves, which reduces stress on the suffering plants.

Caution: it has been speculated that foliar feeding may increase the carcinogen levels in plants.

Space is not only determined by the size of the container the plant is being grown in but by the space the plant has to grow in above the soil line. The root ball of a plant directly determines the size of the plant. The size of the container determines the size of the root ball. In general, the bigger the container, the bigger the plant. Your plant should not be crowded above the soil line, as this will cause your plant to grow up tall and lanky, developing a single main cola. Have your plants spaced at least one foot apart, but outdoors more than 2 feet is preferable, as this will allow your plant to develop properly into a nice bush without having to compete with other plants for light.

Your plants are ready to force flower when you notice pre-flowers developing on the plants. Pre-flowers develop on each node, typically starting above the 4th node. When the plant is young and has developed undifferentiated pre-flowers, this simply means the pre-flowers have not matured enough to determine the sex of the plant.

Male pre-flowers will generally develop before female pre-flowers, usually 3–6 days before, but up to two weeks before females. They will appear as small balls and will develop into "nanners" and will grow a short stem from the node and then droop down. As soon as males have been positively identified, they should be destroyed or isolated from the females if they are to be used for breeding purposes.

For outdoor growers, most males will show their pre-flowers during a heat wave. Pay special attention to these times in order to remove your male plants.

Males are usually distinguishable by being taller, and they generally grow quicker and more robustly than female plants. This is evident in all stages of growth, even seedling. Males are generally taller than the females, so they can grow above the

A fast sexing method is to take a cutting and place it in a cup of water with some Maxicrop or Superthrive in it. Make sure the water is oxygenated and put the lighting at 12/12. In a week you'll see pre-flowers that will indicate the plant's sex.

female and drop their pollen on them. Females are generally shorter and bushier than males so they have greater surface area to catch the pollen. Unlike some popular rumors, you cannot distinguish a male or female plant by the direction of their cotyledons, nor by the dimple, or lack thereof, on the seed husk.

The stipule is a little wispy feather that serves no known purpose except to confuse inexperienced growers. Pre-flowers are usually located behind or above the stipule, are round and not narrow, and are pointed like the stipule.

You should not force flower your plants until you see pre-flowers. This is the plant signaling you that it is mature enough to flower. If you force flower before this signal, your plants will yield less and be generally unhappy-looking and problematic.

If you're anxious to find the sex of a plant, take a cutting and place it in a cup of water, ideally with an air stone, add one tsp of Maxicrop or one drop of Superthrive to the water, and place the cutting in the water. Rest it on the edge, or support it with toothpicks laid across the top of the cup, so it does not go under the water. If you do not have an air stone, pour the water from the cup into another cup, and then back into the original cup daily; this will oxygenate the water. If you do not oxygenate the water, your stem will rot and a foul odor will arise. Put the cutting in 12/12. In one week's time, you should see pre-flowers that indicate the sex of your plant.

Some growers have stated that they can find the sex in three days by leaving the plants in complete darkness, and that for some reason every cutting has been male. The obvious answer is that the stress caused them to become males.

You may also cover a branch with 3X black plastic trash bags and duct tape at the base of the branch. In as little as three days for some plants, they will show sex. After sex is determined, remove the bag from the branch.

Under NO circumstance should you mess with a plant's photoperiod unless you are in search of an XX female. For instance, if you are growing a plant in a vegetative cycle, say 18/6, and then change the cycle to 12/12 for two or so weeks waiting for the plant to sex itself, and then revert back to 18/6, your plant is going to suffer severely from stunted growth and will be a worse plant than what it could have been.

Before you place your plants into the flowering cycle there are some pre-flowering preparations you should make beforehand; you will need about three weeks to accomplish this, so plan ahead.

The first thing you want to do is to transplant your girl into a bigger container containing a flowering soil mixture; these require minimal nitrogen and boosted potassium and phosphorus as well as calcium and magnesium. Refer to the soil chapter for more information on these soil mixes. You want to let your plant adjust to this new container before proceeding; giving it more or less a week before proceeding to the next step is good.

Now you are two weeks from the beginning of the flowering cycle. You want to start removing fan leaves, starting with those blocking lower growth. You only want to remove between 6–10 fan leaves per week. Try to remove older leaves rather than younger leaves, because younger leaves have a higher respiration rate than older leaves. I recommend doing 2 or 3 on day one, and then letting the plant rest for two days, and then removing 2 or 3 again on day four, letting the plant rest for two days, and removing 2 or 3 again on day seven. Repeat this cycle for the entire flowering cycle. For online growers this is known as the Texas Kid Pruning Technique.

Note: removing fan leaves, a.k.a. pruning for higher yields, a.k.a. the Texas Kid Pruning Technique is a highly controversial and hotly debated subject. This book highly recommends the removal of fan leaves as outlined above to increase your yield. Follow the directions to the letter and you will not be disappointed.

Now your plants are ready for the flowering cycle. Remember, bigger plants in vegetation means bigger yields in flowering. Expect a good stretch during the first two to three weeks in flower. This can be easily controlled by training.

These plants are beginning to flower. They will start consuming more water, and they will increase in size drastically.

Chapter 15

Flowering

Now things are getting interesting. This is the most enjoyable time to watch your plants as they are developing their "fruit"—and the fruit of our labor. This is where your plants will really shine and show you their true worth (hopefully). An ugly plant in vegetation can be absolutely gorgeous in flower. Cannabis plants flower because the hormone that controls flower (bud) development, ethylene, has reached critical mass due to continual 12 / 12 photoperiods. This hormone has been present in the plant since it was born but it only becomes active upon consecutive 12 / 12 light cycles. Response time will be slower in some plants because the hormone does not react as quickly to the changed photoperiod as it will in some other plants. Flowering plants need increased water because they have a higher respiration rate than in their vegetative state. The further along in flowering you go, the higher the respiration rate will be, and the more water the plant will need.

When you enter the flowering cycle, you want to double the amount of light your plants receive. Mixing the spectrum with an HPS and MH will yield amazing results.

For the average grower, root growth will stop in the flowering cycle. This is why you transplanted three weeks before entering the flowering cycle.

It is drastically important to keep stress levels as low as possible during flowering. While this is true for all of the growth phases it is vital in flowering; any unnecessary stress will cause hermaphroditic flowers to appear and result in a seeded crop. Stress will also reduce your yield, but may improve your quality.

During the first two to three weeks of flowering, your plants will still grow vegetatively. During this time period you will notice that your plants will stretch— some plants stretch as much as ⅓ more than the height in which they entered the flowering cycle. You can limit this stretch by having ample lighting; also, having the lighting at the right distance is key. Furthermore, it is also important to have the correctly-sized container for the size of the plant (one gallon per one foot of vertical growth) and to keep the temperatures in the optimum range. Having ample nitrogen available during the first two weeks of flowering will also limit stretching.

Starting at the beginning of the flowering cycle, you will want to gradually reduce your pH from 6.5 so that you reach 5.8 by week five. This will lock out nitrogen and force the plant to use its stored nitrogen, resulting in a smoother, tastier smoke. You want to continue to remove the fan leaves. However, you should reduce the number removed to between 4–6 fan leaves during the week. Stop removing fan leaves at week 5. The gradual removal of fan leaves is vital in developing thick, long colas. Direct light to the buds is required to form dense colas—not being shaded by fan leaves. The goal is to grow as much bud as possible—not fan leaves.

Removing large fan leaves will lower the humidity, because those fan leaves retain a lot of moisture. The lower the humidity, the better for budding, especially if you're growing dense colas. The denser the cola, the more prone it is to bud rot because moisture (humidity) becomes trapped inside the cola, which cannot escape. Moisture, lack of ventilation, and darkness are the three main ingredients that cause fungus and mold. Your humidity must be below 50% or you will run a greater risk of developing problems with fungus and mold; 30–40% is ideal. To achieve this, you will most likely have to add a dehumidifier in the room, which will increase the temperatures, so make sure your ventilation is in good running order. Remember, anything above 80°F is going to stress your plants and diminish yield. To compensate for this, you will usually have to run your outtake fan perpetually on its highest setting.

TRICHOMES

Trichomes act as a defense mechanism against extremes in the environment as well as against attacks by predators. Trichomes are often most dense on the calyxes that house any seeds. When insects attack the plant, their mandibles bind together from the sticky resin. When animals, such as deer, attack the plant, the resin's unpleasant spicy characteristics will discourage future attacks—this is not to mention the reaction from the psychoactive properties of the resin itself.

Trichomes are produced to hold in moisture during cases of extreme drought, much like cacti develop a waxy coating that serves as a barrier between the moist plant tissue and the arid desert climate. This jives with what old hippies say: that some of the best pot you can have comes from areas that have experienced an

This insect has tried to eat away at the leaves of the plant, but the sticky trichomes have gummed up his mandibles, thus protecting the plant.

extreme drought. However, extreme cold, around 30°F, also forces trichomes to develop in most Indica-dominant plants.

Trichomes also develop at a greater percentage as a sort of "sun block" from increased levels of UV-B (280–315 nm). Researchers have also found that THC is in a much higher concentration when exposed to UV-B rays. There is also a negative correlation between high temperatures and the amount of THC produced.

The above information is based on the 1994 findings by David Pate, published in the *Journal of the International Hemp Association.*

BEGINNING FLORAL STAGE

This stage is between weeks one and three of flowering cycle.* During the first few days and up to a week, your plant is producing what looks like a series of female pre-flowers in close proximity to each other. These are actually the very beginning of the buds. At this stage, calyxes are small and pistils are straight and white. At this time a great deal of stem will still be exposed—this will be the

The buds will first appear at the top and middle of your plant, like we see here. Then they'll work their way up and down the plant. Make sure it gets lots of water, and get ready for a big harvest.

Here we see a bud developing at a node in the middle of a plant. Bud appears at the most well-established nodes first, and then spreads. Be sure to stake the plant before it gets too heavy.

mainframe of the cola. You should see bud developing at the top and middle of the plant first, and work its way up and down to the bottom of the plant. The most well established nodes will develop bud first. At the beginning you will see mostly non-glandular trichomes, but there are some bulbous trichomes and a few capitate sessile trichomes scattered about. Little to no cannabinoid production is taking place at this time. All the fan leaves should still be green. You should be feeding, as needed, with 600 PPM** of flowering fertilizer and 200 PPM** of Cal Mag—although calcium and magnesium deficiencies are uncommon, you should start using Cal-Mag as a "preemptive strike." You may also add 2 tbsp of molasses per gallon of water.

PEAK FLORAL STAGE

This stage is between weeks four–six of the flowering cycle.* Bud clusters have elongated from the addition of more calyxes and there is less stem exposed.

Toward the middle of week five you will start to see a rapid growth in calyxes. The oldest pistils will have withered away and the oldest calyxes will have begun to swell, though usually only slightly. Leaflets are composed of three blades. There are a majority of capitate sessile trichomes at this time and a few trichomes have turned somewhat milky. There are more and more capitate-stalked trichomes developing and fewer and fewer bulbous trichomes. There will probably be some yellowing of the leaves taking place at this stage. At the beginning of this stage, you want to apply a light flushing to clear any accumulated salts. After the flushing you want to apply 600** PPM of flowering fertilizer and 600** PPM of Cal-Mag, because at this time your plant is using up enormous amounts of calcium and magnesium. As a matter of fact, I typically will just about overdose my plant with Cal/Mag at the first sign of a calcium or magnesium deficiency. This will nip the Cal/Mag issue in the bud (so to speak) before it ever becomes a problem. In week six you should feed with 1,000–1,200** PPM of flowering fertilizer. You should also add about 1–2 tbsp of Black Strap molasses per gallon for every watering you do. Remember to keep a careful eye for hermaphroditic flowers from this point forward.

These are some pistils emerging from the female flowers on the terminal bud. The early stages of flowering are a treat for any grower.

This is how the terminal bud should look a few weeks into flowering. The pistils are emerging and the bud is quickly forming.

This is a good time to add stakes to plants that will not be able to support the weight of the buds. You may want to skip a week of feeding and feed with Liquid Karma and Sweet, around 800–1,000 PPM.**

RIPE FLORAL STAGE

You should start by watching your plants for the peak floral stage—usually around 10 days after the breeder's latest expected finish date. Some plants will mature from bottom to top. As such, you can either stagger your harvest, taking an early "sample," or you could harvest all at once and get both buds with a couch lock high and a more cerebral high from the same plant but from different parts. The opposite is also true in that a plant may mature from top to bottom. This stage is between weeks seven and eight of the flowering cycle.* Rapid growth has slowed around the end of week seven and calyxes begin to swell, as do the trichome heads. This is also when "donkey ears" or "fox tails" emerge— the calyxes that build up on top of each other and protrude from the main bud.

The majority of pistils will have withered away, but a ratio of 80 dead and 20 alive is most likely. At this stage capitate-stalked trichomes are the most abundant trichome and the majority of the heads are cloudy; this is because the resin has stopped being secreted and has frozen. A few heads may still be clear but these are nothing to be concerned with. Towards the end of week seven you will see some amber heads appearing and increasing in number as week eight draws to a close. There should be very little, if any, stem visible if you did a good job controlling the stretch and internodes did not become elongated. At the tops of your colas, you will notice that single blade leaflets have appeared and triple blade leaflets are only located on the middle and lower parts of the cola. Many fan leaves will be yellowing and some leaves even dropping off the plant. This is normal and is a welcome indication that stored nitrogen is being used. During week seven you should apply a heavy flushing to cleanse your plant of any accumulated salts; this will remove any stored nutrients to provide a smoother, cleaner, tastier smoke. After the flushing, you should not water or feed your plant anything, as this will speed up the drying time. You can also add 1 tbsp per gallon of black strap molasses to your flushing mix.

Note: adding black strap molasses will only improve the taste; Sweet, or a similar product, will improve yield.

Note: an experienced large-scale grower has documented that cutting the light back by half one-and-a-half weeks before harvest will increase yield by 15%. Experiments with this technique have proved inconclusive.

Warning: There is a rumor going around that putting your plants in complete

This Ch9 Jack from Ch9 Female Seeds has been staked to ensure that the plant can support the weight of the buds. Ch9 Jack is well known for its bountiful harvests.

darkness 36 to 48 hours before the chop will result in a higher concentration of trichomes. This myth is further perpetuated by growers saying it has worked for them. This has been tried on 30 different strains, with the result that only four out of thirty strains showed a marked higher concentration of trichomes, while the other 26 strains began to herm and the buds looked malformed.

Big Devil from Sweet Seeds is highly impressive in full flower. Notice how the fan leaves have been carefully trimmed to increase the amount of light that hits the cola.

LATE FLORAL STAGE

This stage is between weeks nine and ten of the flowering cycle.* All growth has ceased, calyxes are quite large, and there are more and more amber trichomes developing each day. The majority of fan leaves are dead and more are dying each day. Senescence (decay) is approaching the longer the plant(s) are left alive. The weight of the buds is highest at this point, but the quality has greatly diminished as THC has started to deteriorate.

* Based on a strain that finishes at eight weeks.

** Different strains will be more or less sensitive to fertilizer meaning they will require more or less.

Note: when you hear a grower referring to a strain being at day 52 or week 6, they are referring to when they entered the flowering cycle—not from seed—unless otherwise stated.

Note: some impatient growers start out with 12/12 during the first month or so and then gradually reduce the light to 10/14 two weeks before the actual finishing time of the plants. This fools the plant into thinking that winter is fast approaching and they must hurry up and finish. This does not improve potency or yield; actually, the yield is diminished for the sake of the faster finishing time.

Note the withered and dried trichomes and pistils. These indicate that this bud was harvested some time ago.

Chapter 16

Harvest

That's right, folks, it's time to reap the fruits of your labor. At this stage, you may be feeling a bit mixed up, especially if this is one of your first couple of grows or if you have been especially attached to your plants through the grow cycle—you may be feeling like you don't want to chop them down after all you've put into them. But take out that axe: you'll feel much better once you're toking on those buds!

How do you know if your plants are ready for the chop? The first indication would be the ratio of white vibrant pistils to yellow / orange / red, dead, withered pistils. From about the fourth week of budding onward, you will notice that pistils will begin to wither and die; the average lifespan of a pistil is about four weeks, so the pistils that were the first to emerge (these will be at the bottom of colas) will be the first to die. This cycle will repeat every four weeks. When the plant is one to two weeks shy of harvest, you may notice a sudden surge of white pistils; once these pistils die out, it is a good indication that your plant is ready to be harvested.

Watching the pistils is just one way a grower learns that his crop is nearing its finishing time. The next way is to watch the calyxes. Calyxes will begin to swell as the plant is ripening; calyxes only begin to swell about two to three weeks from the peak harvest period. Watching the calyxes is more important than watching the pistils. As calyxes mature, they will increase your yield; this is not true for pistils. Depending on the strain, calyx size can reach ¼ of an inch. This is an extreme—most will become 2–3mm in length when fully mature. Watching pistils and calyxes are the two ways experienced growers know when their plants are ready for harvest. Foxtails are a good indication of a heavy yielding strain and also that plant is near the chop.

Rookie growers should implement the microscope technique. This is accomplished by purchasing a "pocket" microscope from Radio Shack—very inexpensive at $9.99. This will give you magnification up to 100x. Now the trick with the microscope is to hold it as still as possible; it is next to impossible to look at the trichomes

Reaping the fruits of this Brainstorm Haze will be a true pleasure. This plant experienced a sudden surge of white pistils about a week before harvest.

on the plant, so you will have to take a sample each time. It is best to put the material on a backdrop of a glossy, medium blue color. Now you must place your elbow on something solid while looking at the material so as not to shake your hand. You must experiment just where to hold the microscope. At first you might think it is broken because you may only see black, but with proper adjustment you should be able to see your desired image.

Now what are you looking for? You should first take samples from the beginning of flowering, in the middle, and then at least two times when your plant is nearing the end. This will show you what an immature trichome looks like and how it changes as

420 Scopes are a nice hand held microscope that can do 100x magnification – perfect for examining trichomes closely.

it develops. The changing of clear trichomes to cloudy, and from cloudy to amber, are different stages of development. Even bulbous trichomes will change from clear to cloudy, and this will continue throughout flowering. When trichomes are clear, cannabinoids are still being manufactured; when the trichome turns cloudy, production has ceased for now. When trichomes turn amber, that trichome will not process any more cannabinoids.

As the plant continues to mature, you will notice that the majority of trichomes are milky while some trichomes still remain clear; these are nothing to worry about—some trichomes will always be clear—new trichomes are always developing except in

These bulbous-headed stalks are the trichomes. They process the cannabinoids and store the THC. Watch their coloration and opacity during flowering to determine when to harvest.

senescence. As long as the majority of your trichomes are milky with some amber thrown in, you're golden. However, some growers—especially those growing for medicinal purposes—may wish to have a greater concentration of amber trichomes.

Now, if you look very closely (you will need 100x for this) you will notice that the round heads are starting to become a bit pointed at the top because of the resin that has packed the trichome head. When your plant is at peak ripeness, about 80% of the trichomes will have turned colors and the heads will have "peaks." This is the ideal time to harvest based on trichomes. Now, if you're more focused on yield than a particular type of high, this might not be the right time for you.

If you enjoy more of a couch lock sedative, pain relieving high, then having more amber trichomes—about 20 or 30% more—will be more to your liking. Also, having about 10 or 15% amber trichomes on an Indica or Afghani plant will enhance the effect of the plant.

The same is true for Sativa plants. If you enjoy more of a head high, cerebral and thought provoking, innovative and functional, a day time high, then you should harvest your plant with clear and cloudy heads. This will decrease your yield but will

Use a pocket microscope to look at the trichomes of the plant. The color and maturity of the trichomes are excellent indicators of when to harvest.

contain the type of high that you enjoy.

Now that you have decided when to harvest, it's time to get chopping. You will need some regular heavy-duty scissors to cut stalks, stems, fan leaves, etc. Serrated scissors work best. Next, you will need some small sharp scissors in order to remove sugar leaves and manicure fine bud. You will also need three buckets: one for fan leaves, stems, and stalks; one for sugar leaves; and one for buds.

Note: cannabis buds are transdermal, meaning that THC / Cannabinoids can be absorbed through the skin. There may be times where you may not smoke for months, but may have recently harvested a healthy crop. Once you take your urine analysis, your readings may be as high as 154 PPM of Cannabinoids. Wear double layer latex gloves if this could be a problem for you.

Some people say that all manicuring should be done after the plant has dried because the leaves wrapping around the buds slow the release of chlorophyll, result- ing in smoother smoke, but there has been no documented proof of this. The only definite thing this does is make trimming *much* more difficult.

Warning: this is the smelliest part of growing cannabis: make sure your security is not compromised while wrapping up your grow.

Begin by dissecting the plant into the main branches. Then remove all the fan leaves on the branches. Now you want to trim the sugar leaves off. The easiest way to accomplish this is by laying the scissors against the bud and trimming everything protruding from the cola, forming it into a spear shape; however, the "cannaseur's" preference is to locate the petiole or stem from each fan and sugar leaf, trace the petiole as deep into the bud as possible, and then cut it. Repeat this process for all branches on all plants.

Now you are ready to dry your plants. This is usually done in an area where there

Here we see a very dense and beautiful Margot plant from Green Devil Genetics being harvested. Note the thick latex gloves and good scissors used to trim the sugar leaves and manicure the gorgeous bud.

Lighting and good air circulation are necessary for drying your plants. These colas are hanging from the string by their side buds, but clothespins work well, too.

is lighting with a lot of air circulation. You will need to run a clothes line from wall to wall and either hang the colas on the line via side buds, or attach them via paper clips or string to the clothes line. Clothespins also work surprisingly well (go figure). Try to hang them where they have space between the buds. Have a fan applying a gentle breeze on the buds. For your "popcorn" buds, spread a sheet of newspaper and make sure they are not piled up on top of each other. Come back daily and move the buds around and change the newspaper. You should also have a fan directed across the tops of these "popcorn" buds.

Note: some growers have noticed that having your buds drying in a place where the temperature falls and rises each day will remove more chlorophyll from the buds. This means an un-insulated portion of your house, i.e., a garage, is ideal for drying.

Your buds should hang and dry for between five to seven days, sometimes longer if you have a very wet or dense strain.

Note: if you starved your plant for water four or five days before harvest and maintained low humidity, you will be able to decrease the amount of time needed to dry. You can also decrease the drying time by scoring the stems—the score or cut will release the moisture that is being housed in the stem.

Your buds are ready for curing when you can snap the stem; if it bends, the buds are not ready to be cured yet and need more time to dry. You may think that your

Mason jars are the best for curing bud. Leave a quarter of the jar empty to allow air to circulate. Remember to burp the jars regularly and watch for signs of mold.

stem will never snap and that the buds are dry to the touch; however, there is still a lot of moisture housed inside the buds that will continue to seep out and cause you problems if the buds are sealed. Just be patient and wait for the stems to snap.

Curing dates back centuries. Some African tribes would harvest their cannabis plants and, once dry, would place the buds in the rind of a fruit—usually a banana. They would tie the rind together and bury it in the ground for about a month's time.

When the buds are properly dried you can separate all the side buds and incomplete colas into nice nugs to cure, removing as you do so any unnecessary stem. Now, to cure you must use airtight glass containers—avoid plastic containers, which are porous and therefore undesirable, at all costs. Mason jars work the best, and Wal-Mart carries them as a seasonal spring / summer time item, so stock up while you can. Just ask for canning jars. A case with a dozen pint sized jars runs about 8 dollars.

A word of caution concerning 420 Jars' curing jars. These jars seem like creative ways to store your personal head stash and a decorative way to show them off to your friends. However, I find these jars are dangerous because of the thin glass that 420 Jars uses. I've had two 420 Jars shatter, causing glass shards to contaminate kind buds (therefore having to discard them), and receiving minor injuries. Be gentle if you decide to cure your buds in 420 Jars.

You should only fill your jars up three quarters full so air can get to all the buds. During the first three days, "burp" the jars once a day for about a minute. Shuffle the buds around and make sure they do not feel wet and there is no condensation or mold growing. If there is mold or moisture, remove the infected bud(s) and any buds that were touching it and discard them. Immediately spread the non-infected buds over a couple of sheets of newspaper with a fan circulating on them, and after three days time you should be able to safely place your bud back in the jars, monitoring them closely during the following few days.

After the first three days, you should only burp your jars once a month, making sure to store in a cool, dark place. The longer the cure, the better your herb will taste and smell (and, sometimes, look). The standard cure is three months, but there are people who cure for as long as eighteen months—this is an extreme, however, and few people have the will power for this anyhow. As your bud continues to cure, each time you open the jars you will notice that the aroma has become even more potent and desirable; the aroma will likely have changed from what it was originally. This is because the curing process takes place in cannabinoids, which will isomerize the terpenes and cannabinoids into forming polyterpenes.

Every part of this OG Kush can be harvested and used. Sugar leaves are good for kief and hash, the stalk is good for rope, and the roots can be used for a nutritious tea.

WATER CURING

contributed by Liz_Weir

Water curing is a rather controversial method of curing bud, but it does have its uses. If you have good-tasting bud that has been flushed, you probably won't want to water cure it. Times when water curing will help:

Bad tasting bud: water curing will remove most of the flavor from bud.

Harshness: water curing will help remove a lot of the chemicals from the bud, making it less harsh to smoke and easier on your lungs.

Cooking: water curing removes a lot of the chlorophyll and chemicals from the bud, which helps make better tasting cannabutter or other food items.

Odor: if odor is a problem when drying your bud, water curing eliminates the odor problem.

Time: instead of slow-drying your bud and then curing it in jars for 30–60 days, water curing can reach approximately the same level of cure and smoothness in only 5–10 days.

Advantages

Apart from the above: since water curing removes some of the weight and bulk from the bud, the THC becomes more concentrated. Some claim that water curing makes the bud more potent; that is not true, but you will get more THC per hit because you will be getting less vegetable matter per hit.

Disadvantages

Water curing tends to darken the color of the bud (some varieties can literally almost turn black). This makes the "bag appeal" a lot lower.

It makes the bud weigh less because of the removed gunk, which can be a problem if the bud is destined for sale.

How To

You can water cure fresh bud or already dried bud.

Put the buds loosely into a container. Don't fill the container more than about ⅔ full.

Cover the buds with fresh cool water (not cold, definitely not hot). I prefer to use RO (reverse osmosis) water, but tap water works fine.

Put something on top of the buds to hold them under the water.

Once a day, drain off the water and fill the container with fresh water.

Most of the nasty stuff will be washed out in the first 4–5 days, but you can continue to cure the bud for up to 10 days.

When you are ready to dry the bud, drain as much water off as you can. Lay the buds on top of a couple of towels to let the towels absorb some of the water.

Put the buds loosely on top of a grate or screen so there is lots of airflow. Depending on the quantity of bud and relative humidity, the buds should be dry in about a day. You can use a food dehydrator to dry the buds more quickly, if you have one. Quick drying won't hurt water-cured bud any!

Data

Last time I water cured some bud, I measured the TDS of the runoff each day. This bud was cured using RO water with a starting TDS of 10. These numbers are PPM using .7 conversion.

Day 1: 1,650 PPM

Day 2: 600 PPM

Day 3: 350 PPM

Day 4: 190 PPM

Day 5: 110 PPM

Day 6: 90 PPM

Day 7: 80 PPM

Day 8: 70 PPM

AFTER THE HARVEST

Nothing on the cannabis plant is wasted. The sugar leaves are used to make kief / hash (refer to the hashish and extractions chapter) or cannabutter (refer to the cooking chapter), the stalks can be used to make hemp rope, and the roots may be made into a nutritious tea (a practice common to Africa).

Chapter 17

Revegetation

Revegetation is the process of forcing your harvested plant back into the vegetation cycle. Despite what you may have heard, revegging, as it is most commonly known, is very simple. You may reveg a plant for a number of reasons—the bud was really good, or you want to use it for breeding, or you want to get a jump on the next season. Having the plant's root structure and mainframe intact will save you much more time (up to a month) than having to start from seed again.

You can reveg a plant no matter how long its finishing time.

In order to reveg your plant you will need fresh soil, a blend of worm castings, Black Kow (or another organic fertilizer rich in nitrogen and microbes), Pro Mix BX (preferred; or Sunshine #4), and Plant Tone. Ideally, you should have a bigger container than the one your plant is in. If this is not possible, you should shave the root ball down to size. The most common example would be a 5-gallon container; you would shave at least 2 inches off the sides, and at least 2–3 inches off the bottom.

First, you want to remove all but the branches, leaves, and buds closest to the stalk of your plant. A good rule of thumb is to remove everything outside of a 5 or 6-inch circle from the stalk. Of course, this may not be possible if you were growing a very leggy plant with long internodes. You want at least five branches left on the stalk. You will need to leave at least three nodes with bud on them; these buds are where the new growing shoots will emerge.

Once you have pruned your plant for revegging, it is time to transplant. Grab your new container (if you chose this method), and begin packing in the fresh nitrogen and micro biotic soil. It is also a good idea to mix some mycorrhizae powder in your soil, before adding the plant in, as this will help ease the stress and speed up the revegging process.

Transplant your plant as you normally would, making sure to pack in around the root ball well. You may have to use a ruler or something similar, if your hands

Fish emulsion fertilizer has an NPK ratio of 5-1-1, meaning it is rich in Nitrogen. It also has plenty of microbes, making it ideal for revegging your plants.

Again, like cloning and transplanting, revegetating your plants requires the materials. Good, fresh soil is a good start.

are too big. It is easier to remove a root ball intact when the soil is moist. If too wet, the root ball is heavy and may collapse under the weight of the added water; too dry, and the root ball will flake and break apart. In a five-gallon pot with good aeration and a thorough watering, the ideal time for transplanting will be two days after your last watering.

Once your plant has been transplanted, water thoroughly with a generous amount of Superthrive (or another plant vitamin). One drop per gallon is not nearly enough in my opinion—I have seen no ill results from adding, say, half a teaspoon. pH your water to 6.5 so that nitrogen can be most effectively absorbed.

Ideally, your plant can be placed under a metal halide light, and the light cycle set to 20 on / 4 off.

After your plant(s) dry out from the first watering, feed them with a mild dose of plant food, between 600–800PPM of PBP Grow or a similar vegetative nutrient. You don't want to hit her too hard with too much food, as you don't want to go from one extreme to the other. This is a very stressful time in a plant's life, and you don't need to add any more stress to it. Add a couple of drops of vitamins to this water as well—

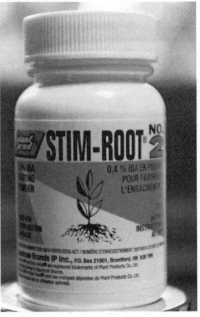

When revegging, transplant your plant as you normally would, and, as always, be sure to pack in well around the roots to avoid air pockets.

Water the plants you are revegetating using a root stimulator. Healthy roots mean a healthy plant.

basically you want to add Superthrive or another supplement every watering during this whole reveg process.

Caution: Avoid using any fertilizer with ammonium nitrate in it; it will wreak havoc on growing roots.

After your plant(s) dry out from the aforementioned feeding, water with a root stimulator. I have found House & Garden's Root Stimulator to be most effective. It is completely organic, which makes it that much better. The reason for adding root stimulator is that it the faster your roots develop below the surface, the faster your plant will develop above the surface. Roots are crucial. Without them, the plant cannot efficiently absorb nutrients or water. Roots dictate the growth above the soil line, so make sure they are healthy in order to have a healthy plant above the surface.

You will not see any change in your plant for between 1½–3 weeks—more or less, depending on how well you followed the instructions, and of course depending on the strain. (Indica and mostly-Indica hybrids seem to respond better and quicker than Sativas.) The first signs you will notice are new white pistils forming on the buds you left on the plant. Congratulations, you just successfully revegged your plant!

After this you will notice the buds starting to stretch or elongate as the stem grows, and what seems like dozens of new branches starting to grow directly from the buds!

Most new leaves emerging are circled, and the ones that aren't are just single blade leaves. Don't worry, this is absolutely normal; the circle leaves are just a form of shock and the single blade leaflets are the plant's way of gathering the most light / energy as soon as possible. Soon after this, you will start seeing three blade leaflets, and then, gradually, the numbers of leaflets will build until they are at the number they were originally on that particular plant. You may need to feed your plants between the single and three-blade leaflet stage, depending on the amount of fertilizer in your soil and the amount of PPMs you gave them on their first feeding. If your plant is developing properly and you see no paling or yellowing on the bottom leaves, you don't need to feed. At this point, when there are enough growing shoots and leaves, you may remove the remaining buds and "sucker" shoots—which are in fact just taking energy away from the main shoots.

Once you see five blade leaflets, this marks the end of the reveg process and you have entered into your regular vegetation stage again. You no longer have to give her any special treatment; you can treat her just as you would any other plant in the vegetation cycle. You will want to give another dose of food at this point—say, 800 PPM of vegetative fertilizer.

The whole process usually takes between 4–5 weeks; it may take longer, as mentioned above, depending on the conditions and the strain. Something to be aware of: some strains may react horribly to even the slightest pH imbalance or deficiency. Revegged plants are more subject to pathogen and bug infestations. Some growers have found that certain strains are very finicky when growing after being revegged, so this is something to be aware of. There have been reports of people revegging a plant more than five times, but again this is just hearsay; it is not recommended to reveg any more than three times. Revegging a plant causes them to become naturally bushier than before, to replace their few big branches with dozens of smaller ones. This process continues until the plant can no longer be used to take healthy clones. This is due to the degradation of the plant's structure, i.e., genetic drift.

An infestation of pests can cause a good grow to go bad very quickly. Be aware of any insects that want to call your plant home, and be prepared to deal with them.

Chapter 18

Pests, Diseases, Deficiencies, and Disorders

PESTS

Insects are a major problem for indoor growers, as extreme weather conditions force insects to seek shelter in a "safer" environment. Insects hitchhike on your clothing and pets to reach your grow room, which is why you should never allow your pets to visit your grow room and why you should take your stroll outside after you check on your plants inside. Below, we will cover the most common indoor pests and diseases. The easiest way to keep your grow room pest free is to never bring them indoors in the first place. The easiest way to accomplish this is to keep your room as clean as possible; hard, but necessary nonetheless. This means cleaning with disinfectant, sweeping, etc. The tiniest insects are often the ones that will ransack your grow rooms. Pay special attention to the cracks and crevices; make sure they are sealed. Standing water is our greatest enemy: eliminate any standing water immediately; stagnant water is a precursor to many kinds of problems. Be sure to quarantine any new clones or seedlings for at least a week's time as far away from your garden as possible.

Aphids

Prevalent throughout the U.S. They can be winged; are green, white, yellow, pink, or black, depending on the species; and they are $1/10$ of an inch in length. They are common on leaf undersides, and feed on your plant's juices and leaves, which in turn become distorted and yellow. Ants and aphids are your enemies; the ants will protect the aphids since they are their source of food. Aphids and spider mites are some of the hardest pests to get rid off. This is partly because most insecticides only work on adult aphids, not on larva and eggs. This means you'll have to spray your whole plant, *thoroughly*, at least three times a week, for several weeks. Cold temperatures below 40°F will eliminate aphids, as will inducing a large population of ladybugs.

Spider Mites

Prevalent all across the southeast and southwestern U.S. in extremely hot, dry, and arid conditions, especially in areas where wintertime temperatures seldom dip below freezing. These tiny insects are yellow, red, or white and are a microscopic $1/64$ of an inch in length. Serious spider mite infections are easy to spot because of the web they weave all over various parts of your plants. Leaves typically have a golden or bronze look to them with a spider mite infection. Keep soil moist and spray plants frequently to prevent them. Treat by using insecticidal soap and/or neem oil. A certain species of ladybug (Stethorus) is especially useful in combating spider mites. Indoors, spider mites are especially hard to get rid of; you may have to resort to chemical insecticides or risk losing your crop. In extreme cases, you may have to use a powerful sulfur bomb to kill these bastards.

Thrips

Many species are prevalent all across the U.S. Thrips are a yellow color and $1/25$ of an inch in length. You probably won't spot the thrips themselves, but may find their droppings—black looking specks on leaf surfaces—or their damage—yellowing lines scarring your plants. Prevent by using diatomaceous Earth. Treat by using neem oil; for a quicker approach, apply pyrethrum, which is derived from the blossoms of chrysanthemums.

Whiteflies

Prevalent throughout the U.S. Whiteflies are translucent in color and $1/16$ of an inch in length. They feed in large numbers on the undersides of leaves. They will fly to other parts of your plant when disturbed. Like other insects, they suck out plant nutrients. Prevent by having excess nitrogen in your soil; also avoid deficiencies in phosphorus and magnesium, which are believed to attract white flies. Treat with insecticidal soap and/or neem oil. A tiny wasp, Encarsia Formosa, is a great predator of white flies, as are spiders.

Fungus Gnats

Prevalent wherever there are shaded, moist areas of soil. Gnats need warm temperatures to reproduce, as well as high humidity. Reducing the temperature to the 60s and reducing the humidity to the 30–40s will combat gnats. Using sterile potting soil is a good way to prevent them. If you notice gnats, try to increase the lighting on the soil (without taking away from the plants). Also, let the medium dry out thoroughly, and on the next watering, water with 2 tsp of 35% hydrogen peroxide per gallon. Yellow sticky traps work wonders for gnats. For immediate results, treat with pyrethrum and / or pheromone traps.

Some insects are very good for your plants, and others are very bad. This ladybug can protect your bud from pests such as aphids. Know the good guys from the bad and you'll have a better chance at a successful grow.

Spreading live ladybugs on your grow can help protect it from pests, such as aphids.

Hanging a praying mantis egg case on your plant can help keep any number of pests away from your bud. Once the mantids hatch, it is hunting season.

This grower should have used insecticidal soap to treat his spider mite infestation. Now his grow is destroyed. Spider mites are one of the most dangerous pests for any grower.

DISEASES

Grey Mold (Botrytis)

Prevalent in grow rooms that do not have ample ventilation systems and / or have excess humidity during the flowering cycle. Moisture gets trapped inside the cola and cannot work its way out, providing heat, humidity, darkness, and lack of evaporation—the ingredients for mold. Treat by removing every part of the botrytis (or "bud rot") and all the plant matter it was or could have been touching. Lower the humidity as much as possible and spray the plants with gliocladium roseum (a microorganism) or trichoderma (another fungi).

Sooty Mold

A direct result of aphid, mealybugs (uncommon indoors), whiteflies, or any other critter that infests your plants. These insects secrete honeydew, which can cause this black mold to develop. Control by first removing the critters and then spray with insecticidal soap.

Powdery Mildew

Appears as a powdery white fungus that coats the upper part of the leaves; it then turns yellow and dries out. Usually affects the older leaves first. Control by using a fungicide that contains sulfur.

At the end of every grow you should do a thorough cleaning, scrubbing every surface with pure bleach. Sweeping out all debris and fumigating for insects. Using human-safe insect and fungus bombs are the easiest way to fumigate a grow room. Use sulfur bombs for any mold / fungus issues.

Notes:

When using Neem oil, dissolve it first in boiling water. Stir and shake to prevent clumping on the surface.

H_2O_2 works well at treating minor fungus issues.

When you are using insect predators (ladybugs, for example) they will be dormant after shipping; awaken them by misting them with lukewarm water and leaving them in the sunlight or HPS.

DEFICIENCIES

There are 13 main nutrients that cannabis uses to grow. Four of these nutrients are mobile, meaning that they can relocate to other parts of the plant as they are needed. Nutrients that show their deficiencies at the bottom / middle of the plant are mobile elements. These include: nitrogen (N), magnesium (Mg), phosphorus (P), and calcium (Ca). The other nine are immobile nutrients, meaning that they will not relocate to other portions of the plants as needed. It is most effective to treat these nutrient deficiencies with foliar feeding rather than through the roots, as normal. However, feeding through both the roots and the leaves is sometimes necessary. In addition, some elements work in synergy with one another, meaning that they aid in absorption by the plant, as is the case with nitrogen and magnesium, magnesium and phosphorus, and potassium, iron and manganese. Likewise, some elements are antagonistic, meaning that they interfere with the absorption of other elements, as is the case with excessive phosphorus, which inhibits the absorption of potassium, zinc, copper, and iron, and excessive calcium, which inhibits the absorption of potassium, magnesium, manganese, iron and zinc.

Sometimes it is necessary to use a sulfur bomb or an inorganic pesticide to save your crop. Know the risks, and best methods of protecting your bud.

This cannabis plant is just beginning to show the effects of a powdery mildew infestation. He needs to control it with a fungicide that contains sulfur.

Nitrogen (N)

Affects the bottom to middle of the plant first, typically with uniform yellowing or paling up; however, paling of new growth will occur as well. Then leaves die and drop, growth is slowed, and leaf margins are not curled up.

Nitrogen and magnesium deficiencies are often confused. Nitrogen deficiencies often occur at the bottom of the plant, progressing their way up the plant. The yellowing is uniform, starting at the leaf tip and working its way to the leaf apex or junction. Nitrogen will cause the entire leaf to yellow, the veins last.

Excess nitrogen will cause overall dark foliage. Plants will lose their vigor and growth will be stunted. Stems will be weak and thin. Excess nitrogen will cause delayed maturity and decreased yields. Older fan leaves will develop the claw and new growth may be deformed.

There are several ways to correct a nitrogen deficiency. The quickest would be to make a tea out of dried blood meal: use 1 cup of dried blood per 5 gallons of water. You can also use 5-1-1 fish emulsion as a foliar feed. And, of course, treating with any organic fertilizer (Pure Blend Pro Grow, Earth Juice Grow, BioBizz grow, or Dr. Hornby's Iguana Juice Grow) via the roots. The concentration of this can range from 300–1,000 PPM, depending on the size and maturity of your plants.

Nitrogen gets locked out of soil and hydro between 4.5–5.5 pH

Nitrogen is best absorbed in soil between 6.3–6.5 pH

Nitrogen is best absorbed in hydroponics between 5.5–6.5 pH

A means of correcting excess nitrogen would be to flush thoroughly with pH balanced water, and/or to use a product like Clearex; in addition, you may wish to reverse foliar feed, which is just spraying your leaves with plain pH water every day. In extreme cases, you may need to transplant into a no nutrient / low nutrient soil or soil-less mix.

Phosphorus (P)

Older leaves are dark green with bluish hues to them. Newer growth has deformed yellowing leaves; edges of the leaves become brown / black and twisted, which closely resembles a fungus issue. Stems also become reddish in color, although some strains may posses the trait naturally. Growth is stunted and overall leaves are smaller.

Cold temperatures and soggy soil make it difficult for the plant to absorb nitrogen and phosphorus.

Correct by making a tea out of bone meal or, preferably, use Jamaican bat guano. You can also use Morbloom, or, of course, commercial fertilizers.

Excess phosphorus inhibits the uptake of potassium, iron, copper, and zinc. The most notable signs of excess phosphorus are the deficiencies of iron and zinc. If you see signs of these deficiencies, it is best to assume you have excess phosphorus.

Correct by flushing with pH'd water or using a product such as Clearex. In extreme cases you may need to transplant to a nutrient-free soil.

Phosphorus is locked out of soil between 4.5–5.5 pH and in hydroponics between 6.0–8.5 pH.

Phosphorus is best absorbed in soil between 6.0–6.8 pH and in hydroponics between 4.0–5.8 pH.

Potassium (K)

The beginnings of potassium deficiencies show twisting / deformed growth. The older leaves will show the signs first, as well as the edges of the leaves. Yellowing will start at the tips and work its way back to the leaf junction along the edges. Leaves will develop necrotic dead spots, primarily along the edges or down the center vein. As the deficiency progresses, these necrotic spots will engulf the leaf tips, moving toward the apex of the leaf. Leaf tips will then curl upwards.

Having too much calcium and ammonium nitrate in your soil will inhibit the absorption of potassium. Also, excess sodium will cause potassium to dissipate too quickly for it to be absorbed by the plant.

Correct by making a tea out of kelp meal or sulfate of potash, or a commercial fertilizer.

Excess potassium leads to high salinity and acid fixation in roots. It also locks out other micronutrients such as iron and magnesium.

Correct by flushing or using a product like Clearex. In extreme cases you may need to transplant to nutrient-free soil.

This plant looks like it was over fed and has excessive salt build up. Remember to flush regularly to prevent salt from building up.

Potassium is locked out of soil between 4.0–5.5 pH and in hydroponics between 4.0–4.5 and 6.0–6.5 pH.

Potassium is best absorbed in soil between 6.0–6.8 pH and in hydroponics between 4.7–5.3 and 6.8–8.5 pH.

Magnesium (Mg)
Magnesium deficiencies will occur on the middle growth most of the time. Not always at the bottom of the plant, but this does happen. It is easiest to tell magnesium deficiencies from nitrogen because nitrogen yellowing is uniform and magnesium is splotchy, but will eventually yellow the entire leaf, excluding the veins, but in extreme cases veins will yellow. More likely, the leaf will not turn pale green but remain a medium / dark shade of green, although yellowing is present. Also, magnesium deficiencies are uncommon in vegetation and extremely common along with cal-

cium deficiencies during mid-flowering.

Correct by using Cal-Mag and foliar feed for quicker results. You may also use 1–2 tsp of Epsom salts dissolved in a cup of hot water before added to a gallon of water. However, Cal-Mag Plus at a concentration of around 800 PPM is most commonly used.*

Magnesium is locked out in soil and hydroponics between 2.0–6.0 pH.

Magnesium is best absorbed in soil and hydroponics between 6.1–7.5 pH.

Calcium (Ca)

Middle–new leaves show deficiencies first. First, your new leaf tips will brown and curl up slightly; then brown spots will develop along most of the serrations around the edge of the leaf; then, as it progresses, the brown spots will spread all over the leaf; finally, young leaves and stems will die, progressing down the plant.

Correct by foliar feeding with 1 tsp of garden lime per quart of water. You can also foliar feed with Cal-Mag plus or prevent by using Cal-Mag plus regularly during flowering, when Calcium deficiencies occur most often. If calcium or magnesium deficiencies do arise, treat with around 800 PPM. Planting with gypsum not only will increase your yields but will prevent most calcium deficiencies.

Excess calcium will inhibit the uptake of potassium. Excess calcium is characterized by weak stems and leaves that develop whitish-brown coloring in between veins. Calcium and magnesium deficiencies often run hand in hand. If you see yellowing and necrotic spots developing at an increasing rate on leaves in the middle of the plant, especially during flower, you know that you are experiencing both calcium and magnesium deficiencies. Just use Cal-Mag Plus as directed but do *not* combine the dosage.

Calcium is locked out in soil between 2.0–6.2 pH and in hydroponics between 2.0–5.3 pH.

Calcium is best absorbed in soil between 6.3–7.5 pH and hydroponics between 5.4–5.8 pH.

Iron (Fe)

Starts with the newer growth and progresses its way down the plant. It begins on the edges of the leaves and works its way inward, causing entire leaves and growing shoots to turn completely white / yellow in color. Excess phosphorus and zinc can lock out iron.

Adding a few non-galvanized nails to the bottom of your pots will ensure that iron deficiency never occurs. Typically any decent nutrients will contain iron. Correct by using Cal-Mag Plus at a normal dosage.

Iron is locked out in soil and hydroponics between 2.0–3.5 pH.

Iron is best absorbed in soil and hydroponics between 5.5–6.8 pH.

Zinc (Zn)

Affects new growth first by causing leaf edges and interveins to become yellow, pale green, or gray.

Correct by having nails in the soil, but any decent nutrient will contain all the zinc you need. Correct by treating with a normal amount of either grow or bloom organic fertilizer.

Zinc is locked out of soil between 4.5–4.7 and 7.5–9.5 pH and in hydroponics between 5.7–8.5 pH.

Zinc is best absorbed in soil between 5.5–6.8 pH and in hydroponics between 5.5–5.8 pH.

Manganese (Mn)

Will develop in the older leaves first, quickly making its way up the plant. First, yellowing will start at the tips and then necrotic dead spots will appear. Leaf fringes / edges will curl downward, as will leaves in general. They will eventually shrivel up entirely and drop off.

Correct by using any decent organic fertilizer at a normal dosage. Foliar feed for faster results.

Manganese is locked out in soil between 2.0–5.0 and in hydroponics between 2.0–4.5 pH.

Manganese is best absorbed in soil between 5.5–6.5 and in hydroponics between 5.0–5.6 pH.

Chlorine (Cl)

Most growers will never have to worry about applying chlorine because tap water contains on average 100 PPM of chlorine. Chlorine's role in cannabis growth is in regulating the cells around the stomata. It is speculated that an abundance of chlorine will help plants retain their moisture and reduce the transpiration rate. Chlorine deficiencies show as yellowing of the leaf, and the leaf will occasionally twist and develop necrotic spots in the middle of the leaf.

Correct by watering with water that contains chlorine.

Chlorine is locked out of soil between 2.5–4.8 pH and in hydroponics between 6.9–8.5 pH.

Chlorine is best absorbed in soil between 6.0–7.4 pH and in hydroponics between 4.9–5.9 pH.

Copper (Cu)

Overall plant will appear blue. The weakest leaves will be affected, usually from the bottom up. It will work from the tips of the leaves, leaving a deforming yellowish brown color, and work its way back to the leaf junction. Excess nitrogen will inhibit copper uptake.

Correct by feeding with any decent fertilizer at the normal dosage and/or foliar feed for quicker results.

Copper is locked out of soil between 2.0–4.5 pH and in hydroponics between 6.5–9.0 pH.

Copper is best absorbed in soil between 5.8–7.0 pH and in hydroponics between 5.0–6.0 pH.

Sulfur (S)

Affects young leaves first, with yellowing starting at the leaf junction and working its way towards the tips of the leaves.

Correct by adding 1–2 tsp of Epsom salts dissolved in hot water before adding to one gallon of water. Prevent by having garden sulfur, sulfate of potash, or gypsum in your soil mix.

Sulfur is locked out of soil and hydroponics between 2.0–5.5 pH.

Sulfur is best absorbed in soil and hydroponics between 5.8–7.0 pH.

Molybdenum (Mo)

Occurs on the older leaves and then moves to the young ones. Is the prettiest of the deficiencies: burgundy / pink along with yellow strips running along the edges and the length of leaves.

Correct by foliar feeding with any decent fertilizer and prevent by adding garden lime to your soil.

Molybdenum is locked out of soil and hydroponics between 2.0–5.5 pH.

Molybdenum is best absorbed in soil between 6.7–7.0 pH and in hydroponics between 6.0–7.5 pH.

Boron (B)

Sometimes confused with light bleach or light burns. A boron deficiency is characterized by a bronze or browning between veins on newest growth. Starts in the middle of the leaf and works to the tip. It mangles the leaf and looks like it is crushing it.

Correct by foliar feeding with 1 tsp of eyewash per gallon of water. Any decent fertilizer will contain boron.

Boron gets locked out of soil and hydroponics between 2.0–5.0 pH.

Boron is best absorbed in soil and hydroponics between 5.5–6.5 pH.

pH ISSUES

Leaves curl under severely and are twisted. Leaves may be pale or develop necrotic spots because plants cannot absorb nutrients when the pH is imbalanced. Flush with pH'd water. If it is a severe case you should transplant into a fresh soil of neutral pH along with flushing. Use lime to raise pH and sulfur to lower pH in soil.

HIGH SALINITY

This is caused by too many nutrients and not enough flushing. Common during late flowering. Apply a moderate to heavy flushing.

OVER FERTILIZATION

Leaves curl under like a claw or ram's horns and are dark green or gold. Leaf fringes / edges curl inwards and it usually progresses from the bottom up. When leaf tips and fringes are burnt, leaves are crispy, and the plant starts smelling like chemicals, chances are you are over fertilizing. Over fertilizing with chemical nutrients will also raise pH. In severe cases, leaves will curl upwards, starting to burn (brown) at the tips and fringes. Apply a heavy flush to correct the problem, as well as reverse foliar feeding (spraying with plain water).

OVERWATERED

Leaves are lifeless and drooped over in most cases the petioles will remain ridged though. Stop watering! Don't apply more water until the soil is dry. Depending on how severe the case of overwatering, let them dry out extensively before watering again. In severe cases you will need to apply $1-1\frac{1}{2}$ tsp of 35% H_2O_2 (hydrogen peroxide) per gallon of water. Overwatering happens because there is not enough oxygen in the soil and roots are suffocating. Even though you watered, the hydrogen peroxide water, with its extra oxygen atom, will get your plants back on track quicker than just waiting for them to dry.

UNDERWATERED

Leaves reach up, seeking to funnel raindrops down to the base of the plant. When cases are progressing, the leaves will drop because the plant does not have enough water to support its cells and the cells are shriveling. One of the best ways to distinguish underwatering from overwatering is by the petioles. In most overwatering cases the petioles will remain ridged and in underwatering they will not. Fix by watering (duh!), lowering the temperatures, and raising the humidity.

VIRUSES

Scientists do not know what causes viruses in cannabis plants. It is thought that poor growing conditions are responsible, although there have been documented cases in completely healthy grow rooms. Since cannabis is not indigenous to North America, cannabis viruses are virtually non-existent here. However, European growers frequently deal with viruses, most commonly Hemp Strike Virus, or HSV. There has been some research that indicates that Tobacco Mosaic Virus can be spread to cannabis. Viruses are almost impossible to get rid of; however, some viruses have been eradicated using copper fungicide. The best practice is to prevent with Citrofresh. You can tell you have a virus when no other deficiencies cover what you see in your plant. Most start with some sort of necrosis developing in the center and have an unpredictable deficiency pattern. Once your plant is infected with a virus, it can spread by seeds and pollen as well, which is why plants should be destroyed immediately, as well as all plants with which they may have come in contact. They most certainly should not be used for breeding.

LIGHT BURN

Also known as bleaching, this occurs through hot spots, which are typically caused by slick chrome reflectors (dimpled reflectors disperse light evenly) or by having radiant heat that is too high. Radiant heat is heat that is emitted by your floors, walls, etc. Radiant heat is higher than air temperature. Your plants are actually hotter than the air temperature. This is why you should not hang your HID lights very close to your plants even if circulation permits you to hang, say, a 400-watt HPS five inches from your plants. While there's no such thing as too much light, having the light too close will cause problems. Correct by simply moving the light away or installing a light mover.

INADEQUATE LIGHTING

While there's no such thing as too much light, the opposite is very true. When plants do not receive adequate lighting, e.g., at least 50 WPSF, they will begin to stretch in search of light. You will notice internodes between 4–8 inches in length and fan leaves will also be bigger than normal in an attempt to absorb the most light as possible. Plants will be long and stretchy with little to no lateral branching. Fix by either moving lights closer to plants and/or adding additional lights.

HEAT STRESS

This is caused by extreme heat. Lower the temperature, increase ventilation, and increase the humidity.

Appropriate lighting will help produce dense colas like this.

Chapter 19

Hydroponics

Contributed by The_Seed

Basically, anything not growing in dirt is hydroponic. Sand, orchid bark, gravel, rockwool, coco-peat, perlite, and vermiculite are all examples of hydroponic media. Soilless growing has been around a long time—allegedly as far back as the Hanging Gardens of Babylon. Hydroponics is a science used in every corner of the world to get more food in less space. It's one of the most important technologies of the new century. There's about to be too many people in the world, and this is how the masses will get fed: with hydroponic food.

There are prefabricated hydroponic systems available on the market for consumers, but hydroponics is also a popular way of growing for the people who like to tinker, build, and fabricate.

PREFABRICATED SYSTEMS AND DIY

Prefabricated systems are made in a variety of styles and shapes. Units on the market come in different heights, different depths, and with different sprayers or misters; all are basically variations on a theme. The most important things to look for in a prefab unit are name and reliability. You'll want to make sure you get all the pieces in the box, and make sure that if you didn't, that it's easy to deal with the manufacturer.

The advantage to a pre-fab system is that everything's ready to go. There are plenty of growers who wished they had just gone and bought a pre-fab system instead of spending endless hours going to the hardware store for bits and pieces. A number of those people ended up buying the pre-fab systems anyway. Even though the pre-fab systems are often expensive, it can be a real bonus to save all those hours.

The DIY person is going to have a shopping list to put together. There are a lot of different approaches to what makes a hydroponics system, but essentially you're going to need a variety of pieces, parts and accessories. This is what makes it such a

A great DIY system with ample lighting, good reflectors, great air circulation, and a nice ScrOG prepared with a good net.

Hydroplex's Spinner hydroponic equipment is an excellent prefabricated hydroponics system. Notice the temperature, gas and nutrient monitor that makes sure everything is at the right level. Perfect.

Good air circulation, organization and cleanliness are vital for a hydroponic grow. Note the control panel and pre-installed ScrOG netting.

great hobby for those people who like to tinker and play with bits and pieces.

You're essentially creating two environments for your hydroponic system: one above the root zone, in the grow room, where the plant is, and one in the chamber with the roots.

Environment #1. Above the media: the grow room itself.

Don't shortcut on lighting! This is the sun for your room; make sure it's the best you can afford. If you don't get the photosynthesis your plant needs, you'll compromise your yield.

This is where the plant is growing, and you'll want to have control of the environment. You're responsible for all the elements in the space.

You want to monitor and maintain temperature and humidity in the room, so having good controllers for that is important. Be sure to maintain the room during the day and also at night. If you need to add heat to keep things warm at night, then get a heater. It can make the difference between getting powdery mildew and not getting it.

Proper intake and exhaust will make all the difference in helping to keep things cool. Don't waste your time with a space if you can't have proper air circulation, etc.

Always keep things clean, clean, and cleaner. Unless you're a hobbyist, or an Australian lettuce grower, avoid a lot of algae on your systems. It's not that it competes with the plant for oxygen, but it's a breeding ground for unfriendly things like fungus gnats. Try to use a "green" cleaning agent if possible. The Earth has enough problems without us poisoning it with more chemicals.

Taking notes is the cornerstone of a hydroponicist. Without them you can end up wasting time and killing plants repeatedly. Monitor and record pH, PPMs, water temperatures, nutrient feedings, additives, CO_2, and so on. If a mistake does happen, you'll be able to insure it doesn't happen again. Organize a log book, and keep those records each time you visit your garden.

Environment #2. In the media: the root zone.
This is where all the hydroponic action comes to play: the root zone.

Keep it clean, keep it dark, and keep good notes.

Check your emitters regularly, make sure that everything is flowing smoothly, and watch for calcification buildup.

Make sure your roots are in good condition and look like healthy roots are supposed to. Nasty things can find their way into a hydroponic reservoir as well, like

This grower has three flood and drain starter trays with rockwool cubes under fluorescent lights and a well-stocked supply of nutrients.

Make sure your roots are in good condition before you add the plant to your hydroponic reservoir. You don't want every plant catching the same disease.

pythium, mold, pathogens and viruses. Keeping everything clean and keeping water temperatures below 72°F will eliminate the opportunity for pythium and other pathogens to develop. This applies for any other pools of water in your room as well.

Clean the chamber thoroughly before using it the next time and rinse thoroughly.

Be sure that any cuttings or plants you put in the system are checked for any problems before you drop them in. Cuttings from strange or unknown places can be the biggest vector for disease.

WATER TEMPERATURE

Water temperatures in chambers and reservoirs must be maintained at no more than 72°F for most crops. Cooler-temperature crops can take a reservoir temperature of around 68°F. If the water is too warm, you invite in all kinds of the nasty things that were mentioned earlier. Always remember that you have two environments to maintain, the one above the root chamber, and the one in the root chamber.

NUTRIENTS

There are plenty of nutrients on the shelves of your local grow shops. For aeroponic

Hy-Pro offers a popular line of hydroponic nutrients. Always measure carefully because over-fertilization is the most common killer of gardens

systems I would recommend something clean and well filtered. Inorganic liquid nutrients are a safe bet, and won't clog your emitters or make the reservoir murky the way some organic solutions do. You might be able to get away with organics in hydroponic systems like NFT or run to waste media systems, but it's not recommended for aeroponics as much. With these systems, particle size is everything. Too big a particle and you can limit the absorption potential of the roots.

There's an endless debate on which nutrient is best, and which brand is better than another. Be prepared, do some research before you shop, and don't believe everything you see and hear. Plants evolved for millions of years without a lot of these additives and supplements, so the rule of thumb is: don't overload your garden with nutrients and additives. Over-fertilization is the most common killer of gardens.

Again, the amount to feed and how often depends on a lot of variables in your grow room. In any hydroponic / aeroponic system you should change your reservoir every 7 days, thoroughly scrubbing it, the whole works. If you are using a medium you should flush your system with plain pH'd water for 12–24 hours, depending on

This Hydroplex spinner gets just the right amount of nutrients and light to the plants to take them from the vegetative to floral states. These plants are just starting to flower.

the strength and how often you feed.

In hydroponics, depending on the medium (rockwool being most common), you should feed for 5 minutes every hour, more or less, depending on how quickly the rockwool dries out and the size of the plant. In pure aeroponics—aero without a medium—you should feed 1 on, 4 off, meaning 30 seconds of feeding and 2–3 minutes off.

VEGETATIVE FORMULA

While this is primarily a hydroponic nutrient formula, it can be used with success in soil. Simply substitute Supernatural Grow Aqua with Supernatural Grow Terra.

Type	User Information
Supernatural Grow Aqua	20-20-20. Start with $\frac{1}{2}$ strength for the first and second week of the vegetative cycle, then move up to $\frac{3}{4}$ or higher by the third and fourth. If you veg longer, then move on to full strength.**HygroZyme** This provides necessary enzymes that roots need to grow. Absorbs nutrients at an increased rate. Use the minimum dose the first and second week of veg and then move up to the maximum dose between the third and fourth (or more) weeks.
HydroGuard	This is derived from several beneficial bacteria and functions as a bio-fungicide. Prevents pathogen infections and diseases from occurring. Apply at $\frac{1}{2}$ strength in the first and second week and then full strength between weeks.
Organics Alive Solution	This is a 100% organic microbial solution. Contains over 30,000 beneficial bacteria, protozoas, fungi, beneficial nematodes, etc. Apply at minimum dose during the first and second week of vegetative growth and run full strength until the second week of flowering.
Silica Blast	This provides beneficial silica to plants, which strengthens plant tissues. Apply at one teaspoon per gallon.
Max Grow	This is not a fertilizer, it is a catalyst that provides Humatic Isolates that aid in nutrient uptake at an accelerated rate. Do not get Max Grow FX; this is something entirely different. Apply at 4ml per gallon throughout veg.

FLOWERING FORMULA

Type	User Information
Supernatural Bloom Aqua	14-8-16. Apply one tsp per gallon and gradually work your way up to $1\frac{1}{2}$ tsp by the third or fourth week of flowering.
Potash +	Contains six different sources of potash. Just follow the instructions on the label.
Max Flower	This is not a fertilizer, it is a catalyst that provides Humatic Isolates that aid in nutrient uptake at an accelerated rate. Do not get Max Flower FX; this is something entirely different. Simply follow the instructions.
Carboload	This provides simple and complex carbohydrates to increase yield. Simply follow the instructions.
Silica Blast	This provides beneficial silica to plants, which strengthens plant tissues. Apply at $\frac{1}{2}$ the recommended dosage.
HydroZyme	This provides enzymes that roots need to grow and absorb nutrients at an increased rate. Apply at $\frac{1}{2}$ the recommended dosage.
Hydroguard	This is derived from several beneficial bacteria and functions as a bio-fungicide. Prevents pathogen infections and diseases from occurring. Apply at full strength.
Banana Manna	Derived from bananas, mangos, guava, and other rich tropical fruit, Banana Manna contains hormones and vitamins and improves taste. Follow the instructions.

The above is your base. You will continue to use all of these in the recommended dosage until it is time for you to flush your plant.

Week 1: Bud Blood 0-39-25. A flowering enhancer. Follow instructions.

Week 2–3: Phosphoload 1-10-2. Derived from coal humates. A flowering enhancer. Follow instructions.

Week 4: Big Bud 1.6-3.6-.86. Contains a specified amount of phosphorus, potassium, magnesium, and amino acids. Follow instructions.

Week 5–7: Over Drive 1-3-4. Contains specified hormones and catalytic agents as well as select sources of phosphorus and potassium. Follow instructions.

Week 8–9: Flush It. It is optional to add Dr. Pepper. A university study has proven

These hydroponic nutrients are specifically designed to help roots and flowers grow bigger, better and stronger.

that it contains more soluble sugars than the plant is able to absorb, more than molasses or any other product. I use two liters to each 50 gallon reservoir.

These formulas must not be altered in any way. They have been designed through trial and error over several years. Do not add or take away from them and you will have excellent results.

ORIGINAL LUCAS FORMULA

contributed by Lucas

G-M-B (Grow-Micro-Bloom)

0-5-10 For Vegetative cycle (18/6)

0-8-16 For Flowering cycle (12/12)

The numbers above indicate the number of milliliters (ml) of Flora Grow, Micro, or Bloom formulas that I use in one gallon of nutrients.

You will notice I don't use any of the Flora "Grow" formula—I don't need to, the Flora "Micro" provides plenty of nitrogen.

There are two ways to work with this formula:

1. Top off the reservoir daily using a pH-corrected water solution as required to maintain full reservoir level. After adding back an amount of water equal to the amount of your reservoir capacity, you should change the reservoir and put in fresh solution.

2. Top off the reservoir daily using a pH-corrected 100% strength nutrient solution as required to maintain full reservoir level. Continue to use this nutrient solution with-

out dumping the tank unless the PPM rises above acceptable levels.

Between vegetative and flowering cycles you should dump your nutrients, flush (possibly with Clearex) to remove salt buildups, and then change to the other feeding program. Always shake your GH nutrient bottles before using them!

For young plants just transplanted into the hydro setup, give them a 50% strength nutrient mix to prevent overfeeding them while they're young. Gradually bring the mix up to full strength as they grow over the next few weeks or so.

The Lucas formula is normally intended for use with reverse osmosis or near 0 PPM water.

Note: The Lucas formula eliminates the need for Epsom salts to correct magnesium deficiencies in most normal feeding programs recommended by manufacturers. Cannabis needs a lot of magnesium to thrive.

The Flora Micro provides the nitrogen and magnesium in proper balance, so there is no need for the Grow formula and little or no room under the maximum acceptable PPM limit of 1,600 @ 0.7 conversion.

CALCULATED EC/TDS LEVELS

EC microsiemen:	TDS @ 0.5 conversion:	TDS @ 0.7 conversion:
0-4-8: 946 µS	0-4-8 = 473 PPM	0-4-8 = 663 PPM
0-5-10: 1,184 µS	0-5-10 = 592 PPM	0-5-10 = 829 PPM
0-8-16: 1,894 µS	0-8-16 = 947 PPM	0-8-16 = 1326 PPM

ADDBACK CALCULATOR (For Advanced Users)

Say you were running the 0-8-16 formula at 0.7 conversion with a 22 gallon reservoir. When you first fill it up, your PPM will be around 1,330.

Now you have been growing for a week, some of the water has been taken up by the plants, some has evaporated, and your reservoir is at 947 PPM. You need to get your PPM from 947 to 1,330. Here is the equation:

((target - current) / target) * 8 ml per gallon * reservoir gallons = Flora Micro (ml). Double this figure to get Flora Bloom (ml).

Example:
((1330 - 947) / 1330) * 8 * 22
(383 / 1330) * 8 * 22
0.3 * 8 * 22 = 53 ml Flora Micro

53 ml Flora Micro; double that and you get 106 ml Flora Bloom. So, 53 ml Flora Micro and 106 ml Flora Bloom to add back to your 22-gallon reservoir gets you from 947 to 1,330.

Ice Cool from Sweet Seeds grows great hydroponically. Check the pH regularly and you could end up with some bud like this.

USING HARD WATER GH MICRO

I had been experimenting with using the hard water Micro as a substitute for the normal Flora Micro to account for my hard 350 PPM water and the lack of a large enough reverse osmosis filter. It has worked well for me. I just kept my reservoir below 1,150 PPM @ 0.5 conversion and it's all good.

One tip: do not pH down this stuff. The hard water micro will drop pH gradually over the next 24 hours. For example, I mix up a batch, it is at 6.2; the next day, it's at 5.6–5.8 after running in the system for a while. If I pH downed to 5.7 before putting it in the system, it ended up as low as 4.8–5.2 by the next day.

My conclusion: the hard water micro buffers the alkaline crud in my water, it just does not do it quickly like phosphoric acid.

pH

pH is measured on a scale from 0 to 14. Values of pH 7.0 indicate a neutral pH; above pH 7.0 is alkaline and below pH 7.0 is acidic. Most soils are within a range of highly acidic pH 4 to alkaline at pH 7.5 to 8.

pH is important in plant growth because it affects the availability of plant foods and also helps prevent the spread of diseases. Check it regularly, at least twice a week, as the pH will drift quite a lot in a short time. Keep good notes on the pH, and you'll begin to see the pattern of drift for your garden.

In hydroponic systems, pH is adjusted with liquid pH up (diluted potassium hydroxide) and pH down (diluted phosphoric acid). They are usually very strong, even diluted, and it only takes a few drops to make the pH drift one direction or another. Depending on the medium, in hydroponics your ideal pH is between 6.0–6.4 and in aeroponics, without media, it is 5.5–6.3, again depending on the stage of the plant's life.

PPM

Parts Per Million (PPM) is a way of expressing percent (%) in small amounts. In hydroponics, it is used to express the quantity of one amount of material dissolved into another (salts into a volume of water). Basically, it measures how much dissolved solids are floating around in your reservoir. The PPM reading includes nutrients, additives, and anything else in the solution. It's an electrical conductivity meter, and measures the electrical current between two probes at the base of the meter.

Smaller plants = fewer PPMs. Bigger plants = more PPMs. Imagine a child that starts out life eating small portions of food, and as the child grows, it eats more and more. The same is true of plants. They don't need so much food when they're younger. As they get older, they need more food to sustain themselves. You might start out with a cutting at 300–500 PPM and end up at 1,000–1,500 PPM, depending on how aggressively you run your solution.

Why get a PPM meter? What does all this boil down to? By knowing exactly how much food your plants eat, you can always keep your reservoir topped off where it needs to be. If you use it faithfully, you won't over-fertilize or under-fertilize with a PPM meter. You can save yourself 30–50% of your nutrients by knowing when to feed and when not to feed. That all adds up to money in your pocket, and properly fed plants.

Every nutrient has its own PPM when it's dissolved in water. Mix a batch of the nutrient up, test it, and you'll have your base starting point to work from. Keep an eye on your plants in case you are under or over feeding.

STYLES OF HYDROPONICS
Aeroponics

This is a style of hydroponics that has the ability to produce phenomenally well— albeit in a properly maintained system. Aeroponics is classically done in a tall, or slant-walled, chamber where the roots hang freely and never touch anything. There's a great example at "The Land," located in the Epcot Center in Florida. It's a pyramid-shaped system where the plants are placed on the angled sides, and the roots grow freely down into the center of the pyramid where they get misted in cycles.

Very often you see the roots hanging into the water, or sometimes even completely submerged. Many gardens die this way, and without the proper education or experience using the systems, failure can follow.

The water in an aeroponic system is delivered through misters most often, and the ideal water droplet size is 5–20 microns. If you looked online, you'd see people saying 5–50 microns or 20–100 microns. When the droplets are smaller than 30 microns, you see it suspended in the air like fog. If the droplets are bigger than 50 microns, they just drop out of the air entirely. So shoot for a droplet size of maybe 20 microns or so and split the difference. There are a lot of sprayers in the marketplace, so choose wisely. Avoid sprayers that you can't open up and clean, otherwise you'll just end up replacing them anytime you get calcification building up on the emitter.

Nutrient Film Technique (NFT)

NFT operates by delivering a thin film of water along the bottom of a feeding trough where the roots are growing into. Plants in these systems get all of their nutrients delivered through this film, and grow surprisingly well for such little water. The troughs for NFT systems are almost like rain gutters, not too wide or deep. Typically, NFT is used for shorter crops like lettuce and strawberries. When growing larger fruits and vegetables, you would want to use a different method because the roots will clog the smaller trough.

This grower is using the nutrient film technique to great effect. The roots will grow into the troughs and will drink from the thin film of nutrient-laden water.

An ebb and flow hydroponic set-up with grow rocks as a medium. Grow rocks won't retain water, so you need to keep the watering rate high.

Ebb and Flow

Just like the name suggests, a tray of plants is flooded with water from the reservoir until the tray is full. Once full, the pump shuts off, and the water drains back into the reservoir by means of gravity. The number of waterings in a day depends on the media you're growing in. Rockwool, for example, holds a lot of water in it and will take a lot longer to dry out completely. Grow rocks will not retain any water, and will need almost constant watering in this style of hydroponics. This is the simplest hydroponic system.

Drip

Drip irrigation is a classic gardening method. Drip line and emitters are laid out and feed the plants. You've all seen it. It's one of the most common forms of hydroponic systems on the market. Be warned, though, some assembly required. You'll be needing: a pump (be sure to get a good filter for your pump, like a "Y" filter,

This grower is using grow rocks and a drip line to feed his plants hydroponically inside of a Tupperware bin.

and to clean routinely), a timer (figure how many times a day you'll water, and get a timer that can be set for all of them), drip emitters (I'd recommend an adjustable 0–4 GPH emitter and one you can take apart and clean), one reservoir, one tubing hole punch, and tubing (½-inch is most popularly used for the primary line, and ¼-inch for the drip feed lines.)

Passive Hydroponics

This is the wick style. It's a classic when it comes to growing passive plants. Forget this style if you have a flowering garden to grow. A wick, placed in the bottom of the plant's container running to the reservoir, carries the nutrient solution to the growing media.

The reservoir is usually topped up manually or with a pump, and the wick draws the nutrient solution upwards by capillary action. This way, the plants can control their own rate of watering.

There are a lot of great soilless mixes that can be used in a tray or in an individually wicked pot directly over the reservoir. The maintenance on all this is minimal, provided the reservoir is topped off. Again, I recommend not growing flowering plants this way.

Aero-hydroponics

This style works by spraying water at the roots, but it happens in a smaller tube where water collects and is recycled. It's oxygenated, but not misted the way an aeroponics system is, so it's called aero-hydroponics. The Aero-Flo from General Hydroponics is a classic example of this style. Aero-hydroponics is a little more finicky than the traditional root suspension chamber style of aeroponics. Water levels have to be watched as roots grow into the solution; submerged for too long, they can kill plants pretty quickly. You lower the level of water as the roots grow into the tubes until there's a thinner film of water eventually left in the bottom. Root mass begins to fill the tubes. The Aero-Flo has been around a long time, and they still sell them to this day. They're used all over the world successfully, and it's not my goal to slam their unit.

Commercial-sized aeroponic systems, ebb and flow, and drip systems are going to require larger pumps, higher pressures, longer manifolds and feed lines, and more fittings, filters, and fertilizers. There's a little math involved in doing all this, or some basic guidelines, at least, to picking the right pump, factoring the total PSI on the system, and total nutrient delivery. It is recommended to break these larger systems into zones, so that not all of a large-scale system is tied to only one pump. In the unlikely event of pump failure, or a disease or whatever, you won't lose everything if all of the systems aren't tied together.

RISKS OF HYDROPONICS

Like any other form of gardening, there are certain risks.

Electrical failure. Pumps and timers require electricity to operate, unless you have allowed for battery backups or generators. If the power fails, you can be sorely inconvenienced. A short outage can reset digital timers, and throw off the cycles even after the lights come back on. A long outage can be more disastrous, and your plants could be dead when you return.

Pump failure. Pump failure can happen; no manufactured thing is perfect. It never hurts to have a spare on hand.

Higher initial startup costs are typically involved: lights, controllers, fans, filters, nutrients, and so on all add up when you're starting out.

Maintaining environmental temperatures and nutrient temperatures. Failure to do so can kill your plants; factor the needed controls into your budget of operations.

BONUSES WITH HYDROPONICS

If your hydroponic system is dialed in, you can enjoy the benefits and rewards of using it successfully. Root development happens at an accelerated rate and nutrient delivery is done with precision. In aeroponics you can look and see how the roots are

OG Kush (Alpine Version) from Alpine Seeds is a great Sativa-dominant plant for hydroponic growers. Look at the resin. Incredible.

growing and monitor their development.

Diseases and pathogens are very easily identifiable and can be removed or cured as needed (hopefully). Most growers report having bigger yields with quicker turns, shaving off a week or more on their total grow times. However, no two grow rooms are quite the same, and you have to take into account the factors in your own personal space.

THE CIRCLE OF HYDROPONICS AND SOIL

Even people who have always grown in soil eventually take a run at hydroponics to see what that has to offer them. The same is true of the die-hard hydro guys; they very often flip over and use soil to find out if they're missing out on something. What am I getting at here? That gardening is an adventure and a hobby, and sometimes a cash-crop that we depend on for our livelihood. It's a hands-on, interactive, scientific, rewarding pastime. It has us looking and watching every day, trying our best to make that plant thrive and prosper.

Whatever you use as a system, whatever media, it is expected that you eventually will want to expand and explore what's next, what the next best thing is, and learning how you can get more yield out of your plant. Take good notes, have fun, expect the unexpected, and your plants will tell you the rest—if you're paying attention.

This AK from Spliff Seeds is a beautiful example of how good genetics, coupled with good organic growing practices, can result in some stellar bud.

Chapter 20

Organic Gardening: Soil and Supplements

In organic gardening, only living or once-living organisms are used to provide nutrients to the plant. With organics you're not so much feeding the plant, as feeding the soil, which in turn feeds the plant. Chemical fertilizers destroy soil ecology; proper organic fertilizing nurtures it. A huge advantage with using organics is that you do not have to pH your water / fertilizer mixture unless they are far out of the acceptable range. The pH is set when you mix the soil and you don't have to worry about it much after that. Organically-grown produce is valued several times higher than its chemical counterpart, and this is because of the great deal of care, time, and expense that goes into producing it. Organically grown produce is sweeter and tastes better, displaying many flavors and smells that have been masked by chemicals. Cannabis is no exception. With organic gardening there is no sacrifice in yield, and a proper organic garden often yields equal to or more than chemically grown crops under the same conditions. The following is a guideline to help the organic grower use organics safely without unknowingly causing harm to one's self or another.

While using organic nutrients / fertilizers, it is also important to remember that without proper composting, those nutrients still contain harmful, potentially deadly bacteria, hormones, pesticides, and other undesirable substances. A special note is that salmonella and E. coli can survive the composting process much better than other types of bacteria. Growers should not use any type of dog, cat, or pig manures to fertilize their crops because of the possibility of transmitting parasites. Do not apply any manure within 60 days of harvest for any plant / fruit that will be eaten without proper cooking. Growers should also note that the application of fresh manure will change the smell and taste of buds. While most manure is a good source of nutrients, specifically phosphorus and potassium, repeated application of certain manures can inhibit the use of micronutrients such as copper, zinc, boron, manganese, and, in some cases, even calcium and magnesium. Continual application of manure will cause pH drift over time, generally making the soil more acidic. When fresh or uncomposted manure is applied to areas where leaching can affect ponds, rivers, and streams, it pollutes said bodies of water enough to mutate frogs. Researches have found that the run off of nitrogen and phosphorus are directly responsible for these mutations. These nutrients encourage the growth of parasitic flatworms that encourage deformities in frogs. Some frogs have been reported to have five or six extra limbs.

(The above is based on reports from George Keupper of the National Sustainable Agriculture Information Service and Pieter Johnson, ecologist and evolutionary biologist, at the University of Colorado.)

Don't let this stop you from entering the wonderful world of organic gardening. Using store bought mushroom compost and soil such as Black Kow will ensure that you stay away from such problems. If you're mixing your own soil using manures, just make sure you know where the manure is coming from, what the animals were eating, and how the feed was treated before using it and that the manure is well composted before use.

SOIL

Healthy soil follows closely behind sunlight as the most important aspect of growing healthy cannabis. Microbes are the essential link between mineral reserves and plant growth. When chemical fertilizers are applied to the soil, the delicate balance becomes interrupted as essential microbes are destroyed. Organic growers strive to maintain healthy soil ecology. However, many organic growers do not fully understand this delicate process, so we will take an in-depth look at it here.

Organic compounds, such as compost and humic substances, provide energy in the form of carbon atoms, as well as many of the nutrient / mineral requirements that feed soil microbes (microorganisms).

Soil microbes lack the ability to capture energy from the sun (photosynthesis) and must survive on nutrients / minerals that contain lingering carbon in the soil or on the soil's surface. Energy is stored in these carbon atoms, which the microbes feed off to perform various metabolic functions.

Various beneficial organisms—algae, bacteria, fungi, and small animals or earthworms—are responsible for many functions that influence soil fertility and dictate plant health, but just how do microbes benefit the plant?

Organic matter contains bacteria. These bacteria release organic acids (humic / fulvic acids, primarily), these acids aid in the solubilization of macro and micronutrients / minerals that had previously been bound in the soil and were not available for use to the plant. These bacteria also release complex sugar-based compounds (polysaccharides) that aid to create soil crumbs. Soil crumbs aerate the soil, resulting in a more desirable soil structure that features increased drainage and access to oxygen.

Other little-known microbes, such as actinomyces, release antibiotics into the soil. These antibiotics are used by the plant to protect itself against pathogens and insect attacks. Actinomyces also aid in maintaining a balance between aerobic and anaerobic microbes.

Beneficial fungi such as the well-known mycorrhizae aid the roots in the uptake of water and nutrients.

Enzymes decompose organic matter, which in the process releases bound nutrients to feed other organisms, which can then, in turn, feed the plant. Much of the organic matter released by fungi and enzymes aids in the formation of humus and soil crumbs.

Small animals such as earthworms create tunnels throughout the soil that allow the soil to readily exchange gases—chiefly oxygen—with the atmosphere. They also create additional microbes by digesting and excreting organic matter.

Organic soil originates all over the world from the decaying process of both plants and animals. When plants and animals die and decompose, they deposit a variety of nutrients and minerals into the ground. This replenishes the soil from the nutrients and minerals that were used by the plants and animals. It is a great big circle. So how do you replicate this process in your containers?

Start by creating a good base for the microbes to thrive. This means adding biologically active soil components that are already rich in microbes and enzymes, such as Black Kow, Ocean Forest, Light Warrior, humus, worm castings, mushroom compost, etc.

In the present day, we have the advantage of adding all the known organic additives, even from places where they would not normally be found. For example, you would not typically have cow remains in the same place that you would have fish and shrimp remains, but by incorporating fish and shrimp meals along with blood and bone meals, you have provided the best of both worlds. Both fish and shrimp meals provide different nutrients, minerals, and microbiotic stimulants than blood and bone meals, and vice versa. By incorporating kelp, alfalfa, and cottonseed meal you are providing the nutrients, minerals, and microbes that decaying plants would contribute. The perfect soil is not complete without the addition of bat and/or bird guano (poop), which stimulates microbes and provides an additional boost in nutrients at the same time. This process is known to organic growers as "feeding the soil to feed the plant."

Ocean Forest, which is made up of earthworm castings, bat guano, Pacific Northwest fish and crab meal, shrimp meal, composed forest humus, sandy loam, and sphagnum peat moss. pH is between 6.3–6.8

Original Planting Mix, which is made up of earthworm castings, bat guano, Norwegian kelp meal, composed forest humus, and sphagnum peat moss.

Light Warrior, which is made up of peat moss, perlite, earthworm castings, mycorrhizae, humic acid, and oyster shells.

Strawberry is an 80% Indica beauty from Spliff Seeds that, like all plants with good genetics, thrives in organic growing conditions.

Notice the NPK on this bag of compost. Always be aware of the levels of Nitrogen, Phosphorus, and Potassium in the nutrients and fertilizers that you use to treat your soil.

Botanicare ReadyGro Moisture, which is made up of perlite, coco coir, compost accelerator, earthworm castings, 72 silica clay, polymere hydro crystals, and rootshield biofungicide.

If you're a serious grower, you'll want to mix your own batch of soil. To do so, you'll want to start with a base. I am a big fan of Pro Mix, especially their BX line. This includes sphagnum peat moss, perlite, vermiculite, mycorrhizae, dolomitic and calcitic limestone, macronutrients, micronutrients, and a wetting agent. There are many other mixes of Pro Mix, some including biofungicide and other organic goodies. You're sure to find the mix that best suits your growing needs. A combination of Pro Mix Mycorrhizae and Pro Mix Biofungicide would do well together. Just visit their website, premierhort.com.

Recently there has been a big trend of using Coco Coir as a base or solely as the inert medium. Coco coir is a byproduct of processed coconut husks; it is the coir fiber pith from the coconut. Coco coir holds water and nutrients well and, because it is so porous, allows for the rapid development of roots. As with all inert or soilless mediums, you will spend an increased amount of money on liquid fertilizers because the medium itself contains no nutrients. There are many suppliers of coco coir, but I have found Botanicare to be the best. Be sure to thoroughly rinse your coco coir before use, as most of the manufacturers incorporate the use of salt water to clean the coco coir, thereby leaving deposits of sodium which will cause problems for your plants.

I've included this organic NPK (nitrogen, phosphorus, potassium) chart so you can experiment and create your own soil recipe. NPK refers to the numbers that are listed on each organic nutrient, fertilizer, and soil amendment. The first number refers to the amount of nitrogen in the product, the second number refers to the amount of Phosphorus in the product, and the third and last number refers to the amount of Potassium. If you wondering why its known as NPK instead of NPP, it's because NPK are the symbols for Nitrogen, Phosphorus, and Potassium on the periodic table.

If you do not wish to create you own soil, you can follow the tried and true recipes below that are sure to do you right, or you may purchase the "complete" soil mixes listed above.

Warning: Be sure to wear surgical gloves and masks when handling / mixing all organic ingredients. While it is unlikely, it is possible to contract diseases from some organic products; additionally, the mask is used to prevent respiratory problems from inhalation of small fibers and particles.

These are some quality blood and bone meal nutrient supplements. Always check the NPK of the products you buy. If the strain you are growing doesn't like nitrogen, don't use a nutrient product that is high in nitrogen. Think it through.

SOIL SUPPLEMENTS

Type	N-P-K	Description
Alfalfa Meal / Pellets	2-1-2	Most often used as animal feed. It does, however, provide a good source of trace elements, and contains trianconatol, which is an organic fatty acid growth stimulant. Slow to release, taking one to four months.
Aragonite	0-0-0	Made of calcium carbonates. Provides little calcium. Not much is known about the effects or benefits of aragonite for agriculture purposes.
Azomit	0-0-2.5	Natural, odorless volcanic minerals. Used for micro and trace elements. Azomite contains over 70 rare minerals and trace elements, as well as calcium, limestone, calcium bentonite, calcium sulfate, and sodium bentonite. Slow release, taking two to four months.
Bat Guano (Nitrogen)	10-3-1*	A.k.a. bat feces, which can be applied directly to soil mix, used in teas, or used as a foliar feed. Stimulates microbes. The nitrogen-heavy bat guano is collected from fruit-eating bats. Moderate release, taking one to two months.

Soil Supplements *continued*

Type	N-P-K	Description
Bat Guano (Phosphorus)	3-10-1*	Phosphorus-heavy bat guano is bat feces collected from mostly insect-eating bats. Stimulates microbes. Moderate release, taking one to two months.
Beef Steer Manure	.7-.3-.4*	Made from the feces of steers. Not recommended because it may contain weeds. If used, it should be hot composted first. Delay planting at least three weeks. Moderate release, taking one to two months.
Bird Guano (Nitrogen)	13-12-2*	Made from the feces of birds. Don't advise its use because of avian flu. Fast and moderate release.
Bird Guano (Phosphorus)	1-10-1*	Made from the fossilized feces of birds. Not likely that it will spread avian flu. Fast and moderate release.
Bird Guano (Peruvian)	10-10-2*	Made from the feces of Peruvian seabirds. It is pelletized, and runs low risk of spreading avian flu. Fast and moderate release.
Blood Meal	12-0-0	Made from the waste of slaughterhouses. Can transmit mad cow disease, so I don't recommend using it; it's also easy to burn. Fast release, taking one to four weeks.
Bone Mea	3-12-0*	Made from the waste of slaughterhouses, e.g., the hooves. Can transmit mad cow disease, so I don't recommend using it Fast release, taking one to four weeks.
Chicken Manure	1.1-.8-.5*	Made from the feces of chickens. Not recommended due to avian flu and its flammability. Breaks down fastest of all manures. Delay planting at least three weeks. Fast release, one to four weeks.
Corn Gluten Meal	9-0-0	High source of nitrogen. Don't use until your seedlings are at least five weeks old, as it will inhibit their growth. Slow to release, taking one to four months. Best to use at the mid-end of the fourth month.
Cottonseed Meal	6-.5-1.5	Good source of nitrogen. Don't recommend using, as cotton is treated with loads of pesticides and this will pass on to the seed and then to your soil medium. Slow to release, taking one to four months.

Soil Supplements *continued*

Type	N-P-K	Description
Cow Manure (Dairy)	.6-.2-.6*	Made from the feces of cows. Not recommended because it may contain weeds. If used, it should be hot composted first. Delay planting at least three weeks. Moderate release, one to three months.
Crab Meal	5-2-.5	Byproduct of the crab industry. Basically it's crabs, ground up. Contains useful microorganisms, namely chitin, which suppresses unwanted nematode activity. Slow release, taking one to four months.
Epsom Salt	0-0-0	Magnesium sulfate, which is magnesium and sulfur. Research has shown that magnesium is a critical mineral for seed germination, and important in the production of chlorophyll. Moderate release, one to three months.
Feather Meal	10-2-1*	Made from the waste of poultry slaughter-houses. Don't recommend using due to the time it takes to release the nitrogen and the risk of avian flu. Very slow to release, taking more than four months.
Fish Emulsion	5-2-2	Made from the waste of fish slaughterhouses. Good source of micronutrients and microbes. Highly soluble and with a fast release, taking one to four weeks. Don't recommend using indoors.
Fishmeal	10-6-2	Fishmeal is ground and heated fish waste. Good source of nitrogen and phosphorus. Slow release, one to four months.
Garden Sulfur	0-0-0	From Espoma. Offers 90% soluble sulfur. Sulfur promotes vigorous, dark green growth and lowers soil pH.
Granite Meal	0-0-5	A good source of potash, which plants need for sugar and starch production. Can be applied in large amounts without affecting the pH. Very slow release, four months or more.
Greensand	0-0-1	Also known as glauconite. Much like azomite, contains rare minerals and trace elements. Primarily iron-potassium silicate.

Soil Supplements *continued*

Type	N-P-K	Description
Gypsum	0-0-0	A soft mineral, calcium sulfate. A source of micronutrients. Loosens clay soils and aids in aeration. Minimizes effects of salt toxicity. Promotes root growth and maximizes fertilizer effectiveness. Moderate release, one to three months.
Horse Manure	.7-.3-.6*	Made from the feces of horses. Not recommend because it may contain weeds. If used, hot compost first. Medium breakdown time; delay planting at least three weeks. Moderate release, one to two months.
Kelp Meal	1-0-4*	Made from brown seaweed found in cold waters around the world. Kelp contains over 70 micro and trace elements, and many growth hormones such as cytokinins and auxins, vitamins, minerals, enzymes, and proteins. Slow release, one to four months.
Kelp (liquid)	1-0-4*	Same as kelp meal, although it is cold processed and so more of the enzymes and overall nutrients are still available to your plants. Very effective as a foliar feed. Very fast release, one to seven days.
Leather Meal	10-0-0	Made of ground tannery waste. Basically, any skin left over from the tanning process. A rich source of nitrogen, it also contains a few amino acids, but because the tanning process uses chromium, a heavy toxic metal, and this may be found in the meal, I would not recommend it.
Limestone (Dolomite)	0-0-0	A sedimentary rock composed mostly of calcium carbonate, as well as different amounts of silica. Used to stabilize / raise pH. Contains 51% calcium and 49% magnesium. Use 2 tbsp to raise your pH from the 5.0 range to the 6.5–7 range.
Limestone (Calcitic)	0-0-0	Same as dolomite lime, except made up of 75% calcium and 25% magnesium. Not recommended as your source of lime.
Potash	0-0-60	An impure form of potassium carbonate mixed with other potassium salts. It is a naturally occurring mineral. Enhances resistances to diseases. Slow release, one to four months.

Soil Supplements *continued*

Type	N-P-K	Description
Rabbit Manure	2.4-1.4-.6	Rabbit feces is the most concentrated of animal manures, and is rumored to be the best. Delay planting for at least three weeks. Fast release, one to four weeks.
Rock Phosphate (Colloidal)	0-3-0	A soft colloidal clay formation that gives away its nutrients slowly; it can also bind to sandy soils and add to their nutrient-holding capability. Contains 11 minerals. Slow release, one to four months.
Rock Phosphate (Super)	0-20-0	Made by treating colloidal rock phosphate with sulfuric acid, which then becomes calcium phosphate, a.k.a. super phosphate. Moderate release, one to two months.
Rock Phosphate (Triple)	0-46-0	Made by treating super phosphate with phosphoric acid. I don't recommend using this product as it bonds with zinc, iron, and magnesium, and plants can't assimilate them. Moderate release, one to three months.
Sheep / Goat Manure	1.4-.5-1.2	Made by the feces of sheep / goats. Not recommended as it may contain weeds. High quality of animal manure, though. Delay planting for at least three weeks. Moderate release, one to two months.
Soybean Meal	7-2-1	Most often used as animal feed. Good source of nitrogen. Slow to release, taking one to four months.
Sulfate of Potash	0-0-52	A natural source of potassium. Sulfate of potash is 51% water-soluble, and contains sulfur, which is a microelement that helps provide a dark green color. Moderate release, taking one to two months.
Worm Castings	3-2-2*	Earthworm feces. Even though the NPK value is low, earthworm castings are essential to any healthy organic garden. There are over 60 trace minerals as well as cytokinins, auxins, and other enzymes, as well as beneficial bacteria. Fast release, taking two to five weeks.

*NPK numbers may vary.

NOTE: avoid using any time-released fertilizers, anything that says "feeds up to three months," etc.

MIXES

These soil mixes are for indoor plants. Because they use a peat-based medium for the majority of the medium, you should add ½–1 tbsp of lime per gallon of soil, except in the seeds and seedling stage, when you should use 1 tsp of lime.

Soil Mix for Seeds and Seedlings (0–3 Weeks)

¼ Pro Mix BX + ¼ Humus + ½ Builders Sand. Sand increases the permeability of the soil, and roots will grow more quickly with the mix. Builders sand contains bigger granules than regular sand. The humus will provide organic nutrients (humates) to your seedlings and is speculated to expand your pH range, although no conclusive evidence of this has been documented. However, the known benefits of humates are numerous and well documented. Pro Mix is a good solid base that will help the aeration of your soil. You may wish to supplement coco coir for Pro Mix—the humus and the mycorrhizae in Pro Mix BX work well together—to create soil teeming with beneficial bacteria. Use 1 x 1 x 4-inch containers or rapid rooters. Favorable results have also been found using a mixture of a 50-pound bag of sand, 1–2 gallons of Pro Mix, 2 gallons of humus, and 1-gallon of worm castings with 4 quarts of extra perlite. This will make enough soil for roughly one hundred and twenty 16-ounce (beer) cups. Avoid rock wool, peat pellets, and jiffy pots.

Soil Mix for Seedlings (3–5 Weeks)

For your more mature seedlings you will want 20% Pro Mix BX (you can supplement with coco coir), 35% Humus, 20% Builders Sand, and 15% worm castings. You may also want to add 1 cup per gallon or so of Chunky Perlite to improve aeration and drainage. You'll want to add two cups earthworm castings and 1 tsp of PSG (Peruvian Seabird Guano) per gallon. Spread the PSG around the bottom of the pot; this will be a nice little boost in growth and nutrients when they are starting to need it most. In most cases, this will be enough to provide all the necessary nutrients for green, healthy, vigorous growth. Transplant into a 1-gallon pot for this stage. We will not be applying any meals in this stage, because we do not want to overwhelm the seedlings. If seedlings begin to yellow slightly, this is normal and we will correct after the next transplant.

Soil Mix for the Entire Vegetative Stage

Use either 3- or 5-gallon containers. We will basically be using the same base as above: 35% Pro Mix BX (you can supplement with coco coir), 35% Humus, 15% Worm Castings, and 15% Builders Sand. I strongly advise growers to add additional Perlite for increased drainage/aeration, as well as two tbsp of PSG (again, applying at the middle or bottom of the container) and 2 tbsp of Plant Tone.

1–1½ months into growing in the 3-gallon containers, it will be time to transplant into 5-gallon containers. For more information on transplanting, see the chapter on transplanting.

Soil Mix for the End of Vegetation / Beginning of Flowering

Transplant into this mix about 3 weeks before you want to induce 12/12. Use either 5- or 10-gallon containers. Mix 35% Pro Mix BX (you can supplement with coco coir), 35% Humus, 15% High Phosphorus Bat Guano, and 15% Builders Sand; add 2 tbsp Black Diamond (amino acids), 1 tbsp Epsom salts, ½ tbsp Plant Tone, 2 tbsp Flower Tone, 1 tbsp gypsum, and 2 tbsp molasses meal per gallon of soil.

With the aforementioned indoor mixes, feeding with liquid fertilizers should be at a minimum. You should feed with Liquid Karma and Sweet or similar products during vegetation and flowering, as well as root stimulators regularly throughout the growth cycles.

I cannot stress enough the importance of adding Leonardite, a.k.a. fulvic acid, a.k.a. Black Diamond, or an equivalent product, to your soil mixes; this goes for any and all soil mixes. For more about the use of fulvic acid, see the advanced techniques chapter.

For substitutes, you may use Black Kow or, if you absolutely cannot find anything else, Miracle Grow Organic potting soil.

Note: do not add clay pellets to the top of your soil containers; for unknown reasons, the clay pellets alter the pH. Instead, add lava rocks or a similar substitute. It needs to have weight so it displaces the water. This will allow the roots to grow into the topsoil. This is an important technique to maximize plant output.

For organic growers, pH is not much of an issue. With organics there is no need to pH your water source unless it is extremely out of whack; the same goes for your fertilizer.

Many pH issues in organic growing can be easily fixed before they are a problem in the medium. Humates add to the organic composition of your soil and in turn will help to stabilize the pH of the medium and the fertilizer that you add or pour into it.

A peat-based medium, such as Pro Mix, will require pulverized lime to raise / buffer the pH. Peat moss, including sphagnum peat moss, is very acidic, with a pH between 3.6–4.2, so it will require a fair amount of lime to raise it.

In addition to helping the pH, the lime will also add magnesium and calcium to your soil mix. Lime, after all, is calcium carbonate. For all soil mixes that are without lime or oyster shells, add roughly two tbsp per gallon or one cup per cubic foot of soil / soilless mix to raise the pH to around 7 pH. Hydrated lime works more quickly than dolomite lime.

Practicing good organic growing methods with an outdoor grow can result in some tasty cannabis.

If, for some bizarre reason, your medium has an abundance of clay, or some other element that causes your soil to have a high alkaline pH, you should use garden sulfur to lower it. However, iron sulfate works more quickly, so I would recommend gypsum only if you're gradually building your soil. For all soil mixes that are without sulfur, add roughly 1–2 tbsp per gallon—note that this measurement can vary greatly depending on the level of alkalinity.

Another advantage of using coco coir-dominant mediums is that they have a near neutral pH (7.0). However, because coco coir has no organic elements to it, you will have to adjust your fertilizer pH.

It is important to always use a soil pH test prior to planting to determine just how much pH work your soil needs, if any at all. Once you are in the proper range, your pH worries will be very few. You will only have to adjust the pH of your liquids if they are extremely out of whack.

When placing soil in your container, mix up a bit of soil that is going to contain most—say ⅔ —of the nutrients, and place this in the bottom ⅓ of the container. Then place the not-so-hot nutrients around the root ball. This will allow the roots to get used to the new nutrient-filled soil slowly, and give it a boost when your plant is going to need it.

OUTDOOR MIXES

Again, you'll want your base to be primarily Pro Mix BX with mycorrhizae and Pro Mix BX with Biofungicide. You'll want to include the biofungicide for growing outdoors as there are more pests and diseases outdoors. Any soil mix that is being used outside should contain a sufficient amount of diatomaceous earth to prevent insect larva from making a home in your soil.

This is the formula for 25 cubic feet of growing space:
- One 25 lb bag of Pro Mix BX mycorrhizae
- One 25 lb bag of Pro Mix BX biofungicide
- One 50 lb bag of mushroom compost
- One 50 lb bag of Black Kow
- One 50 lb bag of sand
- One 50 lb bag of worm castings
- 3 cups of PSG (Peruvian Seabird Guano)
- 3–4 cups of plant tone
- 3 cups of kelp meal
- 4 cups greensand
- 2 cups of flower tone
- 3 cups garden lime
- 3 cups molasses meal
- 2 cups of rare earth
- 4 cups of Black Diamond

Now mix all this really well. Water thoroughly and let sit at least two weeks after drying out from the initial watering. Water with Liquid Karma and Sweet. This mix is for established plants over 6 weeks old.

You can substitute Fox Farm Ocean Forest or Botanicare ReadyGro Moisture for the Pro Mix BX mycorrhizae.

Some important notes:

"Cork plug" perlite is the best perlite available. It gives extra permeability to the soil, letting roots grow faster and with more oxygen. Fox Farm offers a product known as "Big and Chunky Perlite"; it comes in a 4 cubic feet bag.

For a larger scale grow, say 80 cubic feet, this soil mix is the bomb! In 5 days seedlings can grow 4–6 inches, when done correctly. This is also a drought-resistant mix. I would advise it for outdoor use only.

- four bags of solarized compost
- three bags of mushroom compost (white bag)
- one 30 lb. brick of coco coir
- one 3.8 cubic feet unit of peat moss
- four bags of Black Velvet Mushroom Compost (yellow bag)
- two bags of Soil Doctor
- four bags of worm castings
- four bags of Black Kow
- two bags of Pro Mix BX
- three bags of humus
- one bag of Chunky Perlite

Supplements:
- 3 cups plant tone
- 3 cups flower tone
- 2 cups dried blood
- 2 cups bone meal
- 2.5 cups potash
- 2.5 cups Epsom salt
- 4 cups rare earth
- 4 cups Black Diamond
- 5 cups PSG (Peruvian Seabird Guano)
- 40 cups of pulverized lime
- one 5 lb bag of gypsum
- 10 lbs of lime (pulverized)
- one 15 lb bag of diatomaceous earth
- one box of polymer crystals

For this mix it is important to properly layer your mix. Starting with the bottom, gypsum, flower tone, potash, bone meal, Epsom salt, and rare earth should be layered, before a middle section containing plant tone, dried blood, and PSG. The diatomaceous earth, polymer crystals, and lime should be mixed throughout the entire soil mix. The top of your mix should contain only traces of dried blood and plant tone. Top dress with diatomaceous earth.

SOIL MIXES

A special thank you to those growers who compiled these mixes. The soil mixes listed below have been tried and tested by the users who have created them, and the notes are theirs.

Closet Funk's Recipes

- ½ regular organic potting soil
- ¼ perlite
- ¼ worm castings

Amendments (per gallon):

- 2 tsp plant tone (5-3-3) (nitrogen, phosphorus, potassium, and micro-nutrients)
- 1 tsp Epsom Plus (0-0-22) (magnesium, calcium, and potassium source)
- 2 tsp greensand (0-0-1) (potassium source)
- 1 tsp Indonesian bat guano (0-12-0) (phosphorus source, mixed at bottom of pot)
- 2 tsp lime (pH)
- 2 tsp gypsum (soil conditioner)

Feed with Bio-Bloom and guano tea during flowering.

Fredster420's Recipe

- 1 cubic foot of Miracle Grow's new organic potting soil
- ½ cubic foot of Wally World "Expert Perfect" potting soil
- ½ cubic foot of Jeff's all organic soil
- 1 bag of pure sphagnum peat
- 2 cups blood meal
- 3 cups bone meal
- 1 cup sulfate of sulfur
- 1½ cups sulfate of potash
- 4 bags of perlite
- ½ bag of new soil perfecter

This gave Fredster420 a pH of 6.5.

Pig&Pot Farmer's Recipe(s)

I recently started adding gypsum to my mix as I read that it can help in the yield department; I am in the process of harvesting my heaviest grow thus far. It's cheap and effective! I use a big-ass Rubbermaid to do the mixing in, and a 1-gallon and 5-gallon bucket to do my measurements with. My mixes go as follows, and they make around 10 gallons of mix per batch. I mix and soak with 1 tbsp Liquid Karma per gallon of water two weeks prior to using.

Pig&Pot Farmer Seedling Mix:
- 5 gallons Pro Mix
- 3 to 4 gallons perlite
- 1 gallon worm castings
- 1 cup dolomitic lime

Pig&Pot Farmer Veg Mix:
- 5 gallons Pro Mix
- 2 to 3 gallons perlite
- 1 to 1½ gallons worm castings
- 1½ cups blood meal
- 1 cup bone meal
- 1 cup gypsum
- 1 cup dolomitic lime

Pig&Pot Farmer Flower Mix
- 5 gallons Pro Mix
- 2 to 3 gallons perlite
- 1 to 1½ gallons worm castings
- 1 cup blood Meal
- 1 cup bone meal
- 1 cup gypsum
- 1 cup dolomitic lime
- 1 cup Budswell (0-7-0 flowering guano)

Suby's Recipe(s)

Making a good soil mix is a lot like cooking. I like this mix because it is simple, cheap to make, and relatively complete even without the use of teas—at least for a while.
- 60% Pro Mix HP + mycorrhizae
- 30% perlite
- 10% worm castings for micros

To each gallon of this mix I add:
- 2 tbsp per gallon dolomite lime
- 1 tbsp per gallon blood meal
- 2 tbsp per gallon bone meal (for phosphorus; flowering mix only)
- 1 tbsp per gallon kelp meal

The most important step is to compost your soil mix for two weeks before using it.

You want to wet the mix to create an environment where the bacteria in the soil starts munching on the soil elements and creating a stable environment with some nutrients ready to go for a well rooted clone. I use Liquid Karma for a wetting mix at 1 tbsp per gallon, as instructed by the wise ones.

For instance:
- 50% Pro Mix MH with mycorrhizae
- 30% perlite
- 10% worm castings
- 10% Canna Coco

to which I add
- 2 tbsp per gallon dolomite lime
- 1 tbsp per gallon bone meal and blood meal
- 1 tbsp per gallon kelp meal
- 1 tbsp per gallon alfalfa meal

I wet the mix with a bubbled tea that's prebrewed with worm castings, liquid kelp, molasses, and fulvic acid and let it compost for two weeks, stirring every three days.

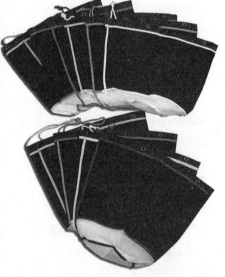

Be aware that there are two versions available: a nitrogen heavy for vegetative, and a phosphorus heavy for flower.

Guano filtration bags can strain particulates out of the guano, ensuring that heavy sediments don't clog your pumps and filters.

Subcool's recipe

- Two 1.5-cubic feet bags Roots Organic (or any high quality potting soil)
- 2 large bales Sunshine Mix #4
- Three 25 lb bags organic worm castings
- 5 lbs steamed bone meal
- 5 lbs Bloom bat guano
- 2.5 lbs blood meal
- ¾ cup Epson salts
- ½ cup sweet lime (dolomite)
- ½ cup azomite (trace elements)

This is the same basic recipe I have used for 15 years; the hardest ingredient to acquire is the worm casting—most people don't even know what worm poop is (what it is, is magic.)

I open all ingredients and place inside a baby pool. I place the Sunshine in first, chopping it up with a rake; then I place the powdered nutrients in a circle around the mound. Then in go the bat poop and the potting soil. The azomite is a granular product I found at a local feed shop for replacing trace elements in soil after a crop. I use this mainly when I replenish my soil. Then it's as simple as my Skipper used to say: "Put your back into it." This is hard work and I am kind of obsessed about breaking up all the clods of soil by hand. I mix for about 15 minutes, then I store it in large Tupperware bins and a few garbage cans.

Once it's placed in the containers, I water it slightly, adding maybe three gallons of water to a large garbage can full. It will make the stirring harder next week, but it will activate the mycorrhizae, and I think it helps all the powders dissolve. I try and buy the highest quality meals and additives as possible I'd hate to ruin a crop just by trying to save $10.

Important note: This soil is really hot and you cannot plant seedlings or clones directly into it. When I do my final transplant into #10 pots, I fill each pot ¾ full with super soil and in the top ¼ I add plain potting soil. This allows the roots to become used to the soil. After a few days the growth on a transplant is amazing.

It is important to remember that creating a soil teeming with billions and billions of beneficial bacteria does not happen overnight. Even using organics, the benefit does not happen immediately; this is especially true when you are using nutrient amendments and correcting pH. Ideally, you should allow your soil to sit for a few weeks to months, depending on the type of amendments. For instance, greensand takes a very long time to reap the full reward of its properties, and the same is true for leonardite. You should keep your soil mixture thoroughly moist during this time period, but not soaking wet; you should allow your soil mix to dry out, but not become bone dry. This destroys the ecological process, as does shifting and stirring the soil. It is a great idea to use Liquid Karma, molasses, or House and Garden's Root Accelerator to speed up this process—and please don't forget to use dechlorided water!

The greater the variety of "goodies" you put into your soil (everything in moderation), the more complete and fertile your soil will be, and healthy fertile soil means healthy fertile plants. You have now created a soil that is superior to that found in nature.

NUTRIENTS

Fertilizers could be called the vitamins of the plant world. The important rule to remember when using fertilizer on a plant is that, just like with vitamins on a human, taking an excess won't increase the rate of growth, it will just cause toxicity and sickness. If you have created a good soil, your plants will not require a lot of fertilizer, what you will be feeding is the soil, not the plant, and by feeding the soil, I mean feeding the microorganisms in the soil. Teas are an excellent way to do this.

A word of caution when using fertilizers: for the most part, fertilizer companies all recommend using more than is necessary. The reason for this is obvious—to sell more product. A good rule of thumb is to cut the manufacturer's dosage by ½ to start out with, and gradually work your way up if needed.

If you're like me, you have a compost bin at home. You can speed up the decomposition of compost by adding compost bin accelerators that can be found at some lawn and garden stores, or a few bottles of beer will work nicely. Keep your compost bin moist, as this will accelerate the decomposition process; also, think about adding a drainpipe so that the interior receives more oxygen.

Why just throw out all those organic leftovers? Composting is a great way of getting rid of some unwanted plant material and soil, if you catch my drift. I don't recommend using homemade compost to plant cannabis in, because of all the potentially harmful pests and diseases, not to mention the weeds.

If you bake it then you lose all the good microbes, bacteria, and helpful insects, as well as the harmful ones. So, what's the solution? Compost tea. To "brew" your own tea, first you will need an old tube sock from your drawer,

Fill that baby up with that "homegrown" compost (roughly 1–2 pounds of compost per gallon of water), and give her a dunk.

(It is *extremely* important when using organics, especially when brewing your own tea, to use water that contains *no* chlorine. All tap water contains chlorine and must sit out in an open air environment for at least 24 hours for chlorine to evaporate. It is best to bubble the water during the time with an air stone.)

You will need an air pump to supply these microbes and bacteria with oxygen during this process. If an air pump is unavailable, add only about half the water to your tea container, and each day add a little bit of water to your tea container. Stir as often as you can during this three to eight day process. You'll want to see whitish / tan foam appear while you're stirring.

Dig under your compost to get down to the good decomposed matter.

Take your spade and funnel the compost into the tube sock

Once you get about ¾ full, zip tie the end so no material can escape.

A popular combination is one-part compost and one-part worm castings.

Another important note is that your brew should not stink. If it stinks, then anaerobic bacteria are present, which are not what you're after. You want the aerobic bacteria. If your brew starts to stink, pour your tea into another container the same size to enrich it with oxygen, leave a little bit out, add fresh water, and stir more frequently. The anaerobic bacteria can't compete with the aerobic bacteria and all the bugs that are bigger than one micron can't pass through the sock. So, basically, you've just eliminated all the unwanted effects of "homegrown" compost while retaining all the wanted ones! Go ahead and pat yourself on the back.

This is the basis for making tea. Now that you know the basics, feel free to add worm castings, bat / bird guano, any well composted cow, horse, goat, sheep, or chicken manure, as well as any other biologically active substrates. You can store your tea indefinitely, provided that you have some form of getting oxygen to the water; once again, an air stone works best.

TEA RECIPES
Here are various tea recipes. A special thank you goes to the growers that contributed them.

Cofi's Tea Recipes
Mixed with one gallon of water and left to brew for 24 hours.
Seedlings mix:
- 5 tbsp Black Strap molasses
- 1 cup worm castings

Vegetative mix:
- 1 tsp Indonesian guano
- 1 tsp Mexican bat guano
- 1 tsp Peruvian seabird guano

- $1/4$ cup worm castings
- 2 tsp Maxicrop powdered kelp extract
- 2 tsp chlorella powder
- 5 tbsp Black Strap molasses
- 1 tsp Epsom salt

Flowering mix:
- 2 tsp worm castings
- 2 tsp Indonesian guano
- 1 tsp Peruvian seabird guano
- 2 tsp Maxicrop powdered kelp extract
- 3 tsp chlorella powder
- 5 tbsp Black Strap molasses

Smokey McPot's Tea Recipe
Roughly one tube sock full of each equals about a pound.
- 1 pound of rich homemade compost
- $1/2$ pound of PSG
- 1 pound of Mushroom Compost

Let sit and soak for three days in a five-gallon bucket; make sure to ring out the tube socks well before removing. Don't forget to add your air stone or stir as much as possible during these three days. Use to fertilize as you would normally.

Guerilla Joe's Tea Recipe
Vegetative cycle:
- 2 cups plant tone
- 2 cups flower tone
- 2 cups kelp meal
- 4 cups worm castings
- 4 cups mushroom compost

Let brew for three–five days, then use as normal fertilizer.

Flowering cycle:
- 2 cups flower tone
- 2 cups kelp meal
- 1 cup high phosphorus guano

Let brew for three–five days; use once every week
Measurements are for 5 gallon batches.

Depending on the strength of the tea and ingredients used, you should use it as a fertilizer. That is, maybe once a week, if that, depending on what your plants are telling you. The majority of those that use teas, including myself, recommend brewing a mild tea of only a few ingredients and using that every time you water your plants. Plants seem to respond better to the latter.

If brewing your own tea isn't for you, here are some helpful step-by-step methods of some of the most popular organic fertilizers. I strongly encourage growers not to use both organic and chemical fertilizers together, because the chemical fertilizers are destroying what the organic fertilizers are doing to your growing medium.

BUYING FERTILIZERS

If brewing your own tea isn't for you, here are some helpful, step-by-step methods for using some of the most popular organic fertilizers.

Earth Juice
by 3LB a.k.a. theFLINTSTONERS

Our favorite among premixed liquid fertilizers is the complete line of Earth Juice products. We've sampled other fertilizers, but always come back to Earth Juice. In our opinion, they are the "premium standard" against which all other organic fertilizers must measure themselves.

The basic line of Earth Juice fertilizers consists of five different products that can all be used in any combination with each other. The ability to mix and match any of the five products gives us the versatility to deal with any nutrient need (or problem) that might arise. Here's a listing of the Earth Juice array:

• Earth Juice Grow
• Earth Juice Bloom
• Earth Juice Catalyst (called Xatalyst in Canada)
• Earth Juice Meta-K
• Earth Juice Microblast

The Grow and Bloom formulas can be used alone or in combination with each other; no big explanation necessary with those names—their intended uses are pretty obvious. Catalyst is basically a jazzed up molasses / carbohydrate product to feed beneficial bacteria and act as a chelate. Meta-K is an awesome potassium supplement, and Microblast is one of the most useful and effective micronutrient products we've had the pleasure of using.

You want to take the compost from the interior of the pile when you make your tea. The stuff on the inside is more decomposed.

Think about adding a drainpipe to your compost heap to help the interior receive more oxygen.

Use the spade to funnel the compost into the tube sock.

A good combination is one-part compost and one-part worm castings. This ensures good nutrient levels.

Once you get about ½ to ¾ full, zip tie the end so no material can escape.

Fill your old tube sock full of compost and dunk them in the water. I suggest using about 1-2 pounds of compost per gallon of water.

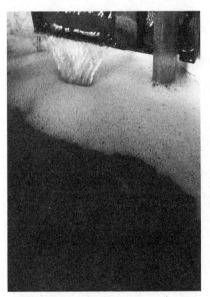

You want to see whitish or tan foam while you stir your tea basin. I'm using a basin with a filter.

If your tea starts to stink, try pouring it from one container to another and adding a little fresh water.

Meet the Earth Juice Lineup

Here's the "scoop," the "tech intell" the "lowdown," the "skinny" on what exactly is in those Earth Juice fertilizers.

Earth Juice Grow 2-1-1
- bat guano
- kelp
- sulfate of potash
- feather meal
- oat bran
- blood meal
- steamed bone meal

This is the jack-of-all-trades among the Earth Juice products, useful throughout all of vegging and the first couple weeks of flowering. Depending on a plant's growth stage, we use the Earth Juice Grow at concentrations of anywhere from 1 tbsp to 2 tbsp per gallon (and we have pushed it to 3 or 4 tbsp without harm for very heavy feeders).

Earth Juice Bloom 0-3-1
- bat guano
- seabird guano
- kelp
- sulfate of potash
- steamed bone meal
- oat bran
- rock phosphate

We love our Earth Juice Bloom as a flowering fertilizer and, because this product has no nitrogen it's especially useful for late stage flowering, when it's desirable to let a plant use up the soil's nitrogen reserves. It's also useful for an added boost of phosphorus at those times when plants need an extra boost. We normally use Earth Juice Bloom at rates between ½ and 2 tbsp per gallon.

Earth Juice Catalyst
- oat bran
- kelp
- wheat malt
- molasses
- yeast

For some odd reason, the Canadian government requires this product to be labeled as "Xatalyst," but whatever it's called where you live you may already know the biggest "secret" to this product is the sweet sticky goodness of molasses. Molasses feeds microbes and acts as a chelating agent to make micronutrients more available to plants. Those extra organic goodies in Catalyst, like wheat malt and oat bran, are just the "icing on the cake."

Earth Juice Meta-K 0-0-10
- sulfate of potash

A pretty simple product with (apparently) only a single active ingredient. It does have a good measure of sulfur, and it's very useful to give an extra boost of potassium when necessary. Many organic fertilizers run a little "lean" on K—especially guano based products, and Earth Juice Meta-K gives us a way to add that needed potassium in controlled amounts, as needed.

Earth Juice Microblast

- kelp meal
- magnesium sulfate
- borax
- cobalt sulfate
- ferrous sulfate
- manganese sulfate
- sodium molybdate
- zinc sulfate

In our experience, Microblast is a great all-around micro-nutrient supplement that resolves almost every potential micronutrient issue likely to arise.

EARTH JUICE RECIPES

Growth Recipes

Which "juice" and how much we use varies from strain to strain, perhaps even from plant to plant, so it's just not possible to set a feeding schedule and ignore the plants. The best gardeners become "at one" with their plants and feed them according to the plant's needs, even anticipating their needs.

Our standard mix for vegging plants is usually (per gallon of water):

- 1 to 2 tbsp Grow
- 1 tsp Bloom
- 1 tsp Catalyst

There are times where we might increase the Bloom portion up to as much as 1 tbsp, especially for plants in the early stages of flowering and we can go as high as 3 or even 4 tbsp of Grow for really N hungry plants—but if we increase the Grow fertilizer above 2 tbsp per gallon we usually leave out Bloom and Catalyst.

We also use what we call our "microblast mix" once or twice during the normal life cycle of vegging plants. No big difference between this and the prior mix, except this one has an extra boost of Meta K and Microblast.

- 1–2 tbsp Grow
- 1 tsp Bloom
- 1 tsp Catalyst
- 1 tsp Meta-K
- 1 tsp Microblast

We also commonly use some kinds of fish fertilizers and kelp concentrates during a plant's early growth stages; we like the combination of enzymes, proteins, and hormones the fish and kelp provide, but it's common for some fish products to be high in heavy metal contaminants like mercury, so the "seafood platter" is a treat we feed our babes and the Earth Juice is their regular diet.

Flowering Recipes

Early stage flowering plants can often use a fair measure of nitrogen as they stretch, so a normal Earth Juice mix in early flowering will look pretty similar to a Grow mix. We like to use something along the lines of the following for the first couple weeks of flowering.

- 1 tbsp Earth Juice Grow
- 1 tbsp Earth Juice Bloom
- 1 tsp Catalyst

As flowering progresses, we forego the nitrogen to let our plants use N reserves from the soil as they finish flowering, so mixing an Earth Juice Bloom formula can be as easy as:

- 1 tbsp Earth Juice Bloom
- 1 tsp Earth Juice Catalyst

For really hungry darlings we'll go as high as 2 tbsp per gallon with the Earth Juice Bloom, but pouring it on that heavy can burn light feeders and even with heavy feeders it's better to build up to stronger concentrations of Earth Juice Bloom over time than to just start in at 2 tbsp per gallon right away as plants begin to flower.

We also have a bloom "micro-mix" that includes Meta-K and Microblast. It's used once in a blooming plant's life (or maybe twice in plants with a long flowering period). Like the growth "microblast mix," it gives an extra boost of potassium and assorted micronutrients to make sure the plants will want for nothing! The flowering micro-mix usually goes like this:

- 1 tbsp Bloom
- 1 tsp Catalyst
- 1 tsp Meta-K
- 1 tsp Microblast

That's about all there is to making an awesome, plant-enriching organic brew with Earth Juice. It's really that simple.

MISCELLANEOUS EARTH JUICE NOTES

In theory, there's no need to "flush" organic soil grown herbs before harvest, and because organic fertilizers are not salt-based like chemical fertilizers, traditional techniques for "flushing" wouldn't carry away nutrient salts in the traditional meaning of the word "flush," anyway. This creates a danger with organic fertilizers that doesn't exist with salt-based chemical fertilizers. With salt fertilizers, over-fertilizing can be pretty severe, but it will show up fairly quickly, and the solution (a good flushing) can be enacted pretty quickly, too. It's probably harder for a grower to over-fertilize using organic fertilizers, but if they do there's no quick solution—organic fertilizers usually can't be flushed away like salt fertilizer's can, so if a grower over-fertilizes they will

A healthy hybrid enjoying its outdoor home.

Notice all the perlite this grower has added? It will help in the aeration and drainage of the soil.

This plant is half way through flower and needs to be flushed. The curling leaves and drooping petioles indicate overfeeding, most likely with excessive Nitrogen.

Different angle, same plant. Now we can see the view!

Young plants ready to be transplanted. Aim for one foot vertical growth per gallon.

These plants are past due for a transplant.

Normal development on a natural plant. No pinching, FIMing, LSTing, or any sort of advanced techniques have been used on this plant.

A little Cannabis seedling growing in harmony with a pink geranium.

This is a typical nitrogen/magnesium / calcium deficiency in late flower. Note the yellow leaves.

Vivid colors are often common with Indica dominant plants, especially when grown in cooler climates.

Proper sunlight is required to grow full colas like the ones on this plant.

An outdoor Swiss garden. Outdoor grows offer enough space for your plants to get nice and bush-like.

Colas bathing in the evening sun. They have great size because of the excellent sunlight available to them.

Cultivating Cannabis in The 21st Century

Here we see two outdoor test grows being conducted side-by-side by No Mercy Supply.

Here we see a great clone being grown outdoors by the medical collective, 420clones.com.

Here we see a very well-organized outdoor grow being conducted by No Mercy Supply. Always remember to stake your plants to help support their weight.

This is an enormous Double Fun plant being grown outdoors by No Mercy Supply. It has a delicious lemon taste and smell. Poke holes in the bottom of the coke bottle for a good, slow-release sugar feed.

Santa Maria from No Mercy Supply is a great indoor/outdoor strain that offers an energetic high and a fruity, sweet taste.

This Double Fun from No Mercy Supply has taken root for an outdoor grow. Double Fun is a very fast and mold resistant strain that is great outdoors and indoors.

Grow bags are a necessity for growing in guerilla locations. It allows you to move the plants in case of emergency, or if the plant needs more light, or even if there are natural predators in the area, like deer.

It is important to keep your grow bags as level as possible to keep your plants from toppling over.

A guerilla grow in a forest clearing. From the air these plants will blend in pretty well with their surroundings.

It is important to clear cut your plot and spray for insects prior to planting and then systematically throughout the life of the crop.

A healthy guerilla garden with easily moveable pots as containers.

Notice how the petioles and leaves are reaching up slightly? This is a great sign of a happy plant.

Notice the yellow/magenta leaves. It's early in flower for this deficiency to be taking place and should be corrected for maximum yields.

Valley growing in the Swiss Alps. Large grows of Cannabis like this one are very beautiful.

Hundreds of flowering female plants basking in the outdoor sun. What a treasure.

Cannabis growers live a simple life. Here we see some cows at pasture right beside a magnificent pot patch.

This is a healthy female cannabis plant being grown outdoors. With good soil and good sunlight, all plants should look like this.

likely have to live with the consequences for a longer term.

When it comes to harvest time we go ahead and put our organic herbs on a "crash" diet. In the past, it's just been pure water for the last two weeks, but lately we've been experimenting with using fulvic acid for the watering during the second week before harvest, and then plain water the final week; this technique really seems to bring out the fullest potential of our babes.

And finally, we need to touch on the practice of premixing and bubbling Earth Juice fertilizers. You may ask:

"Is it absolutely necessary to pre-mix and bubble / aerate Earth Juice fertilizers before use?"

Our simple answer is: no, it's not necessary at all. But, Earth Juice will be more efficiently and effectively used if "brewed" for 24–48 hours before use.

Earth Juice products are generally the cheapest organic fertilizers on the market. Products range from $9.95–$12.95 for a quart and $26.00–$28.95 for a gallon.

The full line of nutrients is available from the good people at plantitearth.com.

BOTANICARE

The Botanicare line that I prefer is Pure Blend Pro Grow and Bloom. This is their reformulated line that offers more nutrients than the original PBP. 100% satisfaction guaranteed.

Note: Botanicare is not OMRI (Organic Materials Review Institute) listed because it is not "certified organic"; the only reason they are not listed is because in the extraction process they use potassium hydroxide.

Pure Blend Pro Grow 3-1.5-4

Derived from: fish meal, composted sea bird guano, kelp, amino acids, rock phosphate, bone meal, potassium carbonate, magnesium carbonate, spirulina, soybean protein extract, fulvic acid, citric acid, B-complex vitamins, and calcium carbonate.

Also contains: 7% humic acid, raw sugar cane, agrimineral 76, silica clay extract, 1.00% of calcium and .05% magnesium.

For seedlings use 7 ml with 4 liters / 1 gallon of water.

For early vegetation use 15 ml with 4 liters / 1 gallon of water.

For mature vegetation use 30 ml / 1 ounce with 4 liters / 1 gallon of water.

Occasionally mist leaves with 7 ml per gallon.

Pure Blend Pro Bloom 1.5-4-5

Derived from: fish meal, composed sea bird guano, kelp, rock phosphate, bone meal, potassium carbonate, magnesium carbonate, spirulina, soybean protein extract, fulvic acid, citric acid, B-complex vitamins, and calcium carbonate.

Also contains: 7% humic acid, 1.00% of calcium, and .05% Magnesium.

For budding mature plants use 30 ml / 1 ounce with 4 liters / 1 gallon of water.

Liquid Karma .1-.1-.5

Derived from: fermented yeast extract and kelp seaweed extract.

Also contains: .01% humic acid, .01% aloe vera extract, and .01% yucca extract.

For seedlings use 5 ml / 1 tsp with 4 liters / 1 gallon of water.

For cuttings use 15–20 ml with 4 liters / 1 gallon of water.

For transplants use 15 ml / 1 tbsp with 4 liters / 1 gallon of water.

For vegetation stage use 10 ml / 2 tsp with 4 liters / 1 gallon of water.

For budding stage use 10–12 ml / 2.25 tsp with 4 liters / 1 gallon of water.

For foliar feeding use 5–7 ml / 1–1.5 tsp with 4 liters / 1 gallon of water.

Liquid Karma contains natural and metabolically active organic compounds that aren't found in plant fertilizers or supplements. Liquid Karma feeds all the microbes and bacteria in your soil, which means accelerated growth under all conditions. It is a stimulant to use in conjunction with PBP Grow or Bloom.

For optimum results use weekly.

Sweet 0-0-0

Derived from: Epsom salt and ferrous sulfate.

Also contains: cane sugar, citric acid, vitamin C, thiamine, riboflavin, pyridoxine, niacin, glycine, alanine, valine, leucine, isoleucine, serine, theronine, aspartic acid, glutamic acid, asparagine, glutamine, lysine, arginine, histidine, cystenine, cystine, methionine, proline, phenylalanine, tyrosine, trytophan, Epsom salt, ferrous sulfate, agrimineral 76 micro complex, 1.50% magnesium, 2.00% sulfur, and .06% iron

For vegetation stage use 10 ml / 2 tsp with 4 liters / 1 gallon of water.

For budding stage use 15–20 ml / 1–1.5 tbsp with 4 liters / 1 gallon of water.

For optimum results use every watering.

Sweet contains all those useful simple and complex carbohydrates that help plant cells generate faster and create more of them, meaning that your plant will basically grow faster and quicker when using Sweet. With Sweet, you're also getting vitamins, amino acids, organic acids, and trace elements that Black Strap molasses doesn't have. When using Sweet you can leave out the BSM.

Cal-Mag Plus 2-0-0

Derived from: calcium, magnesium nitrate, and iron EDTA.

Also contains: iron, boron, zinc, manganese, molybdenum, copper, cobalt and iodine, beneficial vitamins, 20 essential amino acids, and select botanical plant extracts. Also contains 3.2% calcium, 1.2% magnesium, 0.1% iron.

For vegetation or budding, use 5ml per gallon of water.

Cal-Mag Plus corrects the inherent problem of calcium, magnesium and iron deficiencies. Use at the first signs of a calcium or magnesium deficiency; this usually occurs during week 3–5 of budding.

Clearex 0-0-0

Contains: electrolytes, mono and disaccarides, fructose, and sucrose.

For vegetation and budding plants use 30 ml / ½ to 1 ounce with 4 liters / 1 gallon of water.

For pre-harvest plants use 15–30 ml / 1–2 tbsp with 4 liters / 1 gallon of water.

Clearex leaches toxic salts from the growing medium by separating the ionic bond nutrient and grow medium. It also corrects nutrient lock and salt build up. Best used every four weeks. Most growers that use Clearex do not flush at all during the last two weeks of flowering, and continue to feed their plants. They will use Clearex in the last two or three days of growth to flush the plants. They say the buds taste better if not flushed at all and the yield is increased because of increased feeding in the last two weeks.

Silica Blast 0-0-0

Derived from: sodium silica and potassium silicate.

Also contains: 72 silica minerals.

For vegetation and budding plants, use 2–5 ml / ½ –1 tsp with 4 liters / 1 gallon of water.

Helps strengthen plant tissue. Protects against disease, heat stress, drought stress, and frost. For optimum results use every other week.

BOTANICARE NOTES

You can use all Botanicare fertilizers mixed in with one another. When you are fertilizing, just mix them all together beforehand.

Growers have achieved great results mixing 5-gallon batches. Water with this fertilizer mix until the bucket runs dry, then water as normal; on the third or fourth week, mark the flush with Clearex and hydrogen peroxide. Then repeat!

To make 5 gallon batches use as follows:

- 50ml of Liquid Karma
- 45ml of Sweet
- 55–60ml of PBP grow

- 50ml of Cal-Mag
- 25ml of Silica Blast

  Pour all in the 5 gallons of water, let sit overnight, and use in the following days.

Flower mix:
- 50ml of Liquid Karma
- 55–60ml PBP bloom
- 50ml Cal-Mag
- 40ml Sweet
- 25ml Silica Blast

  Pour all in the 5 gallons of water, let sit overnight, and use in the following days.

  If 5 gallons is too much for you, then you can use a 1-gallon recipe as follows:

For vegetation:
- 10–15ml of Liquid Karma
- 10–15ml of Sweet
- 15ml of Pure Blend Pro Grow
- 5ml of Silica Blast
- 10ml of Cal-Mag Plus

For budding:
- 15ml of Liquid Karma
- 15ml of Sweet
- 15ml of Pure Blend Pro Bloom
- 5ml of Silica Blast
- 10–15ml of Cal-Mag Plus

  Pour all in the 1-gallon of water, let sit overnight, and use in the following days.

  Every third or fourth week flush with 30ml of Clearex.

  Botanicare products are some of the best on the market. They balance quality with fair prices. Generally between $11.95–$19.95 for a quart and $29.95–$59.95 for a gallon.

  If you would like to buy wholesale, they sell 2.5 and 5-gallon containers as well.

  All of the products listed above can be found at plantitearth.com

BIO BIZZ

All Bio Bizz products are primarily for soil gardens; they advise not to use in hydroponic gardens.

Bio Grow 1.8-0.1-6.6

Contains: natural sugars (carbohydrates) derived from Dutch beet extract, along with Vitamin B-1, B-2, C, and E, with 70 other trace elements.

For seedlings use 8ml per gallon of water.

For vegetation use 12ml per gallon of water.

For budding use 16ml per gallon of water.

Use can also use Bio Grow during the budding cycle for the carbohydrates / sugars it contains.

Bio Bloom 1.1-2.5-2

Contains: enzymes and amino acids to boost bud growth.

For vegetation use 8–12ml per gallon of water.

For budding use 16ml per gallon of water.

Alg-A-Mic 0-0-0

Contains: seaweed extract, trace elements, hormones, amino acids, and vitamins.

Used to build resistance to stress, bugs and disease.

For seedling use 4ml per gallon.

For vegetation use 8–12ml per gallon of water.

For budding use 16ml per gallon of water.

For foliar feed use 6ml per gallon.

Root Juice 0-0-0

Contains humic acid and seaweed extract.

Used to help roots develop faster and stronger than they normally would. Also said to improve plants' ability to maintain under high salinity content.

For seedling use 4–8ml per gallon of water.

For vegetation use 8ml per gallon.

For budding use 8–10ml per gallon of water.

Top Max 0-0-0

Contains: fulvic and humic acid.

Used to boost yields during budding cycle.

For vegetation use 4ml per gallon of water

For budding use 12ml per gallon of water.

Fish-Mix 2.1-0.2-6.6

Contains: microbes, amino acid, B vitamins, and trace elements.

Is used primarily outdoors because of its strong odor.

For vegetation use 9ml per gallon of water.

For foliar feeding use 5ml per gallon of water.

BIO BIZZ NOTES

I don't like using Bio Bizz products because they just don't perform to the quality I'm used to, and for the price, they should. $15.95–$39.95 for a quart. $44.95–$129.00 for a gallon.

All of the Bio Bizz line can be found at wormsway.com

To view the Bio Bizz feeding schedule visit gchydro.com/pdf/biobizz.pdf

ADVANCED NUTRIENTS

Advanced Nutrients may very well be the best line of fertilizer available in today's market. This theory is certainly reflected in their prices!

Advanced Nutrients Recipes

I've had phenomenal results using the following 5-gallon recipe(s).

For vegetation:
- 12 ml Iguana Juice Grow
- 10 ml Mother Earth Blended Organic Super Tea Grow
- 30 ml Organic-B
- 5 ml Piranha Juice
- 10 ml Voodoo Juice
- 15 ml Scorpion Juice
  and then
- 15 ml SensiZym
- 2.5 ml Tarantula
- 10 ml Fulvic Acid
- 30 ml Seaweed Extract
- 2 ml Emerald Shaman
- 5 ml Carbo Load

For budding:
- 15 ml Iguana Juice Bloom
- 15 ml Mother Earth Blended Organic Super Tea Bloom
- 20 ml Organic-B
- 5 ml Piranha Juice

- 15 ml Voodoo Juice
- 20 ml Scorpion Juice
  and then
- 15 ml SensiZym
- 15 ml Sweet Leaf
- 6 ml Tarantula
- 10 ml Fulvic Acid
- 25 ml Seaweed Extract
- 2 ml Emerald Shaman
- 10 ml Carbo Load

Since 14 ingredients is a lot to mix together, it's good to make separate batches with the measurements from above.

First, feed the soil so it will be ready to use the nutrients it will be receiving in a few days. Start with: Voodoo Juice, Tarantula, Piranha Juice, and SensiZym.

After the medium dries out, add your nutrients: Iguana Juice Grow, Mother Earth Super Tea Grow or Iguana Juice Bloom, Mother Earth Super Tea Bloom, and, depending on your plant stage, Seaweed Extract and Green Shaman.

After your medium dries out from this, water with plain water; after your medium dries from that, it's time for Organic-B, Scorpion Juice and fulvic acid. No need for humic acid, as we have addressed earlier.

After that dries, finish off with Sweet Leaf and Carbo Load, and, if needed, repeat.

Advanced Nutrients Notes

Advanced Nutrients is without a doubt the best line of nutrients available, but they're just so expensive! Not to mention they try to make the extra dollar by not having all the enzymes, microorganisms, microbes, and bacteria in one container.

You can typically find the nutrients listed above for between $12.40 –33.90 for a quart and $63.00–212.00 for a gallon. You get what you pay for, and in this case, let's just average out that you're paying $21.35 for a quart; multiply that by the 13 products listed above, and that equals a whopping $277.55, plus shipping, which will put you well over $325.00. Quite an investment just for nutrients!

Instead of purchasing the whole Advance Nutrients line I suggest purchasing some of the best products, such as: Voodoo Juice, Piranha Juice, Tarantula, and humic and fulvic acids. Add these to the Botanicare line and your total should be around $222.45, which is still a nice chunk of change but a lot better than $325.00. You'll still get phenomenal results using the Advanced Nutrients x Botanicare mix.

This baby was grown outdoors with organic compost tea treatments. This is an incredible looking plant that any grower would be proud of.

A NOTE ABOUT ORGANIC FERTILIZERS

I have heard many growers referring to fertilizers such as Fox Farm, B'Cuzz, and General Hydroponics as organic fertilizers—*they are not*! The reason growers might think this is because of those companies' marketing gimmicks: "organic based" or "natural base" are some of the key phrases used. While they might be organic based, they still contain chemicals and therefore defeat the purpose of organic gardening.

EXPIRED NUTRIENTS

Like everything, nutrients have a shelf life; however, most do not have an expiration date. Here are some tips when buying both organic and chemical nutrients. Unfortunately, these tips are only effective when purchasing the nutrients in person.

When organic nutrients are expiring, the bottles will suck inward because the organisms are using the oxygen inside the bottle. If you see this in a store you may conclude that the store doesn't move much product, the product is at least a year old, and the store is not doing a good job of maintaining supplies.

When chemical nutrients are expiring, the minerals in the nutrients will bond together and sink down to the bottom. When you shake a bottle, you will hear the minerals rattling on the bottom, which sounds like sand or small rocks.

Some nutrients expire faster than others. Earth Juice, for example, degrades faster than others; Botanicare degrades slightly, as with most Advanced Nutrient products; and Biobizz degrades very little.

GETTING THE NUTRIENTS YOU NEED
without Ordering Online or Going to a Hydro Shop

You may be hesitant about ordering nutrients online, or you may not want to spend that much on nutrients for your first or second grow. If this is the case, you can achieve good results by doing the following.

First, you'll need preliminary nutrients for the soil. You can find mushroom compost, Black Kow, and Miracle Grow Organic at any home improvement store, but I would use it only in an emergency. I've only found one business that carries pure Worm Castings and that is an Ace Cowan super center. Pro Mix is even tougher to find, usually only in select "ma and pa" gardening centers. Forget about trying to get worm castings and Pro Mix during the fall and winter months.

Most Epsoma products can be found at most home improvement stores—Lowes and Pikes, primarily, with the exception of Kelp meal. Plant tone and flower tone are key additives. You can also use these to make teas as instructed above in the tea section. You also want to add a ½ tbsp of Dried Blood and Bone meal to your soil because you won't have the nutrients to give them a boost. Using these steps you can have a nice healthy harvest without ordering anything online. Teas are an essential aspect of getting the nutrients and organic goodies you need without purchasing fertilizers from a hydro shop or ordering online.

The Organic Materials Review Institute (OMRI) tests and lists products on their website, OMRI.org. Most products will list the OMRI symbol on their products; if not, you can look up the products online. These products include pesticides and fungicides as well as nutrients.

Also note that the best time to feed your plants is after a nice dry period. The plant will absorb the nutrients better and spread them to more parts of the plant when the plant is "thirsty." It is also better to feed in the morning.

This small hybrid is perfect for inconspicuous outdoor grows.

Chapter 21

Outdoor Gardening

Outdoor growing is the pinnacle of cannabis growing. Indoor growing is just an attempt to create outdoor growing conditions, indoors. Seldom, if ever, has this been successfully accomplished. God just does a better job, hands down. You'll find that the large majority of your strains / plants will taste and grow better; they'll also be much more potent when grown outdoors. The only exception to this rule is if you grow near a busy city. The pollution will clog your plant's stomatas and create sick, unhealthy plants. The cannabis plant absorbs everything in the soil, so growing by a road with oil runoff is very unwise.

CHOOSING YOUR PLOT

The first and most important thing you have to worry about is the security of your chosen plot. Growing a killer crop is nothing but a risk if you don't have a secure place to grow it. All your hard work could disappear and your freedom along with it one day if your plot isn't secure. That is why this is the most important step for growing outdoors.

You want to find a spot secluded from the general public and with good cover plants. I recommend that you be at least 200 yards away from any trail, path, street, or building. Make sure that no artificial light is shining on your plants at night— while this will help in the vegetation cycle, it will wreak havoc during the flowering cycle by delaying or completely stopping your plant from flowering or causing retarded budding structure. Find a spot with some briers and thorn bushes, black-berry bushes, poison ivy, poison oak, stinging nettle, or what have you, as long as it's something to deter uninvited guests. Your spot should also be away from any bright, colorful, inviting plants and blooms. Insects can also be good deterrents. Those pesky flies, bees, wasps, and gnats are great for keeping people from poking their nose around your plants.

This Wildberry plant is camouflaged well by the surrounding brier patch – no tres-
passers, no troubles.

If you are considering growing underneath high voltage power lines, I urge you to reconsider. I know that these places look like prime real estate for growing, but any-where that there are power lines there is annual, if not more frequent, servicing. I would also advise against growing on farmland for the same reasons; if the farmer doesn't find your plants, there is a good chance that the animals will.

A brief word about treetop (canopy) growing. It is a very dangerous form of growing. Not many plants can be grown in one tree, and the plants are heavily shaded by foliage; if they are not, then they are not properly camouflaged. It is extremely hard to tend to plants, hoisting heavy 7–10 gallon containers full of soil and water. This is not to mention the suspicion factor. When it is time to put the plants out in early spring, there is not enough foliage to conceal them and, depending on the strain, the leaves are falling before or during harvest time. Harsh weather can quickly ruin all your labors, and if the weather doesn't get them, then birds and squirrels are very likely to. Too much work, too much risk, for too little reward.

LIGHTING

This may very well be the most important aspect of growing cannabis. Having the required amount of sunlight can become a problem when trying to stay stealthy. In order to grow trichome covered, dense colas, you must have between six and seven hours of direct sunlight. Most "experts" will argue that you only need four or five, but in my (and my colleagues) experiences, this is just not true. Another debatable

Growing on a slope is a good way to maximize the amount of light your plant gets. Notice how the shrub in the foreground has been trimmed to stop it from stealing light from the cannabis plant.

point is whether morning sun is better than afternoon or evening sun. Most will argue that morning sun is better, but it is common sense that the afternoon sun is the most intense, and the more intense the light, the better the growth. In order to get at least seven hours of sunlight, you must have a clearing of 45 yards (depending on the height of surrounding trees and plants) east to west; this will give you direct sunlight for at least seven hours. Natural wood clearings where the trees have fallen make for good areas, with good direct light during the most intense hours of the day and shaded lighting in the morning and late afternoon. Some companies have developed strains that can be grown and produce decent yields under shade. This might be worth checking into if you can't get out into the open. Growing on a hillside facing south will get the best light exposure. Also, planting on the highest possible elevation will allow the plant to have more time in the sun than if they were lower on the slope.

MOBILITY

This is a key part of outdoor growing. Mobility allows you to move your plants if they are ever spotted or you get too paranoid. Another benefit of having your plants mobile is that you can move them to the areas to which the sunlight moves. The standard used to be five gallons, but now most successful outdoor growers will use at least ten-gallon grow containers. Grow bags are the best, seeing as they take up less space, weigh less, and are easier to move than pots. To camouflage your plants, dig a hole big enough to fully submerge your entire pot or bag and proceed to cover it with the surrounding ground cover. This will lower the profile of your plants, which increases its camouflage; you might be surprised at how natural your plants look when their containers are buried in the ground. This will also protect the roots from direct sunlight, which can cook your roots to a crisp.

WATER

Water is one of the key elements of life. It is necessary in large amounts for outdoor growers, especially those in hot, drought-stricken regions. Since you're not planting near a water source (because LEOs look for that), you will have to dig a reservoir to hold the water that you will need to water your crop.

The reservoir should be located a good distance away from your crop, but not too far, as you will have to transport multiple buckets full of water over long distances to your plot. Your reservoir should be at least the size of your plot, but bigger is better. To keep all your water from being absorbed back into the soil, you'll need to line your reservoir with clear plastic at least 5mm thick.

You can do this one of two ways, the easiest of which is to simply take an over-

Grow bags keep your outdoor plants mobile and thus safer. The good outdoor grower also remembers to keep his plants well watered during the hot summer months.

sized portion of clear plastic, at least 5mm thick, put the center of this plastic in the center of the hold, apply some sort of galvanized anchor points (in a pinch, rocks will do) in the corners, and center. Make sure you have at least 2 feet on the outskirts of your reservoir, and secure the whole thing with sod stakes.

To do this, first cut a piece of plastic to fully cover the bottom of the reservoir. Leave enough excess so that the plastic comes up the sides at least a quarter of the way. Use sod stakes to anchor the plastic in place until you finish cutting the rest of the plastic.

Now that you have the bottom portion of your reservoir set up, you can stick the rest of your plastic in place. You may have to get another piece of plastic because your leftover might be insufficient, but take one end of the plastic and overlap at least 6 inches onto the plastic that is already in place on the walls. Use sod stakes to anchor this edge in place— make sure you use the galvanized version so they won't rust and contaminate your water supply. Wrap the inner edge of the plastic all around the inside of your reservoir and anchor it as you go along. Make sure that you that the plastic stays overlapping all around the reservoir. Now that you have the inside secured, anchor down the plastic around the outside of the reservoir.

Bring your caulk gun or silicon sealer that is FISH SAFE so it will not contaminate your water supply. Caulk is preferable to silicon. Seal the overlapping edges, where the plastic layer on the bottom is sealed to the layer of plastic on the top. Do this one-inch below the end of the bottom layer of plastic. Make sure you get a good seal all the way around the reservoir. Double up, if needed. Also, seal the steel that has punctured through the plastic to hold the plastic in place. Make sure you thoroughly coat these as well. Painting the inside of your reservoir with dirt brown or forest green fish safe / waterproof paint will drastically improve the camouflage of your reservoir.

Lastly, place another sheet of clear plastic over your reservoir, with small slits and holes cut in—especially around the center, where water will pool. This serves multiple purposes: to keep rain water in while keeping as much as possible from evaporating, and to keep animals from drinking / bathing in your water supply. Make sure you provide enough anchors so that the plastic does not cave in when water collects on top of the plastic.

Note: if possible, make your reservoir on a hill, the steeper the better, so that you can siphon the water from your reservoir to your plants via a garden hose without the need for buckets. If not, you may use a battery-powered pump.

PESTS AND DISEASES

While pests and disease will vary in different parts of the country, some of the most common outdoor pests, diseases, and treatments are listed below. For all other problems, including indoor pests, see Chapter 18, Pests, Diseases, Deficiencies and Disorders.

PESTS

Offered in order of frequency.

Japanese Beetles

Occur throughout mid- to late-summer. Japanese Beetles are a shiny copper and green color and are a $\frac{1}{2}$-inch in length. These beetles will eat almost anything and are a big problem for growers in the southeast U.S. They can really become a problem for guerilla growers. You can combat these critters by using yellow traps that use pheromones to attract the beetles. Neem oil is fairly effective in treating Japanese Beetles. To prevent them from coming around next season, use parasitic nematodes, diatomaceous earth, or milky spore (a type of bacteria) to destroy their larva.

Cabbage Loopers

Most prevalent in spring. These caterpillars are light green in color and between 1–1½ inches long. In the vegetative stage, these little buggers will chew holes in your leaves, eat tender new shoots, and wreak havoc for young, tender cannabis plants. Combat these critters by spraying Bacillus Thuringiensis, commonly known as Bt; make sure to coat the undersides of leaves well.

Nematodes

Most prevalent throughout the southern U.S. There are many types of nematodes. Some are beneficial, while others can potentially destroy your "healthy" plants and leave you asking, "what the hell went wrong?" especially in hot, dry conditions. Your plants will appear stunted and begin to yellow, a condition which progresses all over the plant, even if treated with nitrogen. You can control nematodes by having high organic matter, which encourages nematode antagonists. If you have high organic content and still suspect nematodes to be the culprit, water with hydrogen peroxide; roughly 1 to 1½ tsp per gallon of 35% H_2O_2 will suffice. Water thoroughly, and then add 1 cup per gallon of diatomaceous earth mixed into your topsoil.

Tomato Hornworms

Prevalent throughout the entire U.S. Hornworms are green, although some have white striping. They have horns on their bodies, which can make them kind of intimidating. Hornworms can get up to 5 inches in length! If you thought inchworms or cabbage loopers where bad for your plants, you ain't seen nothing yet! These monsters have about three times the appetite of those critters. Once again, Bt is your best friend—as are parasitic wasps.

Cutworms

Prevalent throughout most of the U.S., especially in the south. Most commonly known as grubworms. They are yellow, brown, or white, and around ½–2 inches in length when fully extended. There are at least three major varieties: white, yellow, and black colored. They share two common characteristics. They all curl up into a little "c" shape when not active, and they all wreak havoc upon your seedlings. They are active mostly at night and cut your seedlings stalks off right at the soil line. Control with beneficial nematodes and diatomaceous earth.

Aphids

Prevalent throughout the U.S., they can be winged or not, and are green, white, yellow, pink, or black, depending on the species, and they are $\frac{1}{10}$-inch in length. They are common on leaf undersides. They feed on your plants' juices and their leaves will become distorted and yellow. Ants and aphids are your enemies. The ants will protect the aphids, since they are their source of food. Aphids and spider mites are some of the hardest pests to get rid off. This is partly because most insecticides only work on adult aphids, not on larva and eggs. This means you'll have to spray your whole plant, thoroughly, at least three times a week for several weeks. Neem oil, insecticidal soap, and pyrethrum work well in combination with each other, as is true for spider mites. Cold temperatures below 40°F will eliminate aphids. An easy way to find out if you have aphids is to notice if you have an abnormally large number of wasps hanging around your plants—especially on your plants. In this case, wasps are your friends and are eating the aphids, although I must admit it does make it challenging to get work done.

Fire Ants
Prevalent all over the U.S., especially throughout the south. They are generally about $\frac{1}{8}$–$\frac{1}{3}$-inch in length. These critters are big trouble for tender seedlings. Seemingly overnight they will eat the "head" of your newly sprouted seed and leave only a stalk protruding out of the ground. Combat with nematodes, diatomaceous earth, and / or spinocide.

Mealybugs
Prevalent all over the U.S., Mealybugs are white and $\frac{1}{16}$–$\frac{1}{8}$ of an inch in length. These bugs at first appear to be mold appearing on the undersides of leaves and at the internodes. Like aphids, they suck out plant nutrients; you'll notice yellowing and brownish spots developing on the leaves. Controls include use of insecticidal soap or neem oil, a specific ladybug known as *hippodamia convergens*, or lacewing.

Spider Mites
Prevalent all across the southeast U.S., in extreme heat and dry and arid conditions, especially in areas where wintertime temperatures seldom dip below freezing. These tiny insects are yellow, red, or white, and are a microscopic $\frac{1}{64}$ of an inch in length. Keep soil moist and spray plants frequently to prevent. Treat by using insecticidal soap, neem oil, and pyrethrum.

Thrips
Many species are prevalent all across the U.S., Thrips are a yellow color and $\frac{1}{25}$ of an inch in length. You probably won't spot the thrips themselves, but may find their drop-

pings—black looking specks on leaf surfaces—or their damage—yellowing lines that are the scars on your plants. Control by using neem oil and insecticidal soap.

Whiteflies

Prevalent throughout the U.S., White flies are white—sort of translucent—in color and $\frac{1}{16}$ of an inch in length. They feed in large numbers on the underside of leaves. They will fly to other parts of your plant when disturbed. Like other insects, they suck out plant nutrients. Control with insecticidal soap or neem oil.

Grasshoppers

Prevalent all over the U.S., especially in the central and Midwest areas. Grasshoppers come in all colors and can grow up to $2\frac{1}{2}$ inches in length.

In extreme cases, they swarm like locusts, wiping out entire crops. They can be a particular problem for guerilla growers, but backyard gardeners face only one or two that munch on their plants. Control by baiting with protozoan or nosema locustae diseases.

Slugs and Snails

Prevalent all over the U.S., especially in the gulf coast region or in extremely wet and humid conditions. You can quickly determine if you are being invaded by slugs or snails by looking for a clear-colored flaky trail where holes in your leaves are. Stop them before they become a problem by placing copper pipes around the entire perimeter of your plant or plants. Slugs and snails cannot cross copper. If the high price of copper is too much for you, diatomaceous earth will do a good job; again, create a barrier around your plants.

Leafhoppers

Prevalent over the Midwest and Southern U.S., especially in the Southeast. Leafhoppers are light green in color and $\frac{1}{8}$-inch in length. These insects appear on the upper side of leaves and generally do not appear in great number, but extreme infestations have occurred. They are typically green and when they are not using their wings they form a peak or triangle shape giving these insects a very unique profile. Leafhoppers are very quick and will usually fly or hop away to nearby vegetation while you are visiting your plant. They suck out sap from the plant and also secrete honeydew. Spray pyrethrum to kill leafhoppers.

Animals

Small animals and deer are always a problem for outdoor growers, regardless of the

Use fencing to keep animals away from your grow. The wicker border also keeps prying eyes away from your operation.

area. Squirrels will burrow in the soil at the base of the plant, destroying precious roots and sometimes toppling the plant. Rabbits like to munch at the stalks of tender plants and deer like to eat tender plants altogether, as do dogs. Ground red pepper is a powerful deterrent against squirrels and small animals. There are products that you can place around your plants that are made from garlic and other herbs and spices that claim to keep animals away, but I have found that this is untrue, except for the product Liquid Fence—it does a great job but must be applied every three to four weeks for effective control. The only sure-fire way to keep them from getting to your plants is to build a fence around them or place them in a thicket of thorns.

DISEASES
Bacterial Blight
Prevalent across most of the U.S. They first appear to be light green and turn brown; some have a yellow "halo" around them. Prevent by avoiding working in your garden when plants are wet.

Bacterial Wilt
Prevalent across most of the U.S. First signs are that in the heat of the day, the leaves will wilt, but recover later into the evening and into the night. This will repeat the following days until it becomes so severe that parts of the plant will wilt and die. Control with pyrethium.

Downy Mildew
Prevalent across most of the U.S. Appears as irregular brown or yellowish spots on the upper leaf surface. Severely affected leaves die. Prevent by making sure your soil has great drainage. Control by using aerated compost tea, such as foliar spray, or by foliar feeding with a product that has beneficial microbes.

Late Blight
Prevalent all over the U.S. Appears as grayish spots on the upper surface of leaves while white mold grows on the underside. The leaves turn brown, shrivel up, and die. Prevent by not overfeeding; excess nitrogen welcomes the condition.

Powdery Mildew
Prevalent all across the U.S. Appears as a powdery white fungus that coats the upper part of the leaves. It soon turns yellow and dries out, usually affecting the older leaves first. Control by using Safer Fungicide that contains sulfur.

Grey Mold (Botrytis)

Prevalent in the wetter climates of the U.S. On very thick colas it is most prevalent, as moisture gets trapped inside the thick cola and cannot work its way out. Treatment consists of first removing the infected areas and then spraying plants with gliocaldium roseum or trichoderma species.

Sooty Mold

A direct result of aphid, mealybugs, whiteflies and any other critters that infest your plant. These critters secrete honeydew, which can cause black mold to develop. Control by first removing the critters and then spray with insecticidal soap.

OUTDOOR STRAINS

These strains are hardy and are either bred for outdoor climate or are landraces grown only outdoors. *Sown from March 31st.

The following strains finish from early August to mid-August: Legends Ultimate Indica, Hashberry, Speed Queen, Sadhu, Chocolate Chunk, Sweet Tooth #3, Sensi Star, Durga Mata, Top 44, Matanuska Thunderfuck, Ice, Aurora Indica, and pure Indicas.

The following strains finish from late August to mid September: Early Girl, Early Pearl, Early Durban, Early California, Early Sativa, Early Misty, Early Queen, Early Skunk, Early Riser, Hash Plant, Hindu Kush and most Kush hybrids, Northern Lights and most NL hybrids, as well as most Indica / Afghanica plants.

The following strains finish from late September to mid October: Durban, Durban Poison, Durban x Skunk, C99, Blueberry, Jack Herer and Jack Herer hybrids, Jamaican Pearl, Marley's Collie, Kali Mist, Skunk #1, and most Skunk #1 hybrids.

The following strains finish late from late October to mid December: Thai and most Thai hybrids, Malawi, Swazi, Hempstar, Mullumbimby Madness, Nevilles Haze, Original Haze, and most Haze hybrids.

Indicator Plants and Soil Composition

The following information can be used for both guerilla and backyard growing.

These plants will indicate the quality of soil and the amount of nutrients in it.

Look for these when choosing an outdoor plot and you'll have less work ahead of you. Generally, the darker the soil the more available nutrients it will contain.

The soil attributes below are indicated (in practice) by the plants listed.

Rich in overall nutrients: black nightshade, chickweed, coltsfoot, earthsmoke, field pennycress, orache, round leaved dock, sting nettle, thistle, and white leaved goosefoot.

If you are planting your cannabis in sandy soil outdoors, a good idea is to mix some peat moss into the ground to help with absorption.

Poor in overall nutrients: bracken fern, daisies, heather, pansies, ox-eye daisies, white clover, wild onions, and whitlow grass.

Alkaline: chicory, field mustard, meadow pansies, meadow clary, scarlet pimpernel, and wild oats.

Neutral: chamomile.

Acidic: blueberry, blackberries, bracken fern, cranberries, corn spurry, daisies, hemp nettle, holly bushes, ivy-leaved veronica, poison berries, and violet pansies.

Nitrogen Rich: chickweed, couch grass, cow parsnip, dead nettle, elder dandelion, field mustard, fig-leaved goosefoot, orache, and stinging nettle.

Calcium Rich: belladonna (not the cannabis strain), clover, dandelions, dead nettle, field bell flower, field bindweed, field larkspur, hops, liverwort, marigold, meadow clary, red poppy, scarlet pimpernel, and silver thistle.

Potassium Rich: foxtail, orache, and red foxglove.

Magnesium Rich: black hellebore and red foxglove.

Poor Nitrogen: chickweed, gorse, mouse-ear, and whitlow grass.

Poor Calcium: bracken fern, blueberries, cranberries, horsetail, mayweed, and pansies.

Humus: chickweed, dandelion, and thistle.

Humid: alder, bellflower, horsetail, marsh marigold, reed, spearmint, silverweed, and willow.

Soggy: adderwort, coltsfoot, comfrey, dandelion, plantains, spearmint, and silverweed.

Dry: gorse, foxglove, and mullein.

Loose, sandy: chickweed, gorse, heather, pine tree, and red poppy.

Packed clay: dandelion, horsetail, knotgrass, plantain, and spearmint.

SOIL COMPOSITIONS
Sandy
This is a good soil to plant in; it is easy to correct to get the required drainage. It requires at least a 50 lb. bag of humus; adding worm castings would be a good idea as well. It would also be good to mix in some Pro Mix or peat moss for absorption.

Clay Soil
I would not plant in this soil because it takes a lot of work to correct and even then it is still highly acidic. It requires humus, sand, perlite, or vermiculite. Even then the soil may become waterlogged.

Loamy Soil
This is the soil you're looking for. It is light and airy but not so much that it cannot hold water. It is usually rich in nutrients. You will want to add some mushroom compost and PSG to increase microbes and nutrients.

A good soil contains a mix of all types of soil: sand, clay, and loam. It provides good aeration, which keeps a good oxygen-to-water ratio.

You can find out the make up of your soil by taking a sample, say 1 tbsp, and placing it in a test tube or similar glass container for 48 hours. Make sure not to disturb the container during this period. Your bigger, heavier particles will fall to the bottom and the smaller, lighter particles will rise to the top. The muddier the water the more humus is in the soil.

Sand has the heaviest particles, next is silt or loam, and on top is the clay. So on the bottom will be sand, in the middle will be loam / silt, and on the top will be clay.

Obviously, the amounts of sand, loam, and clay will determine the make up of your soil and ultimately what needs to be added to it.

For guerilla and backyard growing, the use of blood and bone meal as well as other meals composed of animal products (i.e. feather meal) will attract carnivorous animals, especially if they are not thoroughly mixed in. Try to keep your animal meal near the bottom of your hole so it will not be easily smelled.

To ward off animal pests that may eat or destroy your crop there are a few natural ways to keep them at bay. Of course, the easiest way is to urinate around your crop. This is very effective for keeping deer and small animals such as rabbits away. The only draw back with this method is that you must re-apply after each rainfall for best results. Storing your urine in a jar for two weeks or longer will make your urine super potent (stinky) and will work even better.

You can also place slivers of Irish Spring body soap around your plants. There are certain pheromones that Irish Spring soap contains that repel animals.

Lastly, you can place hair around your plot. This is very dangerous if you use your own hair or hair of someone closely linked to you; it's dangerous even when you use the hair from your pet. It only takes one strand of hair to link you to the plot. If you do choose to use hair, place it close to the ground, don't leave it hanging on plants, especially tall plants where the hair is easily seen. Don't leave clumps of hair; spread it out well. If you have the courage, your local barbershop will have no problem letting you have all the hair you can carry away. Human hair will keep most animals away, whereas dog hair will only keep deer and small animals away, but will draw other dogs.

GUERILLA GROWING

Depending on who you talk to, this is the most dangerous or most safe form of outdoor growing. The pros would be that it's not on your property, so if you don't leave physical evidence at your plot or they don't take photos of you visiting, there's no evidence it was your plot other than circumstantial evidence so more than likely they will not be able to prosecute you for it.

After all, you were just walking through the woods and found all these beautiful, vibrant cannabis plants, right? More pros would be that you are more able to get the required amount of sunlight easier than with backyard growing. And if you feel particularly safe in your location, then you can have many more plants than a backyard grower might have. The only problem with more plants is the greater possibility of having your patch found. However, the cons can outweigh the pros.

Cons include not being able to watch them closely, which means not being able to adjust to what the plants need as they need it, having to go on someone else's land each time and risk being spotted, as well as risking trespassing charges; having to haul your clones to the location and then haul away enormous amounts of killer bud reeking up your vehicle; possibly frequent trips to water; and usually more pests than backyard growers. Furthermore, you run the risk of having an unwanted seeded crop and you will have to make a trip to remove any possible males (unless growing from female clones).

You have to worry about the possibility of having your patch found by a wandering hunter or hiker. To avoid having a hunter or hiker find your patch, be sure to leave no trail, as people will follow any trail they see in the woods for apparently no reason at all.

Growing in the woods can be very rewarding. I suggest staying away from state parks and that sort of thing where park or forest rangers (who are permitted to carry handguns) patrol. First, get topographical maps that show logging roads marked out, pick out a good location on the maps, and then see how it looks from a satellite image. Earth.google.com is a great source, as is skytracker.com.

Look for a nice open area at least 45 yards wide so you can get a nice chunk of afternoon sunshine. Once again, north or south facing hills are ideal, but also a prime target for LEOs. Most potential plots will need some work, e.g., cutting down a few moderate sized trees, clearing out a bit of brush, etc. When doing this kind of guerilla growing you'll have to find a source of water nearby, but not too close, as bodies of water are high traffic areas where hikers, hunters, and most importantly LEOs patrol for potential cannabis crops. Have at least five or six places marked out because chances are that your first or even third potential plots won't work out.

Some tools you'll need before venturing into the "jungle" include:

- GPS
- Snake bite proof boots that come up to your knees
- Machete
- Handsaw

FURTHER TIPS

You did go to Kinko's and get that fake business card right? Don't forget to bring it and your photography equipment. Make sure to leave a note attached to your vehicle with your business card attached, saying you're photographing *fill in the blank* that is indigenous to this area; note that you know the area, have GPS, and will be back at *fill in the blank* time, and most importantly, do not be late! Leave some film canisters and other obvious photography equipment such as a tripod clearly visible in your car.

Avoid making trails and don't cut or break branches. If you can't get around them, bend them instead of breaking them. Drag some branches behind you to cover your trail, don't walk in a straight line to your plot, and if possible take different paths.

Remember: no planting in straight lines! Also: your shoe pattern and tire pattern are finger prints (so to speak). Make the necessary steps to not leave any behind that can be traced back to you. This means taping the bottom of your shoes in layers so that no print is left and taking a vehicle that cannot be linked back to you.

When transplanting your seedlings or small clones, you can disguise them inside of a large tackle box. Just make sure you bring your fishing pole with you, granted that you are somewhere near a body of water.

OldJoints of thecannacabana.com has this to say about transporting plants to your guerilla spot:

This is a method I designed to get 200 plants in a backpack for a day of guerilla growing. Take plants (sexed or unsexed) at the height of between 12 and 18 inches. Now, take a 5-gallon bucket and fill it about ½ of the way up with lukewarm water, and add a tablespoon of bloom fertilizer. Now, take a plant out of its container, lightly dunk it in the water, and gently shake and swirl it until all soil has been removed. This is called bare-rooting. Take about five pieces of a newspaper, one on top of the other, stretch them out, and wet them down. Now, place the bare-rooted plant and place it on the wet paper. Continue this process until you have about 25 plants in that newspaper. Now wrap newspaper up length-ways around the plants (like a joint) and cut off excess paper, or just fold above and below plants inward, making sure you have enough to cover top and bottom. Now take a pair of pantyhose that are for very large women and cut off one leg. Take rolled newspaper and place it in the pantyhose leg. Tie panty-hose lightly above plants. This will make sure your plants are confined and won't get hurt easily. Your pantyhose with plants in it should now be about the size of a paper towel roll. Continue this process until you have enough to fill your backpack or as few as you want. Always support the bottom when carrying the pantyhose, as damage could occur by just carrying from the top. When remov-ing the plants from pantyhose do not do so against the grain of the way the leaves grow. Have Fun Planting!

BACKYARD GROWING

Nothing's better than having a few cannabis plants scattered around your back-yard. Depending on the layout of your property, you can choose how many and how close to have your plants. Secluded property that is at least 50+ yards away from your neighbors is great; having a wooded part of your lot with heavy under-brush is also ideal, allowing you to disguise some plants in the middle of it. Privacy fences are by far the best. With a fence, your options are limitless, make sure you take into account that an occasional sports ball might stray into your property, along with the child to retrieve it. The fence will provide you cover from the ground; now you just have to work on cover from the air view. I would not attempt backyard growing if you are residing in a subdivision, even if you have a fence. The smell is unmistakable and all it takes is a neighbor to stumble into your yard and the jig is up. With backyard growing you may check on your plants daily and really "get to know" them. You'll be able to provide nutrients as needed and correct any problems that may arise as soon as they occur. I also would strongly advise against patio growing and roof top growing; although these areas get great sunlight, just one pass over by a helicopter or a backdoor delivery by a courier and your safety is compromised. Patio plants stick out like a sore thumb.

Be sure to take into account that routine checks are made to your electrical and water meters when growing in your yard.

DROUGHT GROWING

Over ⅔ of the United States is classified as drought-stricken region. Growing in these areas can be especially challenging, but there are a few things you can do to help keep your plants watered and growing vigorously.

First, your soil mix should contain a heavy amount of Pro Mix, peat moss or coco coir. Coco coir is preferable since it holds nine times its weight in water. Coco is also much lighter to carry to your plot than, say, a 3.8 cubic bag of peat moss. You should also have a good amount of polymer crystals in your mix—polymer crystals absorb water and slowly release it. Use it sparingly—one cup per gallon of soil or two—as polymer crystals can get quite expensive.

Cover your soil with 3 or more inches of mulch, making sure it has been rinsed in fresh water; the same goes for your coco coir, as the majority of it, especially the cheaper, no-name brand, is often rinsed with salt water which will expose your plants to sodium run off / toxicity.

Lastly, you should paint the outside of as many 5-gallon buckets as you need—one for each plant. Make sure you have a lid for these or you will have to make one out of plastic. Paint the bucket green, tan, or brown, depending on which blends in better with your surrounding. At the bottom of the bucket, drill one ⅛-inch hole. Position this hole near the stalk of the plant, mix a weak solution of nutrients and water together, and cover with the lid. These buckets will supply enough water for the plant to last for 10–12 days, in which time they should be refilled.

SECURITY NOTE

No other plant has the same heat signal or IR (infrared) signal as cannabis. Not pine trees, nor tomato plants, as was previously believed. The temperatures inside cannabis leaves can get as hot as 110°F, which is hotter than most other plants. It gives off an IR signal that is very bright on the radar, which means very noticeable.

Californian and Hawaiian growers should know that a few years back the DEA developed a special filter known as the Quantaro Filter. This is a visual filter that can pick out cannabis plants down to the tiniest seedlings. Growers of the Emerald Triangle know this all too well, and the filter has forced them to go indoors with their killer kind bud.

For Georgia growers, there is a special operations unit of the GBI that's sole purpose is to patrol the skies looking for cannabis grows. They operate primarily in the spring, but take to the air again in the fall. They are a specially trained task force that goes to school to learn how to spot even the smallest seedlings with the naked eye. They operate three helicopters—two are blue and white and one is a grayish color. They patrol mostly the mountainous areas of Northern Georgia, any clearings in the woods, and especially near any water source.

Which brings me to my next point: regardless of where in the U.S. you grow, don't grow near a water source. LEOs know you need water. Please don't be a lazy pothead!

For both backyard and guerilla growers it is generally a good idea to surround your plants with fencing. Chicken wire is most typically used for this job; if you do use chicken wire, make sure you buy non-galvanized type. This is so it will rust, which will in turn not draw unnecessary attention. Rust blends in very well against the forest. To accelerate the rusting process you can soak your Chicken wire roll in a 5 or 10-gallon bucket one end at a time. It is best to use a washtub if you have one around; this way you can do the whole roll, or multiple rolls at the same time. Add a whole container of sea salt (preferable) or table salt. This will greatly speed up the corrosion / rust process. In less than a week's time, you should have a thoroughly rusted chicken wire. You may bypass this entire step and paint your chicken wire green, but this can be quite time consuming as well as a pain.

The best option is to buy green vinyl-coated lawn fencing. It is around $30.00 for a 3 x 50-foot roll. It is 2 x 3 inches thick, which keeps out all but the smallest rabbits; it has worked well for growers for years.

You should use thick tree limbs to mount your fencing in place. You should also bury your fencing at least 3-4 feet into the ground to deter moles, rabbits, and other burrowing animals.

This will protect the stalk and mainframe of your plant. If a few branches are hanging over or near the fencing and a deer or other animal snacks on them, just think of it as a natural topping.

There is also a handy product known as Liquid Fence. This product is based from predator urine and it only needs to be applied every three to four weeks. I typically apply every three weeks, just to be on the safe side. It keeps away practically every animal predator that cannabis has. This product is ideal for single plants, or for when fencing is not necessarily an option. One quart is $25.00 and depending on the size of your grow it will usually last for between three and four applications.

It is difficult to have a secure greenhouse. Be careful with where you install a green-house. Notice the open roof panels for ventilation.

Building Your Greenhouse and Cold Frame

Greenhouses provide an excellent way to use natural sunlight while protecting your plants from the elements and casual glances. You can operate your greenhouse year-round by adding HID lights and/or fluoros along with heating and air. These artificial lights will have to be timed according to the light cycle outside. Greenhouses are not stealthy whatsoever, so be sure you out far away from civilization when using them.

Greenhouse growing is one of the least used aspects of cannabis growing. This is due to a few reasons, mostly security, or obscurity, as it may be. It's difficult to have a "secure" greenhouse; anything inside is easily seen and most greenhouses are hard to lock. Even if you do get a lock, LEOs or thieves can easily break inside.

First you need to choose a location with security as your main concern. You should also try to find a location that provides protection against wind while remaining out of the way of the possibility of falling tree limbs and other debris. Your location will obviously have to be flat; either way, you should dig your posts in at least two feet. This will allow your greenhouse to sustain winds up to 70 mph. You're going to need to be able to run power to your greenhouse. The easiest way to do this is to run a heavy-duty weatherproof extension cord to your greenhouse. You may choose to add a surge protector (highly recommended) and plug in your box fan extraction, fluorescent lights, and oscillating fans. However, for HID lighting and heating / air conditioning units you'll need either A) another heavy duty extension cord run off a spread circuit breaker or B) to run your greenhouse's own set of outlets. The exception with any electrical applications outdoors is that all your wiring and electrical outlets will, obviously, have to be weatherproof. You'll have to bury the cable underground, which is most easily accomplished by using a flat shovel to lift and pry the ground up, and simply tucking the cable in the hole, lowering the ground back down and tamping it down afterwards. Now you can either mount your electrical box inside your greenhouse or use a weatherproof box mounted outside.

You can either build your greenhouse from scratch or choose from a variety of different kits from numerous places. Much like constructing your indoor space, you can choose either wood or PVC pipe, but with outdoors you may also want to consider aluminum. Construct your greenhouse to be at least 8 feet tall, because your plants will stretch more outdoors, especially in a greenhouse. Of course, you can also keep them low with LSTing (Low Stress Training). Use the same growing plan as you would indoors, just compensate for them to be at least 8 feet tall. The cheapest way to con-

This aluminum-framed greenhouse is well braced against high winds with strong roof trusses and support beams. It also has a blackout curtain for visual security and photoperiod control.

This greenhouse has been very carefully constructed with solid wood trusses and support beams. See how tall the plants grow trying to get as much of the light from the ceiling panels as possible. This is why it is important to organize the greenhouse interior, with shorter strains protected from the leggier ones.

struct a greenhouse is out of PVC pipe, next easiest is wood, and aluminum is the most expensive.

For the paneling you have a few options: you can use plastic (clear or opaque), corrugated fiberboard (opaque), or a relatively new product known as polycarbonate (clear, opaque, or bronze). However, most growers are opting for Polyethylene, which is very strong and opaque, so your plants are not easily identifiable by helicopter or neighbor. Clear allows for maximum heat and light to pass through. Opaque or white allows for the least amount of heat while still getting a good amount of light. Bronze allows for the most heat and least light. Bronze is most commonly used for decorative purposes. Corrugated fiberboard and polycarbonate are used to diffuse light and offer even lighting. Glass should be the last material to use when constructing your greenhouse. Glass is the most expensive, hardest to work with, and easiest to break material for greenhouses. Glass is not ideal as many types don't diffuse light, creating hot spots that can burn plants.

When constructing a greenhouse, you'll need a few additions to keep your greenhouse operating efficiently. First, you'll need vents, intake and outtake; this will usually be fine for spring and fall. During summer and winter, though, you will need heating and air conditioning units. To find out what size a/c, heating unit, and outtake fan you will need you'll need to calculate your cubic feet. Again, multiply the length x width x height of your greenhouse. This is your cubic foot measurement. For outtake, you'll need a fan rated at least 2x the cubic feet of your greenhouse. You'll also need a floor to prevent weeds and bugs from intruding into your greenhouse, or you may be planting directly into the dirt. In this case, no flooring is needed. Although smart greenhouse growers will put down weed blocker and cut an X where they will put their plants.

Construct your greenhouse to be at least 8 feet tall to accommodate your grow. Outdoor cannabis tends to grow taller.

Notice the opaque paneling on this greenhouse. It lets in just the right amount of light, but doesn't make the interior overheat.

Triangle-shaped roofs are the best for greenhouses, especially if it snows in your region.

The following is a great way to build a greenhouse and typically the cheapest. Go to your local home improvement store and look for the canopies—they are usually marketed as boat / RV canopies. These canopies are great for converting to a greenhouse. Usually around $150 USD, they run about 10 x 20 x 8, giving you plenty of room for your plants. They also have triangle-shaped roofs instead of circular, the latter of which is the least favored. These canopies come with 2-inch aluminum pipes and assemble easily. Store the tarps provided for now. Now, as mentioned above, you can use plastic, fiberboard, or polycarbonate. Plastic is preferable for this application and is sold at most home improvement stores—Finish Factor clear plastic is only $2.89 a roll. These are perfect: 10 x 20, just like our frame. For durability, you want at least four sheets, but for maximum lighting you'll want one. Be warned that these tear very easily, especially when you are mounting with zip ties and pulling taut. You'll need at least six of these drop cloths. Start with the sides first.

Wrap the plastic around the outer poles before zip tying. Using four of the three-foot zip ties per pole should be adequate, though you can always add more. You'll want to get the thickest zip ties you can find; this is to reduce surface tension on the plastic so it is less likely to tear. Reinforce your zip ties with 2-inch box / carton tape. It will be easiest to do this with a friend, as it is rather difficult to pull the plastic taut by yourself. Add three or however many ties to the support braces in the middle as

Notice the blackout curtain at the end of this greenhouse. Use it to block out the sun so that you can control the photoperiod of your grow.

Be aware of the characteristics of the strains you plant in a greenhouse. Because of the inherent space restrictions, shorter strains can get lost and starved of light.

well. Also, remember that plastic shrinks in the cold and expands in the heat. Make sure that you anchor your greenhouse firmly into the ground. This can be done by cementing the poles, or you can use some thin rope and stake it into the ground at all four corners.

Congratulations, you've just constructed the finished frame for your greenhouse!

Now comes the fun part: installing your vents and fans. You have the option of buying outtake fans anywhere above $200 USD, or you can do the budget option. Mount a 20-inch box fan in the upper corner at the end of one side of your greenhouse. In order to do this, drill a hole in the aluminum where you want your fan to be, then screw in a cup hook, hang the fan on the cup hook by the handle (creative zip tie usage could also suffice), cut the plastic slightly smaller than the fan, and have a roll of 2-inch masking tape at the ready. Push the fan through the hole in the plastic; you may have to stretch and pull the plastic to get it to fit, that's OK. Now, tape the edge of the plastic to the back of the fan, and apply one strip of tape after another. You'll want around three or four rows of tape on the fan to make a secure, airtight fit. Keep your fan set on its highest setting. This will provide plenty of airflow through your greenhouse. Now, on the front of your greenhouse, install two passive intake vents. For these you'll have to purchase what is known as a "shutter vent." The standard price is $30 USD for a 20-inch vent. You should also get a bug screen for the vent. Install these vents the same way as the fan.

For your doorway, simply cut a slit in the plastic opposite your extraction fan, about ⅓ of the way down from the top of the plastic. You may either use Velcro strips or purchase a zipper. The zipper is most effective but also more expensive and harder to install. You should also reinforce the plastic around your doorway as this plastic will be the most likely to tear and / or stretch.

Now you have to cover the ground from weeds and bugs. Remember the tarp that came with your canopy set? We'll be using that now. It's the same size as our greenhouse and is either white or grey. You can either lay it flat or anchor it to the foundation poles. If you plan on planting in the ground, you can still use this method, just cut an "X" where you're going to plant a plant, peel back the plastic, and voila! Be sure to use some form of human-friendly sealant around the perimeter of your greenhouse, where the walls meet the floor, ceiling, and other walls; also apply it to the seams of the vents and fans.

If you plan on adding artificial lighting, you can add your fluoros vertically at the foundation poles. The horizontal bar running the length of your greenhouse is strong enough to hold three HID ballasts and fixtures.

Notice how wide this plant is spreading its branches and leaves. It wants to trap as much sunlight as possible.

If you would like to add a blackout curtain so you can control your photoperiod regardless of the lighting outside, simply attach four double thickness black tarps (available at your local home improvement stores) to the top of your greenhouse, and when you want to cover your greenhouse simply roll them down.

If you have the extra money and don't want to deal with the hassle of constructing your own greenhouse there are a wide variety of greenhouses available online. These range from little 5 x 5 x 5 greenhouses made out of plastic, which start at around $100 USD, to beautiful free-standing deluxe model greenhouses that are 30 x 30 x 80 feet and made out of glass, which start at around $5000 USD. Some cost over $10,000 USD. It all depends on your budget and the size of your space. A good-sized greenhouse is available at around $500 USD.

An easy way to both heat greenhouses and cold frames is to place buckets / tubs of water inside the structure. The sunlight heats up the water and the water will give off heat during the night. One smart grower would place bags of uncomposted manure in the inside and outside of his greenhouse along the sides, stacked up to about three feet. During the decomposition (composting) process the manure gives off heat, enough, in fact, to heat his greenhouse during the winter to an acceptable temperature.

If you're seeking a more controlled method of heating and cooling, as I'm sure most of you are, you will have to purchase and install a heating and a/c unit according to the size of your greenhouse. To calculate the number of BTUs needed to heat or cool your greenhouse, first multiply the length x width, then multiply that figure by the height. So 10 x 20 = 200 x 8 = 1,600. That is the volume in cubic feet. Now, if your grow room has poor insulation, which our example does, multiply by 4; if it has adequate insulation, multiply by 3; and if it has good insulation, multiply by 2. 1,600 x 4 = 6,400 BTU. This is only a rough calculation; the variants of your environment will either raise or lower the amount of BTU needed.

Make sure that your heating and air unit does not surpass more than 80% of your circuit breaker's capacity.

COLD FRAMES

Any outdoor growing structure that doesn't have an artificial source of heating or air conditioning is a cold frame. Cold frames are like mini greenhouses, without any source of artificial heat, air conditioning, or lighting. Cold frames are good for starting seedlings and clones early outside, as well as for hardening off clones and seedlings.

Cold frames are easily constructed using common household items. You can make your cold frame any size you would like. It doesn't have to be small; it can be big enough to grow a mature plant(s).

Chapter 23

Advanced Techniques

In this chapter, we will be covering relatively new techniques that all growers may not know about. These are commonly called advanced techniques. These methods are not conventional insofar as a plant does not naturally grow using these procedures; however, by implementing these techniques, you can develop stronger plants that will increase your yield.

TOPPING

Also known as pinching, topping has been passed down from the 60s and 70s. Topping is the most common advanced technique. By simply pinching the new growth at the tips, the plant's energy goes into the side branches. This encourages thicker, bushier plants. In about 4–5 days time you will notice two smaller shoots

This plant was topped using the FIM technique.

This plant was topped during its vegetative state. Those two branches developed after the original growth was pinched off. This is a technique from the 60s and 70s, often used to make plants thicker and bushier, which is ideal for the grower with limited space.

replacing the one you removed. You will find that one of the new shoots will be dominant over the other.

I don't encourage topping because it involves the same principle as having multiple plants in the same container, which takes nutrients away from each other, and can cause neither plant to perform to their full potential. If you choose to top your plants, it should be done approximately four weeks after the seed germinates. Instead of cutting the shoot with scissors or snips, it's best for the plant if you pinch the shoot using your fingernails. This will close off the newly cut shoot from possible pathogen infection. For the most part, growers limit the use of this technique because each time a plant is topped, slow growth or stunting occurs and the yield is reduced. Keep in mind, smaller branches equal smaller buds.

Instead of topping your plants, which many regard as an outdated technique, you may want to consider Low Stress Training (LST). The LST method has more benefits than topping does, and none of the negative impacts.

FIM

FIM, also known as the "Fuck I Missed" technique, was first documented by Kyle Kushman around 1999. This technique is similar to topping except that the newly formed growth is cut at 45-degree angles, leaving about 30% of the growing tip. This method requires a more precise cut, but the reward is greater in that at least three, and as many as seven, new shoots will grow from the main stalk. As with topping, this technique should be done approximately three to four weeks after seed germination and will result in a thicker, bushier plant.

Caution: Fimming causes a great deal of stress to your plants and some strains do not respond well at all. Expect a longer shock period before normal growth resumes.

LOW STRESS TRAINING

Low Stress Training (LST) is a technique that is revolutionizing the cannabis growing scene. LST involves more effort than topping and fimming but is well worth it. The LST method involves using string or twine to bend the plant's branches and place them where you want them.

Begin this technique when your plant has between four to six nodes. At this point, you can use the FIM or topping technique in conjunction with the LST process, as most growers do, but it is certainly not necessary. To anchor the string to the container, drill holes through the pots and attach cup hooks, then tie your string to the hook.

When utilizing grow bags, masking or duct tape can be used to attach the string. Anchor the string to the base of your plant and then to your container. Around the fourth or fifth node, attach another string and pull 180 degrees from your anchor.

Low Stress Training in action. Look at the length some of the branches have bent. Incredible.

The purpose of the anchor is to prevent your plant from being uprooted when pulling the string in the opposite direction. At this point, the plant should be parallel to your container or ground. In as little as a day, the plant top should resume normal vertical growth. Branching will begin to take place in less than a week. When these branches have at least two nodes, you should tie them down. Continue tying down all new branches, spacing each branch evenly around the container so they all receive adequate lighting.

A good LST job is characterized by having the entire container covered with branches, and as a result having an even canopy of growth. The LST technique assures that all branches receive an equal amount of light by having all the growing shoots be the same height, thus allowing you to place the light closer to the plant. The result will be better, bigger buds. At some point you may notice a slowing of growth, which is when you should cut all the ties to allow your plant to grow naturally for a few weeks. During this period of time, you will see an explosion of growth. At the end of the phase, typically two weeks, you will need to start from scratch and LST them again.

"SUPER" LST

This method is performed with a more mature plant typically outdoors, roughly two to five weeks into vegetative growth. The Super LST technique is only to be used once you have an established plant, usually one to two feet in height.

Tie the string two or three nodes down from the top of the plant. Gradually, and with extreme care, pull the plant over until you can tie the string to the base of the plant—say, 3–4 nodes up. After a few days, the plant stalk will look similar to an S-hook. This will cause the auxins to relocate more quickly than when using the regular LST technique, topping or fimming resulting in accelerated lateral growth.

Caution: When LSTing, especially Super LSTing, be sure not to tie the string tightly around branches and stems. As the plant grows, the string will cut into the stems, causing the plants' growth to be stunted. Once more, using thicker string will lessen the chances of harming the plant. Tie the string into a knot instead of tying a knot around the plant. This will reduce the chance of the string cutting into the plant.

All three of these techniques—topping, fimming, and LSTing—relocate/remove auxins inside the plant to different locations. Auxins are one of the key hormones responsible for branch growth. During the day, auxins build at the tips of the plant and retreat to the roots at night. With topping and fimming, the auxins are removed manually, which diffuses them and removes/relocates them to different parts of the plant. The LST method causes the auxins to move naturally to different areas of the plant, without the loss of auxins and the stress caused to the plant.

Here we see a Screen of Green setup with about three plants per square foot. This grower used a large screen to help organize upward growth. Nice.

Be sure to use clones when you execute a ScrOG grow. With the plants all packed in so tightly together, a rogue male could go undetected very easily, so sowing from seed is not an option.

SEA OF GREEN

Commonly referred to as SOG, Sea of Green refers to the practice of having many small plants in the same space instead of a few bigger plants. The theory behind this is that yield will increase with many small plants instead of three or four big plants. The rule of thumb for SOG gardens is generally three plants per square foot, although up to nine plants per square foot have been done. SOG can only be performed with clones, as they are thrown into 12/12 immediately after rooting. If clones are not an option, starting seeds immediately into 12/12 from germination will have a similar effect but they will most likely grow taller and possibly develop lateral growth, which will have to be pruned away. I suggest making clones from these. You will also have to watch for males doing the seed route. Growers typically use either four or six-inch nursery pots. A successful SOG depends highly on the strain chosen. A high yielding SOG is characterized by yielding 12–16 grams of dried bud per plant. A good SOG strain is one that has very little tendency for lateral branching, and produces a nice long main cola. Most Indica dominant strains fit this description. Obviously, you will not top, FIM, or LST your plants.

SCREEN OF GREEN

The Screen of Green technique is basically the opposite of SOG. ScrOG uses fewer plants to increase yield, while SOG uses more. ScrOG requires a bit of ingenuity, but it can be ideal for closet or cab growers. ScrOG gardens often yield the highest gram per watt.

Here we see the Screen of Green technique in use. This one plant will yield an incredible amount of bud thanks to the carefully built screen.

This Screen of Green was constructed using PCV pipe and wire. Remember that you want a minimum of 50 watts of light per square foot during a ScrOG grow.

To begin with, you'll need to construct a screen. Chicken wire is most commonly used, although with a little effort, you can make a screen using PVC pipe and twine. Simply pull the string taut from side to side across the top of your garden, creating a grid. Make sure your screen is as tight as can be, as a loose screen will do absolutely nothing. Typically, the screen is hung eight inches to one-and-a-half feet above your container, but it varies depending on how tall you want your plants to be.

Basic distances between lamp and screen

150w HPS	=	7–8 inches
250w HPS	=	8–10 inches
400w HPS	=	10–12 inches
600w HPS	=	14–16+ inches
1,000w HPS	=	20+ inches

Again, these are just basic distances. Depending on the circulation in your room, you may need your light closer or further away.

First, grow your plant as you would if you were using the LST technique. The size of your screen depends on the size of your lamp. You want a minimum of 50 watts per square foot.

Basic screen sizes per lamp

150w HPS	=	1.75-foot x 1.75-foot screen
250w HPS	=	2.25-foot x 2.25-foot screen
400w HPS	=	2.91-foot x 2.75-foot screen
600w HPS	=	3.45-foot x 3.45-foot screen
1,000w HPS	=	4.50-foot x 4.50-foot screen

Once the shoots reach the height of the screen, train the new growth horizontally, making sure they don't grow up and through just yet. The screen should be roughly sixty to seventy percent full before switching over to 12/12. About five to seven days before the 12/12 conversion, allow the shoots to grow all the way through the panel, about two to four inches above the screen depending on how much your strains stretch during flowering. Once the branches are the appropriate length through the screen, begin gently bending them throughout the screen.

Once the plants have reached optimal height, begin guiding the branches through the screen. Gently pull the new growth through the openings, being especially careful not to break any off any branches. Then continue to work branches through the screen as they continue to grow.

In no time at all, you will find that the entire screen is full of nice, long colas. Be sure to trim all growth below the canopy, as it will steal energy away. The screen's holes provide the maximum circulation and light penetration. ScrOG is one of the best yield-increasing techniques. Strains that are best suited to ScrOG are those that have a higher percentage of Indica / Afghani genetics, and thus a limited stretch.

This ScrOG setup allows the buds to pass through the screen, but keeps them spread out enough that they all get more than enough light to produce ample bud.

This stalk has been super cropped and has regrown even stronger and more capable of transporting nutrients throughout the plant.

SUPER CROPPING

There appears to be some confusion on just exactly what super cropping is. Some say super cropping is a form of pruning in which you remove every bit of the stalk except for the lowest four shoots. This is true; however, super cropping does require a bit of elbow grease as well. Super cropping is one of the most controversial techniques, primarily because it causes excess stress to the plant.

If you wish to super crop, first you need a plant at least two weeks into vegetative growth, with at least four lateral branches. The first step will be cracking the main stalk (stem). On some plants, this can be accomplished using just your fingers. Pliers are needed for bigger, stronger stalks. Using cloth-wrapped pliers, squeeze each side of the stalk until you hear a crack. The plant will take about a week to recover fully. The theory behind cracking the stalk (stem) is similar to the idea of humans working out. You damage, or weaken, the muscle, in order to build it up stronger. With plants, this means increased nutrients and hormones, which result in bigger plants. When the plant rebuilds itself it will be able to transport a greater amount of nutrients and hormones to other parts of the plant, resulting in bigger plants—bigger plants, of course, meaning bigger yield.

After your plant has recovered from the main stalk cropping, repeat on the four lower branches. You know you've done a good job super cropping when all the branches look lifeless and collapse. Don't worry. They'll be better than before in about a week.

Now you should remove all of the plant except for the bottom four branches. This requires removing the meristem (main stalk) and everything else above the fourth branch.

Arrange the remaining four branches so that they are evenly spaced, tying each with string and pulling them in four opposite directions. It is important to have ample air circulation and light penetration to all of the branches. With super cropping, you are focusing all of the plant's energy into the four to six remaining main branches. Remove all other growth. This allows the plant to focus all of its energy into creating long baseball bat colas along those four remaining branches instead of having a greater number of smaller buds.

BONSAI MOMS

Bonsai is a technique first used by the Chinese to make small trees. The word bonsai actually means "plant in a tray." Bonsai gardening will use, at most, one cubic foot of space, making it ideal for small spaces or stealth growers.

To implement this technique, you will need six-inch square containers. This method usually applies to clones, but can be used for seeds as well. Start by LSTing your plant. Try to keep the plant especially close to the container. In about one month, your mom will be as big as you want her. Now, you're most likely asking, how do I keep her this way? The answer is: by not feeding her a lot of food. Only when you see the leaves starting to yellow from lack of nitrogen feed will you feed the plant with half strength PBP Grow or a similar product. This will help to keep her from exploding in growth.

When the growing shoots get too tall, snip them for clones. A good bonsai mom can endure as many as 30 cuttings every two weeks.

For maintaining a bonsai mom, the root ball needs to be trimmed when the container becomes fully root bound. Ordinarily, this only takes four to five weeks, roughly speaking. In order to trim the root ball, a serrated knife is needed. A bread knife is most commonly used. Trim approximately one inch of roots off each side, and approximately two inches off the bottom.

Center the plant and fill in with fresh soil around the roots or the root ball, preferably using Pro Mix or coco coir. Use a stick if necessary to press the soil firmly into narrow spaces. You may also add mycorrhizae powder, which will strengthen the root system and decrease shock time.

Water with Superthrive and in about a week's time your mom will be good as new. Keep the plant from direct sunlight for several days until it recovers from the operation you just performed.

Root trimming is the most important aspect of bonsai moms, so make sure you repeat this process as needed. With proper maintenance, a bonsai mom can be kept alive as long as 15 years!

LEONARDITE, HUMUS, AND HUMIC / FULVIC ACIDS

Leonardite is a naturally occurring hydro-carbon soil amendment that is formed from the decaying remains of both animals and plant matter. These deposits were once buried deep in the ground but manufactures have exhumed the leonardite close to the surface, at which time the leonardite is oxidized by bacteria. The quality of leonardite depends on where the deposit is located. Fresh water leonardite is often thought to be of a higher quality than salt water leonardite because salt water leonardite contains sodium. Some popular sources for the extraction of leonardite are North Dakota, Wyoming, and Arizona.

Leonardite is essentially the raw element which contains humic substances. Humic substances are broken down into three specific but different groups: humins, humic acids, and fulvic acids. Humus, which is an organic compost, contains all of these three specific groups but is not as biologically active as leonardite. Leonardite is basically a coal-like substance whereas humus is a substance that can be used as a growing medium, and I strongly recommend the use of it. Humus also holds seven times its weight in volume and stabilizes pH, to a degree. Humins are not water-soluble and are not widely used in regards to plants because of this fact. Humic Acids (HAs) comprise a mixture of organic acids that are not soluble in acidic water (water below 7.0 pH) but are soluble in alkaline water (water above 7.0 pH). For this reason, I do not recommend the use of humic acids for growing cannabis because cannabis is slightly acidic, and going above 7.0 pH locks out important nutrients. If you do not go above 7.0 pH, your humic acid is doing nothing but wasting your money. (It is interesting to note that when using humic acid along with chemical fertilizers, it bonds with inorganic trace minerals to form salts. These trace minerals are bound to humic acid molecules in a fashion that allows plants to absorb them—essentially, humic acids serve as complex chelators.)

Fulvic Acids (FAs) are a mixture of organic and aromatic acids that are soluble in all types of water—acidic, alkaline, and neutral, which makes them ideal for cannabis growth. The benefits of fulvic acids far outweigh those of humic acids and humins, so we are not missing anything. Fulvic acids contain twice the amount of oxygen as humic acid, and that makes for happy plants. Fulvic acids are much smaller than humic acids, which means they can assimilate into plant roots, stems, and leaves far more easily than humic acids, and when they assimilate into these parts of the plant they are taking trace minerals with them because they have a similar chelating action as humic acids.

For this reason, fulvic acids are incredibly useful for foliar feeding. When you combine fulvic acid with an organic food, liquid kelp for example, they will basically absorb the trace minerals, assimilate into the plant, and transport those trace minerals directly to metabolic sites in plant cells. Fulvic acid can hold 60+ trace minerals in a *single* molecule, all of which are delivered directly to metabolic sites! This process would have taken a considerable amount of time if it had been done through the roots.

Not to say that you should not apply fulvic acid to the roots. Fulvic acid works wonders for soil ecology because it provides energy to those beneficial microbes. Fulvic acid also increases soil fertility and overall plant health in regard to the resistance of pathogens. Humic substances improve the water holding capability of soil because humic substances are heterogeneous substances: humic and fulvic acids are hydrophilic groups that attract water. They also stimulate all facets of plant growth and this has been documented in many vegetables and herbs: beans, corn, cucumbers, grapes, millet, peppers, sugar beets, and tomatoes, just to name a few. Humic substances also stimulate chlorophyll production and an interesting note is that fulvic acids increase chlorophyll density over humic acids by 6%. The use of fulvic acid in the budding / flowering cycle is especially important because it increases the uptake of phosphorus. Perhaps the most important aspect of humic substances is the fact that they buffer (neutralize) soil pH and free CO_2 from the substrate. This has been documented in several field studies performed by Texas A&M University. Their results have concluded that humic substances function to neutralize pH (hydrogen ion) concentration in soil. This is true for both acidic and alkaline soils. This is very important, for once the soil has been buffered (neutralized), trace minerals become available for absorption by the roots of the plant. The same occurs with the release of CO_2.

AUXINS, CYTOKININS, AND GIBBERELLINS

Auxins, cytokinins, and gibberellins are three of the most abundant chemical compounds / hormones that are present in just about all species of plants. These three compounds regulate plant growth as well as perform a variety of other functions. We will be discussing these functions in detail in this section.

Auxins stems from the Greek word *Auxein*, which means *to grow*. Auxins are arguably the most important of the three compounds mentioned above. Auxins are produced in the tips of shoots, which is where they concentrate. It has been speculated that auxins concentrate in the apical growth (the main cola or meristem) during the day, and then sink back to the roots during the night. Like most chemical compounds, Auxins have their advantages and disadvantages. Auxins are primarily a compound that benefits root stimulation and development, and this helps to explain why they sink to the roots at night—because roots grow at night. In one respect, auxins are our enemies when we are trying to grow a bushy plant. When left to grow naturally, the plant will concentrate auxins in the meristem, which will inhibit the lateral growth (the growth of side branches). Auxins also promote cell elongation (stretching or growth of the meristem, main stalk), cell division, root initiation on cuttings, and lateral growth of roots.

Cytokinins primarily stimulate cell growth, meaning plant growth. Cytokinins are produced in the roots. Cytokinins basically act in reverse to auxins: they stimulate stem / bud growth and suppress root growth. They also promote cell division, chloroplast and leaf development, and stimulate morphogenesis (stem imitation / bud formation), growth of lateral buds, leaf expansion, and cell enlargement. Studies have shown that increased cytokinins may increase the size of stomata openings.

Gibberellins are compounds that stimulate seeds and increase germination rates. Gibberellins are produced in both the roots and shoot tips. In the vegetative cycle, gibberellins do not have a very positive effect for most growers, causing male plants, cell division and elongation (spindly plants).

Together, these chemical compounds, as well as others, balance plant growth, carefully balancing the amount of auxins and cytokinins so that the plant grows both proper root and branching structures.

CO_2

You have probably seen the photographs of huge colas that normally grace the centerfolds of *High Times* and other cannabis publications. Most of those were grown using CO_2.

With CO_2, you can raise the temperatures up to 85°F, but it is best to have low humidity. Increased temperatures help the plant's respiration system increase their metabolism to accommodate the increase in CO_2. Because of the increased respiration rate, humidity will increase. CO_2 gardens are susceptible to mold because of this increase in humidity.

Plants use CO_2 to make sugars, which in turn make plant matter. Normal amounts of CO_2 are always present; on average, between 400 to 500 PPM. To truly see increased growth, the CO_2 amounts need to be around 1,200–1,500 PPM. It has been reported that an increase in growth, between one hundred to two hundred percent, has been recorded using CO_2. In order to do this, a sealed room is necessary,

Use an environmental controller like this Xtreme Greenhouse Controller to make sure that your temperature, humidity and carbon dioxide levels are exactly where you need them to be.

meaning air-cooled lights that keep the CO_2 in your room.

Contrary to popular belief, mixing a little baking soda with vinegar will not do the job you are looking for and will be pulled out of the room before it even has a chance to work. If your ventilation system is hooked up to a timer, it could be linked to a CO_2 system, injecting the room with CO_2 periodically. Installing a CO_2 system is quite an undertaking, and not recommended for the closet grower.

There are two main ways to inject CO_2 into your room, the first being bottled CO_2. This is the most common method, and it employs a five-foot or 80-pound tank with a pressure gauge, flow meter, and solenoid valve. Most growers using this method will use PVC pipes with holes drilled into them that are mounted around the top of the grow room. Since CO_2 is heavier than air, it falls down to the plants below. This method would not be ideal for large grows since the tanks have to be refilled regularly, about once a week for a 10 x 10-foot room.

The next method involves using CO_2 generators. CO_2 generators operate on either a natural gas line or with propane tanks. The natural gas line can usually be extended fairly easily from your hot water heater, though you need to seek a professional for this, as it is much too dangerous to attempt on your own. The downfalls of the generators are that they produce heat; however, this isn't always necessarily a bad thing when using CO_2.

With either of these CO_2 systems you will need an environmental controller. Environmental controllers let you set the room size, desired PPM, and cubic feet per minute (CFM) of the emitter. Basically, you plug the fans and CO_2 into the controller. As the CO_2 is released, the fans shut down. The calculations for this action are determined by the information input during installation.

There is also a revolutionary new product known as CO_2 Boost. This product contains enough CO_2 to serve the plants through budding. Be cautious if you decide to use this item, because the PPM emitted initially could potentially cause a headache if you stay in the room. This product is ideal for closet grows, delivering a PPM between 1,200 and 1,400 throughout the budding stage. For a larger space, say a 10 x 10-foot room, at least three buckets are needed. For maximum benefit, the start times for each bucket should be staggered. CO_2 Boost costs $125 for one bucket and is completely biodegradable. The only drawback of this product is the shelf life. It must be used during the time frame specified on the bucket.

To calculate the exact amount of CO_2 needed for your particular grow space you can visit hydroponics.net.

In addition to the above, research is being done on the use of medical grade oxygen in plant growth. So far, the study suggests that it does increase yield, though the results are inconclusive.

CARBOHYDRATES

Carbohydrate is a big word meaning sugar. Plants make their own sugar through photosynthesis. Photosynthesis is the combination of light, water, and CO_2. Plants use carbohydrates for energy, the same as humans. If you increase the number of carbohydrates, or sugars, you will get an increase in energy or increased growth rate.

Before you run and grab that table sugar, let me explain things a bit more. Table sugar is the most refined of all sugars, meaning it has been stripped of vitamins and minerals. This is not the sugar you want to use. Try to find a product called Sucanat. This product is sold at most natural food stores. Sucanat is cheap and has not been refined at all. Another good choice is Turbinado, which is made by steaming Sucanat. Generally speaking, the darker and larger the sugar, the better it is for growing and the more vitamins and minerals it retains. Not only will Sucanat increase the growth rate of your plant, but it will also improve the taste, making each bud sweeter and more enjoyable than any you've ever experienced. Adding Sucanat or a similar product will also increase the beneficial microbes in the soil. You're not only feeding your plant sugars, you're feeding your soil. Sucanat can be utilized at any phase the of plant's life cycle; however, there are some other products available that can be combined for optimal performance.

There are several products on the market that are derived from sugar cane and have added amino acids. One such product is Sweet, from Botanicare. This product is excellent and will enhance the aroma as well as the taste of each plant. Sucanat and Sweet go well together. Sweet provides the nice aroma and amino acids, and Sucanat brings that sweet taste and microbe-stimulating ability.

To use, dissolve one tablespoon of Sucanat in a cup of hot water. Add that mixture to one gallon of water, along with two tablespoons of Sweet. Warning: each tablespoon of Sweet will raise your PPM by around 120.

UV-B LIGHTING

No, I am not talking about those black lights that populated your room when you were in high school. Those lights produce mostly UV-A light, which is not what we are after. The type of lights we are looking for are only available from tanning supply stores. UV-B light is harmful to both humans and plants, but instead of causing skin cancer in plants, it causes an increase in trichomes in cannabis plants. There have been a few studies done on this subject and the findings have been conclusive that UV-B light stimulates trichome production. It is speculated that plants produce trichomes as protection against insect attacks, heat, cold, excess UV light, etc. Some may notice that cannabis grown at higher altitudes is often more potent than cannabis grown at lower altitudes. This is because of the increase in UV light. There have also been side-by-side comparisons done with UV-B lights that support this claim. It is true, however, that UV-B light will retard or mutate growth, so avoid adding the light too early during budding. It is typical for fan leaves to develop a gloss to them, and for pistils to wither within days of inducing the UV-B light. To avoid any loss in bud development, add the light during the last week to week and a half of budding. The plants will pack on trichomes during this time period. If UV-B light is added any earlier the buds will become very dense but small.

TEMPERATURES

Manipulating temperatures can cause trichomes to increase, as well as the plant's color to intensify. The green color you see is a result of a pigment known as chlorophyll. The anthocyanin pigment is responsible for purple colors and carotenoid is responsible for brown, red, orange, and yellow colors. Plants that exhibit colors other than green always have those pigments there, it's just that the green from the chlorophyl masks them. So how do you get those colors to shine through? A naturally colorful strain will color on its own without exposure to colder temperatures, pH fluctuation, or nutrient starvation. Those colors will emerge, usually during the last few weeks of budding. Anything prior to that is truly special. A 20-degree change in temperatures from lights on to lights off will cause the majority of strains to turn colors. I have left strains out in the weather as cold as 28°F without any ill effects other than slowed growth. As a result, a dramatic color change will occur, as well as a huge increase in trichomes. Be advised, after a 30-day cure, most "fake" purple pot will lose its purple coloring.

You may find that using some, if not all, of these techniques works best for you. Most of these methods can be applied to outdoor growing, so (literally) the sky's the limit.

"THE SOUND OF MUSIC"

There have been studies done to determine if certain types of music, or sounds, encourage plant growth and vigor. While most of the results were inconclusive, it has been suggested that music containing a lot of bass, such as heavy metal and rap, impair plant growth. These very same tests suggest that music containing a large number of high pitch notes intensifies plant growth, as with flutes in jazz and classical.

These results coincide with the outcome of other sound studies stating that plants close their stomata when they hear the sound of thunder. It is believed that this occurs to prevent water and debris from clogging the stomata. The bass is comparable to thunder, which indicates to the plant that rain is coming, so they close their stomata. This lowers the respiration rate, which in turn slows the plant's metabolism. In other words, the plant's growth is slowed because it doesn't breathe as much as normal. These studies have also established that the plant's stomata open widest in the morning hours when birds are chirping. This sound is mimicked by certain flutes.

Plants are only affected by the sound when they are above 60 decibels. Based on the results from these studies, it is safe to conclude that it would be beneficial for the plants to play heavy metal, rap, or other music containing a lot of bass approximately 20 minutes before spraying plants with any water or nutrients. Keeping that in mind, locating recordings of birds chirping to play for your plants would also be useful.

On the other hand, 60+ decibels of music or birds chirping, coming from an obscure part of your home, could jeopardize the privacy of your grow room.

The genetics contained in these Ch9 Jack seeds from Ch9 Female Seeds are the culmination of over 20 years of cannabis breeding and research, from California to Europe.

Chapter 24

Breeding

Most growers view breeding as the most learned component of growing cannabis. It is the ultimate test of the grower. Growing is good, but growing strains that you've bred is great. If you think you're proud successfully growing other breeders' strains, just wait for the pride and feeling of accomplishment you'll get when you grow the strains you've bred. Not to mention the feeling you'll receive when you see other growers grow your strains. This breeding chapter will be unlike most articles about breeding you have read, as we will not include any Punnett squares or Mendelian laws or genetic ratios and will simply provide you with the means to achieve your goal(s). The majority of aspiring breeders and most of the established breeders themselves do not use or understand these things, so we will be excluding them and just explaining how to achieve the results. Consider this a layman's guide to breeding great cannabis.

All genetic information is contained and transmitted inside the pollen from the male or hermaphrodite and the ovule from the female. Both the pollen from the male and ovule from the female are known as gametes. The gametes contain genes; typically, each plant will have 1n (haploid with ten chromosomes), or one set of genes. These gametes combine to form a seed in which the seed will have 2n (diploid with twenty chromosomes), with one set of genes from each parent. Cannabis plants contain 19 pairs of normal pairs of chromosomes that are equal in size. However the last chromosome is known as the sex chromosome, either XY, YX, or XX. The male chromosome (Y) is dominant over the female (X).

Now say that we have two true breeding strains; true breeding strains are *homozygous*. True breeding means that every individual in that line will breed true for certain traits. One strain breeds true for higher THC content and yields while the other strain breeds true for webbed leaves. We choose the best plant from each line, one male and one female. Whether you choose a male or female from which line depends on what characteristics you would like to instill in your offspring. It is speculated that males contribute to the overall structure of the plant—to branching, height, roots, etc.—and females contribute to floral aroma and taste. These are the P1 parents; the cross that we just made is the F1 cross (the first filial generation). Since the regular pinnate leaves are most common in cannabis plants it is easily determined that regular pinnate leaves are *dominant* over webbed leaves which are *recessive*. Therefore the offspring will contain mostly plants with regular leaves. However, we now have plants that are *heterozygous*, meaning they contain genes from both parents. Now, in the F1 generation, much breeding cannot take place, and most breeders will typically choose the best-looking plants from the F1 generation, regardless of the phenotypes.

However, in this F1 generation, if you grow enough plants to find a phenotype that expresses the *recessive* traits (in this case webbed leaves), it will make your future selections much easier, in the sense that the webbed phenotypes will appear at a greater percentage.

In the next generation, the F2 generation, you will notice a 3:1 ratio of regular leaves to webbed leaves.

Now, in this generation you can backcross to your original webbed parent to form change the ratio from 2:1 in the F3 cross to 1:1. Backcrossing is a common technique employed by breeders to lock down a certain trait expressed by both the offspring and the parent.

With this backcrossed generation (B1), you should select the phenotypes which demonstrate the traits which we are breeding for. The webbed leaf phenotypes should appear at a pretty common number now and it should be easy to choose the best plant for further crosses. You need to pick the two best plants that possess all the traits we are breeding for; obviously, we will need a male and a female. Now, we cross these plants and the subsequent generation will produce all more potent and high yielding webbed leaf plants. There may still be some varying phenotypes within this generation, in regard to height and finishing time, as well as (most likely) floral development, but if you always selected the heavy yielding, potent, webbed-leaved phenotypes on both the males and females you should have no problem in creating a stable strain for these traits.

For detailed information on ratios please read Robert Connell Clarke's *Marijuana Botany*.

When breeding, avoid the use of polyploids, as this will result in weaker plants and a weak gene pool. Polyploids are plants that contain multiple sets of chromosomes. All polyploids have been proven inferior except tetraploids (4n); however, these are not stable plants and cannot be used for breeding. This means avoiding the use of plants and strains treated with colchicine.

These male cannabis plants have been grown specifically for breeding. The pollen is heavy on the stalk and branches, ready to pollinate a female plant and produce seeds.

This Dark Star from TH Seeds is in full flower, just begging for a male to pollinate her so that she can produce seeds.

Before you start your breeding project you first need to decide what the goal of your project will be. This can be either to stabilize a specific trait or traits, or just to preserve the species. This is known as developing a plan from the "top down."

When you start breeding, you should avoid using seeds and pollen collected from unknown sources. This includes bagseed; however, some of the best and most widely liked strains were developed from bagseeds of unknown origins: Blackberry, Jack Herer, C99, A11, A13, and all the countless crosses from these strains.

Before you start breeding, you should be an experienced grower that knows what traits to look for in plants. You should be able to provide the exact same growing conditions, every time, for all plants. An exact environment is key, without it you cannot unbiasedly determine if certain plants are weaker genetically than others. You need an environment that is the exact same in every aspect. Lighting needs to be equal for all plants. All soil and nutrients must be administered at the same time and at the same concentration. Any deficiencies that show in plants that are grown with the exact same environment are genetically weaker than the others. Likewise, if you are breeding for a strain that shows resistance to a particular disorder, insect, or deficiency you should expose the entire population to this disorder and only continue the line with those individuals that showed the greatest resistance to that disorder, if of course you are breeding for resistance.

In breeding there is no substitute for large populations, no matter how long you have been growing. This is a very common mistake made by some "professional" breeders. This is the first basic principal in breeding: starting with a large selection. You must have a population larger than 100. Shantibaba from Mr. Nice Seeds usually starts with a population of around 10,000. Obviously, this makes breeding in North America extremely dangerous, but there is a way to get around this, it will just take longer. Start, say, 20–30 seeds at a time, pick the best seedlings, and cull the rest. Pick *one* seedling, if that. Don't be afraid to cull them all if none meet the expectations of your breeding program. Start your next batch, so on and so forth, until you either run out of seeds or have a population of the "elite" seedlings. When it is time, clone them and keep them in limbo. Continue to watch these seedlings closely; if any unfavorable traits should arise they must be culled. Once the plants are mature enough to clone you must take clones and make sure to label them. Your next selection process will occur during and after the budding cycle. After harvest, you should select your clones to grow based on what you think are the best tasting and most potent of your harvested buds.

The F1 generation will closely resemble each other; this is nothing special. You can't really count the F1 generation as breeding, since this is simply a cross. True breeding takes place well after the F1 generation. The F1 generation will typically express a trait known as *hybrid vigor*, which usually happens when two plants from different gene pools are crossed for the first time. You will notice that F1 seeds are bigger and the resulting plants will be as well. These plants will perform better than any other generation of plants, which is why most breeders will "cheat" and only sell F1 generations.

The F2 generation will posses much greater variation than the F1 generation. Meaning that you will see many different phenotypes. This generation is likely to posses some of the recessive characteristics from the parental gene pool. Every generation now, including the F2 generation, will be smaller and "weaker" than the F1 generation. This will continue until this new strain is crossed with another. In order to breed properly, your F2 population (as with all your generations) should be as big as possible; your F2 generation should be the biggest of any generation. Selection is one of the most important aspects of breeding. Selection is arguably the most important in the F2 generation; you must choose both male and female plants that meet the ideals of your breeding program. Every generation after the F2 will start shrinking the gene pool of that strain. We will discuss selection in great detail later in this chapter.

Here we see a plant that has been pollinated and gone to seed. This is the end result of the breeding process – seeds containing new genetic material.

Once you reach the F3 generation, you will notice that it has fewer phenotypes than the F2 generation. This is a good sign, as you're starting to lock down your strain. If proper selection has been made in both the F1 and F2 generations, you may start to see a fairly stable strain emerging. At this time you may want to backcross the F3 plant you've selected to a parent whose characteristics you would like to enforce.

Plants will become more stable and uniform until about the F7 or F8 generation. At this time, you will start to see plants becoming smaller and weaker. This is because the gene pool has lost its diversity; you must now integrate some new genes into this pool or risk losing your strain.

You may also find that it is easier to stabilize one trait of the same strain in two different lines. Say you have a Skunk #1 male, which you cross with a Durban Poison female. You want the high THC content of Skunk #1 with the quick finishing time of Durban Poison. You make two lines, one whose goal is to preserve the high THC content and the other whose goal is to have a quick ripening time. You would select for high THC content in each generation in one line, and then for quick finishing time in the other. You would continue to inbreed these lines with each other, at least until the F4 generation, at which time you would cross these two lines to have a strain that was high in THC content and matured rapidly.

It is always a good idea when making your F1 population to select two different lines of the same strain. They can be either a Sativa / Sativa line or a Sativa / Indica line or an Indica / Indica line. The purpose of this line is, when you get to your F7/F8 generation, and your gene pool is shrinking, you can cross these lines together to add a bit of genetic diversity back into your gene pool, but not to the point where you have to start from scratch again. This will only suffice for between one to three more generations, depending on the skill of the breeder. You can gain more time by backcrossing with one of the original parents or an F2 sibling; either of these will add quite a bit of genetic diversity back into your gene pool and prolong the need to do so again for at least five generations, again depending on the skill of the breeder.

Breeding is all about size and selection. The size aspect is difficult in North America, which puts even greater emphasis on selection. However, you can never compensate selection for size, but the smaller the size, the greater the emphasis on selection must be. Selection is also a double-edged sword. If you have high selection standards, you will create the most stable generations, but you will have to add genetic diversity into your shrinking gene pool much sooner than if, say, your methods were a bit lax. Bear this in mind, as this is also the reason why some breeders choose to incorporate three or four different strains into a new strain they are breeding. I would like to add that while making the best selection(s) are key, you should produce a large amount of seeds, especially for your F5 generation, which will most likely be your best generation. Once you have reached the goals of your breeding program, there is no need to make any further crosses. This is when you must clone the last generation of your parental male and females for all future seeds.

PHENOTYPE VS. GENOTYPE

There has been some confusion in the cannabis community as to what constitutes a phenotype and what constitutes a genotype. The phenotype is the expression of observable traits, while the genotypes are the genes that are present in that particular phenotype.

To be more exact, the phenotype is the outward physical representation of the genotype (genes). However, in cannabis, the genotype is only partially responsible for the outward appearance (phenotype). The genotype is 50% responsible for outward appearance; the other 50% is the environment. This explains why clones of the same genotype may look different.

We have all seen the *PP*, *pp*, and *Pp* in biology and breeding books. These are genotypes made possible by alleles "P" and "p." Alleles are different versions of a

This beauty from Short Stuff Seeds is bred to have long, dense colas, and to autoflower.

gene given at a specific point (locus) along a chromosome. P is dominant over p. Meaning P demonstrates the dominant traits: tall plants are dominant over short ones, green is dominant over purple, males are dominant over females, etc. Typically, any mutation, whether favorable or unfavorable, is recessive: p. If you have one parent that is homozygous, meaning it has the same allele, PP, and one parent that is homozygous, for pp. Homozygous means that it is a true breeding strain, it has the same alleles whether they be recessive (pp) or dominant (PP). The majority of hybrid strains are heterozygous (Pp).

This means the majority of the F1 offspring will be PP because P is dominant over p. However, there will be offspring that are heterozygous, meaning they will have one allele of P and one allele of p: Pp. These have both alleles (traits) but the dominant allele (P) will mask the recessive allele (p). Lastly, occurring at a very small percentage, there will be the recessive trait, pp.

Now all the genotypes, PP, pp, and Pp, will have differing phenotypes. Choosing which phenotype of which genotype to breed with is up to you. However, you should use the following criteria to make sure your phenotypes meet breeding requirements. This is the time where breeders will most likely back cross their pp F1 offspring to their pp parent to lock down any recessive traits and have it occur at a higher percentage. While this recessive trait will be "locked down," there will still be altering phenotypes. These phenotypes should again be chosen by what meets your breeding criteria.

FAVORABLE TRAITS

These are traits to look for in choosing which plants make good breeding specimens. These traits should be applied to every plant you choose to breed with. If these traits are not present, move on to the next plant.

Branching

The size of the branches and the space between the branching (internodes) will determine the bud structure of your plant. Shorter internodes with thicker stalks will produce better yields than plants with long internodes and thinner stalks. The thicker the stalk, the more nutrients and water can be transported quickly to other regions of the plant. The thicker stalks and branches will also serve to support the plant.

There is a rumor going around that hollow stems mean better plants. This is completely untrue. A stem becomes "pith filled" when it is exposed to harsh conditions, i.e. wind, rain, and so on. This is just the plant re-enforcing itself so that it can survive. Hollow stems just mean that the plant was not exposed to any harsh weather (i.e., grown indoors) and did not have to develop pith-filled stems to survive. If you were to grow the same "hollow stem" plants outdoors, they would produce piths.

Psicodelicia from Sweet Seeds is bred for high yield and short flowering period, not to mention it's clear, and energetic Sativa high.

OG Kush (Alpine Version feminized/S1) from Alpine Seeds is a backcross from OG Kush – Lemon Larry to the original East Coast Sour Diesel JBL. This strain produces huge buds, a very good yield and extremely resinous buds. Expect a very hard and strong buzz mixed with the typical OG Kush smell. This strain has high medical potency and very high smoke quality and purple, dark red and blue colors and a yield of 600g/square meter (about 21 ounces for 3.5 square feet). –MoD, Breeder of Alpine Seeds.

Disease and Pest Resistance

Similar to hardiness, when plants are exposed to certain insects and fungi, not all of them will be affected, or they will be less affected. You should select these plants to continue your breeding. Insects are drawn to plants from the terpentines that they exhibit. Certain plants of a same strain will give off different terpentines that may or may not draw certain insects.

General Size and Yield

Let's say you're growing a ten pack of breeder's seeds; in this pack, you will see variation between the plants of height and size. If conditions are the same for all ten plants, the size variation will be determined by the genes of said plant. At this time, you should select the plants based on which size is favorable for your breeding practices. Say you're breeding for a strain that stays compact and short, for a cabinet or small space. You should select the smallest *healthy* plant. The yield will also play an important factor in your decision, as well as potency, of course. You'll want both of these factors to be as high as possible.

Hardiness

How a plant responds to extreme temperature / environmental conditions (overwatering, say, or nutritional deficiencies) should be a key determining factor in selecting a plant. Even plants of the same strain will respond differently to deficiencies. Some will react extremely while others will barely be affected. Obviously, you will want to choose the ones that are least affected. It is also a good idea to subject plants to adverse growing conditions to see how they will respond, purposely messing with their environment, much like how companies test their products.

Maturation Rate

Whether plants mature early or late, the most important aspect is even maturation. If you are breeding for a quick maturing strain you will want to choose both parents that mature the fastest. Quickly maturing strains will pass that trait on to the offspring and the same is true for slow-maturing strains. Crossing between these two traits will give a plant intermediate ripening. Even maturation is extremely important so that all of the plant is mature and can be harvested at the same time. It is most common for plants to mature from the middle out. Odd, I know, but in most cases it is true. Other plants will mature from the bottom up, or the top down. It is important to find a plant that matures as evenly as possible. Use withered pistils and trichomes to judge this.

Root Structure

How quickly the roots grow and the size of the roots are two important aspects that determine the size of the plant. After all, a plant can only grow as fast as the roots grow, so selecting a plant that has the biggest roots with the quickest growth is key. I gauge this after the harvest by looking at the number, size, and healthiness of the roots in the top two inches of soil. The top two–three inches of soil is the hardest for roots to grow in, which is why it is a suitable judge for the roots in other areas. You should also pay attention to how quickly the plant's roots grow through the drainage holes after transplanting. Bigger roots, say 2–3 millimeters in diameter, are more for stability, and fine roots uptake water and nutrients.

Vigor

How fast a plant grows and how healthy it is constitute vigor. Only the most vigorous plants should be selected. Vigor in the vegetative phase will translate into vigor during the flowering phase. Leaves should be a rich green color and growth should be at least ¼-inch a day during vegetative cycle. In order to get an accurate reading of vigor, plants should be measured each morning using a sewing tape measure.

Seedling Traits

Seedling traits are basically the same as the ones mentioned above. However, in the seedling stage you should use a "pocket" microscope or good quality camera with a macro lens to observe your seedling and notice how many trichomes are on the leaves and stems of the young seedling. You should start observing your plant as soon as the first serrated single blade leaves appear. You should see some trichomes by the time the second pair of leaves appear; if not, then I would not use that individual.

You may also rub your fingers gently along the stalk of the plant; apply slight pressure with the stalk between your thumb and index finger. Smell the odor that the plant gives off and smell your fingers. If you're breeding for aroma / taste, this will give you a good early indication of the aroma / taste that a given plant will possess. Those seedlings which do not possess a noticeable aroma should be culled, as should seedlings with a hay or grass type of smell.

Also, if you're breeding for color, with normal temperatures you may want to observe some coloring during the seedling stage for the most colorful plants.

FLORAL TRAITS

Calyx Size

The larger the calyx, the more trichomes that calyx can hold, which translates into a higher potency plant. Landrace varieties often have bigger calyxes while hybrid lines generally have many small calyxes. Calyx size depends largely on the maturity of the plant, as calyxes grow every day throughout flowering. The true measure of calyx size should be made when the pistil is still straight and white. A calyx can quadruple in size throughout flowering.

Also, if a plant distributes "donkey ears" or "fox tails" it is a good indication that the plant is a high yielder. Donkey ears or fox tails occur when calyxes build on top of each other and rise up away from the main bud area.

Quality

Bud quality is defined here as the ratio of calyx to leaf. I have seen many pictures of huge colas, but the quality was absolute crap. There were more leaves and pistils than there were resinous calyxes. Calyxes have the highest concentration of resin glands, so obviously, the more calyxes, the higher the quality. Also, a higher calyx-to-leaf ratio means less work trimming.

X-Dog (F1 Hybrid regular) from Alpine Seeds is a cross between an old Netherlands cut from NLx and a male plant from Chemdog dd. This cross has a lot of medical potency and a very strong buzz. X-Dog only has two phenotypes, which are close to the parents NLx and Chemdog. The smell is very special and Chemdog-dominant, but you can also smell a fruity touch from NLx, too. The yield is good, at about 30-35g/100cm plant height (1.5 ounces/40 inches). NLx is a cut between Northern Light x White Widow. A few years ago, we got this cut by another original Netherlands Breeder who made the original NLx. So we selected a great resinous Chemdog Male and crossed the two strains. This is X-Dog. – MoD, Breeder of Alpine Seeds.

Shape

The shape of floral clusters (colas) are determined by the vegetative cycle, specifically by the internodes. The distance of the internodes will either produce long, solid colas, or scattered, wispy colas. Internodal length is 40% genetics and 60% environment. This means that while genetics do play an important role in internodal / cola formation, it is overshadowed by environment. You can control the distance between nodes by having sufficient lighting, training, ventilation, and container size. Obviously, the shape of the cola will also determine the yield.

COLOR

This is the result of an accumulation of either anthocyanin or carotenoid pigments. These pigments have been present throughout the plant's entire life cycle but were masked by chlorophyll, the green pigment. As the plant progresses, chlorophyll begins to dissolve as the plant is using all its stored nitrogen. Also, colder temperatures will cause nitrogen to be locked out and chlorophyll to begin breaking down, letting the anthocyanin, purple or carotenoid, red, orange, and brown pigments to show through. With the coloring, there are different degrees of color; some plants will only develop purple on the calyx, while others will only develop on the leaves (which is common with environmental coloring or false coloring). Still others may turn entirely purple.

Nebu, the breeder of Black Russian and other rich purple strains, was the first to classify varying degrees of purple, and the following is based on his observations.

1st Degree

The 1st degree of purpling is characterized throughout the leaves and petioles (stems); it is pretty to look at while the plant is growing, but does not remain after trimming and curing. A good cure will remove most artificial coloring.

2nd Degree

This purpling develops on the leaves and spreads to the calyxes, but usually only to the tips. Now, this is where bag appeal comes into play, as the calyxes are splashed and in some cases completely covered with purple.

3rd Degree

This is the rarest and truest degree of purple, in which everything is purple: calyxes, leaves, stems, stalks, and even trichomes. This is truly some beautiful herb to behold—and talk about bag appeal.

TASTE AND AROMA

Taste and aroma are closely related by a chain of hydrocarbons. Terpenes (hydrocarbons) are housed in the trichomes of the plants. This explains why the aroma of plants in seedling and veg are less than in flower—because a plant has fewer trichomes in the early stages of life. When the plant is squeezed or rubbed, these trichomes burst, releasing the aromatic terpenes. At least 103 aromatic terpenes are known to affect the smell of cannabis plants. When breeding for a particular aroma or taste you should make notes of how each individual plant smells throughout the vegetative cycle. Make sure your fingers are clean before "sampling" another plant so as not to pollute aromas. The strongest aroma that most resembles what you're

Sweet Pink Grapefruit S1 (feminized) from Alpine Seeds is a clone only Genetic which we got selfed with herself. This next feminized generation has got three phenos. One is identical with the original clone, the second smells like Blueberry and looks like it, too. The third pheno is more Sativa. All three phenotypes have the ground smell from SPG, a fruity, sweet grapefruit-like taste. Between the different phenos are only small aroma variations. All are sweet, but another is more sour and sweet. The S1 Generation is very close to the original SPG clone. With this strain you should expect:
- *Middle hard nuggets*
- *Lots of resin and a high potency / high medical potency*
- *Easy to make cuts*
- *SPG S1 is a very special strain – its original clone mother is 35 years old!*
- *Specialized smell and taste.*

Most people say that SPG is a very sweet pheno from an old NL#1 plant, but there are three phenotypes, so it depends on which you get. This is a SPG x SPG strain. Unfortunately for people buying this seed from us, there is no breeding potential because the seeds are feminized. – MoD, Breeder of Alpine Seeds.

breeding for should be marked, and tabs should be kept on that plant throughout the rest of veg and flowering.

You can get a rough sample of the flavor by taking a sample of the bud or pollen sacks from a male (make sure to use a Happy Chief filter so you don't get a mouth full of pollen) rolling it up as a joint / spliff, and taking a dry hit.

Sweet Chunk F1 (regular) is one of the best strains Alpine Seeds delivers. It is a cross between Sweet Pink Grapefruit and Deep Chunk JBL, and Deep Chunk dominated the cross and gives the plant a 100% homogenized and stable growth. The only difference between the plants are the smell of the buds – some are more Deep Chunk dominated, and others are more Sweet Pink Grapefruit dominated. The smell and taste are the only difference between the plants. With this strain you should expect:
* *Hard and compact nuggets*
* *Yield per plant to be 30-40g at 80cm tall (1.4 ounces for 32 inches)*
* *Easy to make clones (10 days until rooting)*
* *High medical potency (excellent pain killer)*
* *Excellent mold and spider mite resistance*
This strain is great for breeding projects. It is very stable is not a polyhybrid. Deep Chunk is an old Pakistani/Afghani inbred line and SPG is an old Northern Lights #1 Pheno. – MoD, Breeder of Alpine Seeds.

TRICHOME TYPE / RESIN PRODUCTION

There are three different types of secretory trichomes found in cannabis: bulbous, capitate sessile, and capitate stalked. Bulbous trichomes are the "baby" trichomes; these trichomes mature into capitate sessile, then capitate sessile develop into capitate stalked trichomes. Bulbous trichomes have no visible stalk, they appear to be opaque balls on the plant surface; capitate sessile trichomes begin to develop a stalk at which time they mature into capitate stalked trichomes, which have a long stalk; at this time you can separate the head from the stalk to make kief and/or hash.

Naturally, a breeder should look for a plant that has a high concentration of trichomes, but the size of the trichomes should be considered as well. Trichomes vary in size from strain to strain; sativa dominant strains tend to have fewer trichomes, with longer stalks and smaller heads that make for poor hash. Indica dominant plants tend to have a higher concentration of trichomes with smaller stalks and bigger heads. The bigger the head, the better for hash; but the longer the stalk, the easier it is to separate. This means that a hybrid of Sativa / Indica that has bulbous heads and long stalks would be ideal for hash production.

Breeders should look for plants that distribute trichomes underneath the leaves' surface, as this is a somewhat rare quality indicating high trichome content. There are two main phenotypes of trichome coverage, the most common pheno being a wide covering of trichomes on the sugar leaves; leaves protruding from the buds, the other, less common pheno, is when the majority of trichomes congregate on the edges of the sugar leaves. This is typically known as a resin curl.

Growers have found that the less common pheno of the trichomes on the edges typically provides a more potent plant. However, there is a third, extremely rare pheno that distributes the cluster of trichomes down the edge of the leaves while also coating trichomes across the sugar leaf. This is the best pheno to breed with.

MUTATIONS

All-natural mutations are typically "germ line" mutations, meaning they came from the parent plants and are passed on in the seed. These traits can be homozygous or heterozygous, recessive or dominant (but they are typically recessive). There are a few factors which can cause a mutation; we will look at them one by one.

The genotype of a plant is the main cause of germ line mutations. In nature a weak genotype would have died out and not been able to continue its weak genetic structure but indoors so-called breeding has created such plants. All weak plants should be completely *avoided* for breeding and growing purposes.

Stress is more of an individual problem, in which natural stress cannot be passed on to the offspring. However, stress can cause mutations for that plant. The most common of these are leaf mutations.

Breeding with Chemicals

There are many strains out today that are available only in clone form. This is not good from a breeding standpoint, because it means that these genetics are permanently kept from the cannabis gene pool as a whole. This also limits a clone's usefulness to the community at large and limits its breeding potential. For some time now the use of chemicals in breeding has been a very controversial topic with both sides drawing strong supporters. When using chemicals, you are changing the plant's DNA at the molecular and chromosomal level. The long-term effects of using these chemicals on the parents of future strains are not yet known. When using these chemicals in breeding programs, there is a very real danger of unwanted mutations occurring and ruining the entire line and years of work, not to mention wasting money.

It is *extremely* important that *all* safety precautions be followed to the letter. This means wearing protective clothing that covers all areas of exposed skin, eye protection, thick rubber gloves, and a respirator. Proper ventilation should be used at all times when using these chemicals. Never use them in an enclosed space.

Sodium Thiosulfate Solution

Sodium Thiosulfate Solution (STS) is the latest and most effective way to convert female to male plants. This mutagen is fairly simple to make but not as easy to apply as gibberellic acid. What you will need to make STS is:

Part A: 0.5 grams silver nitrate in 500ml distilled water

Part B: 2.5 grams sodium thiosulfate in 500ml distilled water

The silver nitrate dissolves within 15 seconds while the sodium thiosulfate takes 30–45 seconds. Mix the silver nitrate solution into the sodium thiosulfate solution, all the while stirring rapidly. The resulting mixture should be stock silver thiosulfate solution (STS). This stock solution is then diluted to a 1:9 ratio. For example, a 50ml STS solution is added to 450ml of distilled water, which is then sprayed on a selected female.

Some breeders use their solution in a 3:1 ratio, but this does nothing but needlessly burn and stress the plant.

Another formula:

Dissolve 1.58 g of sodium thiosulfate into 100 milliliters of distilled water to create STS stock.

Dissolve 1.7g of silver nitrate into 100 milliliters of distilled water to create $AgNO_3$ stock.

You can store these stock solutions around 40°F in a refrigerator for up to four weeks time.

When you are ready to use your STS solution, mix your sodium thiosulfate and silver nitrate together in a ratio of 4:1. Remember to mix your silver nitrate into the sodium thiosulfate, and not vice versa. Preparation of STS right before use is recommended.

Be sure to spray your converted plants at least twice to ensure that you collect all the pollen that is needed. The first spray will last for 1–1½ weeks, at which time you should spray the plant again. In my experience, any STS concentration is only effec-

Sweet Tooth #4 (S1 feminized) is the third backcross from Sweet Tooth from Spice of Life to the grand Mother Sweet Pink Grapefruit. We used only original genetics, so this Sweet Tooth #4 is not a fake or an F2 Generation. Our Sweet Tooth is original, crossed with true genetics. With this strain you should expect:

- *Hard a compact buds*
- *Lots of resin and a superb sweet smell and grapefruit taste*
- *If the temperature is cold, ST4 can change from the green color into a dark red*
- *The yield is OK, but the smoke quality is the best ever*
- *This is a good strain for more advanced growers – you need to be careful of spidermites when you grow this strain. It is well worth the effort!*

The genetics of this plant are Sweet Tooth #3 Female from SoL crossed with a selfed Sweet Pink Grapefruit clone and then the third Bx to SPG. – MoD, Breeder of Alpine Seeds.

tive at inhibiting ethylene production for three weeks. Around that time period, the plant's natural female hormones (ethylene) will begin to win the battle over the artificially-induced male hormones. When working with an XX female, this process may be accelerated. Combat this by spraying a second and, sometimes, rarely, a third spraying; this will allow the plant to produce plenty of pollen for your breeding purposes.

The selected female plant should be sprayed until the solution runs off. You should spray over a newspaper in a room separate from the flower room. Ventilate the room to get rid of any vapors, even though you may not smell anything. This female plant will now produce male flowers. Once this plant dries it should be immediately placed into 12/12. This should be done 3 to 4 weeks prior to the date that you plan to pollinate your target plant. The time it takes for a plant to produce pollen varies and will be determined through trial. Under this assumption, a plant that takes 8 weeks to produce mature flowers and 3 to 4 weeks to produce mature seeds should have both the reversed plant and the selected female plant put into the flower room at the same time. A plant that takes only 6 weeks to finish flowering should be placed into flower roughly 10 days later than the reversed plant, so the seeds can finish before the plant matures.

A few days after spraying your selected female, some yellowing may occur. This may persist for a couple of weeks. Growth will stop and then resume slowly. Stretch should also be minimal, but this does vary according to the strain / plant. At the end of these two weeks, male clusters should start to form. Once the reversed plant starts to open its clusters, move it closer to your target plant or collect the pollen as outlined below.

A more controlled approach is to put your reversed plant in a separate closet with plastic bags or newspaper sleeves to collect pollen. If you have multiple reversed plants, be sure to not mix the pollen of the different plants. If you used newspaper sleeves, pour the collected pollen in a plastic bag. Slowly remove excess air from the bag, all the while being careful not to release pollen. Carefully slip the pollen bag over a selected branch and tie it off so the pollen is not released. After 4–5 days, remove the bag in a room separate from the flower room and mist the plant with water. Remove excess from the plant before returning it to the flowering room. The resulting seeds are fully viable feminized seeds.

Gibberellic Acid

Gibberellic Acid (GA3) is derived from a fungus known as Gibberella Fujikuroi. Gibberellic acid is a mixture of ethanol, water, and a crystalline powder that contains the gibberellins. Gibberellic acid contains concentrated gibberellins, which are hormones naturally found in plants. (They are discussed in the advanced techniques chapter.) Gibberellin hormones promote growth and elongation of plant cells among increasing seed germination rates. Because GA3 is the concentrated version of a hormone naturally found in plants, plants need very little of it to produce the desired result (increased growth). Excess use can stunt/stop growth because plant cells break down over exhaustion. Most concentrations use between .01–10 milligrams per liter of distilled water, depending on the strain and maturity of the plant, to accelerate growth, while if you are seeking to alter sex it will take a bit more.

To change a female plant into a male plant, spray with 100 PPM of GA3 for five consecutive days; within two weeks male flowers will appear. Some breeders have reported that they have successfully reverted a male into a female plant from the use of GA3. Although the exact concentration is not known, it is interesting to note that this has been found possible with tomatoes, castor beans, and maize, and has also sterilized males in lettuce and pepper.

Colchicine

Colchicine is a tricyclic alkaloid that is derived from the roots of plants in the colchicum genus, specifically the autumn crocus. Early on, colchicine was thought to revert female plants to male plants, but recent experiments have indicated that colchicine is not the best mutagen to accomplish that feat. What colchicine is used for is to promote germ line mutations. Germ line mutations are any detectable, inherited variation in the lineage of germ cells. What this means is that colchicine is used to change diploid plants into polyploid plants via chromosome mutations. This is accomplished by the inhibition of chromosome segregation to the daughter cells and cell wall formation. Chromosome segregation is a part of cell division where chromosomes relocate with similar homologous chromosomes. This causes multiple chromosome sets to form, causing the polyploid condition. Be advised that occasionally a male or female plant treated with colchicine can become sterile, so you should not use colchicine on any plant you are trying to get seeds or pollen from.

To use colchicine you must soak your seeds in a 0.5–1% solution of colchicine (mixed with 99–99.5% distilled water) 24 hours prior to germination. You should be aware that colchicine treated seeds have an extremely poor germination rate, something around 1–5%, because of colchicine's effects on the embryo. This is why breeders use large numbers of seeds when performing any colchicine experiment. If, after the first 24 hour soak, your seeds do not germinate, try soaking for between 6–9 hours more, and if that does not work then you should reduce the strength of your solution.

You may be wondering what the positive effects of colchicine are. Breeders will occasionally use colchicine to produce polyploid plants, as stated before. This means seeds with double, triple, or even quadruple the usual number of chromosomes. In humans and animals, this would be fatal, but plants typically respond very well to this change, growing faster, stronger, and yielding more than their diploid counterparts. In cannabis, the use of colchicine even improves potency by over 100%, according to experiments by H.E. Warmke.

Untrustworthy breeders will use this technique to produce F1 generations that yield phenomenal results, but with germination rates at next to nothing. Breeding with polyploids should never be attempted, as the polyploid condition will usually only last for one generation, which means that breeding a line of polyploid plants as an inherited trait is next to impossible and would require multiple scientific tests to check for polyploid condition. Additionally, polyploids require many more nutrients and water to sustain regular growth and are much more susceptible to fluctuations in the environment.

Indole-3-Acetic Acid

Indole-3-Acetic Acid (IAA) is a phytohormone known as auxins. Phytohormones are chemicals plants naturally produce to regulate growth. Generally speaking, IAA is considered to be the most important auxin. It has been speculated by some that the use of IAA can revert males to females, and a study done by the K.A. Timiryazev Institute of Plant Physiology confirms this to be true. Their study found that 15 milligrams per liter of IAA and distilled water applied to the plant via the root system would revert males to females, and occasionally hermaphrodites. IAA has also been found to stimulate adventitious root growth. Adventitious roots are roots that develop anywhere other than from the taproot / radicle; adventitious roots grow from other roots, and those occasional white bumps at the base of your plant's stalk are the beginnings of adventitious roots. All the root growth from a clone is from adventitious roots because clones have no taproot / radicle.

IAA's close cousin is IBA, Indole-3-Butyric Acid, another member of the auxin family. You may recognize this from the label of some of the better cloning solutions. Concentrations for rooting are from as little as 100 PPM to as much as 10,000 PPM. IBA comes in many sources, including powders that need to be dissolved in 71% + Isopropyl Alcohol, mixtures already dissolved in organic solutions, and water-soluble tablets. IBA dissolved in water is the best for encouraging root growth; in fact, some researchers argue that IBA is more effective in promoting root growth than IAA or NAA. Although its affect on reverting males to females is not known.

Leaf Splitting

This is the most common of all mutations prevalent in equatorial varieties. This is a "germ line" mutation and is not caused by stress. This is a naturally occurring leaf trait in certain strains. It appears to be a leaf growing from another leaf.

Warping

This is a leaf mutation that usually occurs in lines that have been inbred too much or in clones. When these genotypes have been crossed, they produce offspring that have warped leaves. These leaves look disfigured, or as though they have suffered from nutrient deficiencies.

This hermaphrodite plant occurred naturally during an outdoor grow, but some herms can be forced through use of chemicals.

Whorled Phylotaxy

Also known as trilateral branching. Instead of having the normal two branches on each side of the stalk, alternating at each node by 180 degrees, with whorled phylotaxy the plant develops a third branch at each node. Plants that display whorled phylotaxy are usually unstable, polyploid, weak plants; however some plants have been known to increase yield by $\frac{1}{3}$. Whorled phylotaxy is said to be most common in Central and South American varieties.

Twinning

This is a mutation in which two cotyledons emerge from the same seed. If left to grow without being separated, the weaker one will suck nutrients and water away from the stronger one, which will eventually kill them both. Sometimes, if you carefully remove them, you can get them to grow, but the majority of the time neither of them will meet the guidelines for breeding and you should usually cull them out as they are weaker and taking up space that can be used for other healthy plants.

Back Crossing

Back crossing is a technique used by breeders to fix traits in plants by selecting an offspring of that parent and crossing it with the parent. While this is unthinkable for humans, plants respond well to it. Back crossing reinforces parental traits / alleles and is a useful tool in the breeder's arsenal. Back crossing definitely shortens the time and effort of stabilizing the phenotype that expresses the parental characteristics, thus shortening the time to complete your goal. Back crossing can also restore vigor to an inbred line without giving rise to unwanted traits. In order to back cross, you must have your original parent stock alive for all generations; you can either clone them or keep them as mother or father plants. Your first backcross will result in 50% homozygous (stable trait) and 50% heterozygous (unstable trait), instead of 25% homozygous dominant, 25% homozygeous recessive and 50% heterozygeous.

Selfing

Selfing, or self-pollination, is the process of either naturally or chemically stressing a female plant into producing male flowers (becoming a hermaphrodite) and pollinating itself. This can fix many traits, but it has the potential to change genetic structure and turn X (female) into Y (male) chromosomes when a chemical stressing agent is used. It has been said that you should not use "feminized" (selfed) seeds for breeding purposes, and this is true to an extent. However, some breeders are, with selfing, pioneering an individual plant that can fix traits. To do this, they select a male or female of the preceding S1 or F1 population that displays the desired favorable traits, and proceed as normal. When you self a plant, the seeds are "feminized" because they have two X chromosomes instead of an X and Y chromosome. However, you can further increase these odds by using hermaphrodite pollen to pollinate a female plant. When chemicals are used to induce hermaphroditic flowers, this has the potential of carrying mutations to future generations; the same is true for naturally occurring hermaphrodites—most Thai, Southeast Asian strains for example. When you use natural stress in a plant that naturally does not form hermaphroditic flowers, these hermaphroditic tendencies will not pass on to further generations. The problem with using chemicals to stress a plant into selfing is that occasionally those chemicals will change the genetic structure of that plant enough for it to pass on hermaphroditic tendencies, and possible mutations, to future offspring.

Cubing

Find a P1 female and a P1 male and pollinate with these two plants. Collect the seeds and grow them out, collect pollen from all favorable males, and mix them together and pollinate the P1 female. This is the .75 generation.

Grow the .75 generation out, find the best 4 males and mix the pollen together; pollinate the original P1 female. This cross is the .88 generation.

Grow the .88 generation out, find the best 4 males and mix the pollen together; pollinate the original P1 female. This is the .94 generation.

Grow the .94 generation out, find the best 4 males and mix the pollen together; pollinate the original P1 female. This is the .99 generation.

Now you have cubed that strain. You will never be able to reach 100, but with each backcross you're making that strain more stable. This is how most breeders create a true breeding line (TBL).

However, there is a lot of confusion surrounding cubing in the breeding community. Cubing does not stabilize any traits except by accident; there is no selective breeding involved, you are just mixing male pollen together and hoping for the best results. There will still be variations in the phenotypes based on the males used. If you find a phenotype that stands out above the rest, there is no way to stabilize this phenotype, because the male parent is unknown. Not to mention the fact that, when cubing, you kill off the male from the previous generation after you have collected the pollen.

Cubing is the method that was used to create Cinderella 99, and it worked well with that strain because the gene pool was already small to start with, so there was not much variation in the first place. However, with a wider variation in the gene pool, this technique would yield unfavorable results: there is no substitute for selective breeding.

Note: Other "breeders" will refer to cubing as being the third backcross; however, a third backcross has not finished the job. You can still up your "stability" another 5% with the fourth backcross, thus finishing your cube. After all, a cube does have four sides.

XX Female

This is a process developed by a Spanish breeder that goes by the name Mr. XX. Both male and female plants have an X and a Y chromosome. X is the female chromosome and Y is the male chromosome. What this means is that plants have a 50:50 chance of becoming either male or female. However, there are some plants that have both XX chromosomes, as Mr. XX has documented.

Note: Be sure to make clones of the plants before applying this technique.

Mr. XX finds XX females by turning the light cycle to 12/12 for ten days while in the vegetative cycle. Then he will switch the lighting to 24/0 for one day. Then he returns to 12/12 for three–five days, and then back again to 24/0 for one day again. Finally, he returns to 12/12 indefinitely.

If, at the end of this process, you have a plant that does not herm, you have found an XX female. Now, what Mr. XX does when he finds an XX female is he chemically herms that plant for making female seeds. He uses gibberellic acid to cause the female plant to grow male flowers. He mixes .02 grams of GA3 with 30 centiliters of distilled water with two drops of natrium hydroxide. He says these seeds are carbon copies of the mother—cloning through seeds.

However, you can use your XX females slightly differently. Take a first generation backcross and test B1 seeds until you find an XX female; then take a female plant and stress it to the point that it herms. Gather this pollen and pollinate the XX female. Now you will have seeds that will be female and will share common traits. These seeds will all be XX females.

These are all techniques that should be implemented by smart breeders.

Males

The selection of males may very well be more important than the selection of females. The female is easy to select because all of the traits are very visible (smokeable); with males it is not quite as simple.

You should cull out the undesirable males using the traits outlined above. After this has been done, you can really start to get picky with your males. A good male will distribute all the characteristics you're looking for in a female. This means tight clusters and also, if you're breeding for color, purple (or whatever desired color) clusters.

If breeding for color, and if both your male and female posses the color you're breeding for, then this trait is PP against the green color pp. This will make breeding for color much easier, as the purple coloration is dominant over green. It will make the purple genotype occur at a higher rate than the green.

If your male has long, tight clusters of pollen sacks, there is a good chance that this will be passed on to the offspring with a stabilizing of traits; it just seems that male traits show up dominantly over female traits—except for flavor and aroma.

When your male has released its pollen you should gather the empty pollen sacks and roll them into a joint and smoke them. This should be the first smoke of the morning so you can tell if you feel anything from the male; if you do feel a slight buzz, this is a good sign, as the male does have some potency to pass on to the offspring.

The best males to use are ones that shed the majority of their pollen within a short window of time. Males that continue to shed their pollen over, say, a 3–4 month period, will generally produce offspring that have un-even ripening as well as a longer flowering time.

Note: all auto-flowering plants, male or female, should be culled. Auto-flowering means that they flower regardless of the photoperiod.

COLLECTING POLLEN

There are several ways to collect pollen from a male plant. Indoors, you will want to completely isolate the male from the female and each male from other males. Place

Here you see some empty pollen sacks and a whole lot of collected pollen. This will be used for breeding projects.

To collect pollen outdoors, put a breathable synthetic bag, like this Gore-Tex bag, over each branch or floral cluster. Wait a few days for the pollen to collect, and then harvest it."

wax paper around the base of the plant, extending in a 1–1½ foot radius, and have no wind blowing on the plant whatsoever. As the pollen sacks open, they release their pollen and gravity takes care of the rest. When you have collected a sufficient amount of pollen, tap all the leaves that the pollen has collected on, making the pollen fall on to the wax paper.

Fold the wax paper to make a funnel and funnel the pollen into a ziplock bag. Rice should be added to the bag, which acts as a natural desiccant. The bag should then be placed in a deep freeze and will remain viable for about one year. Let the pollen thaw, first in the fridge, then on the countertop, before using. Use immediately after thawing. If at any point during the collecting or storing process your pollen comes in contact with moisture it will be ruined.

Outdoors, things are a bit different. You will have to put a bag over each branch or floral cluster. Ideally, breathable synthetic fibers such as Gore-Tex bags will be used, however, these are difficult to come by, and paper lunch bags are a suitable substitute. You will need to tape the end of each bag with a ½-inch of masking tape. Make sure this is a good seal or your pollen will seep out of the bottom of the bag. After 3–5 days time, there should be enough pollen in the bag(s) for your breeding purposes. At this time, cut the branch and turn the bag over. Now you can go indoors and remove the tape from the bag and, after giving the branch a good shaking, you can remove the branch and discard it. Store the pollen as you would when collecting it indoors.

This Super Star has been seeded in a big way. Notice how the seeds appear at the nodes, like buds, and how the calyxes are bulging.

This Iranian Short Season by Dr. Greenthumb has been pollinated by a male plant. The outdoor grower needs to be aware of any male plants in the vicinity – unless you specifically want to breed the two plants.

WHEN TO SEED

The exact time to pollinate your plant differs from plant to plant. Most seeds take from 4–5 weeks to mature, so you should pollinate your plant at the two-week mark if your plant matures between 6–7 weeks. If your plant matures in 7–8 weeks, you should pollinate at the 3-week mark, etc. The ideal time is when the pistils of your plant are long, white and straight.

If you're only select pollinating—pollinating only one or two branches—you should isolate your plant (usually outdoors) and spray the entire plant down with water, except for the branches you wish to pollinate. Place a large paper (leaf bag) over the plant; make an X incision in the bag, just big enough for the branch to come through. Having the hole a little bit smaller is better than having it too big. With a cheap paintbrush, apply a liberal coating of pollen to all exposed bud sites. Leave isolated for 24 hrs and then thoroughly wash all the remaining pollen away. Remember: when pollen becomes wet it becomes inactive. Instead of pulling the branch back through the hole, simply cut the bag away from the plant. Leave isolated for two to three more days, thoroughly misting the plant each day; then you may return her to the general population. Make sure to keep your branches labeled.

When the pistils are pollinated, they will generally start to change color and wither away, as they have served their purposes.

As the seeds and plants mature, the calyxes will start to bulge as the seed grows. You will see the seed split the calyx, mature, and develop color, etc. Not all plants will split their calyxes when the seed matures, but the majority will. You will need a magnifying glass or a good macro lens. Once your seed has turned a tan or brown color your seed is getting close to harvest.

The seeds sometimes burst out of the calyx when they are ripe. Watch your plants carefully to be sure that seeds don't fall and get lost on the ground.

Here we see some excellent Ch9 Jack seeds from Ch9 Female Seeds. We see seed bracts, husk and calyx here, but these seeds are mature and are ready to be extracted.

Once your seed is mature, the calyx will separate from the husk of the seed. You can slide your fingernail down the side of the husk to remove the calyx and extract the seed. After careful inspection of the seed, you can determine if the rest of the seeds are ripe and ready for harvest. I do not wait for the seed to rattle loosely inside the calyx, as it is too easy for seeds to be dropped and lost. Since you pollinated the whole branch at the same time, all the seeds will be mature at the same time.

Note: It is important to note that when you're pollinating your plant, especially the whole plant, that you have switched your priority from harvesting bud at the right time to harvesting seed at the right time.

STORING SEEDS

Seeds can be stored almost indefinitely if the right techniques are used. When the seeds are first harvested they must be left in the open air for two weeks. This is a sort of "curing" for the seeds. Now place the seeds in an airtight container—film canisters are perfect. Place these film containers in a larger container, say a big pickle jar, and have desiccant placed in the center of the large container. These jars should be placed in a deep freeze. After the first three years, the vitality rate drops from between 2–4% each year, depending on the storage techniques. Remember to change out the desiccant regularly whether using for seeds or pollen.

The Rewards

The powder is un-pressed hash, known as kief. The compressed bars are hash. All of them are made from the resin glands (trichomes) of cannabis plants.

Chapter 25

Hash and Extractions

Hashish, commonly known as hash, is the word used to describe collected and compressed trichomes (resin glands) from cannabis plants / buds (flowers). Until these trichomes are compressed, this powder is known as kief. The best hash has very little to no plant matter in it, giving it a blonde color. As the hash decreases in quality, it will have a more greenish color to it because of the increasing amount of plant matter. The lowest quality of hash is black; this black color is caused by the oxidation of the cannabinoids that are located inside the trichome heads. When these heads rupture because of mishandling, they are exposed to oxygen, which decreases their potency. Black hash is usually hand rubbed.

Hash is usually made from the leftover trim after a harvest; however, hardcore hash enthusiasts will make their hash directly from the buds.

TRADITIONAL PREPARATIONS
Trichome Collection
Hand Rubbing
This is a practice traditionally used by Sadhus of India (traveling medicine men / healers / priests). It is the simplest and easiest method of making hashish and all that it requires is dried buds, two hands, and some friction.

Place a dried bud of fresh cannabis (a cola is preferred over small buds) between the palms of your hands and start rubbing your hands back and forth. The trichomes will begin sticking to your hands and a snowball effect will occur with other trichomes. The heat from the friction of your hands rubbing back and forth will soften the hash and allow it to bind and pick up other hash. Essentially, this can last for as long as you can; when you are finished peel as much of the hash off of your hands as possible and you are ready to enjoy it.

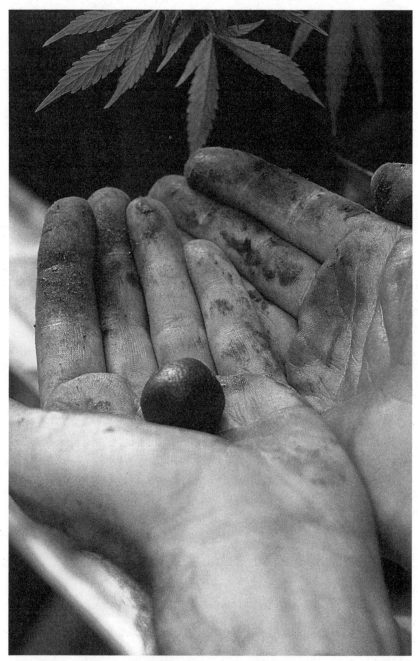

This grower practices the traditional hashish-making style of hand rubbing. The resin collects on his hands, and he rubs it off, exactly as the Sadhus of India did it thousands of years ago.

Dry Sieving

Dry sieving was the method first used by the Lebanese to separate trichomes from plant material. They would place a bowl underneath a zero zero grade of muslin and rub plant matter on the top of the screen in a cold environment. This would separate the heads and stalks from the plant material by filtering it through the screen. Nowadays we can order a 150 micron screen or whatever the desired size and stretch this over a bowl and recreate the same process.

Bubble Man's Bubble Box Dry-Sifting Method

contributed by Bubble Man

Here we will be explaining and introducing you to the first multi-screen, dry-sifting box.

These boxes have been around for years, but until recently only contained a single screen. Single screen dry sifting is an OK method for turning yourself onto dry sifting, but once you have acquired a few of the skills you will want to take it to the next level with multiple screens.

My three-screen box, that I will be detailing here, is made of a Birdseye maple wood, using high-end hinges and locks. The box is not going to fall apart anytime soon. We made sure of that.

The box comes with a bubble man logo engraved inside the top of the lid.

Once you open the box you will find a small wooden lid that sits on top of the first screen; this is mostly to keep contaminant from falling in and out of your box when it's not in use. The top screen is 140u (microns) or 120LPI (lines per inch), depending on the type of screen you purchase.

The top screen is used for breaking up your buds when rolling joints, or, if you are a vaporizer user, you can break vapor material up on this top screen. There will be quite a bit of contaminant that will fall through this screen depending on how much and how hard you work the material. This is OK; I have designed the box especially for this to happen.

If you are not actually using the box to make dry sift, you should be gentle on the top screen; however, because of the multiple screens you can be rough on this top screen if you choose, and still clean the resin up using the second and third screen. Our second screen is an approximate 107u or 140LPI.

You will notice that, as the micron size goes down, the lines per inch number will go up. The Bubble Box's series of screens, pictured below, is a system for removing some of the contaminants that will fall through your top screen.. With the card that comes with the Bubble Box, you can gently rub the material back and forth, pushing the smaller material through and leaving some of the larger plant matter on top. This material, because of its ratio of glands to plant matter, is actually quite nice for vaporizing.

Bubble Man's Bubble Box is made of Birds-eye maple wood. It's tough and durable.

The high-end hinges and locks open to reveal a well-organized interior featuring the Bubble Man brand logo.

The wooden lid inside sits on top of the first screen. Use it to break up your bud or for rolling joints or breaking up vapor material.

Inside the Bubble Box you see a series of screens. These are used to sift the trim and trichomes, leaving trim on top and trichomes on bottom.

Once you have worked your second screen for a bit, it may be lifted out, and work may begin on the third and final screen. This screen is going to be where we find our full melt dry sift. Full melt dry sift is a term used to describe dry sifted hash as shown below. It is of the highest quality. Up until now, we have taken what falls through the screen. However, with this last screen, a 70u or 200LPI, the best resin glands will be found on top, not underneath.

Using the card once again, rub gently back and forth until the plant matter breaks through and goes to the bottom plate. The gland heads (over 70u) will not push through the screen, but will be left sitting on top.

This is where there is some actual work. The process up to now has been quick, but for the last screen you don't really want to rush. I have worked on a three or four gram pile before for more than half an hour and reduced my weight by over 50%. If you want to partake in the joys of hitting some full melt dry sift, you better be willing to take your time. There are methods of getting dry sift that melts without using multiple screens but it involves much smaller amounts and the use of a freezer. The method is basically dry sifting in a freezer, and if you're gentle enough, and have good enough material, you can get a full melt dry sift with one single screen. However, you will guarantee a full melt dry sift if you use the multiple screens, and you won't have to be as delicate.

It's common knowledge amongst heads that full melt dry sift is not your every-day, average smoke. Most people have never had it, and very few have it on a regular basis. With the release of this box, I hope to see that all change.

As you can see from the resin sift on our final screen, when the sift is dropped into the pipe and lit, it melts beautifully into a liquid. The pile below has been worked for no more than 15 minutes, starting with less than a gram. The more you try and work

Use a card to move the dry sift around on top of the screens. As you push it around, the trichomes will break up and the smaller stuff will fall down to the next screen.

Here we see the dry sift that has gone through the larger screen to the smaller screen. It's like panning for gold.

Once you've collected the dry sift, or kief, you can put it straight into a bowl and smoke it, or you can compress it into bars of hash. It's up to you.

The kief bubbles and begins releasing highly potent THC as soon as you put a flame to it. Enjoy.

at a time, the longer you will have to work your final screen. You can try this at home by simply acquiring a few silk screens with the same micron or lines per inch sizes.

You can also smoke what's under the final screen, which will be a collection of 69u (and smaller) heads, along with the capitate stalks and cystolith hair contaminant.

Cleaning out the final layer of sift is also possible with a tighter screen yet, say a 300 LPI or 25u screen. I chose a 70u for my box as these are some very tasty heads, and 70u is usually around the ideal micron size of bubble heads.

Water Sieving

Water sieving is a relatively new technique of using water and ice to separate the trichomes from the plant material and then filtering the water through the bags, removing the collected trichomes and letting them dry before using. A simple water extraction can be made using some dry cannabis trim and a jar partially full of ice water. Fill the jar about ¼ full of trim, twice as much cold water, and five or six ice cubes. Shake extremely thoroughly for as long as you can stand it and let the jar sit for a few minutes until you see the trichome heads at the bottom and the plant material at the top. Use a spoon to scoop out as much of the trim and ice cubes as you can without disturbing the trichomes at the bottom. Now pour the water with the trichomes through a coffee filter and allow that coffee filter to dry completely. Shake and scrape the coffee filter when dry onto a large flat surface so you can collect your trichomes and use accordingly.

Bubble Man's Bubble Now Method

contributed by Bubble Man

In this section we are going to be explaining the newest addition to the bubble family, the Bubblenow.

This unit comes in five and 20-gallon sizes, and both will be discussed here. The five gallon, eight bag kit will also be used to show the process. The unit itself only washes the resin off—but when I say only, don't be fooled: this unit, when packed with the proper amount of ice, will extract your resins extremely effectively.

Over the years, many people have switched from the electric beater / mixer to the wooden spoon that I was promoting some years back as the ultimate full melt maker. I can attest now, after some hundreds of runs with the Bubblenow, that the mixing power and efficiency is not only easier, but more effective than the spoon method.

Also, it makes doing a second rinse almost too easy. As the unit drains into the bucket, you simply fill the Bubblenow half full of water again, turn the dial to 3 minutes, and let her wash.

I put drains on the bottom of my twenty gallon buckets, but you can also do this

An almost ripe outdoor Sour Diesel bud basking in the afternoon sun.

A seedling emerging with the seed husk still holding on. Similar to a scab you should leave the seed husk alone and let it fall off on its own accord.

A healthy, young plant just being transplanted.

Ready to transplant. Remember to tease the roots out so that they spread and the plant isn't root bound.

A little shock after transplant, this plant will bounce back just fine.

Cloning a female plant.

Using powder cloning stimulator.

A female plant bearing seed.

These seeds are about 4-5 weeks from being mature.

Cutting just being set in soil.

Be sure to water and re-tamp the soil so it's not too loose but not too tight.

Always remember to be gentle when handling your plants.

Careful when handling your plants, you don't want to rupture the trichomes.

This plant is being prepared for the FIM technique. Sharp tools are a must.

Extreme fox tailing on this sativa dom. Hybrid. This extreme fox tailing is common with Thai influenced plants.

Turn your bud upside down and remove all the petioles you can see.

It's important to eat right during heavy trim sessions!

Healthy plant in vegetative cycle with natural growth (no topping, FIMing, LSTing or super cropping).

Water your plants thoroughly each time you water, just make sure they need it first!

A sativa dominant hybrid grown outdoors hanging to dry. This grower chose to trim the plants after drying.

The rewards of a successful harvest.

Typical of Thai (haze) strains this mature cola is showing extreme fox tailing and will turn out to be some very heady smoke.

This phototype of Mekong Haze is almost pure sativa, ideal for breeding with a landrace (or as close to it as possible).

The purple kush bud is ready to harvest. Notice all the full bulbous trichomes and all the withered pistils and swollen calyxes. This baby is gonna knock you down!

Notice the amber trichome to clear trichome ratio. It's roughly 40:60 which means that this plant is ready to harvest.

Swollen calyxes are a great way to judge a plant's ripeness.

Durban Poison typically shows unique colors.

Scissor hash! The early rewards of a harvest!

A nice slab wedge of hash butter ready for consumption.

Hand rubbed hash dissected.

A healthy seedling with a garnish of Sour Diesel buds.

to your five gallon buckets; it makes it easier if you want to do your first and second run together (normally I would never consider this if using a mixer to make the bubble, but with the Bubblenow the quality of the second run is extremely close to the first).

So, now I will take you through the process of using the Bubblenow along with the Bubblebag. Keep in mind, for those of you who are confused about the process and how the new unit works, it is only going to wash your resins off, and filter them through a work screen (220u). You will still need bags to drain the water through and separate out the resin glands.

First, we fill our five gallon bucket with our Bubblebag eight bag kit, starting with the 25u, and going through the sequence of screens: 45u, 73u, 90u, 120u, 160u, and 190u.

Note: the work bags that go inside the Bubblenow are triangular in shape, but they have since been redesigned to be barrel shaped. These barrel shapes are much more effective than the triangular ones, and that is why we changed our design.

Once your bags fit snugly into the bucket (a diaper pail, which is about 7 gallons, fits the kit much better than a 5-gallon bucket, as the diaper pails are tapered and taller), you can plug the Bubblenow unit in and get it ready for processing. The all-screen work bags should be stuffed with 100 grams of trim each. The trim used in these photos was Sour Diesel.

I use two work bags for one run, running 200 grams (half a pound) at a time. Once the herb is in the all-screen work bag, you can stuff it full of ice.

The more the merrier: you can't use too much ice, so use a ton. I like the bags to be bulging. You can half fill up the Bubblenow with cold water, the cleaner the better. Throw your all-screen work bags into the Bubblenow.

Add a bit more ice on the outside of the screens, close the lid, and turn the dial to the desired time.

The Bubblenow comes with five different time settings to choose from: 3, 6, 9, 12, and 15.

I played around quite a bit at the beginning with times, choosing the shortest amount and hoping for the highest quality. With some strains I saw a little of that, but I was quite surprised that, when packed with the proper amount of ice, the unit really churned out some excellent quality full melt on 15 minutes, and a second run at 3 minutes added to the same bubble.

For those of you not familiar with the term full melt: it's when the resin is of such high quality, i.e. concentrated and pure, that it melts at the touch of a flame. Often dripping through the tightest of screens, and bubbling up large clear domes. This quality is upwards of around 50% THC.

The Bubblenow water sieving unit works in conjunction with the Bubble Bags system to produce quality hash.

You will need ice. You can't use too much ice with this system, so I always add a ton of it.

Fill the filter bags with trim, or bud, if you like. Fill each bag about half full or so.

Add the ice into the filter bags with the trim. Add lots, but make sure you can close it.

Half fill the Bubblenow unit with clean, cold water.

Throw all of the filter bags into the machine, or as many as you can fit.

Add some more ice on the outside of the bags, and close the lid.

Turn the dial to the desired time. I was in a rush so I chose three minutes.

When it's done, use the hose to fill up your Bubble Bags.

The water comes out fast, so be careful you don't spill.

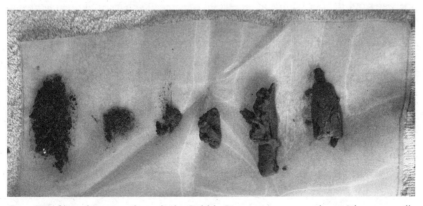

Once you filter the water through the Bubble Bag system, you end up with some really nice grades of hash like this.

Fifteen minutes later, the Bubblenow is ready to drain into five gallon bags. The drain on the five-gallon unit is simple and works by gravity. There is a little hose that hooks onto the top of the unit and plugs into the bottom; you simply lift this off its hook and lower it into the bags, and the water will start coming out immediately.

I suggest putting your thumb over the top of the hose before you lower it, as five gallons of water comes out with a decent amount of force when gravity is working with it.

The color of the water will give you an idea of your quality. When it's extremely gold, you are extremely happy. The darker brown has surprised me with its quality, but not often enough. And, of course, the green can go both ways; sometimes it's green only because fresh material was used.

Once the mixture is poured into the bags you could do your second run. A sink hose is useful for cleaning, as there is a lip around the lid that is hard to get at any other way.

Keep your unit clean and use only cold water to wash it; consider throwing some ice in if you see a lot of resin at the bottom floating around. If you pour clean, fresh water into the Bubblenow, you can drain it through the bags so as to not lose any of those glandular heads.

The screen work bags can be flipped inside out and rinsed with water. If there are tiny bits of leaf still on them towards the end, don't worry: these will come off much more easily when they are dry and brittle.

Now we move forward with the Bubblebags. I like to have cardboard cut and ready for the bubble as I pull it out. So, take some cardboard and write the micron numbers of each bag on separate pieces, leaving a space between each to fit the piles of bubble. Cardboard is good because it acts as a desiccant (moisture remover) and will pull the water out of your bubble more quickly and way more efficiently than air-drying ever could. Place your pressing screens on a towel-covered table; these will absorb the water from the top and bottom as the bubble is gently pressed from each bag.

Even though we already used a work bag screen, I still use my 220u bag to catch any leaf particulate that may have escaped from the bag. Feel free to throw away anything you may have caught in it. Flipping it inside out, use fresh cold water to clean it, and then hang it to dry.

Next up, we have our 190u bag; this bag will produce a very low quality bubble, more contaminant than anything. However, this material can still be vaporized and used for cooking. The medicinal properties are still very much present.

You can use a small plastic or wooden bowl to stretch the bags inside out. This makes for easy scooping out of resin. Clean the 190u bag the same way you did with the 220u, by flipping it inside out, and rinse it with cold, clean water, finally hanging it out to dry.

Next up is the 160u bag. Although I have seen full melt bubble come out of this bag, it's been infrequent. 160u sift is great for vaporizing and cooking. Repeat the steps for cleaning on this bag and hang to dry.

The 120u bag is the first extremely high quality size head in the hierarchy of bags I've developed. The product is always favorable and doesn't usually fall far from the marker. Pull the material out and place it on the pressing screen you have laid out. This process is the same as that you will undertake with the 190u and 160u. Doing all the grades in a line will show you their differences and is well worth doing, even if you end up adding a few grades together in the end.

Press the 120u gently with the screen closed and the towel on both the top and bottom. This allows a lot of the water to be absorbed into the towel.

Next, take the wet paddy of bubble and chop it up into as fine a powder as I can get. If your material is really high quality, press it very lightly in the pressing screen or it will bind and you will have a heck of a time getting it into powder.

The powder will dry within 24 to 36 hours, so checking it every five or six hours is a good idea; you can break up the chunks into smaller pieces as it dries. Also, try to keep this cardboard in a safe place; if you have animals or live in a dusty area, you don't want to risk an accident. I have seen the stove work efficiently for keeping the product out of harm's way. Just don't turn it on.

Next up is the 90u. One of my personal favorites, this is going to be some of the dankest product you produce. Flipping the bag inside out, scoop out the resin and place it on the pressing screen. Take the dirty bag and clean it out in the bubble water so the resin that is still present will be picked up by the 73u bag. Repeat the cleaning steps on your 90u bag, and start pulling your 73u.

At this stage, you should know what to do: just repeat the steps above.

The 45u bag is often one of the first to hold a lot of the water in. Due to the tight size of the screen and the resin blocking the way of much of the screen's surface area, you may find it a bit difficult. For this problem, simply jerk the bag upwards with the top closed. Lifting the water inside the bag will also lift the resin off the screen, allowing for a gush of water to get through (remember to do this over a bucket!). I can drain this bag in under ten seconds by repeating this process, so don't think you have to wait for this bag to drain. Make it happen.

Pull out the material and place it on the pressing screen. Repeat the cleaning steps on this bag after you have rinsed it with the bubble water of the 25u screen. No sense in throwing away viable heads. Hang to dry.

Now we are on our final and most difficult bag to drain. You will need to repeat the upward jerking motion with the bag cinched closed; this will release the water and

Sweet Chunk is a stunning indica-dominant strain from Alpine Seeds that boasts an insane amount of resin production. It is ideal for making hash. Just look at the trichomes.

shouldn't take more than 30 seconds. You will want to get all the resin scraped off the bottom of this screen, as there are no more bags to rinse into. Place the bubble onto the pressing screen, then repeat the cleaning steps and hang the bag to dry.

Now we go back to our pressing screen, which has most of our bubble on it in paddy form.

We will place these wet bubble paddies onto the cardboard next to their appropriate sizes. Chop each paddy of bubble into powder or as small chunks as you can get it into. I use a fairly sharp paring knife for this process, although an X-acto knife will work well, as will (if nothing else is available) a single edged razor blade.

Your pressing screen should be fairly clean if you did your light pressing correctly, but if you find the resin starting to build up on them, you can easily rinse them inside your next batch of bubble. The bubble will dry out over the next 24 plus hours, and then you can place it into containers with the micron size and strain written on the outside. Enjoy.

Bubble Man's 20-Gallon BubbleNow with BubbleBags Method
contributed by Bubble Man

In this section we will be reviewing using the twenty-gallon BubbleNow unit along with the 20-gallon, 8-bag BubbleBag kit.

I have been using these bags for almost 8 years now, and can say that using them with the BubbleNow is much easier than hand mixing. What you will need to process a harvest of 40 pounds:

- Three 30 gallon trash cans
- 1,500 pounds of ice
- Two rakes
- Three electric hand mixers
- Thick rubber gloves
- Multiple squares of thick cardboard labeled for the appropriate quality
- A hose with a cold water sprayer
- Three sets of 20-gallon Bubble Bags 8 bag kits
- A whole mess of trim.
- A scale for measuring each batch is optional but recommended.

I use three sets of BubbleBags with 30-gallon buckets. Most standard garbage cans are around 30 to 32 gallons, even though most assume they are 20. This is OK, as the bags fit well inside, and it makes for an easy second run on the unit, which I will get to later. So the first thing is to take the 30-gallon garbage buckets and add taps to the bottom.

This is an incredible amount of water to work with, so it will make things much easier if you do this. A paddle drill bit is used for this procedure, requiring that you first drill a small starter hole into the bottom of the bucket.

The tool cuts a larger hole into the bottom of the can.

Once the hole is there, you can add the parts of the drain.

The drain screws into itself and works really well.

Once the drain is complete, you can add your hose; make sure it is long enough to reach wherever you need to drain.

Adding a tap is also essential; otherwise your water will not stay in the bucket for long. Once your buckets are ready, add the BubbleBags to the buckets. The order, of course, begins with the smaller sizes of micron hole: first, the 25u, then the 45u, the 73u, the 90u, the 120u, the 160u, the 190u, and finally the work bag, the 220u.

For large scale operations, I use a pallet of ice. If you are running amounts like this all the time, you will want to consider purchasing an ice-making machine. A pallet of ice is $350—a big investment, but the bubble will pay that back in multiple. Store the trim in plastic bags in boxes, separated out by strain.

Believe it or not, this can get pretty messy and if you do it right, and set up the proper space, not only will your work be much easier, but you can collect a small amount of dry sift from each BubbleNow bag you fill; this will only work with dry material.

Each five-gallon BubbleNow bag can fit 200 grams, so use four for each batch and did 800-gram batches. The BubbleNow can take up to a kilo, i.e. 1,000 grams, but it's always nice to leave a little room, especially when you're doing such a big project; using a little less will often get you a little more. Over stuffing and lack of ice is the number one reason people get lower yields and lower quality than they are expecting. Another reason for weighing each batch is that in the end, once you have your bubble dried and weighed, you can figure out your exact ratio of bubble to trim. This is very important to learn, and doing it improperly can spread rumors of false yields. I remember when I first went online, a friend had made a batch, weighed the bubble wet, and decided he had gotten an 18% return. This is very high for a bubble return, and as he posted it more and more people who were *not* getting this return started to feel a little burnt. However, this return was totally inaccurate and should not have been written about, as the amount of water bubble can retain is very high. So, please do not roll up your fresh bubble wet, as the moisture will affect not only the ratio of return, but the quality of the smoke. I will go through proper methods for drying later in this section.

So, now that we had all our tools and our work area set up, we filled our BubbleNow work bags with 200 grams of dry trim each, and then stuffed them to the top with ice. When I say stuffed, I mean stuffed; you cannot have too much ice in this process.

The most important place for the ice to go first is inside the BubbleNow work bag. You can add more ice to the inside of the BubbleNow machine; however, it's the ice on the inside of the barrel-shaped work bag that will do the majority of the work. For those of you who are still a little confused, I will explain: the glandular head of the trichome holds the entire cannabinoid profile (the medicinal part of the plant). The wax membrane that holds it together is key in our extraction: the ice in the mixture will freeze this wax membrane and make it extremely brittle. The large chunks of ice, battering back and forth inside the trim–water mixture, are abrasive enough to knock those brittle little heads off of their stalks. That's the process in a nutshell. Because the resin is dense, it is still affected by gravity, even in water. While most of the plant matter floats, the resin itself sinks down to the bottom of the bags where the screens are. Depending on the size of the gland head, it will fall into the appropriately sized micron screen.

Once the BubbleNow work bags are filled with ice and trim, we place them inside the BubbleNow unit and fill it up with cold water and ice. Turn the dial to the amount of time you want it mixed—usually several 2- and 3-minute runs, but this unit is so even and effective that I run the mixtures for the full time of 15 minutes.

While it's mixing away, and since you're not holding a mixer or a spoon, feeling your back slowly tense up, you can be hitting bong rips of some of the last tasty bubble you made. After a dozen or so bong rips, the mixture will be ready to drain. These units come with a pump that makes it easy to drain. Instead of having to keep the unit higher, using a gravity drain, this unit actually comes with a pump that allows the water to be pumped up and out into the 20-gallon bags.

This is where it becomes cool. Once the first run is drained into the bags, you will see that the water level is still at least 7 to 8 gallons lower than it can hold. So, we rinse the BubbleNow with fresh cold water, fill it up a little less than half way, and turn the dial on for another few minutes. This water will also drain no problem into your bucket, which is, remember, a 32-gallon bucket, not 20. Drain the second run into the first, and you are now ready to get to cleaning your BubbleNow barrel-shaped work bags. I would never normally do my second run into my first, but once again, the mixing on these units is such that your quality will not even be affected—if you are using a high quality trim, that is.

Take each BubbleNow work bag and flip them inside out. We place our wet, used trim into a wheelbarrow and dump it in the back of the yard each time it gets full.

The BubbleNow work bags can also be rinsed with a hose. Cleanliness is an important factor when using these bags, the more you take care of them, the longer they will last and the better they will work for you.

You get into a nice pattern when you work with the same person over time. As the batch finishes its second rinse, we immediately get to cleaning out the BubbleBags.

As you pull each bag, scoop out the product, i.e. the bubble, and place it on your pressing screen.

You should have a pressing screen set up with towels placed under and over the screen; these will absorb the water. I usually wait until all grades are sitting on the pressing screen before I press the water out. This makes for a good idea of what you have just extracted. Showing you all the grades and their differences side by side can be quite powerful.

As you pull each bag and scoop out the bubble, the bag will have to be flipped inside out and rinsed with cold water immediately.

This resin will dry on the screen within minutes, and if you do not undertake this process it will quickly degrade the quality of your bags. I rinse the 190u and 160u with the hose, and when I get to the 120u I rinse it inside the BubbleBags so as to trap the lost resins inside the next BubbleBag to be pulled. This process will be repeated from the 120u all the way down to the 45u bag.

You can also do this with your spoon or scoop after each pull. The bubble, once lightly pressed in the screen, can be taken over to your cardboard section. Gently drop the wet bubble lump onto the cardboard with the according micron number.

We then chop up the lump into a fine powder. Depending on the quality of your bubble, this may or may not be difficult. If it's a super high grade, it will chunk together and not want to powderize; this is no problem—just get it down to as small chunks as you can, and go back every hour to break them up.

The cardboard is key. It works as a desiccant, which pulls the water out from the bottom, using gravity as its ally.

Air drying the bubble on a plate, or on anything that does not absorb water, is next to useless and you will regret it. Doing this simple cardboard method of drying will ensure you get the best, bone dry, powdered bubble possible.

When pressed, bubble tends to burn into an ember and slowly smoke away. Not the kind of hit I enjoy, so I encourage you to leave it loose.

I work the 40 pounds of trim for two days solid. Between two guys, we turned 40 pounds of trim into two pounds of high-grade bubble, that is to say full melt clear dome bubble. Some of the highest quality you can make.

Once your bubble is dry—and this is very easy to tell, as when you first put it on the cardboard it will be darker—mark it down and then place each micron screen size gland heads into their appropriate container. I suggest getting glass containers if you can, however, for this batch we needed too many containers, and weren't able to find glass in time. Cannabis resin does tend to break down plastic, so try and get glass, with glass on glass lids preferably, as the plastic lid on many mason jars will also

Use a precision press to turn your kief into delicious bars of hashish. Or, alternatively, you can just smoke the kief, or sprinkle it inside a joint.

degrade from the contact of the resin over time.

Now finally we get to the smoking process. Too many of you will want to add some of this to a joint. I smoke it through a clean tube bong, i.e., Roor, preferably, or my pocket buddy Roor pipe. Using a clean stainless steel screen gives by far the nicest hits. To each their own, in the end, but I find adding bubble to a joint is a bit wasteful, as most of it burns off on the tip of the joint. However you choose to enjoy your bubble, remember, *if it don't bubble, it ain't worth the trouble!*

PRESSING

Once the kief has been collected, it can then be pressed into hash. Kief needs pressure and warmth to become that dense, lovely, THC-laden wonder called hash. Very small amounts can be pressed between your fingers and rolled into a ball (if done in a piece of cellophane it will help inhibit THC degradation). Alternatively, a precision press can be used; if so, it's important to have it die-fitted to 0.001 inches, unless you want to squeeze a bunch of your hard won kief into the gap in the die. Once pressed, most hash tends to darken on the outside, but remains blond in the middle. Make sure to pre-press water-extracted hash in a piece of cellophane to help get rid of the water.

HASH OIL
TheNewGuy's Method for Making Hash Oil with 91% Isopropyl Alcohol
Materials:
• Any amount of stems, leaf, shake, bud, or whatever you can extract THC from.
• One Mason jar—1 pint will do for small batches.
• 91% isopropyl alcohol
• A large pot
• Stove or an electric eye burner (electric is safer)
• Zip-lock freezer bag
• Scissors
• Coffee filter, or a very fine mesh screen
• Pyrex pan, flat bottomed and big enough to sit on the large pot
Note: ALCOHOL IS VERY FLAMMABLE. VENTILATION IS EXTREMELY IMPORTANT!

These measurements are by volume, so you can make as much or as little as you want.

I start by grinding my trim and cutting the stalks into ¼-inch pieces. Place the desired amount of product into a jar and add alcohol. Simply make sure the alcohol level is higher than the shake to assure that the greens are covered and completely soaked. The better the product, the better the hash. If you used this method with buds, you would have a very potent product on your hands.

After that, shake the jar vigorously for five minutes exactly. Remove the lid from the jar and place a coffee filter over the mouth of the jar. Cut a tiny hole in the corner of a zip-lock freezer bag and place the hole directly over the coffee filter or mesh screen. Usually I just tear the corner right off to make the hole.

Note: shaking any longer than five minutes will result in chlorophyll and plant sugars being extracted into the final product, which lowers quality.

Turn the vent fan on and boil a pot of water. Make sure the water can boil for at least 30 minutes and not go dry. Place the Pyrex pan in an accessible area, as the next step will require filling the pan.

Raise the jar (with the filter and baggie) above the Pyrex pan and flip it upside down. The shake will flop into the filter and the jar can be removed. You can twist the top of the bag to create a seal so that the alcohol won't go spilling out of the top of the bag. Now you should have a zip-lock bag with a drain hole in the

These thin strips of hash have been pressed only recently. Remember, if it is blond in the middle, it is really good stuff.

Not every grow results in a chunk of hashish like this, but, with hard work and practice, you'll be able to produce incredible stash from that trim you used to throw away. Nice.

corner and a filter in front of the hole filtering the stems, leaves, or shake; the filter should be filled with alcohol-covered shake, and it should have started draining into the pan.

Squeeze the bag and the alcohol can be easily extracted from the shake. The reason I like the bag method is that you can squeeze the hell out of the shake and not get your hands all covered in alcohol and wasting product. Simply draining the alcohol isn't enough for me; I want every last drop I can get, so I squeeze hard. You can't do that with a strainer system.

When the water is boiling and the bag is drained, place the Pyrex pan filled with alcohol on top of the boiling pot of water. Monitor closely, make sure to use a low to medium heat. The goal here is to keep the water boiling so the steam lightly heats the pan; this helps to speed the evaporation process along.

Notice the golden rings forming as the alcohol evaporates.

When the moisture is gone, the pan will be covered in a golden film of hash. I use a square pan because it's easy to scrape clean due to the flat bottom, but a rectangular pan will work nicely also.

The hash is easily scraped with a standard razor-blade, and then pressed or rolled for smoking. Scrape the hash from the pan using a razor-blade while it's still warm for easy removal. If it cools down, it is harder to scrape up and it can turn as hard as a rock.

If you just scrape it off the pan, the hash is going to be very warm and gooey and it won't come off very easily. A trick I use to get it off the razor and onto the foil is to cool it down in the freezer for 20–30 seconds. You can just stick your arm in there or you can place the blade on the foil and place them both in there. Either way, I cool down the hash and it becomes more user-friendly. Then take another razor blade and scrape it off. I like to roll mine into a tootsie roll shape, or sometimes a ball, and store it on tin foil. This product is light, sweet, and *very* potent.

A second wash would extract too much chlorophyll and plant sugars. It makes the hash all gooey and green tasting. It can be done, and is sometimes not too bad, but the end product is always of lower quality.

Subcool's incredible Jack the Ripper strain is one of the best types of cannabis for ingestion via food.

Chapter 26

Cooking with Cannabis

Cannabis is a very unique plant in that it may be used in many diverse ways. One of the ways that it has been used just about since its inception is in cooking. Cooking with cannabis is a method for people to medicate themselves—primarily patients with lung disorders that prevent them from smoking cannabis. Ingesting cannabis will not provide such immediate effects as smoking does, and it is not as easy to find the dosage that suits you, but it is the safest way to use cannabis without damage being done to your body. After you finish eating a properly baked cannabis cookie or

Delicious cannabis cookies ready to be enjoyed!

brownie, you should be feeling its effects in about an hour. This time will vary depending on a person's body weight and tolerance.

Eating cannabis raw, with no preparation, is a very unpleasant experience. If you have ever had to eat a bud to "hide the evidence," then you know that raw cannabis has a very hot and spicy taste to it. This is how cannabis defends itself from herbivorous predators. This explains why cannabis is typically prepared with a sweet food—to counteract the hot and spicy resin.

Some strains, such as Jack the Ripper and Jacks Cleaner 2, are most effective when ingested via food. Ingesting cannabis via food also lasts much longer; it is not uncommon for the effects to last for more than eight hours.

In order to cook with cannabis, you will have to remember these five key things.
1. Cannabis is only fat soluble. This means that water will not hold cannabinoids. Milk will hold cannabinoids better than water, but only marginally; if you do use milk, avoid skim milk and go for whole milk. Best, however, are butter, oil, lard, heavy cream, and so on.
2. It is better to simmer cannabis for as long as four to six hours, instead of only for 30 minutes or one hour, as many recipes suggest. This will release more THC, which creates a more potent cannabis recipe.
3. In order for cannabinoids to become active you must use a process known as "decarboxylation." This is a fancy word that means you have to heat cannabis so the cannabinoids are released. Cannabinoids are not active until the cannabis reaches a temperature of 150°F for at least 15 minutes. The boiling point for the

Cannabutter, butter made from Cannabis, is a fundamental ingredient in almost every cannabis recipe. Learn to make it well and have some fun.

Remember to simmer your dried trim for as long as four to six hours. This will release more THC, which makes your recipes more potent. A crock pot is being used here.

majority of active cannabinoids ranges from 260–392°F.

4. Save all your trim and sugar leaves from your harvests to use for cooking.

5. For maximum effect, have an empty stomach when you ingest your medicated foods, if possible.

Most cannabis recipes will require the use of cannabutter. Cannabutter is a term coined by Adam Gottlieb when he wrote *The Art and Science of Cooking with Cannabis* in 1974. When you make cannabutter you can use this for anything that you can apply butter to, including toast, muffins, bagels, cakes, cupcakes, brownies, cookies, fudge, etc. The cannabutter contains all the cannabinoids. You just apply the butter and eat.

I will include two recipes here for cannabutter, one for the normal, small scale cannabis grower and another for the large scale or commercial cannabis grower.

SMALL SCALE CANNABUTTER

Items you will need:

• Two sticks of butter
• A container with a wide mouth (it is ideal to have a conically shaped container; this will make removing the cannabutter much easier in the end)
• Two to four cheesecloths
• One rubber band
• One or one and a half ounces of dried trim, whatever you desire. (Adding more trim of high quality will increase the strength as well as the "green" taste of your butter. If you want a stronger effect, increase the amount of trim and/or decrease the amount of butter.)

Melt your butter down then add the trim. Stir well.

Add water until all the trim is covered, usually about 3–4 cups. Stir well.

Simmer for 3–4 hours. Do not let your temperature rise above 175°F. For most

A medley of delicious cannabis goodies.

ovens this means setting for a low boil. To measure this you will need a food thermometer. Ideally, you want it to simmer as long as possible without letting all the
water evaporate; if it does evaporate, your cannabutter will burn. Too much water is
better than too little.

For a longer cooking time, you must increase the amount of water. A good rule is
one cup of water for every hour of simmering time, five cups for five hours, etc.
Remember, the longer the cooking time the better your butter will be. You must stir

Use the dried trim from your harvested buds as the main ingredient. There is quite a lot here, but you can make some nice foods with much less.

---

regularly during the whole cooking process or you will not get an even mix.

In the past some chefs would have their pot at a full boil, add their butter, wait for the butter to dissolve, mix their trim into the mix of water and butter, cook on high for about 15–20 minutes, and then strain. This does make as potent cannabutter as the method outlined above.

After you are done simmering, place an aluminum sheet down on your counter. Place your container with the secured cheesecloth in the middle of the aluminum sheet. This will reduce the mess.

Strain the mixture of butter, trim, and water through the cheesecloth. Be careful not to burn yourself!

Once all the liquid has passed through the cheesecloth, snip off the rubber band, ball the cheese cloth up, enclosing all of the trim inside, and squeeze the remaining liquid into the container.

Cover with saran wrap and let cool on your counter for about an hour before placing in the refrigerator. Place in the refrigerator for 3–5 hours. During this time the cannabutter will separate from the water and rise to the top as the water will remain below. When the butter has hardened you should remove the container from the refrigerator.

Take a thin knife—a butter knife works perfectly (go figure)—and slide it between the cannabutter and the edge of the container.

You may either pry up the cannabutter or go to your sink and tip the container upside down.

There will be a layer of nasty gunk where the water touched the cannabutter. Take your butter knife, remove this layer, and discard it. You may now either place your cannabutter in a zip lock bag and store it in your freezer for later use, immediately use your cannabutter for a recipe, or repeat the process to continue to remove impurities.

If you would like to remove more impurities, melt your cannabutter down, add more or less one cup of water, and simmer it down for more or less two hours. Repeat the process of straining and refrigerating.

The more you repeat this process, the more it will remove the "green" taste of the butter. It will not, however, affect the potency unless the simmer temperature is greater than 175°F.

LARGE SCALE CANNABUTTER

Items you will need:
- 2–3 pounds of butter
- A 2-gallon bucket or large Tupperware container
- 2–3 window screens
- 2–3 pounds of trim or more, depending on the strength of your cannabutter
- A large pot or a large electric slow cooker

Follow the same directions as you would for the small-scale cannabutter.

Apply as much water as needed for the trim to be covered.

Set on low heat and leave for 16 hours or so, stirring as much as possible during this time period.

Place a trash bag or piece of plastic on your kitchen floor, with the bucket in the middle of the plastic. Carefully place your stew on the screen, pile the trim up, and press down on it (while wearing thick rubber gloves) to squeeze out the remaining liquid from the trim.

If you used the 2-gallon bucket method, transfer the liquid to a smaller container that you can fit inside your fridge. Let it sit for an hour on the counter and then place into your fridge until your butter congeals.

Follow the rest of the instruction for the small-scale cannabutter.

Some hints and tips for making cannabutter

You can increase the quality of your cannabutter by getting the highest fat content butter you can find. This will hold more of the cannabinoids.

Your ideal cannabutter will be a pale yellow color; this will have the fewest impurities and will taste much better on or in whatever you choose. You can usually achieve the pale yellow cannabutter by repeating the process three times.

You can use the cannabutter for whatever recipe calls for butter. Usually, the required amount of butter will get you medicated. If not, then you can always add 1 or 2 more tbsp.

You can store cannabutter indefinitely below 20°F. This preserves the cannabinoids.

Firecrackers taste best if you grind up the bud very fine. You want about one gram per cracker.

FIRECRACKERS

This is one of the most common and most varied cannabis recipes. There are multiple ways to make firecrackers; below is my personal favorite.

You will need:

• Organic peanut butter (if you do not have organic peanut butter, it will not work; the natural fatty acids in organic peanut butter are what hold the cannabinoids)

• One box of Honey Graham crackers

• One cooking sheet

• Aluminum foil

• A butter knife

• You will need one gram of kind (dank) bud per cracker. Use a grinder to grind up the bud; if you do not have a grinder, use a pair of sharp scissors to chop the bud up as fine as possible.

Break the gram cracker into four separate pieces, as indicated by the lines on the cracker.

Spread the organic peanut butter over a cracker with the butter knife. You want the peanut butter to be around ⅛-inch thick. Do one side of two crackers.

Place the gram of cannabis powder or chopped cannabis on one side of the peanut buttered cracker. Use a clean knife to gently press the powder or flakes down into the peanut butter.

Place the other peanut butter cracker on top of this one, making a sandwich out of the crackers with the crackers as the bread. You want to press the crackers down enough so that a bit of peanut butter comes out of the edges. Then wipe down the excess peanut butter from the sides and bevel the edges.

Replace the missing peanut butter from the edges with fresh peanut butter. The reason for this is that when you bake the cracker, the cannabinoids will attempt to escape; the fresh peanut butter traps them.

Preheat your oven to 325°F and place your cookie pan inside the oven while preheating.

When your oven is at 325°F, pull the cookie pan out and carefully lay a layer of aluminum foil down. Quickly place your firecrackers on top of the aluminum foil and pop the pan back in the oven.

Cannabis has a hot and spicy taste to defend it in the wild against herbivorous preda-tors, so, when you cook it, add something sweet, like jam, to make it taste great.

Set your timer for 10 minutes. After the 10 minutes is up, flip your firecrackers over. Then set your timer for 11 minutes. After the 11 minutes is up, pull your firecrackers out and let them cool on the counter for 3 or 4 minutes.

Wrap up the firecrackers in aluminum foil to allow them to come to room temperature slowly. Place them in a zip lock bag in the fridge for 24 hours for maximum potency.

Most people will only eat two or three of these. Stagger eating them to about half an hour apart so you don't get too high.

Hints and tips for making firecrackers

Use creamy peanut butter; crunchy is much harder to work with.

Most of the time when you open a jar of organic peanut butter you will find a pool of oil on the top. *Do not* pour this oil out; this is the fatty acid that holds the cannabinoids in. Mix this oil back in the peanut butter.

You may try chocolate or cinnamon Graham Crackers instead of honey. Whatever suits your taste.

In a pinch, you may use saltine crackers, but it will taste horrible.

PEANUT BUTTER SQUARES

contributed by: ToB

You will need:

- 4 cups of confectioner's sugar
- 2 cups of organic peanut butter
- 1 ½ cups of Graham Crackers, your choice of flavor
- 1 cup of semisweet chocolate chips
- 1 cup of strong cannabutter

Melt 1 cup of cannabutter over low heat. Remove from heat and stir in confectioner's sugar, peanut butter and crumbled Graham Crackers. You may have to add more cracker crumbs than the recipe calls for; it depends on the humidity and consistency of the butter. Mix in enough cracker crumbs that the mixture is no longer sticky and may be patted down in the pan. I also suggest using foil or waxed paper over the pan for ease of removal.

Melt a ½ cup of butter and the chocolate chips and spread over the top of the mixture. Refrigerate for ½ an hour and cut into squares.

I modify this sometimes by using just a couple of tablespoons of butter in the chocolate chip mixture. I form the peanut butter into balls; let them firm up in the fridge for about 30 minutes, then dip. You can also add a tablespoon of beeswax to your mixture if it is warm weather, or humid; it keeps the candies from melting. Or get almond bark at the grocery store. It's ready to melt and dip and is resistant to melting in the candy dish.

Space cookie balls. About two of these and you'll be in a very good place.

SPACE COOKIES

You will need:

- 1 pack of premium cookie mix
- ½ cup of dank cannabutter
- ½ –1 ounce of trim
- Any kief that you have, up to three grams

Make sure your trim is ground up very well, or at least chopped. You want it as close to a powder as possible.

I find it better to melt the cannabutter before mixing it in with the other ingredients, as it will blend more thoroughly this way.

Simply mix together and follow the instructions on the store bought cookie mix.

Most people will be feeling good after ingesting between two–four cookies.

Hints and tips for Space Cookies:

Cookie mixes that call for olive oil or vegetable oil will increase the potency of your cookies.

PEANUT BUTTER COOKIES

You will need:

- 1 pack of premium cookie mix
- ¾ cup of dank cannabutter
- 1 ounce of trim
- Any kief you may have, up to two grams
- 1 cup of organic peanut butter

A mold was used to make these peanut butter cookies into pot leaf shapes. If you eat two of them, you'll be as baked as the cookies.

Again, melt the cannabutter before mixing.

Chop the trim as finely as possible.

Mix the trim and peanut butter together before mixing in with the rest of ingredients.

Follow directions on the cookie mix.

Usually two of these cookies will get you fully baked.

CANNABIS HOT CHOCOLATE

You will need:

- 1 cup of whole milk
- 1 cup of heavy cream
- ⅛ of an ounce of dank bud
- 5 ounces of semi-sweet chocolate
- ½ tsp vanilla extract
- tsp cinnamon
- tsp salt

Mix the milk, sugar and salt in a skillet or saucepan on medium heat. Once the sugar and salt has been dissolved, add the heavy cream, vanilla extract, cinnamon, and finely ground cannabis buds. Simmer to 150°F and add the chocolate. Mix well and stir until the chocolate has melted. Top with little marshmallows or whipped cream.

This makes an excellent winter time drink—with an added surprise.

HEAVENLY HASH FUDGE

You will need:

- 1 cup of heavy cream
- 2 cups of sugar
- 1 tsp of cornstarch
- 2 ounces of semi-sweet chocolate
- 3 grams of hash or 3 tbsp cannabutter
- 1 tbsp of Vanilla Extract

This grower has used some nice hash for these fudge brownies It was well worth it.

Mix the milk, sugar, chocolate and cornstarch together over medium heat. Make sure to stir the mixture well until the temperature reaches 240°F, at which point it should be immediately removed from the heat—leave the thermometer in the mix. Melt your cannabutter in the microwave, and as soon as the butter is melted, mix in your hash. Place it in the microwave again for 30 seconds. This will activate the cannabinoids in the hash. *Do not* pour the cannahash into the mix until the temperature on the thermometer drops to 110°F. When the temperature reaches 110°F, pour the cannahash into the fudge and stir vigorously with a big spoon or kitchen wedge for 10 minutes or so. Stop when it gets really difficult to stir. Spread a piece of wax paper on a cookie sheet and place your fudge balls on the sheet; allow them to cool all the way to room temperature.

Hints and tips on Heavenly Hash Fudge

If you do not have hash you may use 6 tbsp of cannabutter.

BANANA BUD BREAD

You will need:

- 2 eggs
- 1 tsp of lemon juice
- 3 tsps of baking powder
- 1 cup of sugar
- 1 cup of mashed bananas
- 2 cups of sifted flour
- 1 cup of ground cannabis buds
- 2 tbsps of cannabutter
- 1 tsp of salt
- 1 cup of shortening
- 1 cup of chopped pecans (optional)

First, mix the shortening, sugar, and eggs together, and stir well. In a separate bowl, mix the bananas with the lemon juice and add to first mixture of shortening, sugar, and eggs. Finally, mix the sifted flour, salt, baking powder, cannabutter, and powdered buds. Place all of these ingredients in one bowl, making sure to stir well.

Bake in a bread pan for around 1 hour and 30 minutes at 325°F.

Hints and tips for Banana Bud Bread

It is best to use bananas that have the brown, bruised age spots on them. This will increase the flavor of your banana bread.

CANNABIS CHOCOLATE CARAMEL

You will need:

- 1 ½ cup of cannabutter
- 2 ¼ cups of packed brown sugar
- 1 cup of heavy cream
- 1 cup of half and half
- 1 cup of light corn syrup
- 1 tsp vanilla extract
- 6 bags of Hershey's milk chocolate baking pieces
- Candy thermometer
- Double boiler
- Wax paper

First you will need to make the caramel.

In a deep melting pot, melt the cannabutter. You may sprinkle in chopped

These chocolate caramel cannabis treats were made with some very dank Jack the Ripper from Subcool. Delicious and potent.

cannabis flakes or ground cannabis buds for a bit more effect. Add the brown sugar, heavy cream, half and half, and corn syrup. Stir well. Cook on high while making sure to stir very well. Do this until the mixture boils. At this point, reduce the heat to medium and check the temperature—you want your mixture to be at 248°F. It will take around 45 minutes to get to this point.

While you're waiting, wrap a cookie pan in aluminum foil and apply a liberal coat of PAM to the foil.

Remove the pot from the heat and stir in vanilla extract. Quickly but carefully pour the mixture into the prepared cookie pan. After the caramel has adjusted to room temperature, place it in the fridge to harden. It will take the better part of two hours to do so. When hard, cut it into the desired size—usually 1-inch squares work best. After you cut the caramel into squares, place them in a ziplock bag and put them in the freezer overnight. This completes the caramel making process.

You may stop here if you are a caramel lover and don't want your caramel tainted with chocolate.

If not, than grab your double boiler and get her warmed up on the oven. Place your Hershey's chocolate pieces into the double boiler and stir until the chocolate has melted. Once the chocolate has melted, take your caramel squares out of the freezer. You may either drizzle the chocolate onto the squares for a more "refined" look or you may dunk the whole caramel into the chocolate. Place the chocolate caramels onto the cookie pan in the freezer and leave to harden overnight.

The next day, remove them from the freezer and allow them to adjust to room temperature. You will see a bit of moisture escaping from the candies; at this point, you may package them any way you like.

Hints and tips for Cannabis Chocolate Caramel

If a double boiler is not an option, you may re-create, more or less, the same process in the microwave with a microwave-safe dish.

Andre Grossman is one of the greatest cannabis photographers of all time. Known for his carefully planned bud shots, Grossman is an incredible talent.

Chapter 27

Photography

Photos are a great way of capturing memories long after the moment has passed; this includes cannabis. Taking photos of your plants will allow you to remember what each plant looked like long after they're gone. Detailed photographs are especially important when breeding, because, let's face it, your mind isn't what it used to be. Cannabis photos will also give you the option of showing your plants on cannabis forums.

For your cannabis photography, you will need a digital camera; obviously, you can't take your cannabis photos to the 1-hour photo shop to get developed. So what kind of digital camera do you need?

In order for you to take nice crisp photos, you will need at least 5.0 megapixels. Anything below this and quality will greatly diminish. If you want your photos to have a chance of appearing in a cannabis magazine, check the manufacturer's specifications to see how large the resolution is—you need to be able to take "high res" (high resolution) photos. The higher the numbers, the better the quality: 3,072 x 2,304 is a large "high res" size. Very low quality is 640 x 480, which is around 3.2 mega pixels. Typically, the larger the resolution, the higher the dpi (dots per inch); most magazines will not publish anything below 300 dpi. Although this is not often the case, some cameras that have 3,072 x 2,304 resolution are only at 180 dpi. 640 x 480 is 72 dpi. Most of the time dpi is not listed as a manufacturer spec, so it's a game of Russian roulette.

Taking close-up photos is known as macro photography. In its strictest definition, macro photography means photos that are life-size or larger. Having the option of "macro mode" is crucial when purchasing a digital camera. If it does not have a macro setting, then you're out of luck. You will not be able to capture up close photos of trichomes. The minimum macro distance is the feature to watch for when purchasing a digital camera for cannabis photography. Ideally, you will want a camera that has a macro of 1cm or less—the average is 4-cm and a horrible macro is 6-cm or more.

David Strange is known for his incredible ability to photograph the cannabis plant. He has been featured in dozens of magazines, and always manages to capture the side of a plant that no one has ever seen before.

This DSLR camera is more than capable of taking high resolution images of your bud.

This minimum macro distance is the minimum distance you can have your lens from the object you are photographing.

Your camera should also come with a changeable aperture setting. Aperture is defined as the size of the opening beneath the lens, which controls the amount of light reaching the "film," or, in digital cameras, the sensor.

To focus on something up close, i.e., macro photography, for most applications you will want the highest aperture setting that your camera has to offer. Aperture is measured in terms of f-stops. For the most part the higher the aperture, the better for macro photography; the lower the aperture, the better for photographing distant objects. Ideally, you want a camera that has a setting where you can adjust the aperture while in macro mode.

The trick is to get your lens 1 cm away from your object (in your case, buds) and take your photo. Do not zoom in as this will cause blurriness unless you are using a macro lens—just set your tripod up with your camera lens about 1 cm away or within your maximum macro focus range and take your photo.

If possible you will want to set your shutter speed between $1/125 - 1/250$.

Now, if you want to take individual trichome shots you will have to have a camera that has the option of add-on lenses. You will need a macro lens kit with the lens adapter to add them to your camera. Good lenses will typically come from Japan, not China or Taiwan.

When using macro lenses you should use your zoom to zoom all the way in and

Ed Borg has been photographing cannabis for over twenty years. He can capture every aspect of a plant at will and produce a beautiful image of it.

Here is a great 100mm macro lens. Use this to get high resolution close ups of your trichomes."

then gradually physically move the camera back from your object until it is in focus. This will require some experimentation for best results.

Another important aspect of macro photography is the feature of a "flash ring"; this is an adapter that throws the flash in a circle around your buds, creating even lighting with no shadows—a tricky aspect of macro photography. In most cases, having your flash on will "white out" your photo. If your camera has an adjustable flash, it is usually best to set it on its lowest setting, that is, if you use your flash at all. Natural lighting is my preference. Blue CFLs are the best source of artificial lighting.

Let's review how to take your macro photos.

Go to your camera's aperture mode, also known as "Av" mode. Set your aperture at its highest setting.

Turn on your macro feature.

If you have an adjustable ISO setting, set it to 50, or the lowest number.

If you can adjust the shutter speed, adjust it to between $1/125 - 1/250$. Experiment to find what works best for your set-up.

If your camera has an adjustable quality level, set it to its highest level, usually "super-fine."

Set your resolution to the highest available.

Turn off or tone down your flash. You can diffuse your flash with tissue paper folded over a couple of times.

Set your tripod up with your camera lens 1 cm away or at your maximum macro focus distance.

Set the self-timer so you don't move the camera at all when pressing the button to take the photo. This also will allow you to hold your CFL with the lighting where you want it. If available for your camera, you should get a cable release, which will allow you to take your photos by pressing a cable connected to your camera.

Taking macro photos will also let you document trichomes from their first

MG Imaging is one of the premier cannabis photography companies on the planet. They've been documenting this plant for as long as anyone, and they do it very, very well.

Here is the DSLR with macro lens attached. This camera has a 100mm macro.

appearance to the perfect harvesting time, and everywhere in between.

Also note that since you have to come so close to your sticky, trichome-covered buds, you eventually will touch your lens to your buds, creating a blurry spot in each shot you take until you remove the resin on your lens. This is very simple to do— just wrap a Q-tip in a lens-cleaning wipe and dip it in rubbing (isopropyl) alcohol; squeeze out the excess alcohol where the Q-tip is damp and rub on your lens until the resin smear is gone. Dry with another clean lens wipe (with the dry end of the Q-tip) and you're good to go.

SOME BASIC RULES OF CANNABIS PHOTOGRAPHY

Do not photograph your plants with your HID lights on, especially HPS lights. Because of the low CRI, your photos will have colors that your plants don't possess and usually they will just make for some nasty, orange-looking photos. Outdoor lighting on a bright sunny day is the best source of lighting, but if this is not an option blue "daylight" fluoros or CFLs are the next best thing.

Generally, you will not be able to see a camera's maximum macro focus distance when purchasing a digital camera. Dpreview.com is the best source to find out all the specs of a particular camera; not all cameras will be listed, but there is a lot of information available on the many cameras that are.

Another common mistake is that people assume they must have professional, $1,000 SLR cameras to take these kinds of photos. This is not true. Of course, expensive cameras will take the best quality, crystal clear photos, with the best close-ups, but you can certainly take advanced photos by purchasing an advanced "point and shoot" camera. Try to find at least a 6.0 mega pixel with a 1 cm macro. The Internet is your best source for finding a great camera at a reasonable price. One word: eBay! (Some other good sources are froogle.com and amazon.com.)

When photographing, especially outdoors, make sure you don't include anything in your photos that distinguishes your location, such as a unique walkway, parts of your house or yard, street signs, address numbers, fences, etc. The best outdoor backgrounds are woods or just plain grass.

When buying digital cameras, only buy name brand cameras, mostly because they provide warranties with their cameras and have a trusted reputation. Bear in mind, however, there are some companies that make great traditional cameras but their digital models are not quite up to par; one such company is Konica Minolta. Some very good companies are Canon, Nikon, Samsung, and Olympus. (More specifically, the affordable cameras made by these companies include most of Canon's A series, most of Nikon's Coolpix line—such as L5, P4 and P3—most of Samsung's S line, including S1050 and S850, and the Olympus Stylus 750 and 740.

If you want to shoot like the pros, first you'll need about $3,000 dollars. Most of the pros are using Nikon's D line, D40 and D50. Next, you'll need the 105mm bellows lens; this is a really funky-looking macro lens that has a big bellows on the back of it. Lastly, you'll need a flash ring for even lighting without shadows. Taking these extreme close-ups is very difficult without causing shadows, which is where the even lighting from the flash ring comes in to play. Of course, you'll also need a good tripod to hold all this equipment.

Like I said, this is the equipment of the pros, i.e., they earn a living from their photos. If you're just a hobby grower, or a serious grower who has used all your money on growing supplies and paying that heavy electricity bill, then the cameras I mentioned above will do wonderfully for you. They usually come in at around $300 dollars.

Note: don't get discouraged by photos you see online of larger-than-life buds. While they do sometimes occur, most of the time it is just a result of a grower using photoshop to further their reputation and ego. With the use of photoshop you can easily enlarge the size of your bud and shrink the size of a soda can, arm, leg, etc.

Resources

CANNABIS WEBSITES AND FORUMS

ActionTekHD.com – North American Distributor for No Mercy Supply
alpine-seeds.ch/forum.html - Alpine Seeds Grower's Forum
bastadelobby.com – Argentina's HOMEbox supplier
breedbay.co.uk – British Cannabis Website, Forum and Seedbank
cannabis.com – General Cannabis Information Website
cannabis.co.za – South African Cannabis History and Community Site
cannabisculture.com – Cannabis Culture News and Forums
cannabishealth.com – Cannabis Health Website
canamo.cl – Chilean Cannabis Magazine
canamo.net – Spanish Cannabis Magazine
cannaseur.com – Cannabis Forum (Subcool/TGA Seeds)
cogollos-argentinos.com.ar – Argentinian Cannabis Community Site
drugwarfacts.org – Information on the Drug War
erowid.org – Drug Information Website
everyonedoesit.com – Cannabis Forum and Community
fsbookco.com – Online Bookstore
greengrasspub.com.au – Green Grass Publishing
grow.de – German Cannabis Magazine
icmag.com – Cannabis Forum
thcene.com – German Cannabis Magazine
growadvice.com – Cannabis Growing Website
highlife.nl – Dutch Cannabis Magazine
hightimes.com – High Times Magazine
lamarihuana.com/ - Spanish Cannabis Community
legalizace.cz – Czech Cannabis Community

marijuananews.com – Marijuana News and Legal Information
medicalmarijuanainc.com – Medical Marijuana Company
norml.org – National Organization for the Reform of Marijuana Laws
safeaccessnow.org – Americans for Safe Access
skunkmagazine.com – Skunk Magazine
tokeup.com – Online Cannabis Community
weed.co.za – South African Cannabis Forum and Community
weedworld.co.uk – British Cannabis Magazine
yahooka.com – General Cannabis Information Website
420magazine.com – Cannabis Growing Website
420clones.com – Online Medical Cannabis Collective
420genetics.com - Online Cannabis Community
420roomsearch.com - 420 Friendly Room Search
420friendlyrentals.com – 420 Friendly Classifieds

FURTHER READING

Hashish by Robert Connell Clarke, Red Eye Press, 1998
Hemp Diseases and Pests by J.M. McPartland, R.C. Clarke, D.P. Watson, CABI Publishing, September 2000
Invisible Marijuana by Robert Bunch, Green Candy Press, 2008
Marijuana 101 by Professor Lee, Green Candy Press, 2010
Marijuana: A Grower's Lot by Kog, Green Grass Publishing, 1999
Marijuana Gold: Trash to Stash by Ed Rosenthal, Quick American Archives, December 2002
Marijuana Home Grower's Manual by Billy McCann, Green Candy Press, March 2009
Marijuana Horticulture by Jorge Cervantes, Van Patten Publishing, February 2006
Marijuana New School Outdoor Cultivation by Jeff Mowta, Green Candy Press, December 2006
Marijuana Outdoor Grower's Guide by S.T. Oner, Green Candy Press, August 2010
The Cannabible 3 by Jason King, Ten Speed Press, October 2006
The Cannabis Grow Bible 2nd Edition, by Greg Green, Green Candy Press, January 2010
The Cannabis Breeder's Bible by Greg Green, Green Candy Press, April 2005
The Marijuana Chef Cookbook by S.T. Oner, Green Candy Press, December 2001

HASH AND PROCESSING

Biomagno.com – Bio Magno Fertilizers
bubblebag.com – Bubble Bags
greenharvest.ca – North American seller of Pollinator

growlled.com – Growl LED Lighting Systems
hydrohuts.com – Hydro Huts Grow Tents
mixnball.com – Designer Herb Grinders
mmjars.com – Medical Marijuana Jars and Supplies
mg-2.com – MG-2 Lighting Systems
plantasur.com – Wholesale Supplier
pollinator.nl – The Original Pollinator
risingsunhydroponics.com – Grower and Harvester Supplies
hy-pro.nl – Hy-Pro Hydroponics Company

SEEDBANKS AND BREEDERS

aceseeds.org – Ace Seeds (Breeders)
advancedseeds.com – Advanced Seeds (Breeders)
africanseeds.com – African Seeds (Breeders)
afropips.com – Afropips Seeds (Breeders)
almightyseeds.com – Almighty Seeds (Breeders)
alpine-seeds.ch – Alpine Seeds (Breeders)
autofem.com – Autofem Seeds (Breeders)
basilbush.com – Basil Bush Limited Seed Supplier
bigbuddhaseeds.com – Big Buddha Seeds (Breeders)
barneysfarm.com – Barney's Farm Seeds (Breeders)
bcbuddepot.com – BC Bud Depot (Breeders)
bigbuddhaseeds.com – Big Buddha Seeds (Breeders)
bluehemp.ch – Darwin's Seeds (Breeders)
canadianseedexchange.com – Canadian Seed Exchange Seed Bank
cannabismarijuana.com – Emery Seeds (Breeders)
cannapot.at.tc/ - Cannapot Seed Bank
cannaseur.com – Cannaseur Seed Bank
cannaseed.com – Cannaseed Seed Bank
castle-seeds.com – Castle Seeds (Breeders)
celticstone.org – Celtic Stone Seeds (Breeders)
ceresseeds.com – Ceres Seeds (Breeders)
ch9femaleseeds.com– Ch9 Female Seeds (Breeders)
deliciousseeds.com – Delicious Seeds (Breeders)
delta9labs.com – Delta-9 Labs (Breeders)
dinafem-seeds.com – Dinafem Seeds (Breeders)
dnagenetics.com – DNA Genetics (Breeders)
docbushseeds.ca – Doc Bush Seeds (Breeders)

dope-seeds.com – Dope Seeds Seed Bank

dratomicseedbank.com – Dr. Atomic Seeds (Breeders)

drchronic.com – Dr. Chronic Seed Bank

drgreenthumb.com – Dr. Greenthumb (Breeders)

dutch-passion.nl – Dutch Passion Seeds (Breeders)

eliteseeds.com – Elite Seeds (Breeders)

evaseeds.com – Eva Female Seeds (Breeders)

flashseeds.com – Flash Seeds (Breeders)

flyingdutchmen.com – The Flying Dutchmen Seeds (Breeders)

freecannabis.ch – Free Cannabis Seeds (Breeders)

globalamsterdamage.com – Amsterdamage Seed Company

greatcanadianseeds.com – The Great Canadian Seed Company

greendevil.es – Green Devil Genetics (Breeders)

greenfactoryseeds.com – Green Factory Seeds (Breeders)

greenhouseseeds.nl – Green House Seed Co. (Breeders)

greenlifeseeds.com – Green Life Seed Company

growshopalien.com – Grow Shop Alien Seed Company .

gro4me.com – Stoney Girl Gardens Seeds (Breeders)

headsite.com – Head Seed Company

hemcy.at/ - Hemcy Seed Bank

hempdepot.ca – Hemp Depot Canada

high-land.co.uk – The Highland Company

highestseeds.com – Sagarmatha Seeds (Breeders)

homegrown-fantaseeds.com – Homegrown Fantaseeds (Breeders)

kcbrains.com – KC Brains (Breeders)

kindseed.com – Kind Seed Bank (featuring Dr. Atomic)

kiwiseeds.com – Kiwi Seeds (Breeders)

legendsseeds.com – Legends Seeds Company

lightsystems.co.uk – Light Systems (Breeders)

lowryder.co.uk – The Joint Doctor's Lowryder

magusgenetics.com – Magus Genetics (Breeders)

mandalaseeds.com – Mandala Seeds (Breeders)

medicalseeds.com – Enterprise Seeds (Breeders)

ministryofcannabis.com – Ministry of Cannabis (Breeders)

mrnice.nl – Mr. Nice Seeds (Breeders)

nirvanaglobal.com – Nirvana Seeds (Breeders)

nomercy.nl – No Mercy Supply (Breeders)

ogas.ca – Ontario Grower's Association Seeds (Breeders)

paradise-seeds.com – Paradise Seeds (Breeders)

peakseedsbc.com – Peak Seeds (Breeders)

positronicseeds.com – Positronic Seeds (Breeders)

puresativa.com – Pure Sativa Seed Bank

pyramidseeds.com – Pyramid Seeds (Breeders)

resinseeds.net – Resin Seeds (Breeders)

royalqueenseeds.com – Royal Queen Seeds (Breeders)

samenwahl.com/ - Samenwahl Seed Bank

samsaraseeds.com – Samsara Seeds (Breeders)

sanniesshop.com – Sannie's Seed Shop

seedbay.com – Seed Bay Seed Bank

seedboutique.com – Gypsy Nirvana's Seed Boutique

seedfinder.eu/ - Seed Finder Seed Bank

seedmadness.com – Seed Madness Seed Bank

seedsman.com – Seedsman Seed Bank

seedsoflife.biz – Seeds of Life (Breeders)

semenakonopi.cz – Semena Konopi Seeds (Breeders)

sensiseeds.com – Sensi Seeds (Breeders)

seriousseeds.com – Serious Seeds (Breeders)

shortstuffseeds.com – Short Stuff Seeds (Breeders)

sierraseeds.com – Sierra Seeds (Breeders)

somaseeds.nl – Soma Seeds (Breeders)

spiceoflifeseeds.net – Spice of Life Seeds (Breeders)

spliff.nl – Spliff Seeds (Breeders)

supersativaseedclub.com – Super Sativa Seed Club

sweetseeds.es – Sweet Seeds (Breeders)

tessier-ashpool.com – Seed Wholesaler

thcfarmer.com – THC Farmer Seed Bank

thebulldog.com – The Bull Dog Seeds (Breeders)

theharvestmen.co.uk – The Harvestmen Seeds (Breeders)

therealseedcompany.com – The Real Seed Company (Breeders)

thseeds.com – T.H. Seeds (Breeders)

tikiseedbank.ch – Tiki Seed Bank (Breeders)

vancouverseed.com – Vancouver Island Seed Company (Breeders)

vancouverseedbank.ca – Vancouver Seed Bank

victorygardensupply.com – Victory Garden Supply (Breeders)

vulkaniaseeds.com – Vulkania Seed Bank (Breeders)

westcoastgrowers.com – West Coast Growers (Breeders)

willyjack.com – Willy Jack Seeds (Breeders)
worldofseeds.com – World of Seeds Seed Bank (Breeder/Bank)
worldofseeds.eu – World of Seeds (Breeders)
420cannabisseedbank.com – 420 Cannabis Seed Bank

VAPORIZERS
americansmokeless.com – Portable Vaporizer
inavap.com – INAVAP Vaporizers
vaporizergiant.com – Vaporizer Giant
vaportechco.com – Vapor Tech Vaporizer

Index

Index